Marty Alchin

Apress®

Pro Python

ISBN-13 (pbk): 978-1-4302-2757-1

ISBN-13 (electronic): 978-1-4302-2758-8

Printed and bound in the United States of America 9 8 7 6 5 4 3 2 1

President and Publisher: Paul Manning
Lead Editors: Duncan Parkes, Tom Welsh
Technical Reviewer: George Vilches
Editorial Board: Clay Andres, Steve Anglin, Mark Beckner, Ewan Buckingham, Gary Cornell, Jonathan Gennick, Jonathan Hassell, Michelle Lowman, Matthew Moodie, Duncan Parkes, Jeffrey Pepper, Frank Pohlmann, Douglas Pundick, Ben Renow-Clarke, Dominic Shakeshaft, Matt Wade, Tom Welsh
Coordinating Editor: Mary Tobin
Copy Editors: Nancy Sixsmith, Angel Alchin
Compositor: Bytheway Publishing Services
Indexer: John Collin
Cover Designer: Anna Ishchenko

Distributed to the book trade worldwide by Springer Science+Business Media, LLC., 233 Spring Street, 6th Floor, New York, NY 10013. Phone 1-800-SPRINGER, fax (201) 348-4505, e-mail orders-ny@springer-sbm.com, or visit www.springeronline.com.

For information on translations, please e-mail rights@apress.com, or visit www.apress.com.

Apress and friends of ED books may be purchased in bulk for academic, corporate, or promotional use. eBook versions and licenses are also available for most titles. For more information, reference our Special Bulk Sales–eBook Licensing web page at www.apress.com/info/bulksales.

The source code for this book is available to readers at www.apress.com. You will need to answer questions pertaining to this book in order to successfully download the code.

Contents at a Glance

■ Contents iv

■ About the Author xvi

■ About the Technical Reviewer xvii

■ Acknowledgments xviii

■ Introduction xix

■ Chapter 1: Principles and Philosophy 1

■ Chapter 2: Advanced Basics 19

■ Chapter 3: Functions 53

■ Chapter 4: Classes 103

■ Chapter 5: Common Protocols 143

■ Chapter 6: Object Management 169

■ Chapter 7: Strings 191

■ Chapter 8: Documentation 207

■ Chapter 9: Testing 217

■ Chapter 10: Distribution 233

■ Chapter 11: Sheets: A CSV Framework 243

■ PEP 8: Style Guide for Python 283

■ PEP 10: Voting Guidelines 299

■ PEP 20: The Zen of Python 301

■ PEP 257: Docstring Conventions 303

■ PEP 387: Backwards Compatibility Policy 309

■ PEP 3000: Python 3000 313

■ PEP 3003: Python Language Moratorium 317

■ Index 321

Contents

■ Contents iv

■ About the Author xvi

■ About the Technical Reviewer xvii

■ Acknowledgments xviii

■ Introduction xix

■ Chapter 1: Principles and Philosophy 1

The Zen of Python 1

Beautiful Is Better Than Ugly 2

Explicit Is Better Than Implicit 2

Simple Is Better Than Complex 3

Complex Is Better Than Complicated 3

Flat Is Better Than Nested 4

Sparse Is Better Than Dense 5

Readability Counts 5

Special Cases Aren't Special Enough to Break the Rules 6

Although Practicality Beats Purity 6

Errors Should Never Pass Silently 7

Unless Explicitly Silenced 8

In the Face of Ambiguity, Refuse the Temptation to Guess 9

There Should Be One—and Preferably Only One— Obvious Way to Do It 10

Although That Way May Not Be Obvious at First Unless You're Dutch 10

Now Is Better Than Never 11

Although Never Is Often Better Than *Right* Now..11

If the Implementation is Hard to Explain, It's a Bad Idea..11

If the Implementation is Easy to Explain, It May Be a Good Idea...............................11

Namespaces Are One Honking Great Idea— Let's Do More of Those!.........................12

Don't Repeat Yourself 12

Loose Coupling 13

The Samurai Principle..13

The Pareto Principle...14

The Robustness Principle 14

Backward Compatibility...15

The Road to Python 3.0..16

Taking It With You...17

■ **Chapter 2: Advanced Basics** **19**

General Concepts..19

Iteration 19

Caching...20

Transparency...21

Control Flow..21

Catching Exceptions 21

Exception Chains 24

When Everything Goes Right 26

Proceeding Regardless of Exceptions 27

Optimizing Loops 29

The with Statement...29

Conditional Expressions 31

Iteration 33

Sequence Unpacking...34

List Comprehensions 35

Generator Expressions 36

Set Comprehensions 37

Dictionary Comprehensions 37

Chaining Iterables Together 38

Zipping Iterables Together 38

Collections 39

Sets 39

Named Tuples 43

Ordered Dictionaries 44

Dictionaries with Defaults 44

Importing Code 45

Fallback Imports 45

Importing from the Future 46

Using __all__ to Customize Imports 47

Relative Imports 48

The __import__() function 49

The importlib module 51

Taking It With You 52

■ Chapter 3: Functions 53

Arguments 53

Planning for Flexibility 54

Variable Positional Arguments 54

Variable Keyword Arguments 55

Combining Different Kinds of Arguments 56

Invoking Functions with Variable Arguments 59

Preloading Arguments 60

Introspection 61

Example: Identifying Argument Values 62

Example: A More Concise Version 64

Example: Validating Arguments..66

Decorators 67

Closures 69

Wrappers 71

Decorators with Arguments...72

Decorators with—or without—Arguments 74

Example: Memoization 75

Example: A Decorator to Create Decorators 77

Function Annotations 78

Example: Type Safety 79

Factoring Out the Boilerplate..86

Example: Type Coercion 88

Annotating with Decorators..90

Example: Type Safety as a Decorator 90

Generators 94

Lambdas 96

Introspection...97

Identifying Object Types 98

Modules and Packages..98

Docstrings 99

Taking It With You...101

■ Chapter 4: Classes 103

Inheritance...103

Multiple Inheritance...105

Method Resolution Order (MRO) 106

Example: C3 Algorithm 109

Using super() to Pass Control to Other Classes 115

Introspection...117

How Classes Are Created 119

    Creating Classes at Runtime 120

    Metaclasses 121

    Example: Plugin Framework 122

    Controlling the Namespace 125

Attributes 126

    Properties 127

    Descriptors 129

Methods 131

    Unbound Methods 131

    Bound Methods 132

    Class Methods 133

    Static Methods 134

    Assigning Functions to Classes and Instances 135

Magic Methods 135

    Creating Instances 136

    Example: Automatic Subclasses 137

    Dealing with Attributes 138

    String Representations 140

Taking It With You 142

■ Chapter 5: Common Protocols **143**

Basic Operations 143

    Mathematical Operations 144

    Bitwise Operations 148

    Variations 150

Numbers 152

    Sign Operations 154

    Comparison Operations 154

Iterables 155

    Example: Repeatable Generators 158

Sequences 159

Mappings 164

Callables 165

Context Managers 166

Taking It With You 168

■ **Chapter 6: Object Management** **169**

Namespace Dictionary 170

    Example: Borg Pattern 170

    Example: Self-caching properties 173

Garbage Collection 176

    Reference Counting 177

    Cyclical References 178

    Weak References 180

Pickling 182

Copying 186

    Shallow Copies 187

    Deep Copies 188

Taking It With You 190

■ **Chapter 7: Strings** **191**

Bytes 191

    Simple Conversion: chr() and ord() 192

    Complex Conversion: The Struct Module 193

Text 195

    Unicode 196

    Encodings 196

Simple Substitution 198

Formatting 201

    Looking Up Values Within Objects 202

    Distinguishing Types of Strings 202

    Standard Format Specification 203

    Example: Plain Text Table of Contents 204

    Custom Format Specification 205

Taking It With You 206

Chapter 8: Documentation **207**

Proper Naming 207

Comments 208

Docstrings 208

    Describe What the Function Does 209

    Explain the Arguments 209

    Don't Forget the Return Value 209

    Include Any Expected Exceptions 210

Documentation Outside the Code 210

    Installation and Configuration 210

    Tutorials 210

    Reference Documents 210

Documentation Utilities 211

    Formatting 212

    Links 213

    Sphinx 214

Taking It With You 215

Chapter 9: Testing **217**

Test-Driven Development (TDD) 217

Doctests 218

Formatting Code 218

Representing Output.. 218

Integrating With Documentation 219

Running Tests... 220

The unittest module..**221**

Setting Up 221

Writing Tests... 222

Other Comparisons 226

Testing Strings and Other Sequence Content.. 226

Testing Exceptions 227

Testing Identity 229

Tearing Down 229

Providing a Custom Test Class **230**

Changing Test Behavior... 230

Taking It With You...**231**

■ **Chapter 10: Distribution** **233**

Licensing **233**

GNU General Public License (GPL)... 233

Affero General Public License (AGPL) 234

GNU Lesser General Public License (LGPL)... 235

Berkeley Software Distribution (BSD) License... 235

Other Licenses.. 236

Packaging **236**

setup.py.. 237

MANIFEST.in 239

The sdist command 240

Distribution **241**

Taking It With You...**242**

■ Chapter 11: Sheets: A CSV Framework...243

Building a Declarative Framework...244

Introducing Declarative Programming...244

To Build or Not to Build?...245

Building the Framework 246

Managing Options...247

Defining Fields...249

Attaching a Field to a Class 250

Adding a Metaclass 252

Bringing It Together...255

Ordering Fields 256

DeclarativeMeta.__prepare__()...256

Column.__init__()...258

Column.__new__()...262

CounterMeta.__call__()...263

Choosing an Option...264

Building a Field Library 264

StringField...265

IntegerColumn 266

FloatColumn...266

DecimalColumn...266

DateColumn 267

Getting Back to CSV...271

Checking Arguments 272

Populating Values...274

The Reader 276

The Writer...280

Taking It With You...282

■ **PEP 8: Style Guide for Python** **283**

Introduction 283

A Foolish Consistency is the Hobgoblin of Little Minds 283

Code Layout 284

    Indentation...284

    Tabs or Spaces?..284

    Maximum Line Length 284

    Blank Lines 284

    Encodings (PEP 263) 285

Imports 285

Whitespace in Expressions and Statements..286

    Pet Peeves 286

    Other Recommendations 287

Comments..288

    Block Comments..289

    Inline Comments 289

Documentation Strings 289

Version Bookkeeping 290

Naming Conventions...290

    Descriptive: Naming Styles..290

    Prescriptive: Naming Conventions...291

Programming Recommendations 294

Copyright 297

■ **PEP 10: Voting Guidelines** **299**

Abstract 299

Rationale..299

Voting Scores..299

Copyright 300

■ **PEP 20: The Zen of Python** **301**

Abstract 301

The Zen of Python 301

Easter Egg 301

Copyright 302

■ **PEP 257: Docstring Conventions** **303**

Abstract 303

Rationale 303

Specification 303

    What is a Docstring? 303

    One-Line Docstrings 304

    Multi-Line Docstrings 305

    Handling Docstring Indentation 306

Copyright 307

Acknowledgments 307

■ **PEP 387: Backwards Compatibility Policy** **309**

Abstract 309

Rationale 309

Backwards Compatibility Rules 309

Making Incompatible Changes 310

Copyright 311

■ **PEP 3000: Python 3000** **313**

Abstract 313

Naming 313

PEP Numbering 313

Timeline 313

Compatibility and Transition 314

Implementation Language 315

Meta-Contributions 315

Copyright 315

■ PEP 3003: Python Language Moratorium 317

Abstract 317

Rationale 317

Details 318

    Cannot Change 318

    Case-by-Case Exemptions 318

    Allowed to Change 318

Retroactive 319

Extensions 319

Copyright 319

■ Index 321

About the Author

■ **Marty Alchin** is a professional programmer with a passion for the Web. His work with Django, the popular Web framework, led him to write several articles about Python, to speak at PyCon and even to write his first book, *Pro Django*, which was published by Apress in December of 2008.

In addition to writing for print, Marty keeps a blog at http://martyalchin.com/, where he writes about Python, Django and anything else that strikes his fancy.

About the Technical Reviewer

■ **George Vilches** is a software engineer and systems administrator with an unabashed fondness for Python and the Web in both disciplines. In the last three years, he has made several contributions to Django, with a focus on the ORM and administrative side of things. He is a principal engineer with AOL and builds Django applications with Fortune Cookie Studios (`http://fcstudios.com`).

George's personal time is split between tinkering with open source projects and enjoying the company of his wife Kate, their corgi and their two cats (all of whom would prefer he stop tinkering and attend to them more).

Acknowledgments

I wouldn't have even started this project if not for the endless encouragement from my lovely wife, Angel. She's been my sounding board, my task manager, my copy editor and my own personal cheerleader. There's no way I could do anything like this without her help and support.

I'd also like to thank my technical reviewer, George, for everything he's done to help me out. He's gone above and beyond the limits of his role, helping with everything from code to grammar and even a good bit of style. After enjoying his help on *Pro Django*, I wouldn't have even signed on for another book without him by my side.

Lastly, I never would've considered a book like this if not for the wonderful community around Python. The willingness of Python programmers to open their minds and their code is, I believe, unrivaled among our peers. It's this spirit of openness that encourages me every day, leading me to discover new things and push myself beyond the limits of what I knew yesterday.

We learn by doing and by seeing what others have done. I hope that you'll take the contents of this book and do more with it than what I've done. There's no better reward for all this hard work than to see better programmers writing better code.

Introduction

When I wrote my first book, *Pro Django*, I didn't have much of an idea what my readers would find interesting. I had gained a lot of information I thought would be useful for others to learn, but I didn't really know what would be the most valuable thing they'd take away. As it turned out, in nearly 300 pages, the most popular chapter in the book barely mentioned Django at all. It was about Python.

The response was overwhelming. There was clearly a desire to learn more about how to go from a simple Python application to a detailed framework like Django. It's all Python code, but it can be hard to understand based on even a reasonably thorough understanding of the language. The tools and techniques involved require some extra knowledge that you might not run into in general use.

This gave me a new goal with *Pro Python*: to take you from proficient to professional. Being a true professional requires more experience than you can get from a book, but I want to at least give you the tools you'll need. Combined with the rich philosophy of the Python community, you'll find plenty of information to take your code to the next level.

Who This Book Is For

Because my goal is to bring intermediate programmers to a more advanced level, I wrote this book with the expectation that you'll already be familiar with Python. You should be comfortable using the interactive interpreter, writing control structures and a basic object-oriented approach.

That's not a very difficult prerequisite. If you've tried your hand at writing a Python application—even if you haven't released it into the wild, or even finished it—you likely have all the necessary knowledge to get started. The rest of the information you'll need is contained in these pages.

What You'll Need

This book is written with the latest versions of Python in mind, so most of the examples assume that you're already using Python 3.1, which is the latest official release as of the date of publishing. I don't take the jump to Python 3 lightly, though, so there are plenty of compatibility notes along the way, going all the way back to Python 2.5. As long as your copy of Python was released in the last few years, you'll be all set.

Nearly all the packages used in this book come from the Python Standard Library, which ships with every Python installation. Some sections will reference third-party libraries that aren't included in that bundle, but those are strictly informative; you won't lose out if you don't have them installed.

Source Code

The code for all the examples in this book is available at `http://propython.com/`.

■ ■ ■

## CHAPTER 1

Principles and Philosophy

If it seems strange to begin a programming book with a chapter about philosophy, that's actually evidence of why this chapter is so important. Python was created to embody and encourage a certain set of ideals that have helped guide the decisions of its maintainers and its community for nearly 20 years. Understanding these concepts will help you make the most out of what the language and its community have to offer.

Of course, we're not talking about Plato or Nietzsche here. Python deals with programming problems, and its philosophies are designed to help build reliable, maintainable solutions. Some of these philosophies are officially branded into the Python landscape, while others are guidelines commonly accepted by Python programmers, but all of them will help you write code that is powerful, easy to maintain and understandable to other programmers.

The philosophies laid out in this chapter can be read from start to finish here, but don't expect to commit them all to memory in one pass. The rest of this book will refer back here often, by illustrating which concepts come into play in various situations. After all, the real value of philosophy is understanding how to apply it when it matters most.

The Zen of Python

Perhaps the best known collection of Python philosophy was written by Tim Peters, long-time contributor to the language and its newsgroup, `comp.lang.python`.[1] This Zen of Python condenses some of the most common philosophical concerns into a brief list that's been recorded as both its own Python Enhancement Proposal (PEP)[2] and within Python itself. Something of an easter egg, Python includes a module called this.

```
>>> import this
The Zen of Python, by Tim Peters

Beautiful is better than ugly.
Explicit is better than implicit.
Simple is better than complex.
Complex is better than complicated.
Flat is better than nested.
Sparse is better than dense.
Readability counts.
Special cases aren't special enough to break the rules.
Although practicality beats purity.
```

---

[1] http://propython.com/comp-lang-python/
[2] http://propython.coms/pep-20/

```
Errors should never pass silently.
Unless explicitly silenced.
In the face of ambiguity, refuse the temptation to guess.
There should be one-- and preferably only one --obvious way to do it.
Although that way may not be obvious at first unless you're Dutch.
Now is better than never.
Although never is often better than *right* now.
If the implementation is hard to explain, it's a bad idea.
If the implementation is easy to explain, it may be a good idea.
Namespaces are one honking great idea -- let's do more of those!
```

This list was primarily intended as a humorous accounting of Python philosophy, but over the years, numerous Python applications have used these guidelines to greatly improve the quality, readability and maintainability of their code. Just listing the Zen of Python is of little value, though, so the following sections will explain each idiom in more detail.

Beautiful Is Better Than Ugly

Perhaps it's fitting that this first notion is arguably the most subjective of the whole bunch. After all, beauty is in the eye of the beholder, a fact which has been discussed for centuries. It serves as a blatant reminder that philosophy is far from absolute. Still, having something like this in writing provides a goal to strive for, which is the ultimate purpose of all these ideals.

One obvious application of this philosophy is in Python's own language structure, which minimizes the use of punctuation, instead preferring English words where appropriate. Another advantage is Python's focus on keyword arguments, which help clarify function calls that would otherwise be difficult to understand. Consider the following two possible ways of writing the same code, and consider which one looks more beautiful.

```
is_valid = form != null && form.is_valid(true)
is_valid = form is not None and form.is_valid(include_hidden_fields=True)
```

The second example reads a bit more like natural English, and explicitly including the name of the argument gives greater insight into its purpose. In addition to language concerns, coding style can be influenced by similar notions of beauty. The name is_valid, for example, asks a simple question, which the method can then be expected to answer with its return value. A name like validate would've been ambiguous because it would be an accurate name even if no value were returned at all.

Being so subjective, however, it's dangerous to rely too heavily on beauty as a criterion for a design decision. If other ideals have been considered and you're still left with two workable options, certainly consider factoring beauty into the equation, but do make sure that other facets are taken into account first. You'll likely find a good choice using some of the other criteria long before reaching this point.

Explicit Is Better Than Implicit

Though this notion may seem easier to interpret than beauty, it's actually one of the trickier guidelines to follow. On the surface, it seems simple enough: don't do anything the programmer didn't explicitly command. Beyond just Python itself, frameworks and libraries have a similar responsibility because their code will be accessed by other programmers whose goals will not always be known in advance.

Unfortunately, truly explicit code must account for every nuance of a program's execution, from memory management to display routines. Some programming languages do expect that level of detail from their programmers, but Python doesn't. In order to make the programmer's job easier and allow you to focus on the problem at hand, there need to be some trade-offs along the way.

In general, Python asks you to declare your intentions explicitly, rather than issue every command necessary to make that intention a reality. For example, when assigning a value to a variable, you don't need to worry about setting aside the necessary memory, assigning a pointer to the value and cleaning up the memory once it's no longer in use. Memory management is a necessary part of variable assignment, so Python takes care of it behind the scenes. Assigning the value is enough of an explicit declaration of intent to justify the implicit behavior.

On the other hand, regular expressions in the Perl programming language automatically assign values to special variables any time a match is found. Someone unfamiliar with the way Perl handles that situation wouldn't understand a code snippet that relies on it because variables would seem to come from thin air, with no assignments related to them. Python programmers try to avoid this type of implicit behavior in favor of more readable code.

Because different applications will have different ways of declaring intentions, no single generic explanation will apply to all cases. Instead, this guideline will come up quite frequently throughout the book, clarifying how it would be applied to various situations.

Simple Is Better Than Complex

This is a considerably more concrete guideline, with implications primarily in the design of interfaces to frameworks and libraries. The goal here is to keep the interface as straightforward as possible, leveraging a programmer's knowledge of existing interfaces as much as possible. For example, a caching framework could use the same interface as standard dictionaries rather than inventing a whole new set of method calls.

Of course, there are many other applications of this rule, such as taking advantage of the fact that most expressions can evaluate to true or false without explicit tests. For example, the following two lines of code are functionally identical for strings, but notice the difference in complexity between them.

```
if value is not None and value != '':
if value:
```

As you can see, the second option is much simpler to read and understand. All the situations covered in the first example will evaluate to false anyway, so the simpler test is just as effective. It also has two other benefits: it runs faster, having fewer tests to perform, and it also works in more cases, because individual objects can define their own method of determining whether they should evaluate to true or false.

It may seem like this is something of a convoluted example, but it's just the type of thing that comes up quite frequently. By relying on simpler interfaces, you can often take advantage of optimizations and increased flexibility while producing more readable code.

Complex Is Better Than Complicated

Sometimes, however, a certain level of complexity is required in order to get the job done. Database adapters, for example, don't have the luxury of using a simple dictionary-style interface, but instead require an extensive set of objects and methods to cover all of their features. The important thing to remember in those situations is that complexity doesn't necessarily require it to be complicated.

The tricky bit with this one, obviously, is distinguishing between the two. Dictionary definitions of each term often reference the other, considerably blurring the line between the two. For the sake of this guideline, most situations tend to take the following view of the two terms.

- Complex—made up of many interconnected parts.

- Complicated—so complex as to be difficult to understand.

So in the face of an interface that requires a large number of things to keep track of, it's even more important to retain as much simplicity as possible. This can take the form of consolidating methods onto a smaller number of objects, perhaps grouping objects into more logical arrangements or even simply making sure to use names that make sense without having to dig into the code to understand them.

Flat Is Better Than Nested

This guideline might not seem to make sense at first, but it's about how structures are laid out. The structures in question could be objects and their attributes, packages and their included modules or even code blocks within a function. The goal is to keep things as relationships of peers as much possible, rather than parents and children. For example, take the following code snippet, which illustrates the problem.

```
if x > 0:
    if y > 100:
        raise ValueError("Value for y is too large.")
    else:
        return y
else:
    if x == 0:
        return False
    else:
        raise ValueError("Value for x cannot be negative.")
```

In this example, it's fairly difficult to follow what's really going on because the nested nature of the code blocks requires you to keep track of multiple levels of conditions. Consider the following alternative approach to writing the same code, flattening it out.

```
if x > 0 and y > 100:
    raise ValueError("Value for y is too large.")
elif x > 0:
    return y
elif x == 0:
    return False
else:
    raise ValueError("Value for x cannot be negative.")
```

Notice how much easier it is to follow the logic in the second example because all the conditions are at the same level. It even saves two lines of code by avoiding the extraneous else blocks along the way. This is actually the main reason for the existence of the elif keyword; Python's use of indentation means that complex if blocks can quickly get out of hand otherwise.

■ Caution What might not be as obvious is that the refactoring of this example ends up testing x > 0 twice, where it was only performed once previously. If that test had been an expensive operation, such as a database query, refactoring it in this way would reduce the performance of the program, so it wouldn't be worth it. This is covered in detail in a later guideline: Practicality Beats Purity.

In the case of package layouts, flat structures can often allow a single import to make the entire package available under a single namespace. Otherwise, the programmer would need to know the full structure in order to find the particular class or function required. Some packages are so complex that a nested structure will help reduce clutter on each individual namespace, but it's best to start flat and nest only when problems arise.

Sparse Is Better Than Dense

This principle largely pertains to the visual appearance of Python source code, favoring the use of whitespace to differentiate among blocks of code. The goal is to keep highly related snippets together, while separating them from subsequent or unrelated code, rather than simply having everything run together in an effort to save a few bytes on disk.

In the real world, there are plenty of specific concerns to address, such as how to separate module-level classes or deal with one-line if blocks. Though no single set of rules will be appropriate for all projects, PEP-8[3] does specify many aspects of source code layout that help you adhere to this principle. It provides a number of hints on how to format import statements, classes, functions and even many types of expressions.

It's interesting to note that PEP-8 includes a number of rules about expressions in particular, which specifically encourage avoiding extra spaces. Take the following examples, taken straight from PEP-8.

```
Yes: spam(ham[1], {eggs: 2})
No:  spam( ham[ 1 ], { eggs: 2 } )

Yes: if x == 4: print x, y; x, y = y, x
No:  if x == 4 : print x , y ; x , y = y , x

Yes: spam(1)
No:  spam (1)

Yes: dict['key'] = list[index]
No:  dict ['key'] = list [index]
```

The key to this apparent discrepancy is that whitespace is a valuable resource and should be distributed responsibly. After all, if everything tries to stand out in any one particular way, nothing really does stand out at all. If you use whitespace to separate even highly related bits of code like the above expressions, truly unrelated code isn't any different from the rest.

That's perhaps the most important part of this principle and the key to applying it to other aspects of code design. When writing libraries or frameworks, it's generally better to define a small set of unique types of objects and interfaces that can be reused across the application, maintaining similarity where appropriate and differentiating the rest.

Readability Counts

Finally, we have a principle everybody in the Python world can get behind, but that's mostly because it's one of the most vague in the entire collection. In a way, it sums up the whole of Python philosophy in one deft stroke, but it also leaves so much undefined that it's worth examining a bit further.

Readability covers a wide range of issues, such as the names of modules, classes, functions and variables. It includes the style of individual blocks of code and the whitespace between them. It can even

---

[3] http://propython.com/pep-8/

pertain to the separation of responsibilities among multiple functions or classes if that separation is done so that it's more readable to the human eye.

That's the real point here: code gets read not only by computers, but also by humans who have to maintain it. Those humans have to read existing code far more often than they have to write new code, and it's often code that was written by someone else. Readability is all about actively promoting human understanding of code.

Development is much easier in the long run when everyone involved can simply open up a file and easily understand what's going on in it. This seems like a given in organizations with high turnover, where new programmers must regularly read the code of their predecessors, but it's true even for those who have to read their own code weeks, months or even years after it was written. Once we lose our original train of thought, all we have to remind us is the code itself, so it's very valuable to take the extra time to make it easy to read.

The best part is how little extra time it often takes. It can be as simple as adding a blank line between two functions or naming variables with nouns and functions with verbs. It's really more of a frame of mind than a set of rules, though. A focus on readability requires you to always look at your code as a human being would, rather than only as a computer would. Remember the Golden Rule: do for others what you'd like them to do for you. Readability is random acts of kindness sprinkled throughout your code.

Special Cases Aren't Special Enough to Break the Rules

Just as "Readability counts" is a banner phrase for how we should approach our code at all times, this principle is about the conviction with which we must pursue it. It's all well and good to get it right most of the time, but all it takes is one ugly chunk of code to undermine all that hard work.

What's perhaps most interesting about this rule, though, is that it doesn't pertain just to readability or any other single aspect of code. It's really just about the conviction to stand behind the decisions you've made, regardless of what those are. If you're committed to backward compatibility, internationalization, readability or anything else, don't break those promises just because a new feature comes along and makes some things a bit easier.

Although Practicality Beats Purity

And here's where things get tricky. The previous principle encourages you to always do the right thing, regardless of how exceptional one situation might be, where this one seems to allow exceptions whenever the right thing gets difficult. The reality is a bit more complicated, though, and merits some discussion.

Up to this point, it seemed simple enough at a glance: the fastest, most efficient code might not always be the most readable, so you may have to accept subpar performance to gain code that's easier to maintain. This is certainly true in many cases, and much of Python's standard library is less than ideal in terms of raw performance, instead opting for pure Python implementations that are more readable and more portable to other environments, like Jython or IronPython. On a larger scale, though, the problem goes deeper than that.

When designing a system at any level, it's easy to get into a heads-down mode, where you focus exclusively on the problem at hand and how best to solve it. This might involve algorithms, optimizations, interface schemes or even refactorings, but it typically boils down to working on one thing so hard that you don't look at the bigger picture for a while. In that mode, programmers commonly do what seems best within the current context, but when backing out a bit for a better look, those decisions don't match up with the rest of the application as a whole.

It's not always easy to know which way to go at this point. Do you try to optimize the rest of the application to match that perfect routine you just wrote? Do you rewrite the otherwise-perfect function in hopes of gaining a more cohesive whole? Or do you just leave the inconsistency alone, hoping it doesn't trip anybody up? The answer, as usual, depends on the situation, but one of those options will often seem more practical in context than the others.

Typically, it's preferable to maintain greater overall consistency at the expense of a few small areas that may be less than ideal. Again, most of Python's standard library uses this approach, but there are exceptions even there. Packages that require a lot of computational power or get used in applications that need to avoid bottlenecks will often be written in C to improve performance, at the cost of maintainability. These packages then need to be ported over to other environments and tested more rigorously on different systems, but the speed gained serves a more practical purpose than a purer Python implementation would allow.

Errors Should Never Pass Silently

Python supports a robust error-handling system, with dozens of built-in exceptions provided out of the box, but there's often doubt about when those exceptions should be used and when new ones are necessary. The guidance provided by this line of the Zen of Python is quite simple, but as with so many others, there's much more beneath the surface.

The first task is to clarify the definitions of errors and exceptions. Even though these words, like so many others in the world of computing, are often overloaded with additional meaning, there's definite value in looking at them as they're used in general language. Consider the following definitions, as found in the *Merriam-Webster Dictionary*:

- An act or condition of ignorant or imprudent deviation from a code of behavior

- A case to which a rule does not apply

The terms themselves have been left out here to help illustrate just how similar the two definitions can be. In real life, the biggest observed difference between the two terms is the severity of the problems caused by deviations from the norm. Exceptions are typically considered less disruptive and thus more acceptable, but they both amount to the same thing: a violation of some kind of expectation. For the purposes of this discussion, the term exception will be used to refer to any such departure from the norm.

■ **Note** One important thing to realize, though, is that not all exceptions are errors. Some are used to enhance code flow options, such as using StopIteration, which is documented in Chapter 5. In code flow usage, exceptions provide a way to indicate what happened inside a function, even though that indication has no relationship to its return value.

This interpretation makes it impossible to describe exceptions on their own; they must be placed in the context of an expectation that can be violated. Every time we write a piece of code, we make a promise that it'll work in a specific way. Exceptions break that promise, so we need to understand what types of promises we make and how they can be broken. Take the following simple Python function and look for any promises that can be broken.

```python
def validate(data):
    if data['username'].startswith('_'):
        raise ValueError("Username must not begin with an underscore.")
```

The obvious promise here is that of validate() itself: if the incoming data is valid, the function will return silently. Violations of that rule, such as a username beginning with an underscore, are explicitly treated as an exception, neatly illustrating this practice of not allowing errors to pass silently. Raising an exception draws attention to the situation and provides enough information for the code that called this function to understand what happened.

The tricky bit here is to see the other exceptions that may get raised. For example, if the data dictionary doesn't contain a 'username' key, as the function expects, Python will raise a KeyError. If that key does exist, but its value isn't a string, Python will raise an AttributeError when trying to access the startswith() method. If data isn't a dictionary at all, Python would raise a TypeError.

Most of those assumptions are true requirements for proper operation, but they don't all have to be. Let's assume this validation function could be called from a number of contexts, some of which may not have even asked for a username. In those cases, a missing username isn't actually an exception at all, but just another flow that needs to be accounted for.

With that new requirement in mind, validate() can be slightly altered to no longer rely on the presence of a 'username' key to work properly. All the other assumptions should stay intact, however, and should raise their respective exceptions when violated. Here's how it might look after this change.

```python
def validate(data):
    if 'username' in data and data['username'].startswith('_'):
        raise ValueError("Username must not begin with an underscore.")
```

And just like that, one assumption has been removed and the function can now run just fine without a username supplied in the data dictionary. Alternately, you could now check for a missing username explicitly and raise a more specific exception if truly required. How the remaining exceptions are handled depends on the needs of the code that calls validate(), and there's a complementary principle to deal with that situation.

Unless Explicitly Silenced

Like any other language that supports exceptions, Python allows the code that triggers exceptions to trap them and handle them in different ways. In the preceding validation example, it's likely that the validation errors should be shown to the user in a nicer way than a full traceback. Consider a small command-line program that accepts a username as an argument and validates it against the rules defined previously.

```python
import sys

def validate(data):
    if 'username' in data and data['username'].startswith('_'):
        raise ValueError("Username must not begin with an underscore.")

if __name__ == '__main__':
    username = sys.argv[1]
    try:
        validate({'username': username})
    except TypeError, ValueError as e:
        print e
```

Compatibility: Prior to 3.0

The syntax used to catch the exception and store it as the variable `e` in this example was made available in Python 3.0. Previously, the `except` clause used commas to separate exception types from each other and to distinguish the name of the variable to hold the exception, so the example here would read `except (TypeError, ValueError), e`. To resolve this ambiguity, the `as` keyword was added to Python 2.6, which makes blocks like this much more explicit.

The comma syntax will work in all Python versions up to and including 2.7, while Python 2.6 and higher support the as keyword shown here. Python 2.6 and 2.7 support both syntaxes in an effort to ease the transition.

In this example, all those exceptions that might be raised will simply get caught by this code, and the message alone will be displayed to the user, not the full traceback. This form of error handling allows for complex code to use exceptions to indicate violated expectations without taking down the whole program.

Explicit is better than implicit

In a nutshell, this error-handling system is a simple example of the previous rule favoring explicit declarations over implicit behavior. The default behavior is as obvious as possible, given that exceptions always propagate upward to higher levels of code, but can be overridden using an explicit syntax.

In the Face of Ambiguity, Refuse the Temptation to Guess

Sometimes, when using or implementing interfaces between pieces of code written by different people, certain aspects may not always be clear. For example, one common practice is to pass around byte strings without any information about what encoding they rely on. This means that if any code needs to convert those strings to Unicode or ensure that they use a specific encoding, there's not enough information available to do so.

It's tempting to play the odds in this situation, blindly picking what seems to be the most common encoding. Surely it would handle most cases, and that should be enough for any real-world application. Alas, no. Encoding problems raise exceptions in Python, so those could either take down the application or they could be caught and ignored, which could inadvertently cause other parts of the application to think strings were properly converted when they actually weren't.

Worse yet, your application now relies on a guess. It's an educated guess, of course, perhaps with the odds on your side, but real life has a nasty habit of flying in the face of probability. You might well find that what you assumed to be most common is in fact less likely when given real data from real people. Not only could incorrect encodings cause problems with your application, those problems could occur far more frequently than you realize.

A better approach would be to only accept Unicode strings, which can then be written to byte strings using whatever encoding your application chooses. That removes all ambiguity, so your code doesn't have to guess anymore. Of course, if your application doesn't need to deal with Unicode and can simply pass byte strings through unconverted, it should accept byte strings only, rather than you having to guess an encoding to use to produce byte strings.

There Should Be One—and Preferably Only One— Obvious Way to Do It

Though similar to the previous principle, this one is generally applied only to development of libraries and frameworks. When designing a module, class or function, it may be tempting to implement a number of entry points, each accounting for a slightly different scenario. In the byte string example from the previous section, for example, you might consider having one function to handle byte strings and another to handle Unicode strings.

The problem with that approach is that every interface adds a burden on developers who have to use it. Not only are there more things to remember, but it may not always be clear which function to use even when all the options are known. Choosing the right option often comes down to little more than naming, which can sometimes be a guess in and of itself.

In the previous example, the simple solution is to accept only Unicode strings, which neatly avoids other problems, but for this principle, the recommendation is broader. Stick to simpler, more common interfaces like the protocols illustrated in Chapter 5 where you can, adding on only when you have a truly different task to perform.

You might have noticed that Python itself seems to violate this rule sometimes, most notably in its dictionary implementation. The preferred way to access a value is to use the bracket syntax, `my_dict['key']`, but dictionaries also have a `get()` method, which seems to do the exact same thing. Conflicts like this come up fairly frequently when dealing with such an extensive set of principles, but there are often good reasons if you're willing to consider them.

In the dictionary case, it comes back to the notion of raising an exception when a rule is violated. When thinking about violations of a rule, we have to examine the rules implied by these two available access methods. The bracket syntax follows a very basic rule: return the value referenced by the key provided. It's really that simple. Anything that gets in the way of that, such as an invalid key, a missing value or some additional behavior provided by an overridden protocol, results in an exception being raised.

The `get()` method, on the other hand, follows a more complicated set of rules. It checks to see whether the provided key is present in the dictionary; if it is, the associated value is returned. If the key isn't in the dictionary, an alternate value is returned instead. By default, the alternate value is `None`, but that can be overridden by providing a second argument.

By laying out the rules each technique follows, it becomes clearer why there are two different options. Bracket syntax is the common use case, failing loudly in all but the most optimistic situations, while `get()` offers more flexibility for those situations that need it. One refuses to allow errors to pass silently, while the other explicitly silences them. Essentially, providing two options allows dictionaries to satisfy both principles.

More to the point, though, is that the philosophy states there should only be one *obvious* way to do it. Even in the dictionary example, which has two ways to get values, only one—the bracket syntax—is obvious. The `get()` method is available, but it isn't very well known, and it certainly isn't promoted as the primary interface for working with dictionaries. It's okay to provide multiple ways to do something as long as they're for sufficiently different use cases, and the most common use case is presented as the obvious choice.

Although That Way May Not Be Obvious at First Unless You're Dutch

This is a nod to the homeland of Python's creator and Benevolent Dictator for Life, Guido van Rossum. More importantly, though, it's an acknowledgment that not everyone sees things the same way. What seems obvious to one person might seem completely foreign to somebody else, and though there are any number of reasons for those types of differences, none of them are wrong. Different people are different, and that's all there is to it.

The easiest way to overcome these differences is to properly document your work, so that even if the code isn't obvious, your documentation can point the way. You might still need to answer questions beyond the documentation, so it's often useful to have a more direct line of communication with users, such as a mailing list. The ultimate goal is to give users an easy way to know how you intend them to use your code.

Now Is Better Than Never

We've all heard the saying, "Don't put off 'til tomorrow what you can do today." That's a valid lesson for all of us, but it happens to be especially true in programming. By the time we get around to something we've set aside, we might have long since forgotten the information we need to do it right. The best time to do it is when it's on our mind.

Okay, so that part was obvious, but as Python programmers, this antiprocrastination clause has special meaning for us. Python as a language is designed in large part to help you spend your time solving real problems rather than fighting with the language just to get the program to work.

This focus lends itself well to iterative development, allowing you to quickly rough out a basic implementation and then refine it over time. In essence, it's another application of this principle because it allows you to get working quickly rather than trying to plan everything out in advance, possibly never actually writing any code.

Although Never Is Often Better Than *Right* Now

Even iterative development takes time. It's valuable to get started quickly, but it can be very dangerous to try to finish immediately. Taking the time to refine and clarify an idea is essential to get it right, and failing to do so usually produces code that could be described as—at best—mediocre. Users and other developers will generally be better off not having your work at all than having something substandard.

We have no way of knowing how many otherwise useful projects never see the light of day because of this notion. Whether in that case or in the case of a poorly made release, the result is essentially the same: people looking for a solution to the same problem you tried to tackle won't have a viable option to use. The only way to really help anyone is to take the time required to get it right.

If the Implementation is Hard to Explain, It's a Bad Idea

This is something of a combination of two other rules already mentioned, that simple is better than complex, and that complex is better than complicated. The interesting thing about the combination here is that it provides a way to identify when you've crossed the line from simple to complex or from complex to complicated. When in doubt, run it by someone else and see how much effort it takes to get them on board with your implementation.

This also reinforces the importance of communication to good development. In open source development, like that of Python itself, communication is an obvious part of the process, but it's not limited to publicly contributed projects. Any development team can provide greater value if its members talk to each other, bounce ideas around and help refine implementations. One-man development teams can sometimes prosper, but they're missing out on crucial editing that can only be provided by others.

If the Implementation is Easy to Explain, It May Be a Good Idea

At a glance, this seems to be just an obvious extension of the previous principle, simply swapping "hard" and "bad" for "easy" and "good." Closer examination reveals that adjectives aren't the only things that changed. A verb changes its form as well: "is" became "may be." That may seem like a subtle, inconsequential change, but it's actually quite important.

Although Python highly values simplicity, many very bad ideas are easy to explain. Being able to communicate your ideas to your peers is valuable, but only as a first step that leads to real discussion. The best thing about peer review is the ability for different points of view to clarify and refine ideas, turning something good into something great.

Of course, that's not to discount the abilities of individual programmers. One person can do amazing things all alone, there's no doubt about it. But most useful projects involve other people at some point or another, even if only your users. Once those other people are in the know, even if they don't have access to your code, be prepared to accept their feedback and criticism. Even though you may think your ideas are great, other perspectives often bring new insight into old problems, which only serves to make it a better product overall.

Namespaces Are One Honking Great Idea— Let's Do More of Those!

In Python, namespaces are used in a variety of ways—from package and module hierarchies to object attributes—to allow programmers to choose the names of functions and variables without fear of conflicting with the choices of others. Namespaces avoid collisions without requiring every name to include some kind of unique prefix, which would otherwise be necessary.

For the most part, you can take advantage of Python's namespace handling without really doing anything special. If you add attributes or methods to an object, Python will take care of the namespace for that. If you add functions or classes to a module, or a module to a package, Python takes care of it. But there are a few decisions you can make to explicitly take advantage of better namespaces.

One common example is wrapping module-level functions into classes. This creates a bit of a hierarchy, allowing similarly named functions to coexist peacefully. It also has the benefit of allowing those classes to be customized using arguments, which can then affect the behavior of the individual methods. Otherwise, your code might have to rely on module-level settings that are modified by module-level functions, restricting how flexible it can be.

Not all sets of functions need to be wrapped up into classes, though. Remember that flat is better than nested, so as long as there are no conflicts or confusion, it's usually best to leave those at the module level. Similarly, if you don't have a number of modules with similar functionality and overlapping names, there's little point in splitting them up into a package.

Don't Repeat Yourself

Designing frameworks can be a very complicated process, often expecting programmers to specify a variety of different types of information. Sometimes, though, the same information might need to be supplied to multiple different parts of the framework. How often this happens depends on the nature of the framework involved, but having to provide the same information multiple times is always a burden and should be avoided wherever possible.

Essentially, the goal is to ask your users to provide configurations and other information just once and then use Python's introspection tools, described in detail in later chapters, to extract that information and reuse it in the other areas that need it. Once that information has been provided, the programmer's intentions are explicitly clear, so there's still no guesswork involved at all.

It's also important to note that this isn't limited to your own application. If your code relies on the Django web framework, for instance, you have access to all the configuration information required to work with Django, which is often quite extensive. You might only need to ask your users to point out which part of their code to use and access its structure to get anything else you need.

In addition to configuration details, code can be copied from one function to another if they share some common behaviors. In accordance with this principle, it's often better to move that common code out into a separate utility function, Then, each function that needs that code can defer to the utility function, paving the way for future functions that need that same behavior.

This type of code factoring showcases some of the more pragmatic reasons to avoid repetition. The obvious advantage to reusable code is that it reduces the number of places where bugs can occur. Better yet, when you find a bug, you can fix it in one place, rather than worry about finding all the places that same bug might crop up. Perhaps best of all, having the code isolated in a separate function makes it much easier to test programmatically, to help reduce the likelihood of bugs occurring in the first place. Testing is covered in detail in Chapter 9.

This is also one of the most commonly abbreviated principles, given that its initials spell a word so clearly. Interestingly, though, it can actually be used in a few different ways, depending on context.

- An adjective—"Wow, this feels very DRY!"

- A noun—"This code violates DRY."

- A verb—"Let's DRY this up a bit, shall we?"

Loose Coupling

Larger libraries and frameworks often have to split their code into separate subsystems with different responsibilities. This is typically advantageous from a maintenance perspective, with each section containing a substantially different aspect of the code. The concern here is about how much each section has to know about the others because it can negatively affect the maintainability of the code.

It's not about having each subsystem completely ignorant of the others, nor is it to avoid them ever interacting at all. Any application written to be *that* separated wouldn't be able to actually do anything of interest. Code that doesn't talk to other code just can't be useful. Instead, it's more about how much each subsystem relies on how the other subsystems work.

In a way, you can look at each subsystem as its own complete system, with its own interface to implement. Each subsystem can then call into the other ones, supplying only the information pertinent to the function being called and getting the result, all without relying on what the other subsystem does inside that function.

There are a few good reasons for this behavior; the most obvious being that it helps make the code easier to maintain. If each subsystem only needs to know its own functions work, changes to those functions should be localized enough to not cause problems with other subsystems that access them. You're able to maintain a finite collection of publicly reliable interfaces while allowing everything else to change as necessary over time.

Another potential advantage of loose coupling is how much easier it is to split off a subsystem into its own full application, which can then be included in other applications later on. Better yet, applications created like this can often be released to the development community at large, allowing others to utilize your work or even expand on it if you choose to accept patches from outside sources.

The Samurai Principle

The samurai warriors of ancient Japan are known for following the code of Bushido, which governed most of their actions in wartime. One particularly well-known aspect of Bushido is that warriors should return from battle victorious or they should not return at all. The parallel in programming, as may be indicated by the word return is the behavior of functions in the event that any exceptions are encountered along the way.

It's not a unique concept among those listed in this chapter, but rather an extension of the ideas that errors should never pass silently and to avoid ambiguity. If something goes wrong while executing a function that ordinarily returns a value, any return value could be misconstrued as a successful call, rather than identifying that an error occurred. The exact nature of what occurred is very ambiguous and may produce errors down the road, in code that's unrelated to what really went wrong.

Of course, functions that don't return anything interesting don't have a problem with ambiguity because nothing is relying on the return value. Rather than allowing those functions to return without raising exceptions, they're actually the ones that are most in need of exceptions. After all, if there's no code that can validate the return value, there's no way of knowing that anything went wrong.

The Pareto Principle

In 1906, Italian economist Vilfredo Pareto noted that 80% of the wealth in Italy was held by just 20% of its citizens. In over a century since then, this idea has been put to the test in a number of fields beyond economics, and similar patterns have been found. The exact percentages may vary, but the general observation has emerged over time: the vast majority of effects in many systems are a result of just a small number of the causes.

In programming, this principle can manifest in a number of different ways. One of the more common is in regard to early optimization. Donald Knuth, the noted computer scientist, once said that premature optimization is the root of all evil, and many people take that to mean optimization should be avoided until all other aspects of the code have been finished.

Knuth, however, was referring to a focus solely on performance too early in the process. It's useless to try to tweak every ounce of speed out of a program until you've verified that it even does what it's supposed to. As a more practical matter, the Pareto Principle teaches us that a little bit of work at the outset can have a large impact on performance.

Striking that balance can be difficult, but there are a few easy things that can be done while designing a program, which can handle the bulk of the performance problems with little effort. Some such techniques are listed throughout the remainder of this book, under sidebars labeled Optimization.

Another application of the Pareto Principle involves prioritization of features in a complex application or framework. Rather than trying to build everything all at once, it's often better to start with the minority of features that will provide the most benefit to your users. Doing so allows you to get started on the core focus of the application and get it out to the people who need to use it, while you can refine additional features based on feedback.

The Robustness Principle

During early development of the Internet, it was evident that many of the protocols being designed would have to be implemented by countless different programs and they'd all have to work together in order to be productive. Getting the specifications right was important, but getting people to implement them interoperably was even more important.

In 1980, the Transmission Control Protocol was updated with RFC 761,[4] which included what has become one of the most significant guidelines in protocol design: be conservative in what you do; be

---

[4] http://propython.com/rfc-761

liberal in what you accept from others. It was called "a general principle of robustness," but it's also been referred to as Postel's Law, after its author, Jon Postel.

It's easy to see how this principle would be useful when guiding the implementations of protocols designed for the Internet. Essentially, programs that follow this principle will be able to work much more reliably with programs that don't. By sticking to the rules when generating output, that output is more likely to be understood by software that doesn't necessarily follow the specification completely. Likewise, if you allow for some variations in the incoming data, incorrect implementations can still send you data you can understand.

Moving beyond protocol design, an obvious application of this principle is in functions. If you can be a bit liberal in what values you accept as arguments, you can accommodate usage alongside other code that provides different types of values. A common example is a function that accepts floating point numbers, which can work just as well when given an integer or a decimal because they can both be converted to floats.

The return value is also important to the integration of a function with the code that calls it. One common way this comes into play is when a function can't do what it's supposed to and thus can't produce a useful return value. Some programmers will opt to return None in these cases, but then it's up to the code that called the function to identify that and handle it separately. The samurai principle recommends that in these cases, the code should raise an exception rather than return an unusable value. Because Python returns None by default, if no other value was returned, it's important to consider the return value explicitly.

It's always useful, though, to try to find some return value that would still satisfy requirements. For example, for a function that's designed to find all instances of a particular word within a passage of text, what happens when the given word can't be found at all? One option is to return None; another is to raise some WordNotFound exception.

If the function is supposed to return *all* instances, though, it should already be returning a list or an iterator, so finding no words presents an easy solution: return an empty list or an iterator that produces nothing. The key here is that the calling code can always expect a certain type of value, and as long as the function follows the robustness principle, everything will work just fine.

If you're unsure which approach would be best, you can provide two different methods, each with a different set of intentions. For example, Chapter 5 will explain how dictionaries can support both get() and __getitem__() methods, each reacting differently when a specified key doesn't exist.

In addition to code interaction, robustness also applies when dealing with the people who use the software. If you're writing a program that accepts input from human beings, whether it be text- or mouse-based, it's always helpful to be lenient with what you're given. You can allow command-line arguments to be specified out of order, make buttons bigger, allow incoming files to be slightly malformed or anything else that helps people use the software without sacrificing being explicit.

Backward Compatibility

Programming is iterative in nature, and nowhere is that more noticeable than when you distribute your code for other people to use in their own projects. Each new version not only comes with new features but also the risk that existing features will change in some way that will break code that relies on its behavior. By committing yourself to backward compatibility, you can minimize that risk for your users, giving them more confidence in your code.

Unfortunately, backward compatibility is something of a double-edged sword when it comes to designing your application. On one hand, you should always try to make your code the best it can be, and sometimes that involves changes to repair decisions that were made early on in the process. On the other hand, once you make major decisions, you need to commit to maintaining those decisions in the long run. The two sides run contrary to each other, so it's quite a balancing act.

Perhaps the biggest advantage you can give yourself is to make a distinction between public and private interfaces. Then, you can commit to long-term support of the public interfaces, while leaving the private interfaces for more rigorous refinement and change. Once the private interfaces are more finalized, they can then be promoted to the public API and documented for users.

Documentation is one of the main differentiators between public and private interfaces, but naming can also play an important role. Functions and attributes that begin with an underscore are generally understood to be private in nature, even without documentation. Adhering to this will help your users look at the source and decide which interfaces they'd like to use, taking on the risk themselves if they choose to use the private ones.

Sometimes, though, even the publicly safe interfaces might need to change in order to accommodate new features. It's usually best to wait until a major version number change, though, and warn users in advance of the incompatible changes that will occur. Then, going forward, you can commit to the long-term compatibility of the new interfaces. That's the approach Python took while working toward its long-awaited 3.0 release.

The Road to Python 3.0

At the turn of the century, Guido van Rossum decided it was time to start working toward a significant change in how Python handles some of its core features, such as how it handles strings and integers, favoring iterators over lists and several seemingly minor syntax changes. During the planning of what was then called Python 3000—at the time, it was unclear what version number would actually implement the changes—the Python team realized just how much of a burden those backward incompatible changes would place on programmers.

In an effort to ease the transition, features were divided into those that could be implemented in a backward compatible way and those that couldn't. The backward compatible features were implemented in the 2.x line, while the rest were postponed for what would eventually become Python 3.0. Along the way, many of the features that would eventually change or be removed were marked as deprecated, indicating developers should begin preparations for moving to the new code when it arrives.

When everything was ready, versions 2.6 and 3.0 were released back to back, with Python 2.6 being compatible with the rest of the 2.x line, while Python 3.0 would be a new beginning for the codebase and its users. Python 2.6 also included a special execution mode, invoked by supplying the -3 option, which would report warnings for using those features that would change in Python 3.0.

In addition, a separate tool, called 2to3, is able to automatically convert most Python source files from using the 2.x features to the 3.0 features that would replace them. It can't read your mind, of course, but many of the changes can be made without programmer intervention. Others, such as choosing the right string type to use, may require explicit hints to be provided by a programmer in order for 2to3 to make the right choices. These hints will be explained in more detail in Chapter 7.

This transition is particularly well-suited for individual projects converting from Python 2.6 to Python 3.0, but that still leaves the question of distributed applications, especially those libraries and frameworks with very large audiences. In those cases, you can't be sure what version of Python your users will be using, so you can't just convert the codebase over and expect everyone to follow along. After all, their work may be relying on multiple applications at once, so moving some to Python 3.0 means abandoning those that have yet to make the transition.

The seemingly obvious solution is to provide both 2.x and 3.0 versions of the codebase simultaneously, but that's often very difficult to maintain, given live access to a development version between official releases. Essentially, each modification of the codebase would need to be run through the 2to3 conversion, so that both versions are always up to date. With automated tools integrated with a source management system, this would be possible, but very fragile, because not all changes can have the conversion fully automated.

A more pragmatic approach is to actively maintain support for the version of Python used by the majority of users, with more occasional releases that undergo the conversion to the other version used by the minority. This also means regularly polling the users to determine which version is more common and making the change in support once the shift takes place.

Taking It With You

The principles and philosophies presented in this chapter represent many of the ideals that are highly valued by the Python community at large, but they're of value only when applied to actual design decisions in real code. The rest of this book will frequently refer to this chapter, explaining how these decisions went into the code described. First up, let's examine some of the more fundamental techniques that you can build on to put these principles to work in your code.

■ ■ ■

## CHAPTER 2

Advanced Basics

Like any other book on programming, the remainder of this book relies on quite a few features that may or may not be considered commonplace by readers. You, the reader, are expected to know a good deal about Python and programming in general, but there are a variety of lesser-used features that are extremely useful in the operations of many techniques shown throughout the book.

Therefore, as unusual as it may seem, this chapter will focus on a concept of advanced basics. The tools and techniques in this chapter aren't necessarily common knowledge, but they form a solid foundation for more advanced implementations to follow. Let's start off with some of the general concepts that tend to come up often in Python development.

General Concepts

Before getting into more concrete details, it's important to get a feel for the concepts that lurk behind the specifics covered later in this chapter. These are different from the principles and philosophies from the first chapter in that they are concerned more with actual programming techniques, while those discussed previously are more generic design goals.

In this regard, you can look at the first chapter as a design guide, while the concepts presented here are more of an implementation guide. Of course, there's only so specific a description like this can get without bogging down in too many details, so this section will defer to more detailed chapters throughout the rest of the book for more information.

Iteration

Although there is a nearly infinite number of different types of sequences that might come up in Python code—more on that later in this chapter and in Chapter 5—most code that uses them can be placed in one of two categories: those that actually use the sequence as a whole and those that just need the items within it. Most functions use both approaches in various ways, but the distinction is important in order to understand what tools Python makes available and how they should be used.

Looking at things from a purely object-oriented perspective, it's easy to understand how to work with sequences that your code actually needs to use. You'll have a concrete object, such as a list, set or dictionary, which not only has data associated with it, but also has methods that allow for accessing and modifying that data. You may need to iterate over it multiple times, access individual items out of order or return it from the function for other code to use, all of which works well with more traditional object usage.

On the other hand, you may not actually need to work with the entire sequence as a whole; you may be interested solely in each item within it. This is often the case when looping over a range of numbers, for instance, because what's important is having each number available within the loop, not having the whole list of numbers available.

The difference between the two approaches is primarily about intention, but there are technological implications as well. Not all sequences need to be loaded in their entirety in advance, and many don't even need to have a finite upper limit at all. This category includes such things as the set of positive odd numbers, squares of integers and the Fibonacci sequence, all of which are infinite in length and easily computable. Therefore, they're best suited for pure iteration, without the need to populate a list in advance.

The main benefit to this is memory allocation. A program designed to print out the entire range of the Fibonacci sequence only needs to keep a few variables in memory at any given time, because each value in the sequence can be calculated from the two previous values. Populating a list of the values, even with a limited length, requires loading all the included values into memory before iterating over them. If the full list will never be acted on as a whole, it's far more efficient to simply generate each item as it's necessary and discard it once it's no longer required in order to produce new items.

Python as a language offers a few different ways to iterate over a sequence without pushing all its values into memory at once. As a library, Python uses those techniques in many of its provided features, which may sometimes lead to confusion. After all, both approaches allow you to write a `for` loop without a problem, but many sequences won't have the methods and attributes you might expect to see on a list.

The section on iteration later in this chapter will cover some of the more common ways to create iterable sequences and also a simple way to coerce those sequences to lists when you truly do need to operate on the sequence as a whole. Sometimes, though, it's useful to have an object that can function in both respects, which requires the use of caching.

Caching

Outside of computing, a cache is a hidden collection, typically of items either too dangerous or too valuable to be made publicly accessible. The definition in computing is related, with caches storing data in a way that doesn't impact a public-facing interface. Perhaps the most common real-world example is a Web browser, which downloads a document from the Web when it's first requested, but keeps a copy of that document. When the user requests that same document again at a later time, the browser loads the private copy and displays it to the user instead of hitting the remote server again.

In the browser example, the public interface could be the address bar, an entry in the user's favorites or a link from another Web site, where the user never has to indicate whether the document should be retrieved remotely or accessed from a local cache. Instead, the software uses the cache to reduce the number of remote requests that need to be made, as long as the document doesn't change quickly. The details of Web document caching are beyond the scope of this book, but it's a good example of how caching works in general.

More specifically, a cache should be looked at as a time-saving utility that doesn't explicitly need to exist in order for a feature to work properly. If the cache gets deleted or is otherwise unavailable, the function that utilizes it should continue to work properly, perhaps with a dip in performance because it needs to re-create the items that were lost. That also means that code utilizing a cache must always accept enough information to generate a valid result without the use of the cache.

The nature of caching also means that you need to be careful about ensuring the cache is as up-to-date as your needs demand. In the Web browser example, servers can specify how long a browser should hold on to a cached copy of a document before destroying the local copy and requesting a fresh one from the server. In simple mathematical examples, the result can be cached theoretically forever, because the result should always be the same, given the same input. Chapter 3 covers a technique called memoization that does exactly that.

A useful compromise is to cache a value indefinitely, but update it immediately when the value is updated. This isn't always an option, particularly if values are retrieved from an external source, but when the value is updated within your application, updating the cache is an easy step to include, which saves the trouble of having to invalidate the cache and retrieve the value from scratch later on. Doing so can incur a performance penalty, though, so you'll have to weigh the merits of live updates against the speed you might lose by doing so.

Transparency

Whether describing building materials, image formats or government actions, transparency refers to the ability to see through or inside of something, and its use in programming is no different. For our purposes, transparency refers to the ability of your code to see—and in many cases, even edit—nearly everything that the computer has access to.

Python doesn't support the notion of private variables in the typical manner, so all attributes are accessible to any object that requests them. Some languages consider that type of openness to be a risk to stability, instead allowing the code that powers an object to be solely responsible for that object's data. While that does prevent some occasional misuses of internal data structures, Python doesn't take any measures to restrict access to that data.

Although the most obvious use of transparent access is in object attributes—which is where many other languages allow more privacy—Python allows you to inspect a wide range of aspects of objects and the code that powers them. In fact, you can even get access to the compiled bytecode that Python uses to execute functions. Here are just a few examples of information available at runtime.

- Attributes on an object

- The names of attributes available on an object

- The type of an object

- The module where a class or function was defined

- The filename where a module was loaded

- The bytecode for a given function

Most of this information is only used internally, but it's available because there are potential uses that can't be accounted for when code is first written. Retrieving that information at run-time is called introspection and is a common tactic in systems that implement principles like DRY.

The rest of this book will contain many different introspection techniques in the sections where such information is available. For those rare occasions where data should indeed be protected, Chapters 3 and 4 show how data can show the intent of privacy or be hidden entirely.

Control Flow

Generally speaking, the control flow of a program is the path the program takes during execution. The more common examples of control flow are the `if`, `for` and `while` blocks, which are used to manage the most fundamental branches your code could need. Those blocks are also some of the first things a Python programmer will learn, so this section will instead focus on some of the lesser-used and under-utilized control flow mechanisms.

Catching Exceptions

Chapter 1 explained how Python philosophy encourages the use of exceptions wherever an expectation is violated, but expectations often vary between different uses. This is especially common when one application relies on another, but it's also quite common within a single application. Essentially, any time one function calls another, it can add its own expectations on top of what the called function already handles.

Exceptions are raised with a simple syntax using the **raise** keyword, but catching them is slightly more complicated because it uses a combination of keywords. The **try** keyword begins a block where you expect exceptions to occur, while the **except** keyword marks a block to execute when an exception is raised. The first part is easy, since **try** doesn't have anything to go along with it, and the simplest form of **except** also doesn't require any additional information.

```
def count_lines(filename):
    """
    Count the number of lines in a file. If the file can't be
    opened, it should be treated the same as if it was empty.
    """
    try:
        return len(open(filename, 'r').readlines())
    except:
        # Something went wrong reading the file
        # or calculating the number of lines.
        return 0
```

Any time an exception gets raised inside the **try** block, the code in the **except** block will be executed. As it stands, this doesn't make any distinction among the many various exceptions that could be raised; no matter what happens, the function will always return a number. It's actually fairly rare that you'd want to do that, though, because many exceptions should in fact propagate up to the rest of the system— errors should never pass silently. Some notable examples are **SystemExit** and **KeyboardInterrupt**, both of which should usually cause the program to stop running.

In order to account for those and other exceptions that your code shouldn't interfere with, the **except** keyword can accept one or more exception types that should be caught explicitly. Any others will simply be raised as if you didn't have a **try** block at all. This focuses the **except** block on just those situations that should definitely be handled, so your code only has to deal with what it's supposed to manage.

```
def count_lines(filename):
    """
    Count the number of lines in a file. If the file can't be
    opened, it should be treated the same as if it was empty.
    """
    try:
        return len(open(filename, 'r').readlines())
    except IOError:
        # Something went wrong reading the file.
        return 0
```

By changing the code to accept **IOError** explicitly, the **except** block will only execute if there was a problem accessing the file from the filesystem. Any other errors, such as a **filename** that's not even a string, will simply raise outside of this function, to be handled by some other piece of code.

If you need to catch multiple exception types, there are two approaches. The first and easiest is to simply catch some base class that all the necessary exceptions derive from. Since exception handling matches against the specified class and all its subclasses, this approach works quite well when all the types you need to catch do have a common base class. In the line counting example, you could encounter either **IOError** or **OSError**, both of which are descendants of **EnvironmentError**.

```python
def count_lines(filename):
    """
    Count the number of lines in a file. If the file can't be
    opened, it should be treated the same as if it was empty.
    """
    try:
        return len(open(filename, 'r').readlines())
    except EnvironmentError:
        # Something went wrong reading the file.
        return 0
```

■ **Note** Even though we're only interested in `IOError` and `OSError`, all subclasses of `EnvironmentError` will get caught as well. In this case, that's fine because those are the only subclasses of `EnvironmentError`, but in general you'll want to make sure you're not catching too many exceptions.

Other times, you may want to catch multiple exception types that don't share a common base class or perhaps limit it to a smaller list of types. In these cases, you need to specify each type individually, separated by commas. In the case of **count_lines()**, there's also the possibility of a **TypeError** that could be raised if the filename passed in isn't a valid string.

```python
def count_lines(filename):
    """
    Count the number of lines in a file. If the file can't be
    opened, it should be treated the same as if it was empty.
    """
    try:
        return len(open(filename, 'r').readlines())
    except (EnvironmentError, TypeError):
        # Something went wrong reading the file.
        return 0
```

If you need access to the exception itself, perhaps to log the message for later, you can get it by adding an **as** clause and supplying a variable to contain the exception object.

```python
import logging

def count_lines(filename):
    """
    Count the number of lines in a file. If the file can't be
    opened, it should be treated the same as if it was empty.
    """
    try:
        return len(open(filename, 'r').readlines())
    except (EnvironmentError, TypeError) as e:
        # Something went wrong reading the file.
        logging.error(e)
        return 0
```

Multiple **except** clauses can also be combined, allowing you to handle different types of exceptions in different ways. For example, `EnvironmentError` uses two arguments, an error code and an error message, that combine to form its complete string representation. In order to log just the error message in that case, but still correctly handle the `TypeError` case, two **except** clauses could be used.

```python
import logging

def count_lines(filename):
    """
    Count the number of lines in a file. If the file can't be
    opened, it should be treated the same as if it was empty.
    """
    try:
        return len(open(filename, 'r').readlines())
    except TypeError as e:
        # The filename wasn't valid for use with the filesystem.
        logging.error(e)
        return 0
    except EnvironmentError as e:
        # Something went wrong reading the file.
        logging.error(e.args[1])
        return 0
```

Exception Chains

Sometimes, while handling one exception, another exception might get raised along the way. This can happen either explicitly with a **raise** keyword or implicitly through some other code that gets executed as part of the handling. Either way, this situation brings up a question of which exception is important enough to present itself to the rest of the application. Exactly how that question is answered depends on how the code is laid out, so let's take a look at a simple example, where the exception handling code opens and writes to a log file.

```python
>>> def get_value(dictionary, name):
>>>     try:
```

```
>>>         return dictionary[name]
>>>     except Exception as e:
>>>         log = open('logfile.txt', 'w')
>>>         log.write('%s\n' % e)
>>>         log.close()
>>>
```

If anything should go wrong when writing to the log, a separate exception will be raised. Even though this new exception is important, there was already an exception in play that shouldn't be forgotten. To retain the original information, the file exception gains a new attribute, called **__context__**, which holds the original exception object. Each exception can possibly reference one other, forming a chain that represents everything that went wrong, in order. Consider what happens when **get_value()** fails, but **logfile.txt** is a read-only file.

```
>>> get_value({}, 'test')
Traceback (most recent call last):
  ...
KeyError: 'test'

During handling of the above exception, another exception occurred:

Traceback (most recent call last):
  ...
IOError: [Errno 13] Permission denied: 'logfile.txt'
>>>
```

This is an implicit chain, because the exceptions are linked only by how they're encountered during execution. Sometimes you'll be generating an exception yourself, and you may need to include an exception that was generated elsewhere. One common example of this is validating values using a function that was passed in. Validation functions, as will be described in Chapters 3 and 4, generally raise a **ValueError**, regardless of what was wrong.

This is a great opportunity to form an explicit chain, so we can raise a **ValueError** directly, while retaining the actual exception behind the scenes. Python allows this by including the **from** keyword at the end of the **raise** statement.

```
>>> def validate(value, validator):
...     try:
...         return validator(value)
...     except Exception as e:
...         raise ValueError('Invalid value: %s' % value) from e
...
>>> def validator(value):
...     if len(value) > 10:
...         raise ValueError("Value can't exceed 10 characters")
...
>>> validate('test', validator)
>>> validate(False, validator)
Traceback (most recent call last):
  ...
TypeError: object of type 'bool' has no len()
```

The above exception was the direct cause of the following exception:

```
Traceback (most recent call last):
    ...
ValueError: invalid value: False
```

Since this wraps multiple exceptions up together into a single object, it may seem ambiguous as to which exception is really being passed around. A simple rule to remember is that the most recent exception is the one being raised, with any others available by way of the __context__ attribute. This is easy to test by wrapping one of these functions in a new **try** block and checking the type of the exception.

```
>>> try:
...     validate(False, validator)
... except Exception as e:
...     print(type(e))
...
<class 'ValueError'>
>>>
```

When Everything Goes Right

On the other end of the spectrum, you may find that you have a complex block of code, where you need to catch exceptions that may crop up from part of it, but code after that part should proceed without any error handling. The obvious approach is to simply add that code outside of the **try**/**except** blocks. Here's how we might adjust the count_lines() function to contain the error-generating code inside the **try** block, while the line counting takes place after the exceptions have been handled.

```
import logging

def count_lines(filename):
    """
    Count the number of lines in a file. If the file can't be
    opened, it should be treated the same as if it was empty.
    """
    try:
        file = open(filename, 'r')
    except TypeError as e:
        # The filename wasn't valid for use with the filesystem.
        logging.error(e)
        return 0
    except EnvironmentError as e:
        # Something went wrong reading the file.
        logging.error(e.args[1])
        return 0
    return len(file.readlines())
```

In this particular case, the function will work as expected, so all seems fine. Unfortunately, it's misleading because of the nature of this specific case. Because each of the **except** blocks explicitly returns a value from the function, the code after the error handling will only be reached if no exceptions were raised.

■ **Note** We could place the file reading code directly after the file is opened, but then if any exceptions are raised there, they'd get caught using the same error handling as the file opening. Separating them is a way to better control how exceptions are handled overall. You may also notice that the file isn't closed anywhere here. That will be handled in later sections, as this function continues expanding.

If, however, the **except** blocks simply logged the error and moved on, Python would try to count the lines in the file, even though no file was ever opened. Instead, we need a way to specify a block of code should be run only if no exceptions were raised at all, so it doesn't matter how your **except** blocks execute. Python provides this feature by way of the **else** keyword, which defines a separate block.

```python
import logging

def count_lines(filename):
    """
    Count the number of lines in a file. If the file can't be
    opened, it should be treated the same as if it was empty.
    """
    try:
        file = open(filename, 'r')
    except TypeError as e:
        # The filename wasn't valid for use with the filesystem.
        logging.error(e)
        return 0
    except EnvironmentError as e:
        # Something went wrong reading the file.
        logging.error(e.args[1])
        return 0
    else:
        return len(file.readlines())
```

■ **Caution** Raising an exception isn't the only thing that tells Python to avoid the **else** block. If the function returns a value at any time inside the **try** block, Python will simply return the value as instructed, skipping the **else** block altogether.

Proceeding Regardless of Exceptions

On yet another hand, many functions perform some kind of setup or resource allocation that must be cleaned up before returning control to external code. In the face of exceptions, the cleanup code might not always be executed, which can leave files or sockets open or perhaps leave large objects in memory when they're no longer needed.

To facilitate this, Python also allows the use of a **finally** block, which gets executed every time the associated **try**, **except** and **else** blocks finish. Since **count_lines()** opens a file, best practice would suggest that it also explicitly close the file, rather than waiting for garbage collection to deal with it later. Using `finally` provides a way to make sure the file always gets closed.

There is still one thing to consider though. So far, `count_lines()` only anticipates exceptions that could occur while trying to open the file, even though there's a common one that comes up when reading the file: `UnicodeDecodeError`. Chapter 7 covers a bit of Unicode and how Python deals with it, but for now, just know that it comes up fairly often. In order to catch this new exception, it's necessary to move the `readlines()` call back into the `try` block, but we can still leave the line counting in the `else` block.

```python
import logging

def count_lines(filename):
    """
    Count the number of lines in a file. If the file can't be
    opened, it should be treated the same as if it was empty.
    """
    file = None  # file must always have a value
    try:
        file = open(filename, 'r')
        lines = file.readlines()
    except TypeError as e:
        # The filename wasn't valid for use with the filesystem.
        logging.error(e)
        return 0
    except EnvironmentError as e:
        # Something went wrong reading the file.
        logging.error(e.args[1])
        return 0
    except UnicodeDecodeError as e:
        # The contents of the file were in an unknown encoding.
        logging.error(e)
        return 0
    else:
        return len(lines)
    finally:
        if file:
            file.close()
```

Of course, it's not very likely that you'd have this much error handling in a simple line counting function. After all, it really only exists because we wanted to return 0 in the event of any errors. In the real world, you're much more likely to just let the exceptions run their course outside of `count_lines()`, letting other code be responsible for how to handle it.

■ **Tip** Some of this handling can be made a bit simpler using a `with` block, described later in this chapter.

Optimizing Loops

Since loops of some kind or another are very common in most types of code, it's important to make sure they can run as efficiently as possible. The iteration section later in this chapter covers a variety of ways to optimize the design of any loops, while Chapter 5 explains how you can control the behavior of for loops. Instead, this section focuses on the optimization of the while loop.

Typically, while is used to check a condition that may change during the course of the loop, so that the loop can finish executing once the condition evaluates to false. When that condition is too complicated to distill into a single expression or when the loop is expected to break due to an exception, it makes more sense to keep the while expression always true and end the loop using a break statement where appropriate.

Although any expression that evaluates to true will induce the intended functionality, there is one specific value you can use to make it even better. Python knows that True will always evaluate to true, so it makes some additional optimizations behind the scenes to speed up the loop. Essentially, it doesn't even bother checking the condition each time; it just runs the code inside the loop indefinitely, until it encounters an exception, a break statement or a return statement.

```python
def echo():
    """Returns everything you type until you press Ctrl-C"""

    while True:
        try:
            print(input('Type Something: '))
        except KeyboardInterrupt:
            print()  # Make sure the prompt appears on a new line.
            break
```

Compatibility: Prior to 3.0

Before Python 3.0 was released, True and False weren't reserved as constants. Because you were allowed to assign to them, such as True = 0, their values could only be determined when actually executing the code. The optimization used for while loops relies on knowing, in advance, that the value will always be true, so it wasn't available in older versions.

If you need to maintain compatibility with Python versions prior to 3.0, you can use while 1 for loops such as the one listed in this section. It's slightly less readable than the newer alternative, but it's still quite straightforward, and the performance gains will be worth it, especially if it's a commonly used function that may need to perform many iterations of the loop's contents.

The with Statement

The finally block covered in the exception handling section previously in this chapter is a convenient way to clean up after a function, but sometimes that's the only reason to use a try block in the first place. Sometimes you don't want to silence any exceptions, but you still want to make sure the cleanup code executes, regardless of what happens. Working solely with exception handling, a simpler version of count_lines() might look something like this.

```python
def count_lines(filename):
    """Count the number of lines in a file."""

    file = open(filename, 'r')
    try:
        return len(file.readlines())
    finally:
        file.close()
```

If the file fails to open, it'll raise an exception before even entering the `try` block, while everything else that could go wrong would do so inside the try block, which will cause the `finally` block to clean up the file. Unfortunately, it's something of a waste to use the power of the exception handling system just for that. Instead, Python provides another option that has some other advantages over exception handling as well.

The `with` keyword can be used to start a new block of code, much like `try`, but with a very different purpose in mind. By using a `with` block, you're defining a specific context, in which the contents of the block should execute. The beauty of it, though, is that the object you provide in the `with` statement gets to determine what that context means.

For example, you can use `open()` in a `with` statement to run some code in the context of that file. In this case, `with` also provides an `as` clause, which allows an object to be returned for use while executing in the current context. Here's how we could rewrite the new version of `count_lines()` to take advantage of all of this.

```python
def count_lines(filename):
    """Count the number of lines in a file."""

    with open(filename, 'r') as file:
        return len(file.readlines())
```

That's really all that's left of `count_lines()` after switching to use the `with` statement. The exception handling gets done by the code that manages the `with` statement, while the file closing behavior is actually provided by the file itself, by way of a context manager. Context managers are special objects that know about the `with` statement and can define exactly what it means to have code executed in their context.

In a nutshell, the context manager gets a chance to run its own code before the `with` block executes; then gets to run some more cleanup code after it's finished. Exactly what happens at each of those stages will vary; in the case of `open()`, it opens the file and closes it automatically when the block finishes executing.

With files, the context obviously always revolves an open file object, which is made available to the block using the name given in the `as` clause. Sometimes, though, the context is entirely environmental, so there is no such object to use during execution. To support those cases, the `as` clause is optional.

In fact, you can even leave off the `as` clause in the case of `open()` without causing any errors. Of course, you also won't have the file available to your code, so it'd be of little use, but there's nothing in Python that prevents you from doing so. If you include an `as` clause when using a context manager that doesn't provide an object, the variable you define will simply be populated with `None` instead, because all functions return `None` if no other value is specified.

There are several context managers available in Python, some of which will be detailed throughout the rest of this book. In addition, Chapter 5 will show how you can write your own context managers, so you can customize the contextual behavior to match the needs of your own code.

Conditional Expressions

Fairly often, you may find yourself needing to access one of two values, and which one you use depends on evaluating an expression. For instance, it's quite common to display one string to a user if the a value exceeds a particular value and a different one otherwise. Typically, this would be done using an `if`/`else` combination, as follows.

```python
def test_value(value):
    if value < 100:
        return 'The value is just right.'
    else:
        return 'The value is too big!'
```

Rather than writing this out into four separate lines, it's possible to condense it down to a single line using a conditional expression. By converting the `if` and `else` blocks into clauses in an expression, Python does the same effect much more concisely.

```python
def test_value(value):
    return 'The value is ' + ('just right.' if value < 100 else 'too big!')
```

Readability Counts

If you're used to this behavior from other programming languages, Python's ordering may seem unusual at first. Most other languages implement something of the form, `expression ? value_1 : value_2`. That is, the expression to test comes first, followed by the value to use if the expression is true, then the value to use if the expression is false.

Instead, Python attempts to use a form that more explicitly describes what's really going on. The expectation is that the expression will be true most of the time, so the associated value comes first, followed by the expression, then the value to use if the expression is false. This takes the entire statement into account by putting the more common value in the place it would be if there were no expression at all. For example, you end up with things like `return value ...` and `x = value ...`.

Because the expression is then tacked on afterward, it highlights the notion that the expression is just a qualification of the first value. "Use this value whenever this expression is true; otherwise, use the other one." It may seem a little odd if you're used to another language, but it makes sense when thinking about the equivalent in plain English.

There's another approach that is sometimes used to simulate the behavior of the conditional expression described in this section. This was often used in older Python installations where the `if`/`else` expression wasn't yet available. In its place, many programmers relied on the behavior of the **and** and **or** operators, which could be made to do something very similar. Here's how the previous example could be rewritten using only these operators.

```
def test_value(value):
    return 'The value is ' + (value < 100 and 'just right.' or 'too big!')
```

This puts the order of components more in line with the form used in other programming languages. That fact may make it more comfortable for programmers used to working with those languages, and it certainly maintains compatibility with even older versions of Python. Unfortunately, it comes with a hidden danger that is often left unknown until it breaks an otherwise working program with little explanation. To understand why, let's examine what's going on.

The **and** operator works like the **&&** operator in many languages, checking to see if the value to the left of the operator evaluates to true. If it doesn't, **and** returns the value to its left; otherwise, the value to the left is evaluated and returned. So, if a value of 50 was passed into **test_value()**, the left side evaluates to true, so the **and** clause evaluates to the string, **'just right.'** Factoring in that process, here's how the code would look.

```
    return 'The value is ' + ('just right.' or 'too big!')
```

From here, the **or** operator works similarly to **and**, checking the value to its left to see if it evaluates to true. The difference is that if the value is true, that value is returned, without even evaluating the right-hand side of the operator at all. Looking at the condensed code here, it's clear that **or** would then return the string, **'just right.'**

On the other hand, if the value passed into the **test_value()** function was 150, the behavior is changed. Since **150 < 100** evaluates to false, the **and** operator returns that value, without evaluating the right-hand side. In that case, here's the resulting expression.

```
    return 'The value is ' + (False or 'too big!')
```

Since **False** is obviously false, the the **or** operator returns the value to its right instead, **'too big!'** This behavior has led many people to rely on the **and/or** combination for conditional expressions. But have you noticed the problem? One of the assumptions being made here causes the whole thing to break down in many situations.

The problem is in the **or** clause when the left side of the **and** clause is true. In that case, the behavior of the **or** clause depends entirely on the value to the left of the operator. In the case shown here, it's a non-empty string, which will always evaluate to true, but what happens if you supply it an empty string, the number 0 or, worst of all, a variable that could contain a value you can't be sure of until the code executes?

What essentially happens is that the left side of the **and** clause evaluates to true, but the right side evaluates to false, so the end result of that clause is a false value. Then, when the **or** clause evaluates, its left side is false, so it returns the value to its right. In the end, the expression will always return the item to the right of the **or** operator, *regardless of the value at the beginning of the expression.*

Because no exceptions are raised, it doesn't look like anything is actually broken in the code. Instead, it simply looks like the first value in the expression was false, because it's returning the value that you would expect in that case. This may lead you to try to debug whatever code defines *that* value, rather than looking at the real problem, which is the value between the two operators.

Ultimately, what makes it so hard to pin down is that you have to distrust your own code, removing any assumptions you may have had about how it should work. You have to really look at it the way Python sees it, rather than how a human would see it.

Iteration

There are generally two ways of looking at sequences: as a collection of items or as a way to access a single item at a time. These two aren't mutually exclusive, but it's useful to separate them in order to understand the different features available in each case. Working on the collection as a whole requires that all the items be in memory at once, but accessing them one at a time can often be done much more efficiently.

Iteration refers to this more efficient form of traversing a collection, working with just one item at a time before moving on to the next. Iteration is an option for any type of sequence, but the real advantage comes in special types of objects that don't need to load everything in memory all at once. The canonical example of this is Python's built-in `range()` function, which iterates over the integers that fall within a given range.

```
>>> for x in range(5):
...     print(x)
...
0
1
2
3
4
```

At a glance, it may look like `range()` returns a list containing the appropriate values, but it doesn't. This shows if you examine its return value on its own, without iterating over it.

```
>>> range(5)
range(0, 5)
>>> list(range(5))
[0, 1, 2, 3, 4]
```

The `range` object itself doesn't contain any of the values in the sequence. Instead, it generates them one at a time, on demand, during iteration. If you truly want a list that you can add or remove items from, you can coerce one by passing the `range` object into a new `list` object. This internally iterates just like a `for` loop, so the generated list uses the same values that are available when iterating over the `range` itself.

Compatibility: Prior to 3.0

In Python 3.0, many functions were changed to rely on iteration rather than returning complete lists. The `range()` example in this section will simply return a list in an earlier version. Prior to version 3.0, some of these sequence-creating functions had alternatives that offered iteration instead. These variations are often prefixed with an x, so the iterable option that was available in earlier versions was `xrange()`.

Now that `range()` behaves the way `xrange()` used to, `xrange()` has been removed. If you simply need compatibility with Python installations both before and after 3.0, you can simply use `range()`, allowing the older installations to simply lose the performance benefits. If the efficiency gains are important to the application, though, you can check for the existence of `xrange()` and use that if it's available, falling back to `range()` otherwise.

Chapter 5 shows how you can write your own iterable objects that work similarly to `range()`. In addition to providing iterable objects, there are a number of ways to iterate over these objects in different situations, for different purposes. The `for` loop is the most obvious technique, but Python offers other forms of syntax as well, which are outlined in this section.

Sequence Unpacking

Generally, you would assign one value to one variable at a time, so when you have a sequence, you would assign the entire sequence to a single variable. When the sequences are small and you know how many items are in the sequence and what each item will be, this is fairly limiting, because you'll often end up just accessing each item individually, rather than dealing with them as a sequence.

This is particularly common when working with tuples, where the sequence often has a fixed length and each item in the sequence has a pre-determined meaning. Tuples of this type are also the preferred way to return multiple values from a function, which makes it all the more annoying to have to bother with them as a sequence. Ideally, you should be able to retrieve them as individual items directly when getting the function's return value.

To allow for this, Python supports a special syntax called sequence unpacking. Rather than specifying a single name to assign a value, you can specify a number of names as a tuple on the left side of the = operator. This will cause Python to unpack the sequence on the right side of the operator, assigning each value to the related name on the left side.

```
>>> 'propython.com'.split('.')
['propython', 'com']
>>> components = 'propython.com'.split('.')
>>> components
['propython', 'com']
>>> domain, tld = 'propython.com'.split('.')
>>> domain
'propython'
>>> tld
'com'
>>> domain, tld = 'www.propython.com'.split('.')
Traceback (most recent call last):
  ...
ValueError: too many values to unpack
```

The error shown at the end of this example illustrates the only significant limitation of this approach: the number of variables to assign must match the number of items in the sequence. If they don't match, Python can't properly assign the values. If you look at the tuple as being similar to an argument list, though, there's another option available.

If you add an asterisk before the final name in the variable list, Python will keep a list of any values that couldn't be put into one of the other variables. The resulting list is stored in the final variable, so you can still assign a sequence that contains more items than you have explicit variables to hold them. This only works if you have more items in the sequence than you have variables to assign to. If the reverse is true, you'll still run into the `TypeError` shown previously.

```
>>> domain, *path = 'propython.com/example/url'.split('/')
>>> domain
'propython.com'
>>> path
['example', 'url']
```

■ **Note** Chapter 3 will show how a similar syntax applies to function arguments as well.

List Comprehensions

When you have a sequence with more items than you really need, it's often useful to generate a new list and add just those items that meet a certain criteria. There are a few ways to do that, the most obvious being to use a simple **for** loop, adding each item in turn.

```
>>> output = []
>>> for value in range(10):
...     if value > 5:
...         output.append(str(value))
...
>>> output
['6', '7', '8', '9']
```

Unfortunately, that adds four lines and two levels of indentation to your code, even though it's an extremely common pattern to use. Instead, Python offers a more concise syntax for this case, which allows you to express the three main aspects of that code into a single line.

- A sequence to retrieve values from

- An expression that's used to determine whether a value should be included

- An expression that's used to provide a value to the new list

These are all combined into a syntax called list comprehensions. Here's how the preceding example would look, when rewritten to use this construct. The three basic segments of this form have been highlighted for clarity.

```
>>> output = [str(value) for value in range(10) if value > 5]
>>> output
['6', '7', '8', '9']
```

As you can see, the three portions of the overall form have been rearranged slightly, with the expression for the final value coming first, followed by the iteration and ending with the condition for deciding which items are included. You may also consider the variable that contains the new list to be its own fourth portion of the form, but since the comprehension is really just an expression, it doesn't have to be assigned to a variable. It could just as easily be used to feed a list into a function.

```
>>> min([value for value in range(10) if value > 5])
6
```

Of course, this seems to violate the whole point of iteration that was pointed out earlier. After all, the comprehension returns a full list, only to have it thrown away when **min()** processes the values. For these situations, Python provides a different option: generator expressions.

Generator Expressions

Instead of creating an entire list based on certain criteria, it's often more useful to leverage the power of iteration for this process as well. Instead of surrounding the compression in brackets, which would indicate the creation of a proper list, you can instead surround it in parentheses, which will create a generator. Here's how it looks in action.

```
>>> gen = (value for value in range(10) if value > 5)
>>> gen
<generator object <genexpr> at 0x...>
>>> min(gen)
6
>>> min(gen)
Traceback (most recent call last):
  ...
ValueError: min() arg is an empty sequence
>>> min(value for value in range(10) if value > 5)
6
```

Okay, so there are a few things going on here, but it's easier to understand once you've seen the output, so you have a frame of reference. First off, a generator is really just an iterable object that you don't have to create using the explicit interface. Chapter 5 shows how you can create iterators manually and even how to create generators with more flexibility, but the generator expression is the simplest way to deal with them.

When you create a generator—whether a generator expression or some other form—you don't immediately have access to the sequence. The generator object doesn't yet know what values it'll need to iterate over; it won't know that until it actually starts generating them. So if you view or inspect a generator without iterating over it, you won't have access to the full range of values.

In order to retrieve those values, all you need to do is iterate over the generator like you ordinarily would and it'll happily spit out values as needed. This step is implicitly performed inside many built-in functions, such as min(). If those functions are able to operate without building a complete list, you can use generators to dramatically improve performance over the use of other options. If they do have to create a new list, you're not losing anything by delaying until the function really needs to create it.

But notice what happens if you iterate over the generator twice. The second time through, you get an error that you tried to pass in an empty sequence. Remember, a generator doesn't contain all the values; it just iterates over them when asked to do so. Once the iteration is complete and there are no more values left to iterate, the generator doesn't restart. Instead, it simply returns an empty list each time it's called thereafter.

There are two main reasons behind this behavior. First, it's not always obvious how it should restart the sequence. Some iterables, such as range(), do have an obvious way to restart themselves, so those do restart when iterated multiple times. Unfortunately, because there are any number of ways to create generators—and iterators in general—it's up to the iterable itself to determine when and how the sequence gets reset. Chapter 5 will explain this behavior, and how you can customize it for your own needs, in more detail.

Second, not all sequences should be reset once they complete. For example, you might implement an interface for cycling through a collection of active users, which may change over time. Once your code finishes iterating over the available users, it shouldn't simply reset to the same sequence over and over again. The nature of that ever-changing set of users means that Python itself can't possibly guess at how to control it. Instead, that behavior is controlled by more complex iterators.

One final note to point out about generator expressions is that, even though they must always be surrounded by parentheses, those parentheses don't always need to be unique to the expression. The last expression in this section's example simply use the parentheses from the function call to enclose the generator expression, which also works just fine.

This form may seem a little odd at first, but in this simple case, it saves you from having an extra set of parentheses hanging around. However, if the generator expression is just one of multiple arguments or if it's part of a more complex expression, you still need to include explicit parentheses around the generator expression itself, to make sure Python knows your intent.

Set Comprehensions

Sets—described in more detail in their own section under Collections—are very similar to lists in their construction, so you can build a set using a comprehension in basically the same way as lists. The only significant difference between the two is the use of curly braces instead of brackets surrounding the expression.

```
>>> {str(value) for value in range(10) if value > 5}
{'6', '7', '8', '9'}
```

■ **Note** Unlike sequences, sets are unordered, so different platforms may display the items in a different order. The only guarantee is that the same items will be present in the set, regardless of the platform.

Compatibility: Prior to 3.0

Just as set literals were introduced in Python 3.0, set comprehensions were first made available in that version. In older versions, you'll can use the built-in `set()` function, combined with a generator expression. The example provided in this section could be converted to the older style as follows:

```
set(str(value) for value in range(10) if value > 5)
```

Dictionary Comprehensions

There's certainly a theme developing with the construction of comprehensions for different types, and it's limited solely to one-dimensional sequences. Dictionaries can also be a form of sequence, but each item is really a pair of a key and its value. This is reflected in the literal form, by separating each key from its value by the use of a colon.

Since that colon is the factor that distinguishes the syntax for dictionaries from that of sets, the same colon is what separates dictionary comprehensions from set comprehensions. Where you would ordinarily include a single value, simply supply a key/value pair, separated by a colon. The rest of the comprehension follows the same rules as the other types.

```
>>> {value: str(value) for value in range(10) if value > 5}
{8: '8', 9: '9', 6: '6', 7: '7'}
```

■ **Note** Remember, dictionaries are unordered, so their keys work a lot like sets. If you need a dictionary with keys that can be reliably ordered, see the Ordered Dictionaries section later in this chapter.

Compatibility: Prior to 3.0

Dictionaries have had a literal syntax in Python for a long time, but the comprehension syntax wasn't added until version 3.0. In older installations, you could use a slightly more verbose syntax to achieve the same effect, combining `dict()` with a generator expression. This doesn't support the use of a colon to separate keys from values, though, so you'll have to create a sequence of 2-tuples, which `dict()` can use to join keys and values together. This syntax is equally valid after Python 3.0 as it was before, so this will suffice even in cases where compatibility with both must be maintained.

```
dict((value, str(value)) for value in range(10) if value > 5)
```

Chaining Iterables Together

Working with one iterable is useful enough in most situations, but sometimes you'll need to access one right after another, performing the same operation on each. The simple approach would be to just use two separate loops, duplicating the code block for each loop. The logical next step would be to factor that code out into a function, but now you have an extra function call in the mix for something that really only needs to be done inside the loop.

Instead, Python provides the `chain()` function, as part of its `itertools` module. The `itertools` module includes a number of different utilities, some of which are described in the following sections. The `chain()` function, in particular, accepts any number of iterables and returns a new generator that will iterate over each one in turn.

```
>>> import itertools
>>> list(itertools.chain(range(3), range(4), range(5)))
[0, 1, 2, 0, 1, 2, 3, 0, 1, 2, 3, 4]
```

Zipping Iterables Together

Another common operation involving multiple iterables is to merge them together, side by side. The first items from each iterable would come together to form a single tuple as the first value returned by a new generator. All the second items become part of the second tuple in the generator, and so on. The built-in `zip()` function provides this functionality when needed.

```
>>> list(zip(range(3), reversed(range(5))))
[(0, 4), (1, 3), (2, 2)]
```

Notice here that even though the second iterable has five values, the resulting sequence only contains three values. When given iterators of varying lengths, `zip()` goes with the least common denominator, so to speak. Essentially, `zip()` makes sure that each tuple in the resulting sequence has exactly as many values as there are iterators to join together. Once the smallest sequence has been exhausted, `zip()` simply stops looking through the others.

This functionality is particularly useful in creating dictionaries, because one sequence can be used to supply the keys, while another supplies the values. Using `zip()` can join these together into the proper pairings, which can then be passed directly into a new `dict()`.

```
>>> keys = map(chr, range(97, 102))
>>> values = range(1, 6)
>>> dict(zip(keys, values))
{'a': 1, 'c': 3, 'b': 2, 'e': 5, 'd': 4}
```

Collections

There are a number of well-known objects that come standard with the Python distribution, both as built-ins available to all modules and as part of the standard package library. Objects such as integers, strings, lists, tuples and dictionaries are in common use among nearly all Python programs, but others, including sets named tuples and some special types of dictionaries, are used less often and may be unfamiliar to those who haven't already needed to discover them.

Some of these are built-in types that are always available to every module, while others are part of the standard library included with every Python installation. There are still more that are provided by third-party applications, some of which have become fairly commonly installed, but this section will only cover those included with Python itself.

Sets

Typically, collections of objects are represented in Python by tuples and lists, but sets provide another way to work with the same data. Essentially, a set works much like a list, but without allowing any duplicates, making it useful for identifying the unique objects in a collection. For example, here's how a simple function might use a set to determine which letters are used in a given string.

```
>>> def unique_letters(word):
...     return set(word.lower())
...
>>> unique_letters('spam')
{'a', 'p', 's', 'm'}
>>> unique_letters('eggs')
{'s', 'e', 'g'}
```

There are a few things to notice here. First, the built-in **set** type takes a sequence as its argument, which populates the set with all the unique elements found in that sequence. This is valid for any sequence, such as a string as shown in the example as well as lists, tuples, dictionary keys or custom iterable objects.

In addition, notice that the items in the set aren't ordered the same way they appeared in the original string. Sets are concerned solely with membership. They keep track of items that are in the set, without any notion of ordering. That seems like a limitation, but if you need ordering, you probably want a list anyway. Sets are very efficient when you only need to know if an item is a member of a collection, without regard to where it is in the collection or how many times it has otherwise appeared.

The third thing to notice is the representation showed when displaying the set in the interactive shell. As these representations are intended to be formatted in the same way as you can type into your source file, this indicates a syntax for declaring sets as literals in your code. It looks very similar to a dictionary, but without any values associated with the keys. That's actually a fairly accurate analogy, because a set works very much like the collection of keys in a dictionary.

Compatibility: Prior to 3.0

Although Python versions as far back as 2.4 have had a built-in named `set()`—and it was available as part of the `sets` module even before that—it wasn't until Python 3.0 that you could use curly braces to define sets as literals in your code. They're functionally identical, but set literals are much more convenient and readable if you already know at least some of the items that will go in the set. Now that `set()` is a built-in, the `sets` module has been removed from the Python standard library.

Since sets are designed for a different purpose than sequences and dictionaries, the available operations and methods are a bit different than you might be used to. To start, though, let's look at the way sets behave fairly similarly to other types. Perhaps the most common use of sets is to determine membership, a task often asked of both lists and dictionaries as well. In the spirit of matching expectations, this uses the **in** keyword, familiar from other types.

```
>>> example = {1, 2, 3, 4, 5}
>>> 4 in  example
True
>>> 6 in  example
False
```

In addition, items can be added to or removed from the set later on. The list's **append()** method isn't suitable for sets, because to append an item is to add it at the end, which then implies that the order of items in the collection is important. Since sets aren't at all concerned with ordering, they instead use the **add()** method, which just makes sure that the specified item ends up in the set. If it was already there, **add()** does nothing; otherwise, it adds the item to the set, so there are never any duplicates.

```
>>> example.add(6)
>>> example
{1, 2, 3, 4, 5, 6}
>>> example.add(6)
>>> example
{1, 2, 3, 4, 5, 6}
```

Dictionaries have the useful **update()** method, which adds the contents of a new dictionary to one that already exists. Sets have an **update()** method as well, performing the same task.

```
>>> example.update({6, 7, 8, 9})
>>> example
{1, 2, 3, 4, 5, 6, 7, 8, 9}
```

On the other side, removing items from the set can be done in a few different ways, each serving a different need. The most direct complement to **add()** is the **remove()** method, which removes a specific item from the set. If that item wasn't in the set in the first place, it raises a **KeyError**.

```
>>> example.remove(9)
>>> example.remove(9)
Traceback (most recent call last):
  ...
KeyError: 9
>>> example
{1, 2, 3, 4, 5, 6, 7, 8}
```

Many times, though, it doesn't matter whether the item was already in the set or not; you may only care that it's not in the set when you're done with it. For this purpose, sets also have a **discard()** method, which works just like **remove()** but without raising an exception if the specified item wasn't in the set.

```
>>> example.discard(8)
>>> example.discard(8)
>>> example
{1, 2, 3, 4, 5, 6, 7}
```

Of course, **remove()** and **discard()** both assume you already know what object you want to remove from the set. To simply remove any item from a set, use the **pop()** method, which again is borrowed from the list API, but differs slightly. Since sets aren't explicitly ordered, there's no real end of the set for an item to be popped off. Instead, the set's **pop()** method picks one arbitrarily, returning it for use outside the set.

```
>>> example.pop()
1
>>> example
{2, 3, 4, 5, 6, 7}
```

Lastly, sets also provide a way to remove all items in one shot, resetting it to an empty state. The **clear()** method is used for this purpose.

```
>>> example.clear()
>>> example
set()
```

■ **Note** The representation of an empty set is set(), rather than {}, because Python needs to maintain a distinction between sets and dictionaries. In order to preserve compatibility with older code written before the introduction of set literals, empty curly braces remain dedicated to dictionaries, so sets use their name instead.

In addition to methods for modifying the contents in-place, sets also provide operations where two sets combine in some way to return a new set. The most common of these is a union, where the contents of two sets are joined together, so the resulting new set contains all items that were in both of the original sets. It's essentially the same as using the **update()** method, except that none of the original sets is altered.

The union of two sets is a lot like a bit-wise OR operation, so Python represents it with the pipe character (|), which is the same as is used for bit-wise OR. In addition, sets offer the same functionality using the `union()` method, which can be called from either set involved.

```
>>> {1, 2, 3} | {4, 5, 6}
{1, 2, 3, 4, 5, 6}
>>> {1, 2, 3}.union({4, 5, 6})
{1, 2, 3, 4, 5, 6}
```

The logical complement to that operation is the intersection, where the result is the set of all items common to the original sets. Again, this is analogous to a bit-wise operation, but this time it's the bit-wise AND, and again, Python uses the ampersand (&) to represent the operation as it pertains to sets. Sets also have an `intersection()` method which performs the same task.

```
>>> {1, 2, 3, 4, 5} & {4, 5, 6, 7, 8}
{4, 5}
>>> {1, 2, 3, 4, 5}.intersection({4, 5, 6, 7, 8})
{4, 5}
```

You can also determine the difference between two sets, resulting in a set of all the items that exist in one of the sets but not the other. By removing the contents of one set from another, it works a lot like subtraction, so Python uses the subtraction operator (-) to perform this operation, along with the `difference()` method.

```
>>> {1, 2, 3, 4, 5} - {2, 4, 6}
{1, 3, 5}
>>> {1, 2, 3, 4, 5}.difference({2, 4, 6})
{1, 3, 5}
```

In addition to that basic difference, Python sets offer a variation, called a symmetric difference, using the `symmetric_difference()` method. Using this method, the resulting set contains all items that were in either set, but not in both. This is equivalent to the bit-wise exclusive OR operation, commonly referred to as XOR. Since Python uses the caret (^) to represent the XOR operation elsewhere, sets use the same operator as well as the method.

```
>>> {1, 2, 3, 4, 5} ^ {4, 5, 6}
{1, 2, 3, 6}
>>> {1, 2, 3, 4, 5}.symmetric_difference({4, 5, 6})
{1, 2, 3, 6}
```

Lastly, it's possible to determine whether all the items in one set also exist in another. If one set contains all the items of another, the first is considered to be a superset of the other, even if the first set contains additional items not present in the second. The inverse, where all the items in first are contained in the second, even if the second has more items, means the first set is a subset of the second.

Testing to see if one set is a subset or a superset of another is performed by two methods, `issubset()` and `issuperset()`, respectively. The same test can be performed manually, by subtracting one set from the other and checking to see if any items remain. If no items are left, the set evaluates to `False`, and the first is definitely a subset of the second, and testing for a superset is as simple as swapping the two sets in the operation. Using these methods avoids creating a new set just to have it reduce to a Boolean anyway.

```
>>> {1, 2, 3}.issubset({1, 2, 3, 4, 5})
True
>>> {1, 2, 3, 4, 5}.issubset({1, 2, 3})
False
>>> {1, 2, 3}.issuperset({1, 2, 3, 4, 5})
False
>>> {1, 2, 3, 4, 5}.issuperset({1, 2, 3})
True

>>> not ({1, 2, 3} - {1, 2, 3, 4, 5})
True
>>> not ({1, 2, 3, 4, 5} - {1, 2, 3})
False
```

■ **Note** Looking at how subsets and supersets can be determined using subtraction, you might notice that two identical sets will always subtract to an empty set, and the order of the two sets is irrelevant. This is correct, and because {1, 2, 3} - {1, 2, 3} is always empty, each set is both a subset and a superset of the other.

Named Tuples

Dictionaries are extremely useful, but sometimes you may have a fixed set of possible keys available, so you don't need that much flexibility. Instead, Python uses named tuples, which provide some of the same functionality, but they're much more efficient because the instances don't need to contain any of the keys, only the values associated with them.

Named tuples are created using a factory function from the **collections** module, called **namedtuple()**. Rather than returning an individual object, **namedtuple()** returns a new class, which is customized for a given set of names. The first argument is the name of the tuple class itself, but the second is, unfortunately, less straightforward. It takes a string of attribute names, which are separated by either a space or a comma.

```
>>> from collections import namedtuple
>>> Point = namedtuple('Point', 'x y')
>>> point = Point(13, 25)
>>> point
Point(x=13, y=25)
>>> point.x, point.y
(13, 25)
>>> point[0], point[1]
(13, 25)
```

As an efficient trade-off between tuples and dictionaries, many functions that need to return multiple values can do so using named tuples to be as useful as possible. There's no need to populate a full dictionary, but values can still be referenced by useful names rather than integer indexes.

Ordered Dictionaries

If you've ever iterated over the keys of a dictionary or printed its contents to the interactive prompt, as has been done previously in this chapter, you'll notice that its keys don't always follow a predictable order. Sometimes they may look like they're sorted numerically or alphabetically, but other times it seems completely random.

Dictionary keys, like sets, are considered to be unordered. Even though there may occasionally appear to be patterns, these are merely the byproduct of the implementation and aren't formally defined. Not only is the ordering inconsistent from one dictionary to another, variations are even more significant when using a different Python implementation, such as Jython or IronPython.

Most of the time, what you're really looking for from a dictionary is a way to map specific keys to associated values, so the ordering of the keys is irrelevant. Sometimes, though, it's also useful to be able to iterate over those keys in a reliable manner. To offer the best of both worlds, Python offers the `OrderedDict` class by way of its `collections` module. This provides all the features of a dictionary, but with reliable ordering of keys.

```
>>> from collections import OrderedDict
>>> d = OrderedDict((value, str(value)) for value in range(10) if value > 5)
>>> d
OrderedDict([(6, '6'), (7, '7'), (8, '8'), (9, '9')])
>>> d[10] = '10'
>>> d
OrderedDict([(6, '6'), (7, '7'), (8, '8'), (9, '9'), (10, '10')])
>>> del d[7]
>>> d
OrderedDict([(6, '6'), (8, '8'), (9, '9'), (10, '10')])
```

As you can see, the same construction used previously now results in a properly-ordered dictionary that does the right thing even as you add and remove items.

■ **Caution** In the example here, notice that the values for the dictionary are provided using a generator expression. If you supply a standard dictionary, that means your supplied values are unordered prior to going into the ordered database, which will then assume that order was intentional and preserve it. This also occurs if you supply values as keyword arguments, because those are passed as a regular dictionary internally. The only reliable way to supply ordering to `OrderedDict()` is to use a standard sequence, such as a list or a generator expression.

Dictionaries with Defaults

Another common pattern using dictionaries is to always assume some default value in the event that a key can't be found in the mapping. This behavior can be achieved either by explicitly catching the `KeyError` raised when accessing the key or by using the available `get()` method, which can return a suitable default if the key wasn't found. One such example of this pattern is using a dictionary to track how many times each word appears in some text.

```
def count_words(text):
```

```
count = {}
for word in text.split(' '):
    current = count.get(word, 0) # Make sure we always have a number
    count[word] = current + 1
return count
```

Instead of having to deal with that extra `get()` call, the `collections` module provides a `defaultdict` class that can handle that step for you. When you create it, you can pass in a callable as the single argument, which will be used to create a new value when a requested key doesn't exist. In most cases, you can just supply one of the built-in types, which will provide a useful basic value to work with. In the case of `count_words()`, we can use `int`.

```
from collections import defaultdict

def count_words(text):
    count = defaultdict(int)
    for word in text.split(' '):
        count[word] += 1
    return count
```

Essentially any callable can be used, but the built-in types tend to provide optimal default values for whatever you need to work with. Using `list` will give you an empty list, `str` returns an empty string, `int` returns 0 and `dict` returns an empty dictionary. If you have more specialized needs, any callable that can be used without any arguments will work. Chapter 3 will introduce lambda functions, which are convenient for cases like this.

Importing Code

Complex Python applications are typically made up of a number of different modules, often separated into packages to supply more granular namespaces. Importing code from one module to another is a simple matter, but that's only part of the story. There are several additional features available for more specific situations that you're likely to run into.

Fallback Imports

By now, you've seen several points where Python changes over time, sometimes in backward-incompatible ways. One particular change that tends to come up occasionally is when a module gets moved or renamed, but still does essentially the same thing as before. The only update needed to make your code work with it is to change to the import location, but you'll often need to maintain compatibility with versions both before and after the change.

The solution to this problem exploits Python's exception handling to determine whether the module exists at the new location. Since imports are processed at run-time, like any other statement, you can wrap them in a `try` block and catch an `ImportError`, which is raised if the import failed. Here's how you might import a common hash algorithm both before and after the change in Python 2.5, which moved its import location.

```
try:
    # Use the new library if available. Added in Python 2.5
    from hashlib import md5
```

```
except ImportError:
    # Compatible functionality provided prior to Python 2.5
    from md5 import new as md5
```

Notice here that the import prefers the newer library first. That's because changes like this usually have a grace period, where the old location is still available, but deprecated. If you check for the older module first, you'll find it long after the new module became available. By checking for the new one first, you take advantage of any newer features or added behaviors as soon as they're available, falling back to older functionality only when necessary. Using the **as** keyword allows the rest of the module to simply reference the name md5 either way.

This technique is just as applicable to third-party modules as it is to Python's own standard library, but third-party applications often require different handling. Rather than determining which module to use, it's often necessary to distinguish whether the application is available at all. This is determined the same way as the previous example, by wrapping the import statement in a **try** block.

What happens next, however, depends on how your application should behave if the module is unavailable. Some modules are strictly required, so if it's missing, you should raise an exception directly inside the **except ImportError** block or simply forgo exception handling altogether. Other times, a missing third-party module simply means a reduction in functionality. In this case, the most common approach is to assign **None** to the variable that would otherwise contain the imported module.

```
try:
    import docutils  # Common Python-based documentation tools
except ImportError:
    docutils = None
```

Then, when your code needs to utilize features in the imported module, it can use something like **if docutils** to see if the module is available, without having to re-import it.

Importing from the Future

Python's release schedule often incorporates new features, but it's not always a good idea to just introduce them out of nowhere. In particular, syntax additions and behavior changes may break existing code, so it's often necessary to provide a bit of a grace period. During the transition, these new features are made available by way of a special kind of import, letting you choose which features are updated for each module.

The special __future__ module allows you to name specific features that you'd like to use in a given module. This provides a simple compatibility path for your modules, since some modules can rely on new features while other modules can use existing features. Typically, the next release after a feature was added to __future__, it becomes a standard feature available to all modules.

As a quick example, Python 3.0 changed the way integer division worked. In earlier versions, dividing one integer from another always resulted in an integer, which often resulted in a loss of precision if the result would normally produce a remainder. That makes sense to programmers who are familiar with the underlying C implementation, but it's different than what happens if you perform the same calculation on a standard calculator, so it caused a lot of confusion.

The behavior of division was changed to return floating point values if the division would contain a remainder, thus matching how a standard calculator would work. Before making the change across all of Python, however, the **division** option was added to the __future__ module, allowing the behavior to be changed earlier if necessary. Here's how an interactive interpreter session might look in Python 2.5.

```
>>> 5 / 2  # Python 2.5 uses integer-only division by default
2
```

```
>>> from __future__ import division  # This updates the behavior of division
>>> 5 / 2
2.5
```

There are a number of such features made available through the __future__ module, with new options being added with each release of Python. Rather than trying to list them all here, the remainder of this book will mention them when the features being described were recent enough to need a __future__ import in older versions of Python, back to Python 2.5. Full details on these feature changes can always be found on the "What's New" page of the Python documentation.[1]

■ **Note** If you try to import a feature from __future__ that already exists in the version of Python you're using, it doesn't do anything. The feature is already available, so no changes have to be made, but it also doesn't raise any exceptions.

Using __all__ to Customize Imports

One of the lesser-used features of Python imports is the ability to import the namespace from one module into that of another. This is achieved by using an asterisk as the portion of the module to import.

```
>>> from itertools import *
>>> list(chain([1, 2, 3], [4, 5, 6]))
[1, 2, 3, 4, 5, 6]
```

Ordinarily, this would just take all the entries in the imported module's namespace that don't begin with an underscore and dump them into the current module's namespace. It can save some typing in modules that make heavy use of the imported module, because it saves you from having to include the module name every time you access one of its attributes.

Sometimes, though, it doesn't make sense for every object to be made available in this way. In particular, frameworks often include a number of utility functions and classes that are useful within the framework's module, but don't make much sense when exported out into external code. In order to control what objects get exported when you import a module like this, you can specify __all__ somewhere in the module.

All you need to do is supply a list—or some other sequence—that contains the names of objects that should get imported when the module is imported using an asterisk. Additional objects can still be imported by either importing the name directly or by just importing the module itself, rather than anything inside of it. Here's how an example module might supply its __all__ option.

```
__all__ = ['public_func']

def public_func():
    pass

def utility_func():
    pass
```

---

[1] http://propython.com/whats-new/

Of course, there would be useful code in both of those functions in the real world. For the purposes of illustration, though, here's a quick run-down of the different ways you could import that module, which we'll call example.

```
>>> import example
>>> example.public_func
<function public_func at 0x...>
>>> example.utility_func
<function utility_func at 0x...>
>>> from example import *
>>> public_func
<function public_func at 0x...>
>>> utility_func
Traceback (most recent call last):
  ...
NameError: name 'utility_func' is not defined
>>> from example import utility_func
>>> utility_func
<function utility_func at 0x...>
```

Notice how, in the final case, you can still import it directly using the from syntax, as long as you specify it explicitly. The only time __all__ comes into play is if you use an asterisk.

Explicit is Better than Implicit

It's generally considered bad form to import using the asterisk notation in the first place; PEP-8, the Python Style Guide, specifically recommends against it. The main issue with it is that it's not immediately obvious where the contents of that module came from. If you see a function used without a module namespace, you can usually look at the top of the module to see if it was imported; if not, you can safely assume it was defined in the module. If it was imported with the asterisk notation, you'd have to either scan the entire module to see if it was defined or open up the source for the related module to see if it was defined there.

On occasion, it can still be useful to import using an asterisk, but it's best to only do so when you're wrapping it in another namespace. As will be illustrated in Chapter 11, you might allow your users to import a single root namespace that incorporates objects from several different modules. Rather than having to update the imports every time something new is added, you can use asterisk imports in the main module, without introducing any ambiguity in your users' modules.

Relative Imports

When starting out with a project, you'll spend most of your time importing from external packages, so every import is absolute; its path is rooted in your system's PYTHONPATH. Once your projects start growing to several modules, you'll be importing from one another regularly. And once you establish a hierarchy, you might realize that you don't want to include the full import path when sharing code between two modules at similar parts of the tree.

Python allows you to specify a relative path to the module you'd like to import, so you can move around an entire package, if necessary, with minimal modifications required. The preferred syntax for this is to specify part of the module's path with one or more periods, indicating how far up the path to look for the module. For example, if the `acme.shopping.cart` module needs to import from `acme.billing`, the two following import patterns are identical.

```
from acme import billing
from .. import billing
```

A single period allows you to import from the current package, so `acme.shopping.gallery` could be imported as `from . import gallery`. Alternatively, if you're looking to just import something from that module, you could instead simply prefix the module path with the necessary periods, then specify the names to import as usual: `from .gallery import Image`.

The __import__() function

You don't always have to place your imports at the top of a module. In fact, sometimes you might not be able to write some of your imports in advance at all. You might be making decisions about which module to import based on user-supplied settings or perhaps you're even allowing users to specify modules directly. These user-supplied settings are a convenient way to allow for extensibility without resorting to automatic discovery.

In order to support this functionality, Python allows you to import code manually, using the `__import__()` function. It's a built-in function, so it's available everywhere, but using it requires some explanation, because it's not as straightforward as some of the other features provided by Python. There are a possible five arguments that can be used to customize how a module gets imported and what contents are retrieved.

- `name`—The only argument that is always required, this accepts the name of the module that should be loaded. If it's part of a package, just separate each part of the path with a period, just like when using `import path.to.module`.

- `globals`—A namespace dictionary that is used to define the context in which the module name is resolved. In standard `import` cases, the return value from the built-in `globals()` function is used to populate this argument.

- `locals`—Another namespace dictionary, ideally used to help define the context in which the module name is resolved. In reality, however, current implementations of Python simply ignore it. In the event of future support, the standard import provides the return value from the built-in `locals()` function for this argument.

- `fromlist`—A list of individual names that should be imported from the module, rather than importing the full module.

- `level`—An integer indicating how the path should be resolved with respect to the module that calls `__import__()`. A value of -1 allows both absolute and implicit relative imports; 0 allows only absolute imports; positive values indicate how many levels up the path to use for an explicit relative import.

Even though that may seem simple enough, the return value contains a few traps that can cause quite a bit of confusion. It always returns a module object, but it can be surprising to see which module is returned and what attributes are available on it. Since there are a number of different ways to import modules, these variations are worth understanding. First, let's examine how different types of module names impact the return value.

In the simplest case, you'd pass in a single module name to `__import__()`, and the return value is just what you'd expect: the module referenced by the name provided. The attributes available on that module object are the same as you'd have available if you imported that name directly in your code: the entire namespace that was declared in that module's code.

When you pass in a more complex module path, however, the return value may not match expectations. Complex paths are provided using the same dot-separated syntax used in your source files, so importing os.path, for instance, would be achieved by passing in 'os.path'. The returned value in that case is os, but the path attribute lets you access the module you're really looking for.

The reason for that variation is that __import__() mimics the behavior of Python source files, where import os.path makes the os module available under that name. You can still access os.path, but the module that goes into the main namespace is os. Since __import__() works essentially the same way as a standard import, what you get in the return value is what you would have in the main module namespace ordinarily.

In order to get just the module at the end of the module path, there are a couple different approaches you can take. The most obvious, though not necessarily direct, would be to split the given module name on periods, using each portion of the path to get each attribute layer from the module returned by __import__(). Here's a simple function that would do the job.

```
>>> def import_child(module_name):
...     module = __import__(module_name)
...     for layer in module_name.split('.')[1:]:
...         module = getattr(module, layer)
...     return module
...
>>> import_child('os.path')
<module 'ntpath' from 'C:\Python31\lib\ntpath.py'>
>>> import_child('os')
<module 'os' from 'C:\Python31\lib\os.py'>
```

■ **Note** The exact name of the module referenced by os.path will vary based on the operating system under which it's imported. For example, it's called ntpath on Windows, while most Linux systems use posixpath. Most of the contents are the same, but they may behave slightly differently depending on the needs of the operating system, and each may have additional attributes that are unique to that environment.

As you can see, it works for the simple case as well as more complex situations, but it still goes through a bit more work than is really necessary to do the job. Of course, the time spent on the loop is fairly insignificant compared to the import itself, but if the module had already been imported, our import_path() function comprises most of the process. An alternate approach takes advantage of Python's own module caching mechanism to take the extra processing out of the picture.

```
>>> import sys
>>> def import_child(module_name):
...     __import__(module_name)
...     return sys.modules[module_name]
...
>>> import_child('os.path')
<module 'ntpath' from 'C:\Python31\lib\ntpath.py'>
>>> import_child('os')
<module 'os' from 'C:\Python31\lib\os.py'>
```

The `sys.modules` dictionary maps import paths to the module objects that were generated when importing them. By looking up the module in that dictionary, there's no need to mess around with the particulars of the module name.

Of course, this is really only applicable to absolute imports. Relative imports, no matter how they are referenced, are resolved relative to the module where the import statement—or in this case, the `__import__()` function call—is located. Since the most common case is to place `import_path()` in a common location, relative imports would be resolved relative to that, rather than the module that called `import_path()`. That could mean importing the completely wrong module.

The importlib module

In order to address the issues that are raised by using `__import__()` directly, Python also includes the `importlib` module, which provides a more intuitive interface to import modules. The `import_module()` function is a much simpler way to achieve the same effect as `__import__()`, but in a way that more closely matches expectations.

For absolute imports, `import_module()` accepts the module path, just like `__import__()`. The difference, however, is that `import_module()` always returns the last module in the path, while `__import__()` returns the first one. The extra handling that was added in the previous section is made completely unnecessary because of this functionality, so this is a much better approach to use.

```
>>> from importlib import import_module
>>> import_module('os.path')
<module 'ntpath' from 'C:\Python31\lib\ntpath.py'>
>>> import_module('os')
<module 'os' from 'C:\Python31\lib\os.py'>
```

Compatibility: Prior to 2.7/3.1

The `importlib` module, in its entirety, was added in Python 3.1, then backported for inclusion in Python 2.7. This means that, even though it looks like `importlib` was added in 2.7, not all higher versions of Python include the module. In particular, the Python 3.0 does *not* include `importlib`. Any higher version number can be expected to include `importlib`, without any problems.

In addition, `import_module()` takes relative imports into account by also accepting a `package` attribute that defines the reference point from which the relative path should be resolved. This is easily done when calling the function, simply by passing in the always-global `__name__` variable, which holds the module path that was used to import the current module in the first place.

```
import_module('.utils', package=__name__)
```

■ **Caution** Relative imports don't work directly inside the interactive interpreter. The module the interpreter runs in isn't actually in the filesystem, so there are no relative paths to work with.

Taking It With You

The features laid out in this chapter are just a taste of what Python has to offer if you're willing to take the time to learn it. The rest of this book will rely heavily on what was laid out here, but each chapter will add another layer for future chapters to build on as well. In that spirit, let's continue on to what you thought was one of the most basic, unassuming features of Python: functions.

CHAPTER 3

■■■

Functions

At the core of any programming language is the notion of functions, but we tend to take them for granted. Sure, there's the obvious fact that functions allow code to be encapsulated into individual units, which can be reused rather than being duplicated all over the place. But Python takes this beyond just the notion of code, with functions being full-fledged objects that can be passed around in data structures, wrapped up in other functions or replaced entirely by new implementations.

In fact, Python provides enough flexibility with functions that there are actually several different types of functions, reflecting the various forms of declaration and purposes. Understanding each of these types of functions will help you decide which is appropriate for each situation you encounter while working with your own code. This chapter will explain each of them in turn, as well as a variety of features you can take advantage of to extend the value of each function you create, regardless of its type.

At their core, all functions are essentially equal, regardless of which of the following sections they fit into. The built-in `function` type forms their basis, containing all the attributes necessary for Python to understand how to use them.

```
>>> def example():
...     pass
...
>>> type(example)
<class 'function'>
>>> example
<function example at 0x...>
```

Of course, there are still a number of different types of functions and as many different ways of declaring them. First off, let's examine one of the most universal aspects of functions.

Arguments

Most functions need to take some number of arguments in order to do anything useful. Normally, that means defining them in order in the function; then supplying them in the same order when calling that function later. Python supports that model, but also supports passing keyword arguments and even arguments that won't be known until the function is called.

One of the most common advantages of Python's keyword arguments is that you can pass arguments in a different order than the way they were defined in the function. You can even skip arguments entirely, as long as they have a default value defined. This flexibility helps encourage the use of functions that support lots of arguments with default values.

One way Python's keyword arguments encourage being explicit is to only allow arguments to be passed out of order if they're passed by keyword. Without keywords, Python needs to use the position of the argument to know which name to give it when the function runs. Since keywords are just as explicit as positions, the ordering requirement can be lifted without introducing ambiguity.

In fact, keywords are even more explicit than positions when working with arguments, because the function call documents the purpose of each argument. Otherwise, you'd have to look up the function definition in order to understand its arguments. Some arguments may be understandable in context, but most optional arguments aren't obvious at a glance, so passing them with keywords makes for more readable code.

Planning for Flexibility

Argument planning is particularly important for functions intended to be called by someone who didn't write them, such as those in distributed applications. If you don't know the exact needs of the users who will eventually be using your code, it's best to move any assumptions you may have into arguments that can be overridden later.

As an extremely simple example, consider a function that assigns a prefix to a string:

```python
def add_prefix(string):
    """Adds a 'pro_' prefix before the string provided."""
    return 'pro_' + string
```

The `'pro_'` prefix here may make sense for the application it was written for, but what happens when anything else wants to use it? Right now, the prefix is hard-coded into the body of the function itself, so there's no available alternative. Moving that assumption into an argument makes for an easy way to customize the function later.

```python
def add_prefix(string, prefix='pro_'):
    """Adds a 'pro_' prefix before the string provided."""
    return prefix + string
```

The default function call—without the **prefix** argument—doesn't need to change, so existing code works just fine. The section on preloading arguments later in this chapter shows how even the prefix can be changed and still be used by code that doesn't know about it.

Of course, this example is far too simple to provide much real-world value, but the functions illustrated throughout the rest of this book will take advantage of plenty of optional arguments, showing their value in each situation.

Variable Positional Arguments

Most functions are designed to work on a specific set of arguments, but some can handle any number of objects, acting on each in turn. These may be passed into a single argument as a tuple, list or other iterable, but that makes things a little odd if the function call knows in advance how many items will be passed in.

Take a typical shopping cart, for example. Adding items to the cart could be done one at a time or in batches. Here's how it *could* be done, using a standard argument.

```
class ShoppingCart:
    def add_to_cart(items):
        self.items.extend(items)
```

That would certainly do the trick, but now consider what that means for all the code that has to call it. The common case would be to add just a single item, but since the function always accepts a full list, it would end up looking something like this.

```
cart.add_to_cart([item])
```

So we've basically sabotaged the majority case in order to support the minority. Worse yet, if add_to_cart() originally supported just one item and was changed to support multiples, this syntax would break any existing calls, requiring you to rewrite them just to avoid a TypeError.

Ideally, the method should support the standard syntax for single arguments, while still supporting multiple arguments. By adding an asterisk before an argument name, you can specify that it should accept all positional arguments that didn't get assigned to anything before it. In this case, there are no other arguments, so variable positional arguments can make up the entire argument list.

```
def add_to_cart(*items):
    self.items.extend(items)
```

Now, the method can be called with any number of positional arguments, rather than having to group those arguments first into a tuple or list. The extra arguments are bundled up into a tuple automatically before the function starts executing. This cleans up the common case, while still enabling more arguments as needs require. Here are a few examples of how the method could be called.

```
cart.add_to_cart(item)
cart.add_to_cart(item1, item2)
cart.add_to_cart(item1, item2, item3, item4, item5)
```

There is still one more way to call this function that allows the calling code to support any number of items as well, but it's not specific to functions that are designed to accept variable arguments. See the section on invoking functions with variable arguments for all the details.

Variable Keyword Arguments

Other times, functions may need to take extra configuration options, particularly if passing those options to some other library further down the line. The obvious approach would be to accept a dictionary, which can map configuration names to their values.

```
class ShoppingCart:
    def __init__(self, options):
        self.options = options
```

Unfortunately, that ends up with a problem similar to the one we encountered with positional arguments described in the previous section. The simple case where you only override one or two values gets fairly complicated. Here are two ways the function call could look, depending on preference.

```
options = {'currency': 'USD'}
cart = ShoppingCart(options)

cart = ShoppingCart({'currency': 'USD'})
```

Of course, this approach doesn't scale any prettier than the list provided in the positional argument problem from the previous section. Also like the previous problem, this can be problematic. If the function you're working with was previously set up to accept some explicit keyword arguments, the new dictionary argument would break compatibility.

Instead, Python offers the ability to use variable keyword arguments by adding two asterisks before the name of the argument that will accept them. This allows for the much friendlier keyword argument syntax, while still allowing for a fully dynamic function call.

```
def __init__(self, **options):
    self.options = options
```

Now consider what that same function from earlier would look like, given that the function now takes arbitrary keyword arguments.

```
cart = ShoppingCart(currency='USD')
```

■ **Caution** When working with variable arguments, there's one difference between positional and keyword arguments that can cause problems. Positional arguments are grouped into a tuple, which is immutable, while keyword arguments are placed into a dictionary, which is mutable. That property of dictionaries can be useful, but if you're not careful, you can accidentally lose data.

Beautiful is better than ugly

The second function call example here is a classic example of code that would generally be considered ugly by many Python programmers. The sheer volume of punctuation—quotation marks around both the key and value, a colon between them and curly braces around the whole thing—inside the already-necessary parentheses make it very cluttered and difficult to process at a glance.

By switching to keyword arguments, as shown in this section, the appearance of the code is considerably better aligned with Python's core values and philosophy. Beauty may be subjective in its very nature, but certain subjective decisions are praised by the vast majority of the programmers.

Combining Different Kinds of Arguments

These options for variable arguments combine with the standard options, such as required and optional arguments. In order to make sure everything meshes nicely, Python has some fairly specific rules about how arguments are laid out in the function definition. There are only four types of arguments, listed here in the order they generally appear in functions.

- Required arguments

- Optional arguments

- Variable positional arguments

- Variable keyword arguments

Putting the required arguments first in the list ensures that positional arguments satisfy the required arguments prior to getting into the optional arguments. Variable arguments can only pick up values that didn't fit into anything else, so they naturally get defined at the end. Here's how this would look in a typical function definition.

```
def create_element(name, editable=True, *children, **attributes):
```

This same ordering can be used when calling functions as well, but it has one shortcoming. In this example, you'd have to supply a value for editable as a positional argument in order to pass in any children at all. It'd be better to be able to supply them right after the name, avoiding the optional editable argument entirely most of the time.

To support this, Python also allows variable positional arguments to be placed in among standard arguments. Both required and optional arguments can be positioned after the variable argument, but now they must be passed by keyword. All the arguments are still available, but the less common ones become more optional when not required and more explicit when they do make sense.

In the face of ambiguity, refuse the temptation to guess

By allowing positional arguments in the middle of a list of explicit arguments, Python might have introduced a considerable ambiguity. Consider a function defined to pass commands through to an arbitrary argument: perform_action(action, *args, log_output=False). Ordinarily, you can supply enough positional arguments to reach even the optional arguments, but in this case, what would happen if you supplied three or more values?

One possible interpretation is to give the first value to the first argument, the last value to the last argument and everything else to the variable argument. That could work, but then it comes down to a guess as to the intent of the programmer making the call. Once you consider a function with even more arguments behind the variable argument, the possible interpretations become quite numerous.

Instead, Python strictly enforces that everything after the variable argument becomes accessible by keyword only. Positional argument values beyond those explicitly defined in the function go straight into the variable argument, whether just one or dozens were provided. The implementation becomes easy to explain by having just one way to do it, and it's even more explicit by enforcing the use of keywords.

An added feature of this behavior is hat explicit arguments placed after variable positional arguments can still be required. The only real difference between the two types of placement is the requirement of using keyword arguments; whether the argument requires a value still depends on whether you define a default argument.

```
>>> def join_with_prefix(prefix, *segments, delimiter):
...     return delimiter.join(prefix + segment for segment in segments)
```

```
...
>>> join_with_prefix('P', 'ro', 'ython')
Traceback (most recent call last):
    ...
TypeError: join_with_prefix() needs keyword-only argument delimiter
>>> join_with_prefix('P', 'ro', 'ython', ' ')
Traceback (most recent call last):
    ...
TypeError: join_with_prefix() needs keyword-only argument delimiter
>>> join_with_prefix('P', 'ro', 'ython', delimiter=' ')
'Pro Python'
```

■ **Note** If you want to accept keyword-only arguments, but you don't have a good use for variable positional arguments, simply specify a single asterisk without an argument name. This will tell Python that everything after the asterisk is keyword-only, without also accepting potentially long sets of positional arguments. One caveat is that if you also accept variable keyword arguments, you must supply at least one explicit keyword argument. Otherwise, there's really no point in using the bare asterisk notation, and Python will raise a SyntaxError.

In fact, remember that the ordering requirements of required and optional arguments is solely intended for the case of positional arguments. With the ability to define arguments as being keyword-only, you're now free to define them as required and optional in any order, without any complaints from Python. Ordering isn't important when calling the function, so it's also not important when defining the function. Consider rewriting the previous example to require the prefix as a keyword argument, while also making the delimiter optional.

```
>>> def join_with_prefix(*segments, delimiter=' ', prefix):
...         return delimiter.join(prefix + segment for segment in segments)

>>> join_with_prefix('ro', 'ython', prefix='P')
'Pro Python'
```

■ **Caution** Be careful taking advantage of this level of flexibility because it's not very straightforward compared to how Python code is typically written. It's certainly possible, but it runs contrary to what most Python programmers will expect, which can make it difficult to maintain in the long run.

In all cases, though, variable keyword arguments must be positioned at the end of the list, after all other types of arguments.

Invoking Functions with Variable Arguments

In addition to being able to define arguments that can accept any number of values, the same syntax can be used to pass values into a function call. The big advantage to this is that it's not restricted to arguments that were defined to be variable in nature. Instead, you can pass variable arguments into any function, regardless of how it was defined.

The same asterisk notation is used to specify variable arguments, which are then expanded into a function call as if all the arguments were specified directly. A single asterisk specifies positional arguments, while two asterisks specify keyword arguments. This is especially useful when passing in the return value of a function call directly as an argument, without assigning it to individual variables first.

```
>>> value = 'ro ython'
>>> join_with_prefix(*value.split(' '), prefix='P')
```

This example seems obvious on its own, because it's a variable argument being passed in to a variable argument, but the same process works just fine on other types of functions as well. Since the arguments get expanded before getting passed to the function, it can be used with any function, regardless of how its arguments were specified. It can even be used with built-in functions and those defined by extensions written in C.

■ **Note** You can only pass in one set of variable positional arguments and one set of variable keyword arguments in a function call. If you have two lists of positional arguments, for example, you'll need to join them together yourself and pass that combined list into the function instead of trying to use the two separately.

Preloading Arguments

When you start adding a number of arguments to functions, many of which are optional, it becomes fairly common to know some of the argument values that will need to be passed, even if it's still long before the function will actually be called. Rather than having to pass in all the arguments at the time the call is made, it can be quite useful to apply some of those arguments in advance, so fewer can be applied later.

This concept is officially called partial application of the function, but the function doesn't get called at all yet, so it's really more a matter of preloading some of the arguments in advance. When the preloaded function is called later, any arguments passed along are added to those that were provided earlier.

What About Currying?

If you're familiar with other forms of functional programming, you may have heard of currying, which may look very similar to preloading arguments. Some frameworks have even provided functions named curry() that can preload arguments on a function, which leads to even more confusion. The difference between the two is subtle, but important.

With a truly curried function, you must call it as many times as necessary to fill up all of the arguments. If a function accepts three arguments and you call it with just one argument, you'd get back a function that accepts two more arguments. If you call that new function, it still won't execute your code, but will instead load in the next argument and return another function that takes the last remaining argument. Calling that function will finally satisfy all the arguments, so the actual code will be executed and return a useful value.

Partial application returns a function that, when called later, will at least try to execute code, no matter how many arguments may remain. If there are required arguments that haven't gotten a value yet, Python will raise a TypeError just like it would if you had called it with missing arguments any other time. So even though there are certainly similarities between the two techniques, it's important to understand the difference.

This behavior is provided as part of the built-in **functools** module, by way of its **partial()** function. By passing in a callable and any number of positional and keyword arguments, it will return a new callable that can be used later to apply those arguments.

```
>>> import os
>>> def load_file(file, base_path='/', mode='rb'):
...     return open(os.path.join(base_path, file), mode)
...
>>> f = load_file('example.txt')
>>> f.mode
'rb'
>>> f.close()

>>> import functools
>>> load_writable = functools.partial(load_file, mode='w')
>>> f = load_writable('example.txt')
>>> f.mode
'w'
>>> f.close()
```

■ **Note** The technique of preloading arguments is true for the `partial()` function, but the technique of passing one function into another to get a new function back is generally known as a decorator. Decorators, as you'll see later in this chapter, can perform any number of tasks when called; preloading arguments is just one example.

This is commonly used to customize a more flexible function into something simpler, so it can be passed into an API that doesn't know how to access that flexibility. By preloading the custom arguments beforehand, the code behind the API can call your function with the arguments it knows how to use, but all the arguments will still come into play.

■ **Caution** When using `functools.partial()`, you won't be able to provide any new values for those arguments that were previously loaded. This is, of course, standard behavior any time you try to supply multiple values for a single argument, but the situation comes up much more often when you're not supplying them all in the same function call. For an alternative approach that addresses this issue, see the Decorators section of this chapter.

Introspection

Python is very transparent, allowing code to inspect many aspects of objects at run-time. Since functions are objects like any others, there are several things that your code can glean from them, including the argument specification. Obtaining a function's arguments directly requires going through a fairly complicated set of attributes that describe Python's bytecode structures, but thankfully Python also provides some functions to make it easier.

Many of Python's introspection features are available as part of the standard `inspect` module, with its `getfullargspec()` function being of use for function arguments. It accepts the function to be inspected and returns a named tuple of information about that function's arguments. The returned tuple contains values for every aspect of an argument specification.

- `args`—A list of explicit argument names

- `varargs`—The name of the variable positional argument

- `varkw`—The name of the variable keyword argument

- `defaults`—A tuple of default values for explicit arguments

- `kwonlyargs`—A list of keyword-only argument names

- `kwonlydefaults`—A dictionary of default values for keyword-only arguments

- `annotations`—A dictionary of argument annotations, which will be explained later in this chapter

To better illustrate what values are present in each part of the tuple, here's how it maps out to a basic function declaration.

```
>>> def example(a:i nt, b=1, *c, d, e=2, **f) -> str:
...     pass
...
>>> import inspect
>>> inspect.getfullargspec(example)
FullArgSpec(args=['a', 'b'], varargs='c', varkw='f', defaults=(1,), kwonlyargs=[
'd', 'e'], kwonlydefaults={'e': 2}, annotations={'a': <class 'int'>, 'return': <
class 'str'>})
```

Compatibility: Prior to 3.0

Advanced argument features like keyword-only arguments and annotations were introduced in Python 3.0, and `inspect.getfullargspec()` was added to support those features. Earlier versions used `inspect.getargspec()`, which only knows about the features that were available at the time.

Specifically, `getargspec()` returns a named tuple with only four values: `args`, `varargs`, `keywords` and `defaults`, which are identical to the first four values returned by `getfullargspec()`. In order to preserve backward compatibility, `getargspec()` is still available in Python 3.0 and later.

Example: Identifying Argument Values

Sometimes it can be useful to log what arguments a function will receive, regardless of which function it is or what its arguments look like. This behavior often comes into play in systems that generate argument lists based on something other than a Python function call. Some examples include instructions from a template language and regular expressions that parse text input.

Unfortunately, positional arguments present a bit of a problem because their values don't include the name of the argument they'll be sent to. Default values also pose a problem because the function call doesn't need to include any values at all. Since the log should include all the values that will be given to the function, both of these problems will need to be addressed.

First, the easy part. Any argument values passed by keyword don't need to be matched up with anything manually, since the argument names are provided right with the values. Rather than concerning ourselves with logging at the outset, let's start with a function to get all the arguments in a dictionary that can be logged. The function accepts a function, a tuple of positional arguments and a dictionary of keyword arguments.

```
def get_arguments(func, args, kwargs):
    """
    Given a function and a set of arguments, return a dictionary
    of argument values that will be sent to the function.
    """

    arguments = kwargs.copy()
    return arguments

>>> get_arguments(example, (1,), {'f': 4})
{'f': 4}
```

That really was easy. The function makes a copy of the keyword arguments instead of just returning it directly because we'll be adding entries to that dictionary soon enough. Next, we have to deal with positional arguments. The trick is to identify which argument names map to the positional argument values, so those values can be added to the dictionary with the appropriate names. This is where `inspect.getfullargspec()` comes into play, using `zip()` to do the heavy lifting.

```python
import inspect
def get_arguments(func, args, kwargs):
    """
    Given a function and a set of arguments, return a dictionary
    of argument values that will be sent to the function.
    """

    arguments = kwargs.copy()
    spec = inspect.getfullargspec(func)
    arguments.update(zip(spec.args, args))

    return arguments

>>> get_arguments(example, (1,), {'f': 4})
{'a': 1, 'f': 4}
```

Now that the positional arguments have been dealt with, let's move on to figuring out default values. If there are any default values that weren't overridden by the arguments provided, the defaults should be added to the argument dictionary, since they will be sent to the function.

```python
import inspect

def get_arguments(func, args, kwargs):
    """
    Given a function and a set of arguments, return a dictionary
    of argument values that will be sent to the function.
    """

    arguments = kwargs.copy()
    spec = inspect.getfullargspec(func)
    arguments.update(zip(spec.args, args))

    if spec.defaults:
        for i, name in enumerate(spec.args[-len(spec.defaults):]):
            if name not in arguments:
                arguments[name] = spec.defaults[i]

    return arguments

>>> get_arguments(example, (1,), {'f': 4})
{'a': 1, 'b': 1, 'f': 4}
```

Since optional arguments must come after required arguments, this addition uses the size of the `defaults` tuple to determine the names of the optional argument. Looping over them, it then assigns only those values that weren't already provided. Unfortunately, this is only half of the default value situation. Because keyword-only arguments can take default values as well, **getfullargspec()** returns a separate dictionary for those values.

```python
import inspect

def get_arguments(func, args, kwargs):
    """
    Given a function and a set of arguments, return a dictionary
    of argument values that will be sent to the function.
    """
    arguments = kwargs.copy()
    spec = inspect.getfullargspec(func)
    arguments.update(zip(spec.args, args))

    for i, name in enumerate(spec.args[-len(spec.defaults)]):
        if name not in arguments:
            arguments[name] = spec.defaults[i]

    if spec.kwonlydefaults:
        for name, value in spec.kwonlydefaults.items():
            if name not in arguments:
                arguments[name] = value

    return arguments

>>> get_arguments(example, (1,), {'f': 4})
{'a': 1, 'b': 1, 'e': 2, 'f': 4}
```

Since default values for keyword-only arguments also come in dictionary form, it's much easier to apply those because the argument names are known in advance. With that in place, **get_arguments()** can produce a more complete dictionary of arguments that will be passed to the function. Unfortunately, because this returns a dictionary and variable positional arguments have no names, there's no way to add them to the dictionary. This limits its usefulness a bit, but it's still valid for a great many function definitions.

Example: A More Concise Version

The previous example is certainly functional, but it's a bit more code than is really necessary. In particular, it takes a fair amount of work supplying default values when explicit values aren't provided. That's not very intuitive, though, because we usually think about default values the other way around: they're provided first, then overridden by explicit arguments.

The **get_arguments()** function can be rewritten with that in mind by bringing the default values out of the function declaration first, before replacing them with any values passed in as actual arguments. This avoids a lot of the checks that have to be made to make sure nothing gets overwritten accidentally.

The first step is to get the default values out. Because the **defaults** and **kwonlydefaults** attributes of the argument specification are set to **None** if no default values were specified, we actually have to start by setting up an empty dictionary to update. Then, the default values for positional arguments can be added in.

Because this only needs to update a dictionary this time, without regard for what might be in it already, it's a bit easier to use a different technique to get the positional defaults. Rather than using a complex slice that's fairly difficult to read, we can use a similar **zip()** to what was used to get the explicit argument values. By first reversing the argument list and the default values, they still match up starting at the end.

```
def get_arguments(func, args, kwargs):
    """
    Given a function and a set of arguments, return a dictionary
    of argument values that will be sent to the function.
    """

    arguments = {}
    spec = inspect.getfullargspec(func)

    if spec.defaults:
        arguments.update(zip(reversed(spec.args), reversed(spec.defaults)))

    return arguments

>>> get_arguments(example, (1,), {'f': 4})
{'b': 1}
```

Adding default values for keyword arguments is much easier because the argument specification already supplies them as a dictionary. We can just pass that straight into an **update()** of the argument dictionary and move on.

```
def get_arguments(func, args, kwargs):
    """
    Given a function and a set of arguments, return a dictionary
    of argument values that will be sent to the function.
    """

    arguments = {}
    spec = inspect.getfullargspec(func)

    if spec.defaults:
        arguments.update(zip(reversed(spec.args), reversed(spec.defaults)))
    if spec.kwonlydefaults:
        arguments.update(spec.kwonlydefaults)

    return arguments

>>> get_arguments(example, (1,), {'f': 4})
{'b': 1, 'e': 2}
```

Now all that's left is to add in the explicit argument values that were passed in. The same techniques used in the earlier version of this function will work here, with the only exception being that keyword arguments are passed in an **update()** instead of being copied to form the argument dictionary in the first place.

```
def get_arguments(func, args, kwargs):
    """
    Given a function and a set of arguments, return a dictionary
```

```
of argument values that will be sent to the function.
"""

arguments = {}
spec = inspect.getfullargspec(func)

if spec.defaults:
    arguments.update(zip(reversed(spec.args), reversed(spec.defaults)))
if spec.kwonlydefaults:
    arguments.update(spec.kwonlydefaults)
arguments.update(zip(spec.args, args))
arguments.update(kwargs)

return arguments

>>> get_arguments(example, (1,), {'f': 4})
{'a': 1, 'b': 1, 'e': 2, 'f': 4}
```

With that, we have a much more concise function that works the way we normally think of default argument values. This type of refactoring is fairly common after you get more familiar with the advanced techniques available to you. It's always useful to look over old code to see if there's an easier, more straightforward way to go about the task at hand. This will often make your code faster as well as more readable and maintainable going forward.

Example: Validating Arguments

Unfortunately, that doesn't mean that the arguments returned by `get_arguments()` are capable of being passed into the function without errors. As it stands, `get_arguments()` assumes that any keyword arguments supplied are in fact valid arguments for the function, but that isn't always the case. In addition, any required arguments that didn't get a value will cause an error when the function is called. Ideally, we should be able to validate the arguments as well.

We can start with `get_arguments()`, so we have a dictionary of all the values that will be passed to the function, then we have two validation tasks: make sure all arguments have values and make sure no arguments were provided that the function doesn't know about. The function itself may impose additional requirements on the argument values, but as a generic utility, we can't make any assumptions about the content of any of the provided values.

Let's start off with making sure all the necessary values were provided. We don't have to worry as much about required or optional arguments this time around, since `get_arguments()` already makes sure optional arguments have their default values. Any argument left without a value is therefore required.

```
import itertools

def validate_arguments(func, args, kwargs):
    """
    Given a function and its arguments, return a dictionary
    with any errors that are posed by the given arguments.
    """

    arguments = get_arguments(func, args, kwargs)
    spec = inspect.getfullargspec(func)
    declared_args = spec.args[:]
```

```
    declared_args.extend(spec.kwonlyargs)
    errors = {}

    for name in declared_args:
        if name not in arguments:
            errors[name] = "Required argument not provided."

    return errors
```

With the basics in place to validate that all required arguments have values, the next step is to make sure the function knows how to deal with all the arguments that were provided. Any arguments passed in that aren't defined in the function should be considered an error.

```
import itertools

def validate_arguments(func, args, kwargs):
    """
    Given a function and its arguments, return a dictionary
    with any errors that are posed by the given arguments.
    """

    arguments = get_arguments(func, args, kwargs)
    spec = inspect.getfullargspec(func)
    declared_args = spec.args[:]
    declared_args.extend(spec.kwonlyargs)
    errors = {}

    for name in declared_args:
        if name not in arguments:
            errors[name] = "Required argument not provided."

    for name in arguments:
        if name not in declared_args:
            errors[name] = "Unknown argument provided."

    return errors
```

Of course, because this relies on get_arguments(), it inherits the same limitation of variable positional arguments. This means validate_arguments() may sometimes return an incomplete dictionary of errors. Variable positional arguments present an additional challenge that can't be addressed with this function. A more comprehensive solution is provided in the section on function annotations.

Decorators

When dealing with a large codebase, it's very common to have a set of tasks that need to be performed by many different functions, usually before or after doing something more specific to the function at hand. The nature of these tasks is as varied as the projects that use them, but here are some of the more common examples of where decorators are used.

- Access control

- Cleanup of temporary objects

- Error handling

- Caching

- Logging

In all of these cases, there's some boilerplate code that needs to be executed before or after what the function's really trying to do. Rather than copying that code out into each function, it'd be better if it could be written once and simply applied to each function that needs it. This is where decorators come in.

Technically, decorators are just simple functions designed with one purpose: accept a function and return a function. The function returned can be the same as the one passed in or it could be completely replaced by something else along the way. The most common way to apply a decorator is using a special syntax designed just for this purpose. Here's how you could apply a decorator designed to suppress any errors during the execution of a function.

```
import datetime
from myapp import suppress_errors

@suppress_errors
def log_error(message, log_file='errors.log'):
    """Log an error message to a file."""

    log = open(log_file, 'w')
    log.write('%s\t%s\n' % (datetime.datetime.now(), message))
```

This syntax tells Python to pass the `log_error()` function as an argument to the `suppress_errors()` function, which then returns a replacement to use instead. It's easier to understand what happens behind the scenes by examining the processed used in older versions of Python, before the @ syntax was introduced in Python 2.4.

```
import datetime
from myapp import suppress_errors

def log_error(message, log_file='errors.log'):
    """Log an error message to a file."""

    log = open(log_file, 'w')
    log.write('%s\t%s\n' % (datetime.datetime.now(), message))
log_error = suppress_errors(log_error)
```

Don't Repeat Yourself/Readability Counts

When using the older decoration approach, notice that the name of the function is written three different times. Not only is this some extra typing that seems unnecessary; it complicates matters if you ever need to change the function name, and it only gets worse the more decorators you add. The newer syntax can apply a decorator without repeating the function name, no matter how many decorators you use.

Of course, the @ syntax does have one other benefit, which greatly helps its introduction: it keeps decorators right near the function's signature. This makes it easy to see at a glance which decorators are applied, which more directly conveys the total behavior of the function. Having them at the bottom of the function requires more effort to understand the complete behavior, so by moving decorators up to the top, readability is greatly enhanced.

The older option is still available and behaves identically to the @ syntax. The only real difference is that the @ syntax is only available when defining the function in the source file. If you want to decorate a function that was imported from elsewhere, you'll have to pass it into the decorator manually, so it's important to remember both ways it can work.

```
from myapp import log_error, suppress_errors

log_error = suppress_errors(log_error)
```

To understand what commonly goes on inside decorators like `log_error()`, it's first necessary to examine one of the most misunderstood and underutilized features of Python—and many other languages as well—closures.

Closures

Despite their usefulness, closures can seem to be an intimidating topic. Most explanations assume prior knowledge of things like lexical scope, free variables, upvalues and variable extent. Also, because so much can be done without ever learning about closures, the topic often seems mysterious and magical, as if it's the domain of experts, unsuitable for the rest of us. Thankfully, closures really aren't as difficult to understand as the terminology may suggest.

In a nutshell, a closure is a function that's defined inside another function, but is then passed outside that function where it can be used by other code. There are some other details to learn as well, but it's still fairly abstract at this point, so here's a simple example of a closure.

```
def multiply_by(factor):
    """Return a function that multiplies values by the given factor"""

    def multiply(value):
        """Multiply the given value by the factor already provided"""

        return value * factor

    return multiply
```

As you can see, when you call `multiply_by()` with a value to use as a multiplication factor, the inner `multiply()` gets returned to be used later on. Here's how it would actually be used, which may help explain why this is useful.

```
>>> times2 = multiply_by(2)
>>> times2(5)
10
>>> times2(10)
20
>>> times3 = multiply_by(3)
>>> times3(5)
15
>>> times2(times3(5))
30
```

This behavior looks a bit like the argument preloading feature of `functools.partial()`, but you don't need to have a function that takes both arguments at once. The interesting part of about how this works, though, is that the inner function doesn't need to accept a **factor** argument of its own; it essentially inherits that argument from the outer function.

The fact that an inner function can reference the values of an outer function often seems perfectly normal when looking at the code, but there are a couple of rules about how it works that might not be as obvious. First, the inner function must be defined within the outer function; simply passing in a function as an argument won't work.

```
def multiply(value):
    return value * factor

def custom_operator(func, factor):
    return func

multiply_by = functools.partial(custom_operator, multiply)
```

On the surface, this looks mostly equivalent to the working example shown previously, but with the added benefit of being able to provide a callable at run-time. After all, the inner function gets placed inside the outer function and gets returned for use by other code. The problem is that closures only work if the inner function is actually defined inside the outer function, not just anything that gets passed in.

```
>>> times2 = multiply_by(2)
>>> times2(5)
Traceback (most recent call last):
  ...
NameError: global name 'factor' is not defined
```

This almost contradicts the functionality of `functools.partial()`, which works much like the `custom_operator()` function described here, but remember that `partial()` accepts all the arguments at the same time as it accepts the callable to be bundled with them. It doesn't try to pull in any arguments from anywhere else.

Wrappers

Closures come into play heavily in the construction of wrappers, the most common use of decorators. Wrappers are functions designed to contain another function, adding some extra behavior before or after the wrapped function executes. In the context of the closure discussion, a wrapper is the inner function, while the wrapped function is passed in as an argument to the outer function. Here's the code behind the suppress_errors() decorator shown in the previous section.

```
def suppress_errors(func):
    """Automatically silence any errors that occur within a function"""

    def wrapper(*args, **kwargs):
        try:
            return func(*args, **kwargs)
        except Exception:
            pass

    return wrapper
```

There are a few things going on here, but most of them have already been covered. The decorator takes a function as its only argument, which isn't executed until the inner wrapper function executes. By returning the wrapper instead of the original function, we form a closure, which allows the same function handle to be used even after suppress_errors() is done.

Since the wrapper has to be called as if it were the original function, regardless of how that function was defined, it must accept all possible argument combinations. This is achieved by using variable positional and keyword arguments together and passing them straight into the original function internally. This is a very common practice with wrappers because it allows maximum flexibility, without caring what type of function it's applied to.

The actual work in the wrapper is quite simple: just execute the original function inside a try/except block to catch any errors that are raised. In the event of any errors, it just continues merrily along, implicitly returning None instead of doing anything interesting. It also makes sure to return any value returned by the original function, so that everything meaningful about the wrapped function is maintained.

In this case, the wrapper function is fairly simple, but the basic idea works for many more complex situations as well. There could be several lines of code both before and after the original function gets called, perhaps with some decisions about whether it gets called at all. Authorization wrappers, for instance, will typically return or raise an exception without ever calling the wrapped function, if the authorization failed for any reason.

Unfortunately, wrapping a function means some potentially useful information is lost. Chapter 5 shows how Python has access to certain attributes of a function, such as its name, docstring and argument list. By replacing the original function with a wrapper, we've actually replaced all of that other information as well. In order to bring some of it back, we turn to a decorator in the functools module called wraps.

It may seem odd to use a decorator inside a decorator, but it really just solves the same problem as anything else: there's a common need that shouldn't require duplicate code everywhere it takes place. The functools.wraps() decorator copies the name, docstring and some other information over to the wrapped function, so at least some of it gets retained. It can't copy over the argument list, but it's better than nothing.

```
import functools

def suppress_errors(func):
    """Automatically silence any errors that occur within a function"""

    @functools.wraps(func)
    def wrapper(*args, **kwargs):
        try:
            return func(*args, **kwargs)
        except Exception:
            pass

    return wrapper
```

What may seem most odd about this construction is that `functools.wraps()` takes an argument besides the function it's applied to. In this case, that argument is the function to copy attributes from, which is specified on the line with the decorator itself. This is often useful for customizing decorators for specific tasks, so next we'll examine how to take advantage of custom arguments in your own decorators.

Decorators with Arguments

Ordinarily, decorators only take a single argument, the function to be decorated. Behind the scenes, though, Python evaluates the @ line as an expression before applying it as a decorator. The result of the expression is what's actually used as a decorator. In the simple case, the decorator expression is just a single function, so it evaluates easily. Adding arguments in the form used by `functools.wraps()` makes the whole statement evaluate like this.

```
wrapper = functools.wraps(func)(wrapper)
```

Looking at it this way, the solution becomes clear: one function returns another. The first function accepts the extra arguments and returns another function, which is used as the decorator. This makes implementing arguments on a decorator more complex because it adds another layer to the whole process, but it's easy to deal with once you see it in context. Here's how everything works together in the longest chain you're likely to see.

- A function to accept and validate arguments

- A decorator to accept a user-defined function

- A wrapper to add extra behavior

- The original function that was decorated

Not all of that will happen for every decorator, but that's the general approach of the most complex scenarios. Anything more complicated is simply an expansion of one of those four steps. As you'll notice, three of the four have already been covered, so the extra layer imposed by decorator arguments is really the only thing left to discuss.

This new outermost function accepts all the arguments for the decorator, optionally validates them and returns a new function as a closure over the argument variables. That new function must take a single argument, functioning as the decorator. Here's how the `suppress_errors()` decorator might look if it instead accepted a logger function to report the errors to, rather than completely silencing them.

```
import functools

def suppress_errors(log_func=None):
    """Automatically silence any errors that occur within a function"""

    def decorator(func):
        @functools.wraps(func)
        def wrapper(*args, **kwargs):
            try:
                return func(*args, **kwargs)
            except Exception as e:
                if log_func is not None:
                    log_func(str(e))

        return wrapper

    return decorator
```

This layering allows `suppress_errors()` to accept arguments prior to being used as a decorator, but it removes the ability to call it without any arguments. Since that was the previous behavior, we've now introduced a backward incompatibility. The closest we can get to the original syntax is to actually call `suppress_errors()` first, but without any arguments.

Here's an example function that processes updates files in a given directory. This is a task that's often performed on an automated schedule, so that if something goes wrong, it can just stop running and try again at the next appointed time.

```
import datetime
import os
import time
from myapp import suppress_errors

@suppress_errors()
def process_updated_files(directory, process, since=None):
    """
    Processes any new files in a `directory` using the `process` function.
    If provided, `since` is a date after which files are considered updated.

    The process function passed in must accept a single argument: the absolute
    path to the file that needs to be processed.
    """

    if since is not None:
        # Get a threshold that we can compare to the modification time later
        threshold = time.mktime(since.timetuple()) + since.microsecond / 1000000
    else:
        threshold = 0

    for filename in os.listdir(directory):
        path = os.path.abspath(os.path.join(directory, filename))
        if os.stat(path).st_mtime > threshold:
            process(path)
```

Unfortunately, this is still a strange situation to end up with, and it really doesn't look like anything Python programmers are used to. Clearly we need a better solution.

Decorators with—or without—Arguments

Ideally, a decorator with optional arguments would be able to be called without parentheses if no arguments are provided, while still being able to provide the arguments when necessary. This means supporting two different flows in a single decorator, which can get tricky if you're not careful. The main problem is that the outermost function must be able to accept arbitrary arguments *or* a single function, and it must be able to tell the difference between the two and behave accordingly.

That brings us to the first task: determining which flow to use when the outer function is called. One option would be to inspect the first positional argument and check to see if it's a function, since decorators always receive the function as a positional argument. But since things like `functools.wraps()` accept a function as a non-decorator argument, that method falls apart pretty quickly.

Interestingly, a pretty good distinction can be made based on something mentioned briefly in the previous paragraph. Decorators always receive the decorated function as a positional argument, so we can use that as its distinguishing factor. For all other arguments, we can instead rely on keyword arguments, which are generally more explicit anyway, thus making it more readable as well.

We could do this by way of using `*args` and `**kwargs`, but since we know the positional argument list is just a fixed single argument, it's easier to just make that the first argument and make it optional. Then, any additional keyword arguments can be placed after it. They'll all need default values, of course, but the whole point here is that all arguments are optional, so that's not a problem.

With the argument distinction squared away, all that's left is to branch into a different code block if arguments are provided, rather than a function to be decorated. By having an optional first positional argument, we can simply test for its presence to determine which branch to go through.

```python
import functools

def suppress_errors(func=None, log_func=None):
    """Automatically silence any errors that occur within a function"""

    def decorator(func):
        @functools.wraps(func)
        def wrapper(*args, **kwargs):
            try:
                return func(*args, **kwargs)
            except Exception as e:
                if log_func is not None:
                    log_func(str(e))

        return wrapper

    if func is None:
        return decorator
    else:
        return decorator(func)
```

This now allows `suppress_errors()` to be called with or without arguments, but it's still important to remember that arguments *must* be passed with keywords. This is an example where an argument looks identical to the function being decorated. There's no way to tell the difference by examining them, even if we tried.

If a logger function is provided as a positional argument, the decorator will assume it's the function to be decorated, so it'll actually execute the logger immediately, with the function to be decorated as its argument. In essence, you'll end up logging the function you wanted to decorate. Worse yet, the value you're left with after decorating the function is actually the return value from the logger, not the decorator. Since most loggers don't return anything, it'll probably be None—that's right, your function has vanished.

```
>>> def print_logger(message):
...     print(message)
...
>>> @suppress_errors(print_logger)
... def example():
...     return variable_which_does_not_exist
...
<function example at 0x...>
>>> example
>>>
```

This is a side-effect of the way the decorator works, and there's little to be done besides documenting it and making sure you always specify keywords when applying arguments.

Example: Memoization

To demonstrate how decorators can copy out common behavior into any function you like, consider what could be done to improve the efficiency of deterministic functions. Deterministic functions always return the same result given the same set of arguments, no matter how many times they're called. Given such a function, it should be possible to cache the results of a given function call, so if it's called with the same arguments again, the result can be looked up without having to call the function again.

Using a cache, a decorator can store the result of a function using the argument list as its key. Dictionaries can't be used as keys in a dictionary, so only positional arguments can be taken into account when populating the cache. Thankfully, most functions that would take advantage of memoization are simple mathematical operations, which are typically called with positional arguments anyway.

```
def memoize(func):
    """
    Cache the results of the function so it doesn't need to be called
    again, if the same arguments are provided a second time.
    """
    cache = {}

    @functools.wraps(func)
    def wrapper(*args):
        if args in cache:
            return cache[args]

        # This line is for demonstration only.
        # Remove it before using it for real.
        print('Calling %s()' % func.__name__)

        result = func(*args)
```

```
            cache[args] = result
            return result

    return wrapper
```

Now, whenever you define a deterministic function, you can use the `memoize()` decorator to automatically cache its result for future use. Here's how it would work for some simple mathematical operations.

```
>>> @memoize
... def multiply(x, y):
...     return x * y
...
>>> multiply(6, 7)
Calling multiply()
42
>>> multiply(6, 7)
42
>>> multiply(4, 3)
Calling multiply()
12
>>> @memoize
... def factorial(x):
...     result = 1
...     for i in range(x):
...         result *= i + 1
...     return result
...
>>> factorial(5)
Calling factorial()
120
>>> factorial(5)
120
>>> factorial(7)
Calling factorial()
5040
```

■ **Caution** Memoization is best suited for functions with a few arguments, which are called with relatively few variations in the argument values. Functions that are called with a large number of arguments or have a lot of variety in the argument values that are used will quickly fill up a lot of memory with the cache. This can slow down the entire system, with the only benefit being the minority of cases where arguments are reused. Also, functions that aren't truly deterministic will actually cause problems because the function won't be called every time.

Example: A Decorator to Create Decorators

Astute readers will have noticed something of a contradiction in the descriptions of the more complex decorator constructs. The purpose of decorators is to avoid a lot of boilerplate code and simplify functions, but the decorators themselves end up getting quite complicated just to support features like optional arguments. Ideally, we could put that boilerplate into a decorator as well, simplifying the process for new decorators.

Since decorators are Python functions, just like those they decorate, this is quite possible. As with the other situations, though, there's something that needs to be taken into account. In this case, the function you define as a decorator will need to distinguish between the arguments meant for the decorator and those meant for the function it decorates.

```python
def decorator(declared_decorator):
    """Create a decorator out of a function, which will be used as a wrapper."""

    @functools.wraps(declared_decorator)
    def final_decorator(func=None, **kwargs):
        # This will be exposed to the rest
        # of your application as a decorator

        def decorated(func):
            # This will be exposed to the rest
            # of your application as a decorated
            # function, regardless how it was called
            @functools.wraps(func)
            def wrapper(*a, **kw):
                # This is used when actually executing
                # the function that was decorated
                return declared_decorator(func, a, kw, **kwargs)

            return wrapper

        if func is None:
            # The decorator was called with arguments,
            # rather than a function to decorate
            return decorated
        else:
            # The decorator was called without arguments,
            # so the function should be decorated immediately
            return decorated(func)

    return final_decorator
```

With this in place, you can define your decorators in terms of the wrapper function directly; then just apply this decorator to manage all the overhead behind the scenes. Your declared functions must always accept three arguments now, with any additional arguments added on beyond that. The three required arguments are shown in the following list.

- The function that will be decorated, which should be called if appropriate

- A tuple of positional arguments that were supplied to the decorated function

- A dictionary of keyword arguments that were supplied to the decorated function

With these arguments in mind, here's how you might define the `suppress_errors()` decorator described previously in this chapter.

```
>>> @decorator
... def suppress_errors(func, args, kwargs, log_func=None):
...     try:
...         return func(*args, **kwargs)
...     except Exception as e:
...         if log_func is not None:
...             log_func(str(e))
...
>>> @suppress_errors
... def example():
...     return variable_which_does_not_exist
...
>>> example() # Doesn't raise any errors
>>> def print_logger(message):
...     print(message)
...
>>> @suppress_errors(log_func=print_logger)
... def example():
...     return variable_which_does_not_exist
...
>>> example()
global name 'variable_which_does_not_exist' is not defined
```

Function Annotations

There are typically three aspects of a function that don't deal with the code within it: a name, a set of arguments and an optional docstring. Sometimes, though, that's not quite enough to fully describe how the function works or how it should be used. Static-typed languages—like Java, for example—also include details about what type of values are allowed for each of the arguments, as well as what type can be expected for the return value.

Python's response to this need is the concept of function annotations. Each argument, as well as the return value, can have an expression attached to it, which describes a detail that can't be conveyed otherwise. This could be as simple as a type, such as `int` or `str`, which is analogous to static-typed languages, as shown in the following example.

```
def prepend_rows(rows:list, prefix:str) -> list:
    return [prefix + row for row in rows]
```

The biggest difference between this example and traditional static-typed languages isn't a matter of syntax; it's that in Python, annotations can be *any* expression, not just a type or a class. You could annotate your arguments with descriptive strings, calculated values or even inline functions—see this chapter's section on lambdas for details. Here's what the previous example might look like if annotated with strings as additional documentation.

```python
def prepend_rows(rows:"a list of strings to add to the prefix",
                 prefix:"a string to prepend to each row provided",
                 ) -> "a new list of strings prepended with the prefix":
    return [prefix + row for row in rows]
```

Of course, this flexibility might make you wonder about the "intended" use for function annotations, but there isn't one, and that's deliberate. Officially, the intent behind annotations is to encourage experimentation in frameworks and other third-party libraries. The two examples shown here could be valid for use with type checking and documentation libraries, respectively.

Compatibility: Prior to 3.0

Function annotations were added in Python 3.0; prior to that, declaring them in a function would've resulted in a `SyntaxError`. The following two examples rely entirely on built-in annotation support, so it's not possible to rework in a way that will work for previous versions of Python. However, at the end of this chapter, the examples are rewritten as decorators, which will be compatible with older versions.

Example: Type Safety

To illustrate how annotations can be used by a library, consider a basic implementation of a type safety library that can understand and utilize the function described previously. It would expect argument annotations to specify a valid type for any incoming arguments, while the return annotation would be able to validate the value returned by the function.

Since type safety involves verifying values before and after the function is executed, a decorator is the most suitable option for the implementation. Also, since all the type hinting information is provided in the function declaration, we don't need to worry about any additional arguments, so a simple decorator will suffice. The first task, though, is to validate the annotations themselves, since they must be valid Python types in order for the rest of the decorator to work properly.

```python
import inspect

def typesafe(func):
    """
    Verify that the function is called with the right argument types and
    that it returns a value of the right type, according to its annotations
    """

    spec = inspect.getfullargspec(func)

    for name, annotation in spec.annotations.items():
        if not isinstance(annotation, type):
            raise TypeError("The annotation for '%s' is not a type." % name)

    return func
```

So far, this doesn't do anything to the function, but it does check to see that each annotation provided is a valid type, which can then be used to verify the type of the arguments referenced by the annotations. This uses isinstance(), which compares an object to the type it's expected to be. More information on isinstance() and on types and classes in general can be found in Chapter 4.

Now that we can be sure all the annotations are valid, it's time to start validating some arguments. Given how many types of arguments there are, let's take them one at a time. Keyword arguments are the easiest to start out with, since they already come with their name and value tied together, so that's one less thing to worry about. With a name, we can get the associated annotation and validate the value against that. This would also be a good time to start factoring some things out, since we'll end up having to use some of the same things over and over again. Here's how the wrapper would look to begin with.

```python
import functools
import inspect

def typesafe(func):
    """
    Verify that the function is called with the right argument types and
    that it returns a value of the right type, according to its annotations
    """

    spec = inspect.getfullargspec(func)
    annotations = spec.annotations

    for name, annotation in annotations.items():
        if not isinstance(annotation, type):
            raise TypeError("The annotation for '%s' is not a type." % name)

    error = "Wrong type for %s: expected %s, got %s."

    @functools.wraps(func)
    def wrapper(*args, **kwargs):
        # Deal with keyword arguments
        for name, arg in kwargs.items():
            if name in annotations and not isinstance(arg, annotations[name]):
                raise TypeError(error % (name,
                                         annotations[name].__name__,
                                         type(arg).__name__))

        return func(*args, **kwargs)
    return wrapper
```

By now, this should be fairly self-explanatory. Any keyword arguments provided will be checked to see if there's an associated annotation. If there is, the provided value is checked to make sure it's an instance of the type found in the annotation. The error message is factored out because it'll get reused a few more times before we're done.

Next up is dealing with positional arguments. Once again, we can rely on zip() to line up the positional argument names with the values that were provided. Since the result of zip() is compatible with the items() method of dictionaries, we can actually use chain() from the itertools module to link them together into the same loop.

```python
import functools
import inspect
from itertools import chain

def typesafe(func):
    """
    Verify that the function is called with the right argument types and
    that it returns a value of the right type, according to its annotations
    """
    spec = inspect.getfullargspec(func)
    annotations = spec.annotations

    for name, annotation in annotations.items():
        if not isinstance(annotation, type):
            raise TypeError("The annotation for '%s' is not a type." % name)

    error = "Wrong type for %s: expected %s, got %s."

    @functools.wraps(func)
    def wrapper(*args, **kwargs):
        # Deal with keyword arguments
        for name, arg in chain(zip(spec.args, args), kwargs.items()):
            if name in annotations and not isinstance(arg, annotations[name]):
                raise TypeError(error % (name,
                                         annotations[name].__name__,
                                         type(arg).__name__))

        return func(*args, **kwargs)
    return wrapper
```

Even though that takes care of both positional and keyword arguments, it's not everything. Since variable arguments can also accept annotations, we have to account for argument values that don't line up as nicely with defined argument names. Unfortunately, there's something else that must be dealt with before we can do much of anything on that front.

If you're paying really close attention, you might notice a very subtle bug in the code as it stands. In order to make the code a bit easier to follow and to account for any arguments that are passed by keywords, the wrapper iterates over the kwargs dictionary in its entirely, checking for associated annotations. Unfortunately, that leaves us with the possibility of an unintentional name conflict.

To illustrate how the bug could be triggered, first consider what would be expected when dealing with variable arguments. Since we can only apply a single annotation to the variable argument name itself, that annotation must be assumed to apply to all arguments that fall under that variable argument, whether passed positionally or by keyword. Without explicit support for that behavior yet, variable arguments should just be ignored, but here's what happens with the code as it stands.

```python
>>> @typesafe
... def example(*args:int, **kwargs:str):
...     pass
...
>>> example(spam='eggs')
>>> example(kwargs='spam')
```

```
>>> example(args='spam')
Traceback (most recent call last):
  ...
TypeError: Wrong type for args: expected int, got str.
```

Interestingly, everything works fine unless the function call includes a keyword argument with the same name as the variable positional argument. Though it may not seem obvious at first, the problem is actually in the set of values to iterate over in the wrapper's only loop. It assumes that the names of all the keyword arguments line up nicely with annotations.

Basically, the problem is that keyword arguments that are meant for the variable argument end up getting matched up with annotations from other arguments. For the most part, this is acceptable because two of the three types of arguments won't ever cause problems. Matching it with an explicit argument name simply duplicates what Python already does, so using the associated annotation is fine, and matching the variable keyword argument name ends up using the same annotation that we were planning on using anyway.

So the problem only crops up when a keyword argument matches the variable positional argument name because that association never makes sense. Sometimes if the annotation is the same as that of the variable keyword argument, the problem might never show up, but it's still there, regardless. Since the code for the wrapper function is still fairly minimal, it's not too difficult to see where the problem is occurring.

In the main loop, the second part of the iteration chain is the list of items in the kwargs dictionary. That means everything passed in by keyword is checked against named annotations, which clearly isn't always what we want. Instead, we only want to loop over the explicit arguments at this point, while still supporting both positions and keywords. That means we'll have to construct a new dictionary based on the function definition, rather than taking the easy way out and relying on kwargs, as we are now. The outer typesafe() function has been removed from the listing here to make the code easier to digest in print.

```python
def wrapper(*args, **kwargs):
    # Populate a dictionary of explicit arguments passed positionally
    explicit_args = dict(zip(spec.args, args))

    # Add all explicit arguments passed by keyword
    for name in chain(spec.args, spec.kwonlyargs):
        if name in kwargs:
            explicit_args[name] = kwargs[name]

    # Deal with explicit arguments
    for name, arg in explicit_args.items():
        if name in annotations and not isinstance(arg, annotations[name]):
            raise TypeError(error % (name,
                                     annotations[name].__name__,
                                     type(arg).__name__))

    return func(*args, **kwargs)
```

With that bug out of the way, we can focus on properly supporting variable arguments. Since keyword arguments have names but positional arguments don't, we can't manage both types in one pass like we could with the explicit arguments. The processes are fairly similar to the explicit arguments, but the values to iterate over are different in each case. The biggest difference, though, is that the annotations aren't referenced by the name of the arguments.

In order to loop over just the truly variable positional arguments, we can simply use the number of explicit arguments as the beginning of a slice on the positional arguments tuple. This gets us all positional arguments provided after the explicit arguments or an empty list if only explicit arguments were provided.

For keyword arguments, we have to be a bit more creative. Since the function already loops over all the explicitly declared arguments at the beginning, we can use that same loop to exclude any matching items from a copy of the kwargs dictionary. Then we can iterate over what's left over to account for all the variable keyword arguments.

```python
def wrapper(*args, **kwargs):
    # Populate a dictionary of explicit arguments passed positionally
    explicit_args = dict(zip(spec.args, args))
    keyword_args = kwargs.copy()

    # Add all explicit arguments passed by keyword
    for name in chain(spec.args, spec.kwonlyargs):
        if name in kwargs:
            explicit_args[name] = keyword_args.pop(name)

    # Deal with explicit arguments
    for name, arg in explicit_args.items():
        if name in annotations and not isinstance(arg, annotations[name]):
            raise TypeError(error % (name,
                                     annotations[name].__name__,
                                     type(arg).__name__))

    # Deal with variable positional arguments
    if spec.varargs and spec.varargs in annotations:
        annotation = annotations[spec.varargs]
        for i, arg in enumerate(args[len(spec.args):]):
            if not isinstance(arg, annotation):
                raise TypeError(error % ('variable argument %s' % (i + 1),
                                         annotation.__name__,
                                         type(arg).__name__))

    # Deal with variable keyword arguments
    if spec.varkw and spec.varkw in annotations:
        annotation = annotations[spec.varkw]
        for name, arg in keyword_args.items():
            if not isinstance(arg, annotation):
                raise TypeError(error % (name,
                                         annotation.__name__,
                                         type(arg).__name__))

    return func(*args, **kwargs)
```

Now we've covered all explicit arguments as well as variable arguments passed in by position and keyword. The only thing left is to validate the value returned by the target function. Thus far, the wrapper just calls the original function directly, without regard for what it returns, but by now, it should be easy to see what needs to be done.

```
    def wrapper(*args, **kwargs):
        # Populate a dictionary of explicit arguments passed positionally
        explicit_args = dict(zip(spec.args, args))
        keyword_args = kwargs.copy()

        # Add all explicit arguments passed by keyword
        for name in chain(spec.args, spec.kwonlyargs):
            if name in kwargs:
                explicit_args[name] = keyword_args(name)

        # Deal with explicit arguments
        for name, arg in explicit_args.items():
            if name in annotations and not isinstance(arg, annotations[name]):
                raise TypeError(error % (name,
                                         annotations[name].__name__,
                                         type(arg).__name__))

        # Deal with variable positional arguments
        if spec.varargs and spec.varargs in annotations:
            annotation = annotations[spec.varargs]
            for i, arg in enumerate(args[len(spec.args):]):
                if not isinstance(arg, annotation):
                    raise TypeError(error % ('variable argument %s' % (i + 1),
                                             annotation.__name__,
                                             type(arg).__name__))

        # Deal with variable keyword arguments
        if spec.varkw and spec.varkw in annotations:
            annotation = annotations[spec.varkw]
            for name, arg in keyword_args.items():
                if not isinstance(arg, annotation):
                    raise TypeError(error % (name,
                                             annotation.__name__,
                                             type(arg).__name__))

        r = func(*args, **kwargs)
        if 'return' in annotations and not isinstance(r, annotations['return']):
            raise TypeError(error % ('the return value',
                                     annotations['return'].__name__,
                                     type(r).__name__))
        return r
```

With that, we have a fully functional type safety decorator, which can validate all arguments to a function as well as its return value. There's one additional safeguard we can include to find errors even more quickly, though. Similarly to how the outer **typesafe()** function already validates that the annotations are types, that part of the function is also capable of validating the default values for all provided arguments. Since variable arguments can't have default values, this is much simpler than dealing with the function call itself.

```
import functools
import inspect
```

```python
from itertools import chain

def typesafe(func):
    """
    Verify that the function is called with the right argument types and
    that it returns a value of the right type, according to its annotations
    """
    spec = inspect.getfullargspec(func)
    annotations = spec.annotations

    for name, annotation in annotations.items():
        if not isinstance(annotation, type):
            raise TypeError("The annotation for '%s' is not a type." % name)

    error = "Wrong type for %s: expected %s, got %s."
    defaults = spec.defaults or ()
    defaults_zip = zip(spec.args[-len(defaults):], defaults)
    kwonlydefaults = spec.kwonlydefaults or {}

    for name, value in chain(defaults_zip, kwonlydefaults.items()):
        if name in annotations and not isinstance(value, annotations[name]):
            raise TypeError(error % ('default value of %s' % name,
                                     annotations[name].__name__,
                                     type(value).__name__))

    @functools.wraps(func)
    def wrapper(*args, **kwargs):
        # Populate a dictionary of explicit arguments passed positionally
        explicit_args = dict(zip(spec.args, args))
        keyword_args = kwargs.copy()

        # Add all explicit arguments passed by keyword
        for name in chain(spec.args, spec.kwonlyargs):
            if name in kwargs:
                explicit_args[name] = keyword_args.pop(name)

        # Deal with explicit arguments
        for name, arg in explicit_args.items():
            if name in annotations and not isinstance(arg, annotations[name]):
                raise TypeError(error % (name,
                                         annotations[name].__name__,
                                         type(arg).__name__))

        # Deal with variable positional arguments
        if spec.varargs and spec.varargs in annotations:
            annotation = annotations[spec.varargs]
            for i, arg in enumerate(args[len(spec.args):]):
                if not isinstance(arg, annotation):
                    raise TypeError(error % ('variable argument %s' % (i + 1),
                                             annotation.__name__,
                                             type(arg).__name__))
```

```
        # Deal with variable keyword arguments
        if spec.varkw and spec.varkw in annotations:
            annotation = annotations[spec.varkw]
            for name, arg in keyword_args.items():
                if not isinstance(arg, annotation):
                    raise TypeError(error % (name,
                                            annotation.__name__,
                                            type(arg).__name__))

        r = func(*args, **kwargs)
        if 'return' in annotations and not isinstance(r, annotations['return']):
            raise TypeError(error % ('the return value',
                                    annotations['return'].__name__,
                                    type(r).__name__))
        return r
    return wrapper
```

Factoring Out the Boilerplate

Looking over the code as it stands, you'll notice a lot of repetition. Each form of annotation ends up doing the same things: checking if the value is appropriate and raising an exception if it's not. Ideally, we'd be able to factor that out into a separate function that can focus solely on the actual task of validation. The rest of the code is really just boilerplate, managing the details of finding the different types of annotations.

Since the common code will be going into a new function, the obvious way to tie it into the rest of the code is to create a new decorator. This new decorator will be placed on a function that will process the annotation for each value, so we'll call it annotation_processor. The function passed into annotation_processor will then be used for each of the annotation types throughout the existing code.

```
import functools
import inspect
from itertools import chain

def annotation_decorator(process):
    """
    Creates a decorator that processes annotations for each argument passed
    into its target function, raising an exception if there's a problem.
    """

    @functools.wraps(process)
    def decorator(func):
        spec = inspect.getfullargspec(func)
        annotations = spec.annotations

        defaults = spec.defaults or ()
        defaults_zip = zip(spec.args[-len(defaults):], defaults)
        kwonlydefaults = spec.kwonlydefaults or {}

        for name, value in chain(defaults_zip, kwonlydefaults.items()):
            if name in annotations:
                process(value, annotations[name])
```

```
    @functools.wraps(func)
    def wrapper(*args, **kwargs):
        # Populate a dictionary of explicit arguments passed positionally
        explicit_args = dict(zip(spec.args, args))
        keyword_args = kwargs.copy()

        # Add all explicit arguments passed by keyword
        for name in chain(spec.args, spec.kwonlyargs):
            if name in kwargs:
                explicit_args[name] = keyword_args.pop(name)

        # Deal with explicit arguments
        for name, arg in explicit_args.items():
            if name in annotations:
                process(arg, annotations[name])

        # Deal with variable positional arguments
        if spec.varargs and spec.varargs in annotations:
            annotation = annotations[spec.varargs]
            for arg in args[len(spec.args):]:
                process(arg, annotation)

        # Deal with variable keyword arguments
        if spec.varkw and spec.varkw in annotations:
            annotation = annotations[spec.varkw]
            for name, arg in keyword_args.items():
                process(arg, annotation)

        r = func(*args, **kwargs)
        if 'return' in annotations:
            process(r, annotations['return'])
        return r

    return wrapper

return decorator
```

■ **Note** Because we're making it a bit more generic, you'll notice that the initial portion of the decorator no longer checks that the annotations are valid types. The decorator itself no longer cares what logic you apply to the argument values, since that's all done in the decorated function.

Now we can apply this new decorator to a much simpler function to provide a new **typesafe()** decorator, which functions just like the one in the previous section.

```
@annotation_decorator
def typesafe(value, annotation):
    """
```

```
    Verify that the function is called with the right argument types and
    that it returns a value of the right type, according to its annotations
    """
    if not isinstance(value, annotation):
        raise TypeError("Expected %s, got %s." % (annotation.__name__,
                                                  type(value).__name__))
```

The benefit of doing this is that it's much easier to modify the behavior of the decorator in the future. In addition, you can now use `annotation_processor()` to create new types of decorators that use annotation for different purposes, such as type coercion.

Example: Type Coercion

Rather than strictly requiring that the arguments all be the types specified when they're passed into the function, another approach is to coerce them to the required types inside the function itself. Many of the same types that are used to validate values can also be used to coerce them directly into the types themselves. In addition, if a value can't be coerced, the type it's passed into raises an exception, usually a `TypeError`, just like our validation function.

Robustness Principle

This is one of the more obvious applications of the robustness principle. Your function requires an argument be of a specific type, but it's much nicer to accept some variations, knowing that they can be converted to the right type before your function needs to deal with them. Likewise, coercion also helps ensure that the return value is always of a consistent type that the external code knows how to deal with.

The decorator presented in the previous section provides a good starting point for adding this behavior to a new decorator, and we can use it to modify the incoming value according to the annotation that was provided along with it. Since we're relying on the type constructor to do all the necessary type checking and raise exceptions appropriately, this new decorator can be much simpler. In fact, it can be expressed in just one actual instruction.

```
@annotation_decorator
def coerce_arguments(value, annotation):
    return annotation(value)
```

In fact, this is so simple that it doesn't even require the annotation be a type at all. Any function or class that returns an object will work just fine, and the value returned will be passed into the function decorated by `coerce_arguments()`. Or will it? If you look back at the `annotation_decorator()` function as it stands, there's a minor problem that prevents it from working the way this new decorator would need it to.

The problem is that, in the lines that call the `process()` function that was passed into the outer decorator, the return value is thrown away. If you try to use `coerce_arguments()` with the existing decorator, all you'll get is the exception-raising aspect of the code, not the value coercion aspect. So in order to work properly, we'll need to go back and add that feature to `annotation_processor()`.

There are a few things that need to be done overall, though. Because the annotation processor will be modifying the arguments that will be eventually sent to the decorated function, we'll need to set up a new list for positional arguments and a new dictionary for keyword arguments. Then we have to split up the explicit argument handling, so that we can distinguish between positional and keyword arguments. Without that, the function wouldn't be able to apply variable positional arguments correctly.

```python
def wrapper(*args, **kwargs):
    new_args = []
    new_kwargs = {}
    keyword_args = kwargs.copy()

    # Deal with explicit arguments passed positionally
    for name, arg in zip(spec.args, args):
        if name in annotations:
            new_args.append(process(arg, annotations[name]))

    # Deal with explicit arguments passed by keyword
    for name in chain(spec.args, spec.kwonlyargs):
        if name in kwargs and name in annotations:
            new_kwargs[name] = process(keyword_args.pop(name),
                                       annotations[name])

    # Deal with variable positional arguments
    if spec.varargs and spec.varargs in annotations:
        annotation = annotations[spec.varargs]
        for arg in args[len(spec.args):]:
            new_args.append(process(arg, annotation))

    # Deal with variable keyword arguments
    if spec.varkw and spec.varkw in annotations:
        annotation = annotations[spec.varkw]
        for name, arg in keyword_args.items():
            new_kwargs[name] = process(arg, annotation)

    r = func(*new_args, **new_kwargs)
    if 'return' in annotations:
        r = process(r, annotations['return'])
    return r
```

With those changes in place, the new `coerce_arguments()` decorator will be able to replace the arguments on the fly, passing the replacements into the original function. Unfortunately, if you're still using `typesafe()` from before, this new behavior causes problems because `typesafe()` doesn't return a value. Fixing that is a simple matter of returning the original value, unchanged, if the type check was satisfactory.

```python
@annotation_decorator
def typesafe(value, annotation):
    """
    Verify that the function is called with the right argument types and
    that it returns a value of the right type, according to its annotations
    """
```

```
    if not isinstance(value, annotation):
        raise TypeError("Expected %s, got %s." % (annotation.__name__,
                                                  type(value).__name__))
    return value
```

Annotating with Decorators

The natural question to ask is: what happens if you want to use two libraries together? One might expect you to supply valid types, while the other expects a string to use for documentation. They're completely incompatible with each other, which forces you to use one or the other, rather than both. Furthermore, any attempt to merge the two, using a dictionary or some other combined data type, would have to be agreed on by both libraries, since each would need to know how to get at the information it cares about.

Once you consider how many other frameworks and libraries might take advantage of these annotations, you can see how quickly the official function annotations fall apart. It's still too early to see which applications will actually use it or how they'll work together, but it's certainly worth considering other options which can bypass the problems completely.

Since decorators can take arguments of their own, it's possible to use them to provide annotations for the arguments of the functions they decorate. This way, the annotations are separate from the function itself and provided directly to the code that makes sense of them. And since multiple decorators can be stacked together on a single function, it's already got a built-in way of managing multiple frameworks.

Example: Type Safety as a Decorator

To illustrate the decorator-based approach to function annotations, let's consider the type safety example from earlier. It already relied on a decorator, so we can extend that to take arguments, using the same types that the annotations provided previously. Essentially, it'll look something like this.

```
>>> @typesafe(str, str)
... def combine(a, b):
...     return a + b
...
>>> combine('spam', 'alot')
'spamalot'
>>> combine('fail', 1)
Traceback (most recent call last):
  ...
TypeError: Wrong type for b: expected str, got int.
```

It works almost exactly like the true annotated version, except that the annotations are supplied to the decorator directly. In order to accept arguments, we're going to just change the first portion of the code a bit, so we can get the annotations from the arguments instead of inspecting the function itself.

Since annotations come in through arguments to the decorator, we have a new outer wrapper for receiving them. When the next layer receives the function to be decorated, it can match up the annotations with the function's signature, providing names for any annotations passed positionally. Once all the available annotations have been given the right names, they can be used by the rest of the inner decorator, without any further modifications.

```
import functools
import inspect
from itertools import chain
```

```python
def annotation_decorator(process):
    """
    Creates a decorator that processes annotations for each argument passed
    into its target function, raising an exception if there's a problem.
    """

    def annotator(*args, **kwargs):
        annotations = kwargs.copy()

        @functools.wraps(process)
        def decorator(func):
            spec = inspect.getfullargspec(func)
            annotations.update(zip(spec.args, args))

            defaults = spec.defaults or ()
            defaults_zip = zip(spec.args[-len(defaults):], defaults)
            kwonlydefaults = spec.kwonlydefaults or {}

            for name, value in chain(defaults_zip, kwonlydefaults.items()):
                if name in annotations:
                    process(value, annotations[name])

            @functools.wraps(func)
            def wrapper(*args, **kwargs):
                new_args = []
                new_kwargs = {}
                keyword_args = kwargs.copy()

                # Deal with explicit arguments passed positionally
                for name, arg in zip(spec.args, args):
                    if name in annotations:
                        new_args.append(process(arg, annotations[name]))

                # Deal with explicit arguments passed by keyword
                for name in chain(spec.args, spec.kwonlyargs):
                    if name in kwargs and name in annotations:
                        new_kwargs[name] = process(keyword_args.pop(name),
                                                   annotations[name])

                # Deal with variable positional arguments
                if spec.varargs and spec.varargs in annotations:
                    annotation = annotations[spec.varargs]
                    for arg in args[len(spec.args):]:
                        new_args.append(process(arg, annotation))

                # Deal with variable keyword arguments
                if spec.varkw and spec.varkw in annotations:
                    annotation = annotations[spec.varkw]
                    for name, arg in keyword_args.items():
                        new_kwargs[name] = process(arg, annotation)
```

```
            r = func(*new_args, **new_kwargs)
            if 'return' in annotations:
                r = process(r, annotations['return'])
            return r

        return wrapper

    return decorator

return annotator
```

That handles most of the situation, but it doesn't handle return values yet. If you try to supply a return value using the right name, `return`, you'll get a syntax error because it's a reserved Python keyword. Trying to provide it alongside the other annotations would require each call to pass annotations using an actual dictionary, where you can provide the return annotation without upsetting Python's syntax.

Instead, we'll need to provide the return value annotation in a separate function call, where it can be the sole argument, without any reserved name issues. When working with most types of decorators, this would be easy to do: just create a new decorator that checks the return value and be done with it. Unfortunately, since the eventual decorator we're working with is created outside the control of our code, it's not so easy.

If we completely detached the return value processing from the argument processing, the programmer who's actually writing something like the `typesafe()` decorator would have to write it twice; once to create the argument-processing decorator and again to create the return-value-processing decorator. Since that's a clear violation of DRY, let's see if we can reuse as much of their work as possible.

Here's where some design comes into play. We're looking at going beyond just a simple decorator, so we need to figure out how to best approach it, so it makes sense to those who have to use it. Thinking about the available options, one solution springs to mind fairly quickly. If we can add the extra annotation function as an attribute of the final decorator, you'd be able to write the return value annotator on the same line as the other decorator, but right afterward, in its own function call. Here's what it might look like, if we went that route.

```
@typesafe(int, int).returns(int)
def add(a, b):
    return a + b
```

Unfortunately, this isn't actually an option, for reasons that can be demonstrated without even adding the necessary code to support it. The trouble is, this formation isn't allowed as Python syntax. If `typesafe()` hadn't taken any arguments, it would work, but there's no support for calling two separate functions as part of a single decorator. Instead of supplying the return value annotation in the decorator itself, let's look somewhere else.

Another option is to use the generated `typesafe()` decorator to add a function as an attribute to the wrapper around the `add()` function. This places the return value annotation at the end of the function definition, closer to where the return value is specified. In addition, it helps clarify the fact that you can use `typesafe()` to supply argument decorators without bothering to check the return value, if you want to. Here's how it would look.

```
@typesafe(int, int)
def add(a, b):
    return a + b
add.returns(int)
```

It's still very clear and perhaps even more explicit than the syntax that doesn't work anyway. As an added bonus, the code to support it is very simple, requiring just a few lines be added to the end of the inner `decorator()` function.

```python
def decorator(func):
    from itertools import chain

    spec = inspect.getfullargspec(func)
    annotations.update(zip(spec.args, args))

    defaults = spec.defaults or ()
    defaults_zip = zip(spec.args[-len(defaults):], defaults)
    kwonlydefaults = spec.kwonlydefaults or {}

    for name, value in chain(defaults_zip, kwonlydefaults.items()):
        if name in annotations:
            process(value, annotations[name])

    @functools.wraps(func)
    def wrapper(*args, **kwargs):
        new_args = []
        new_kwargs = {}
        keyword_args = kwargs.copy()

        # Deal with explicit arguments passed positionally
        for name, arg in zip(spec.args, args):
            if name in annotations:
                new_args.append(process(arg, annotations[name]))

        # Deal with explicit arguments passed by keyword
        for name in chain(spec.args, spec.kwonlyargs):
            if name in kwargs and name in annotations:
                new_kwargs[name] = process(keyword_args.pop(name),
                                           annotations[name])

        # Deal with variable positional arguments
        if spec.varargs and spec.varargs in annotations:
            annotation = annotations[spec.varargs]
            for arg in args[len(spec.args):]:
                new_args.append(process(arg, annotation))

        # Deal with variable keyword arguments
        if spec.varkw and spec.varkw in annotations:
            annotation = annotations[spec.varkw]
            for name, arg in keyword_args.items():
                new_kwargs[name] = process(arg, annotation)

        r = func(*new_args, **new_kwargs)
        if 'return' in annotations:
            r = process(r, annotations['return'])
        return r
```

```
def return_annotator(annotation):
    annotations['return'] = annotation
wrapper.returns = return_annotator

return wrapper
```

Since this new `returns()` function will be called before the final `typesafe()` function ever will, it can simply add a new annotation to the existing dictionary. Then, when `typesafe()` does get called later, the internal wrapper can just continue working like it always did. This just changes the way the return value annotation is supplied, which is all that was necessary.

Because all of this behavior was factored out into a separate decorator, you can apply this decorator to `coerce_arguments()` or any other similarly purposed function. The resulting function will work the same way as `typesafe()`, only swapping out the argument handling with whatever the new decorator needs to do.

Generators

Chapter 2 introduced the concept of generator expressions and stressed the importance of iteration. While generator expressions are useful for simple situations, you'll often need more sophisticated logic to determine how the iteration should work. You may need finer-grained control over the duration of the loop, the items getting returned, possible side-effects that get triggered along the way or any number of other concerns you may have.

Essentially, you need a real function, but with the benefits of a proper iterator and without the cognitive overhead of creating the iterator yourself. This is where generators come in. By allowing you to define a function that can produce individual values one at a time, rather than just a single return value, you have the added flexibility of a function and the performance of an iterator.

Generators are set aside from other functions by their use of the `yield` statement. This is somewhat of an analog to the typical `return` statement, except that `yield` doesn't cause the function to stop executing completely. It pushes one value out of the function, which gets consumed by the loop that called the generator, then when that loop starts over, the generator starts back up again. It picks up right where it left off, running until it finds another yield statement or the function simply finishes executing.

The basics are best illustrated by an example, so consider a simple generator that returns the values in the Fibonacci sequence. The sequence begins with 0 and 1; each following number is produced by adding up the two numbers before it in the sequence. Therefore, the function only ever needs to keep two numbers in memory at a time, no matter how high the sequence goes. In order to keep it from continuing on forever, though, it's best to require a maximum number of values it should return, making a total of three values to keep track of.

It's tempting to set up the first two values as special cases, yielding them one at a time before even starting into the main loop that would return the rest of the sequence. That adds some extra complexity, though, which can make it pretty easy to accidentally introduce an infinite loop. Instead, we'll use a couple other seed values, -1 and 1, which can be fed right into the main loop directly. They'll generate 0 and 1 correctly when the loop's logic is applied.

Next, we can add a loop for all the remaining values in the sequence, up until the count is reached. Of course, by the time the loop starts, two values have already been yielded, so we have to decrease `count` by 2 before entering the loop. Otherwise, we'd end up yielding two more values than were requested.

```
def fibonacci(count):
    # These seed values generate 0 and 1 when fed into the loop
```

```
a, b = -1, 1

while count > 0:
    # Yield the value for this iteration
    c = a + b
    yield c

    # Update values for the next iteration
    a, b = b, c
    count -= 1
```

Optimization: Size or Speed?

For a simple Fibonacci sequence, it may not be worth looking at optimization, but mathematical tasks like this tend to crop up often and get relied on a lot, so it's often worth it to get them right. As mentioned, this function only really needs to keep three values in memory at a time: a, b and count, but you'll notice that the example also uses c to store the newest value before shifting the values around. You'll also notice, though, that c is used once to yield the value and again to update the values for the next run.

Without storing it away as a variable, we'd have to recalculate it when updating the values. Like any optimization, it's a tradeoff; in this case, it's between size (in terms of memory footprint) and speed. Since it's just a single value, this example has taken the optimization for speed instead of size, but your own needs may vary, so you may want to go the other way around. It's a very small optimization either way, though; don't worry too much about it unless you're having problems with performance.

With the generator in place, you can iterate over the values it produces, simply by treating it like you would any other sequence. Generators are iterable automatically, so a standard **for** loop already knows how to activate it and retrieve its values.

```
>>> for x in fibonacci(3):
...     print(x)
...
0
1
1
>>> for x in fibonacci(7):
...     print(x)
...
0
1
1
2
3
5
8
```

Unfortunately, the main benefit of generators can also, at times, be somewhat of a burden. Because there's no complete sequence in memory at any given time, generators always have to pick up where they left off. Most of the time, though, you'll completely exhaust the generator when you iterate over it the first time, so when you try to put it into another loop, you won't get anything back at all.

```
>>> fib = fibonacci(7)
>>> list(fib)
[0, 1, 1, 2, 3, 5, 8]
>>> list(fib)
[]
```

This behavior can seem a bit misleading at first, but most of the time, it's the only behavior that makes sense. Generators are often used in places where the entire sequence isn't even known in advance or it may change after you iterate over it. For example, you might use a generator to iterate over the users currently accessing a system. Once you've identified all the users, the generator automatically becomes stale and you need to create a new one, which refreshes the list of users.

■ **Note** If you've used the built-in `range()` function (or `xrange()` prior to Python 3.0) often enough, you may have noticed that it does restart itself if accessed multiple times. That behavior is provided by moving one level lower in the iteration process, by implementing the iterator protocol explicitly. It can't be achieved with simple generators, but Chapter 5 shows you can have greater control over iteration of the objects you create.

Lambdas

In addition to providing features on their own, functions are often called upon to provide some extra minor bit of functionality to some other feature. For example, when sorting a list, you can configure Python's behavior by supplying a function that accepts a list item and returns a value that should be used for comparison. This way, given a list of **House** objects, for instance, you can sort by price.

```
>>> def get_price(house):
...     return house.price
...
>>> houses.sort(key=get_price)
```

Unfortunately, this seems like a bit of a waste of the function's abilities, plus it requires a couple of extra lines of code and a name that never gets used outside of the **sort()** method call. A better approach would be if you could specify the **key** function directly inline with the method call. This not only makes it more concise, it also places the body of the function right where it will be used, so it's a lot more readable for these types of simple behaviors.

In these situations, Python's lambda form is extremely valuable. Python provides a separate syntax, identified by the keyword **lambda**. This allows you to define a function without a name as a single expression, with a much simpler feature set. Before diving into the details of the syntax, here's what it looks like in the house sorting example.

```
>>> houses.sort(key=lambda h: h.price)
```

As you can see, this is a considerably compressed form of a function definition. Following the **lambda** keyword is a list of arguments, separated by commas. In the sort example, only one argument is needed, and it can be named anything you like, like any other function. They can even have default values if necessary, using the same syntax as regular functions. Arguments are followed by a colon, which notes the beginning of the lambda's body. If no arguments are involved, the colon can be placed immediately after the lambda keyword.

```
>>> a = lambda: 'example'
>>> a
<function <lambda> at 0x. .>
>>> a()
'example'
>>> b = lambda x, y=3: x + y
>>> b()
Traceback (most recent call last):

TypeError: <lambda>() takes at least 1 positional argument (0 given)
>>> b(5)
8
>>> b(5, 1)
6
```

As you'll have likely discovered by now, the body of the lambda is really just its return value. There's no explicit return statement, so the entire body of the function is really just a single expression used to return a value. That's a big part of what makes the lambda form so concise, yet easily readable, but it comes at a price: only a single expression is allowed. You can't use any control structures, such as try, with or while blocks, you can't assign variables inside the function body and you can't perform multiple operations without them also being tied to the same overall expression.

This may seem extremely limiting, but in order to still be readable, the function body must be kept as simple as possible. In situations where you need the additional control flow features, you'll find it much more readable to specify it in a standard function, anyway. Then, you can pass that function in where you might otherwise use the lambda. Alternatively, if you have a portion of the behavior that's provided by some other function, but not all of it, you're free to call out to other functions as part of the expression.

Introspection

One of the primary advantages of Python is that nearly everything can be examined at run-time, from object attributes and module contents to documentation and even generated bytecode. Peeking at this information is called introspection, and it permeates nearly every aspect of Python. The following sections define some of the more general introspection features that are available, while more specific details are given in the remaining chapters.

The most obvious introspective aspect of any function is its name. It's also one of the simplest, made available simply at the __name__ attribute. The return is the string used to define the function. In the case of lambdas, which have no names, the __name__ attribute is populated with the standard string, '<lambda>'.

```
>>> def example():
...     pass
...
>>> example.__name__
```

```
'example'
>>> (lambda: None).__name__
'<lambda>'
```

Identifying Object Types

Python's dynamic nature can sometimes make it seem difficult to ensure you're getting the right type of value or to even know what type of value it is. Python does provide some options for accessing that information, but it's necessary to realize those are two separate tasks, so Python uses two different approaches.

The most obvious requirement is to identify what type of object your code was given. For this, Python supplies its built-in **type()** function, which accepts an object to identify. The return value is the Python class that was used to create the given object, even if that creation was done implicitly, by way of a literal value.

```
>>> type('example')
<class 'str'>
>>> class Test:
...     pass
...
>>> type(Test)
<class 'type'>
>>> type(Test())
<class '__main__.Test'>
```

Chapter 4 explains in detail what you can do with that class object once you have it, but the more common case is to compare an object against a particular type you expect to receive. This is a different situation because it doesn't really matter exactly what type the object is. As long as the value is an instance of the right type, you can make correct assumptions about how it behaves.

There are a number of different utility functions available for this purpose, most of which will be covered in Chapter 4. This section and the next chapter will make use of one of them fairly frequently, so it merits some explanation here. The **isinstance()** function accepts two arguments: the object to check and the type you're expecting it to be. The result is a simple **True** or **False**, making it suitable for if blocks.

```
>>> def test(value):
...     if isinstance(value, int):
...         print('Found an integer!')
...
>>> test('0')
>>> test(0)
Found an integer!
```

Modules and Packages

Functions and classes that are defined in Python are placed inside of modules, which in turn are often part of a package structure. Accessing this structure when importing code is easy enough, using documentation or even just peeking at the source files on disk. Given a piece of code, however, it's often useful to identify where it was defined in the source code.

For this reason, all functions and classes have a __module__ attribute, which contains the import location of the module where the code was defined. Rather than just supplying the name of the module, the __module__ string also includes the full path to where the module resides. Essentially, it's enough information for you to pass it straight into any of the dynamic importing features shown in Chapter 2.

Working with the interactive interpreter is something of a special case because there's no named source file to work with. Any functions or classes defined there will have the special name '__main__' returned from the __module__ attribute.

```
>>> def example():
...     pass
...
>>> example
<function example at 0x...>
>>> example.__module__
'__main__'
```

Docstrings

Since you can document your functions with docstrings included right alongside the code itself, Python also stores those strings as part of the function object. By accessing the __doc__ attribute of a function, you can read a docstring into code, which can be useful for generating a library's documentation on the fly. Consider the following example, showing simple docstring access on a simple function.

```
>>> def example():
...     """This is just an example to illustrate docstring access."""
...     pass
...
>>> example.__doc__
'This is just an example to illustrate docstring access.'
>>> def divide(x, y):
...     """
...     divide(integer, integer) -> floating point
...
...     This is a more complex example, with more comprehensive documentation.
...     """
...     return float(x) / y # Use float()for compatibility prior to 3.0
...
>>> divide.__doc__
'\n    divide(integer, integer) -> floating point\n\n    This is a more complex ex
ample, with more comprehensive documentation.\n    '
>>> print(divide.__doc__)

    divide(integer, integer) -> floating point

    This is a more complex example, with more comprehensive documentation.

>>>
```

As you can see, simple docstrings are easy to handle just by reading in __doc__ and using it however you need to. Unfortunately, more complex docstrings will retain all whitespace, including newlines, making them more challenging to work with. Worse yet, your code can't know which type of docstring you're looking at without scanning it for certain characters. Even if you're just printing it out to the interactive prompt, you still have an extra line before and after the real documentation, as well as the same indentation as was present in the file.

To more gracefully handle complex docstrings like the one shown in the example, the inspect module mentioned previously also has a `getdoc()` function, designed to retrieve and format docstrings. It strips out whitespace both before and after the documentation, as well as any indentation that was used to line up the docstring with the code around it. Here's that same docstring again, but formatted with `inspect.getdoc()`.

```
>>> import inspect
>>> print(inspect.getdoc(divide))

divide(integer, integer) -> floating point
This is a more complex example, with more comprehensive documentation.
>>>
```

We still have to use `print()` at the interactive prompt because the newline character is still retained in the result string. All `inspect.getdoc()` strips out is the whitespace that was used to make the docstring look right alongside the code for the function. In addition to trimming the space at the beginning and end of the docstring, `getdoc()` uses a simple technique to identify and remove whitespace used for indentation.

Essentially, `getdoc()` counts the number of spaces at the beginning of each line of code, even if the answer is 0. Then, it determines the lowest value of those counts and removes that many characters from each line that remains after the leading and trailing whitespace has been removed. This allows you to keep other indentation in the docstring intact, as long as it's greater than what you need to align the text with the surrounding code. Here's an example of an even more complex docstring, so you can see how `inspect.getdoc()` handles it.

```
>>> def clone(obj, count=1):
...     """
...     clone(obj, count=1) -> list of cloned objects
...
...     Clone an object a specified number of times, returning the cloned
...     objects as a list. This is just a shallow copy only.
...
...     obj
...         Any Python object
...     count
...         Number of times the object will be cloned
...
...     >>> clone(object(), 2)
...     [<object object at 0x12345678>, <object object at 0x87654321>]
...     """
...     import copy
...     return [copy.copy(obj) for x in count]
...
>>> print(inspect.getdoc(clone))
clone(obj, count=1) -> list of cloned objects

Clone an object a specified number of times, returning the cloned
```

```
objects as a list. This is just a shallow copy only.

obj
    Any Python object
count
    Number of times the object will be cloned

  >>> clone(object(), 2)
  [<object object at 0x12345678>, <object object at 0x87654321>]
>>>
```

Notice how the descriptions of each argument are still indented four spaces, just like they appeared to be in the function definition. The shortest lines had just four total spaces at the beginning, while those had eight, so Python stripped out the first four, leaving the rest intact. Likewise, the example interpreter session was indented by two extra spaces, so the resulting string maintains a two-space indentation.

Oh, and don't worry too much about the **copy** utility just yet. Chapter 6 will describe in detail how to make and manage copies of objects when necessary.

Taking It With You

Although Python functions may seem to be quite simple on the surface, you now know how to define and manage them in ways that really fit your needs. Of course, you're probably looking to incorporate functions into a more comprehensive object-oriented program, and for that, we'll need to look at how Python's classes work.

CHAPTER 4

■ ■ ■

Classes

Although functions allow you to define code that can be reused, it's often more useful to combine those functions into logical groupings that define the behavior of a particular type of object. This is standard object-oriented programming, which is implemented in Python by way of types and classes. These, like functions, may seem simple enough on the surface, but there's a considerable amount of power behind them that you can leverage.

The most basic idea of a class is that it encapsulates the behavior of an object, while an instance of the class represents the data for the object. Therefore, even though data may well change from one instance to another, behavior determined by the underlying class will remain the same across those instances. Defining, extending and altering that behavior is the focus of this chapter.

Inheritance

The simplest way to use classes is to define a single class for a single type of object. That works well for many simple applications, but you're likely to find the need for finer-grained control over the behavior of objects. In particular, it's common to have a single common set of behaviors for a large collection of objects, but then need to modify them or add new ones for a smaller set of more specific objects.

To facilitate this, Python allows each class to specify one or more base classes that will provide the fundamental behavior. Then, the new class being defined can add new behaviors or override any existing ones. By default, all objects descend from the built-in `object` type, though that doesn't really do anything useful on its own. It's really just a foundation type that underpins the entire system, as everything else inherits from it.

Compatibility: New-style vs. Old-style

Traditionally, Python treated built-in types as fundamentally different from classes defined in Python code. Simple features worked the same between the two, but more complex usage revealed subtle differences that could be quite difficult to track down. These were labeled as "old-style" and "new-style" classes, with old-style classes used by default. Classes could be marked as new-style by inheriting from the built-in object, either directly or somewhere down the inheritance chain.

In Python 3, old-style classes were removed, so there's no longer any need to inherit from object except to support backward compatibility with older versions of Python. Therefore, in general, classes mentioned in this book are assumed to be new-style unless otherwise noted. The differences between the two are too numerous to list here, but they'll be mentioned throughout this chapter as necessary.

Like most object-oriented languages, Python lets you define as many subclasses as you'd like for a given class, and you can subclass those as well, going as many levels deep as necessary. This vertical approach to inheritance is appropriate for most applications, because it maximizes the usefulness of the base classes. When a single, typically large, set of behaviors needs to be reused across a variety of other classes, vertical inheritance proves quite useful.

Consider a common scenario involving a contact management application. At the root of all else, you would have a contact class, since, by definition, everything in the application is a contact. It would have a set of fields and behaviors associated with it, which cover only those things that are pertinent to all contacts, according to the needs of your application.

```python
class Contact:
    name = TextField()
    email = EmailAddressField()
    phone = PhoneNumberField()

    def send_mail(self, message):
        # Email sending code would go here
```

For now, don't worry about the specifics of where each of the Field classes come from or how they work in the application. If you're interested anyway, Chapter 11 demonstrates one possible framework for writing classes like this. The key for now is that each of the fields represents a single piece of data relating to the class at hand. Values might be provided by user input, results from a database query or even random value generator; what's important is the structure of the class and how subclasses will work with it.

Even with just a contact in place, you can create a useful application based on those core fields and behaviors. Providing additional features means adding support for different types of contacts. For instance, real people have a first name, last name and perhaps a cell phone, while companies will often have only a single name and phone number. Likewise, companies will do business in particular industries, which wouldn't make any sense in the case of individuals.

```python
class Person(Contact):
    first_name = TextField()
    last_name = TextField()
    name = ComputedString('%(last_name)s, %(first_name)s')
    cell_phone = PhoneNumberField()

class Company(Contact):
    industry = TextField()
```

Now we have a basic hierarchy beginning to take shape. People are different from companies, and they each have different fields that are appropriate to each case. Python's inheritance system automatically pulls the fields from the Contact class and makes them available on the Person and Company classes. You can subclass these as well, providing such Person types as Employee, Friend, FamilyMember.

```python
class Employee(Person):
    employer = RelatedContact(Company)
    job_title = TextField()
    office_email = EmailAddressField()
    office_phone = PhoneNumberField()
    extension = ExtensionField()
```

```
class Friend(Person):
    relationship = TextField()

class FamilyMember(Person):
    relationship = TextField()
    birthday = DateField()
```

Notice here that, even though both `Friend` and `FamilyMember` have relationship fields that work identically to each other, `FamilyMember` doesn't inherit from `Friend`. It's not necessarily true that a family member will also be a friend, so the class structure reflects that. Each new subclass is automatically considered to be a more specific example of the class it extends, so it's important that the inheritance scheme reflects the actual relationships being codified.

This may seem like a philosophical detail, but it has real ramifications in code as well. As will be shown in the introspection portion of this section, Python code can take a look at the inheritance structure of classes, so any mismatches can cause your code to confuse one type of class for another. The best way to avoid those problems is to think about how the objects you're representing actually relate to one another and try to re-create those relationships in code.

Multiple Inheritance

Python also supports a horizontal approach to class inheritance, by allowing a subclass to define more than one base class at a time. This way, a class can obtain behaviors from many various classes without having to go several levels deep. Of course, that means taking a different logical approach because you're no longer defining classes by increasing specificity. Instead, you're essentially building up each class as a set of components.

Building up classes like this is particularly well-suited for applications where your classes share some common behaviors, but where they're not otherwise related to each other in a hierarchical manner. In order to make sense, this typically requires a large number of classes to be built from a reasonably large number of components. Because that's not the way most applications are put together, it's rarely used this way in the wild.

Instead, multiple inheritance is often called on to apply support classes, called mixins. Mixin classes don't provide full functionality on their own; they instead supply just a small add-on feature that could be useful on a wide range of different classes. One example might be a mixin that returns `None` when you try to access any attribute that isn't available on the object, rather than raising an `AttributeError`.

```
class NoneAttributes:
    def __getattr__(self, name):
        return None
```

The `__getattr__()` method, which will be described in more detail in the Magic Methods section later in this chapter, is called whenever an attribute is requested that isn't already available on the object. Since it works as a fallback, it's an obvious choice for a mixin; the real class provides its own functionality, with the mixin adding onto that where applicable.

```
>>> class Example(BaseClass, NoneAttributes):
...     pass
...
>>> e = Example()
>>> e.does_not_exist
>>>
```

In typical applications, a vertical hierarchy will provide most of the functionality, with mixins adding some extras where necessary. Because of the potential number of classes involved when accessing attributes, it becomes even more important to fully understand how Python decides which class is used for each attribute and method that was accessed. To put it another way, you need to know the order in which Python resolves which method to use.

Method Resolution Order (MRO)

Given a class hierarchy, Python needs to determine which class to use when attempting to access an attribute by name. To do this, Python has rules that govern how to order a set of base classes when a new class is processed. For most basic usage of classes, you don't really need to know how this works, but if you work with multi-level or multiple inheritance, the details in this section will help you understand what's really going on.

In the simple vertical-only scenario, it's easy to imagine how the MRO would be created. The class you're actually working with would be first in line, followed by its base class, followed by the base class of the base class, and so on down the line until you get back to the root object type.

At each step in the chain, Python checks to see if the class has an attribute with the name being requested, and if it does, that's what you get. If not, it moves on to the next one. This is easy to see with a simple example.

```
>>> class Book:
...     def __init__(self, title):
...         self.title = title
...         self.page = 1
...     def read(self):
...         return 'There sure are a lot of words on page %s.' % self.page
...     def bookmark(self, page):
...         self.page = page
...
>>> class Novel(Book):
...     pass
...
>>> class Mystery(Novel):
...     def read(self):
...         return "Page %s and I still don't know who did it!" % self.page
...
>>> book1 = Book('Pro Python')
>>> book1.read()
'There sure are a lot of words on page 1.'
>>> book1.bookmark(page=52)
>>> book1.read()
'There sure are a lot of words on page 52.'
>>> book2 = Novel('Pride and Prejudice')
>>> book2.read()
'There sure are a lot of words on page 1.'
>>> book3 = Mystery('Murder on the Orient Express')
>>> book3.read()
"Page 1 and I still don't know who did it!"
>>> book3.bookmark(page=352)
>>> book3.read()
"Page 352 and I still don't know who did it!"
```

As you can see, when calling **read()** on a **Mystery** object, you get the method that's defined directly on that class, while using **bookmark()** on that same class uses the implementation from **Book**. Likewise, **Novel** doesn't define anything on its own—it's just there to make for a more meaningful hierarchy—so all the methods you have access to actually come from **Book**. To put it more directly, the MRO for **Mystery** is [Mystery, Novel, Book], while the MRO for **Novel** is simply [Novel, Book].

So what happens when you take a horizontal approach using multiple inheritance? For the sake of simplicity, we'll start with just a single layer of inheritance for each of the supplied base classes, so it's a purely horizontal approach. In this case, Python goes from left to right, in the order the classes were defined as base classes. Here's what the previous example looks like once we add a **purchase()** method, which would allow the user to buy a copy of the book.

```
>>> class Product:
...     def purchase(self):
...         return 'Wow, you must really like it!'
...
>>> class BookProduct(Book, Product):
...     pass
...
>>> class MysteryProduct(Mystery, Product):
...     def purchase(self):
...         return 'Whodunnit?'
...
>>> product1 = BookProduct('Pro Python')
>>> product1.purchase()
'Wow, you must really like it!'
>>> product2 = MysteryProduct('Murder on the Orient Express')
>>> product2.purchase()
'Whodunnit?'
```

Thus far, each MRO has been very straightforward and easy to understand, even if you didn't know what was going on behind the scenes. Unfortunately, things get more complex when you start combining both forms of inheritance. It doesn't even take a very complicated example to illustrate the problem; consider what happens when you inherit from one class that has a base class of its own and a mixin that stands alone.

```
class A:
    def test(self):
        return 'A'

class B(A):
    pass

class C:
    def test(self):
        return 'C'
```

This is simple enough, but if you create a new class, D, which subclasses both B and C, what would happen if you call its **test()** method? As always, it's easy enough to test this out in the interactive interpreter, where you'll see that the answer depends on which one you put first.

```
>>> class D(B, C):
...     pass
...
>>> D().test()
'A'
>>> class D(C, B):
...     pass
...
>>> D().test()
'C'
```

On the surface, it seems easy to assume that Python simply goes depth first; it looks at the first base class and follows it all the way down, looking for the requested attribute, moving on to the next base class only when it can't find what it needs. That observation is certainly true for this and many other cases, but it's still not the whole story. What's really going on takes the whole inheritance scheme into account.

Before clarifying the full algorithm, though, let's get one thing out of the way. The first namespace Python looks at is always the instance object. If the attribute isn't found there, it goes to the actual class that provides that object's behavior. These two namespaces are always the first two to be checked, regardless of any inheritance structure that may be in use. Only if the attribute isn't found there will Python try to locate it through class inheritance.

Rather than looking at the whole inheritance structure as a kind of tree, Python tries to flatten it out to a single list, with each class appearing just once. This is an important distinction because it's possible for two base classes to subclass the same class deeper in the chain, but looking at that class twice would only cause confusion later on. To resolve this and other potential issues, there needs to be a single, flat list to work with.

The first step is to identify all the different paths that can be taken to get from a class to its basemost class. There will always be at least one path, even if there's no base class, for two reasons. For one, the MRO for a given class always includes the class itself in the first position. This may seem obvious from earlier descriptions, but the rest of the algorithm will make it clear why this is important to state explicitly. Also, every class implicitly inherits from **object**, so that's at the end of every MRO.

So, for just a simple class, A, which doesn't inherit from anything, its MRO is just a simple two-element list: `[A, object]`. If you have another class, B, which subclasses A, its MRO becomes fairly obvious as well, being `[B, A, object]`. Once you introduce a bit of multiple inheritance, it's possible for the same class to appear more than once in the overall tree, so we need some extra work in order to sort out the MRO.

Consider a new class, C, which inherits from both B and A. Now A shows up under two different branches and at two different distances from the new class, C.

■ **Note** It might not make sense to do this because B already inherits from A. Remember, though, that you may not always know in advance what the base classes are doing behind the scenes. You might extend classes that were passed into your code from elsewhere or were generated dynamically, such as will be shown later in this chapter. Python doesn't know how your classes are laid out, so it has to be able to account for all the possibilities.

```
>>> class A:
...     pass
...
```

```
>>> class B(A):
...     pass
...
>>> class C(B, A):
...     pass
...
```

The MRO for object is obviously just [object], and A has already been shown to be [A, object] as you would expect. B is clearly [B, A, object], but what about C? Looking at it depth-first, you might guess [C, B, A, object] once the duplicate A is removed. Taking a breadth-first (horizontal before vertical) approach, you'd come up with [C, A, B, object].

So which way does Python go? The truth is, neither of those is accurate; Python uses an algorithm called C3.[1] This algorithm takes all the inheritance into account, reducing it by one layer at a time, until only a single list remains. At each level, C3 processes the class lists that were created for all of that level's parent classes. Because of this, it starts at the most generic class, object, and continues outward from there.

With C in place, we can finally see how the algorithm works in detail. By the time Python encounters C, both A and B have already been processed, so their MROs are known. In order to combine them, C3 looks at the first class in each of the parent MROs to see if it can find a candidate for inclusion in the MRO for C. Of course, that begs the question of what exactly constitutes a valid candidate.

The only criteria used to identify a candidate class is whether it exists in only the first position in any of the MRO lists being considered. It doesn't have to be in all of them, but if it's present, it must be the first in the list. If it's in any other position in any of the lists, C3 will skip it until its next pass. Once it finds a valid entry, it pulls that into the new MRO and looks for the next one using the same procedure.

Example: C3 Algorithm

Since algorithms are really just code, let's put together a simple C3 function that will perform the necessary linearization—reducing the inheritance tree into a single list. Before diving into the full implementation, though, let's first take a look at what the function call would look like, so we know what data it'll be working with. For C, it would look like this:

```
C3(C, [B, A, object], [A, object], [B, A])
```

The first argument is the class itself, which is followed by the known MRO lists for its parent classes, in the order they were defined on the class. The last argument, though, is simply the list of parent classes themselves, without their full MROs. As will be shown in a slight modification of C later, this extra argument is necessary to resolve some extra ambiguities.

As with any function, there are a few boring details that need to be put in place before the real heavy lifting can be done. In the case of C3, there will be some modification of the MRO lists along the way, and we don't want those modifications to affect the code that called the C3 function, so we have to make copies of them to work with. In addition, we need to set up a new list to contain the final MRO being generated by the algorithm.

```
def C3(cls, *mro_lists):
    # Make a copy so we don't change existing content
    mro_lists = [list(mro_list[:]) for mro_list in mro_lists]
```

[1] http://propython.com/mro/

```
# Set up the new MRO with the class itself
mro = [cls]

# The real algorithm goes here.

return mro
```

We can't just use mro_list[:] here because that only copies the outer list. All the other lists that were contained inside that list would remain, so any modifications to them would be visible outside the function. By using a list comprehension and copying each of the internal lists, we get copies of all the lists involved, so they can be safely altered.

The Robustness Principle

If you're already aware of Python's copy module—or you've skipped ahead to Chapter 6—you may wonder why we don't just use copy.deepcopy(mro_list) instead. At the very least, you may be wondering what that extra list(mro_list[:]) is for, since we're passing in lists already. By explicitly casting each of the internal sequences to lists and wrapping it all in a list comprehension, we can allow the function to accept any valid sequence types, including tuples, which aren't able to be modified. This makes the C3 function much more liberal in what it accepts.

With the housekeeping out of the way, we can move on to the main algorithm. Since we don't know in advance how many classes are in each MRO, it's best to wrap the main workload in a simple while True loop, which will execute indefinitely, so we can control its flow using break and continue. Of course, this means you shouldn't try executing this code until a bit later on, until we have the necessary control code in place.

The first task inside that loop will be to loop over each MRO list, get its first class and see if it's in any position other than first in any of the other lists. If it is, that class isn't a valid candidate yet and we need to move on to the first class in the next list. Here's the loop necessary to perform those first steps.

```
import itertools

def C3(cls, *mro_lists):
    # Make a copy so we don't change existing content
    mro_lists = [list(mro_list[:]) for mro_list in mro_lists]

    # Set up the new MRO with the class itself
    mro = [cls]

    while True:
        for mro_list in mro_lists:
            # Get the first item as a potential candidate for the MRO.
            candidate = mro_list[0]

            if candidate in itertools.chain(*(x[1:] for x in mro_lists)) :
                # The candidate was found in an invalid position, so we
                # move on to the next MRO list to get a new candidate.
```

```
        continue

    return mro
```

The chain used here reduces all the non-first classes in all the MRO lists down to a single list, so it's easier to test whether the current candidate is valid or not. Of course, the current code only responds if the candidate is invalid. If it wasn't found in that chain, it's a valid candidate and can be promoted to the final MRO right away.

In addition, we need to remove that candidate from the MRO list where it was found as well as any of the others it might be found in. This is made a bit easier by the fact that we know it can only be the first item in any of the lists and that it won't be in any of them that were already processed this round. We can therefore just look at each of the remaining candidates and remove the class that was promoted. In any case, none of the other MRO lists should be processed for a new candidate this time around, so we also need to add a continue.

```
while True:
# Reset for the next round of tests
    candidate_found = False

    for mro_list in mro_lists:
        if not len(mro_list):
            # Any empty lists are of no use to the algorithm.
            continue

        # Get the first item as a potential candidate for the MRO.
        candidate = mro_list[0]

        if candidate_found:
            # Candidates promoted to the MRO are no longer of use.
            if candidate in mro:
                mro_list.pop(0)
            # Don't bother checking any more candidates if one was found.
            continue

        if candidate in itertools.chain(*(x[1:] for x in mro_lists)) :
            # The candidate was found in an invalid position, so we
            # move on to the next MRO list to get a new candidate.
            continue

        else:
            # The candidate is valid and should be promoted to the MRO.
            mro.append(candidate)
            mro_list.pop(0)
            candidate_found = True
```

■ **Note** Now that we're removing items from the MRO lists, we also have to add in an extra bit of code to handle the situation where one of the lists was completely emptied. Since there's nothing of value in an empty list, the loop just moves on to the next one.

With the candidate selection now complete, the only things left are to tell the algorithm when its job is done and it should exit the loop. As it stands, it'll empty the lists completely, but continue looping through them forever, without ever returning the new MRO. The key to identifying this situation is that it will indeed empty all the lists. Therefore, we can check the remaining MRO lists to see if any classes remain. If not, it's done and can end the loop.

```python
    while True:
        # Reset for the next round of tests
        candidate_found = False

        for mro_list in mro_lists:
            if not len(mro_list):
                # Any empty lists are of no use to the algorithm.
                continue

            # Get the first item as a potential candidate for the MRO.
            candidate = mro_list[0]

            if candidate_found:
                # Candidates promoted to the MRO are no longer of use.
                if candidate in mro:
                    mro_list.pop(0)
                # Don't bother checking any more candidates if one was found.
                continue

            if candidate in itertools.chain(*(x[1:] for x in mro_lists)) :
                # The candidate was found in an invalid position, so we
                # move on to the next MRO list to get a new candidate.
                continue

            else:
                # The candidate is valid and should be promoted to the MRO.
                mro.append(candidate)
                mro_list.pop(0)
                candidate_found = True

        if not sum(len(mro_list) for mro_list in mro_lists):
            # There are no MROs to cycle through, so we're all done.
            break
```

This loop, inside the C3 function mentioned already, can successfully create an MRO for any valid Python inheritance scheme. Going back to the function call for the C class mentioned previously, we'd get the following result. Notice that we're using strings here instead of the actual classes, to make it easier to illustrate. Nothing about the C3 algorithm is actually tied to classes anyway, it's all just about flattening out a hierarchy that may contain duplicates.

```
>>> C3('C', ['B', 'A', 'object'], ['A', 'object'], ['B', 'A'])
['C', 'B', 'A', 'object']
```

That's all well and good, but there's another related situation that needs some attention as well: what happens when C inherits from A before B? One would logically assume that any attributes found on A would be used before those on B, even though B's MRO puts B before A. That would violate an important consistency in class inheritance: the order of items in an MRO should be preserved in all of its future subclasses.

Those subclasses are allowed to add new items to their MRO, even inserting them in between items in the MRO of the base class, but all the MROs involved should still retain the same ordering they had originally. So when doing something like C(A, B), the correct result would actually be inconsistent with user expectations.

That's why the C3 algorithm requires that the base classes themselves be added to the list of MROs that are passed in. Without them, we could invoke the C3 algorithm with this new construct and get the same result that was obtained with the original ordering.

```
>>> C3('C', ['B', 'A', 'object'], ['A', 'object'])
['C', 'B', 'A', 'object']
>>> C3('C', ['A', 'object'], ['B', 'A', 'object'])
['C', 'B', 'A', 'object']
```

Even though it seems like the two should do different things, they would actually end up doing the same thing. By adding in the extra class list at the end, though, the behavior of C3 changes a bit. The first candidate is A, which is found in the second position in the MRO of B, so A is skipped for this round. The next candidate is B, which is found in the list added in the final argument, so that's skipped too. When the final list is examined, A is skipped once again.

This means C3 completes a full loop without finding any valid candidates, which is how it detects inappropriate constructs like C(A, B). Without a valid candidate, no items are removed from any of the lists and the main loop would run again with exactly the same data. Without any extra handling for the invalid case, our current Python implementation of C3 will simply continue on indefinitely. It'd be better to raise an exception. First, though, let's validate this assumption by examining Python's own behavior with C(A, B).

```
>>> class A:
...     pass
...
>>> class B(A):
...     pass
...
>>> class C(A, B):
...     pass
...
Traceback (most recent call last):
  ...
TypeError:  Cannot create a consistent method resolution
order (MRO)  for bases B, A
```

Sure enough, Python's class system disallows this construct in an effort to force developers to only make classes that make sense. Duplicating this functionality in our own C3 class is fairly easy, now that we know how to identify an invalid situation. All we have to do is check at the end of the loop and see whether a valid candidate was found. If not, we can raise a **TypeError**.

```python
import itertools

def C3(cls, *mro_lists):
    # Make a copy so we don't change existing content
    mro_lists = [list(mro_list[:]) for mro_list in mro_lists]

    # Set up the new MRO with the class itself
    mro = [cls]

    while True:
        # Reset for the next round of tests
        candidate_found = False

        for mro_list in mro_lists:
            if not len(mro_list):
                # Any empty lists are of no use to the algorithm.
                continue

            # Get the first item as a potential candidate for the MRO.
            candidate = mro_list[0]

            if candidate_found:
                # Candidates promoted to the MRO are no longer of use.
                if candidate in mro:
                    mro_list.pop(0)
                # Don't bother checking any more candidates if one was found.
                continue

            if candidate in itertools.chain(*(x[1:] for x in mro_lists)) :
                # The candidate was found in an invalid position, so we
                # move on to the next MRO list to get a new candidate.
                continue

            else:
                # The candidate is valid and should be promoted to the MRO.
                mro.append(candidate)
                mro_list.pop(0)
                candidate_found = True

        if not sum(len(mro_list) for mro_list in mro_lists):
            # There are no MROs to cycle through, so we're all done.
            break

        if not candidate_found:
            # No valid candidate was available, so we have to bail out.
            break
```

```
raise TypeError("Inconsistent MRO")

return mro
```

With this last piece in place, our C3 implementation matches the behavior of Python's own, covering all the bases. Most arbitrary class inheritance structures can be reduced to a valid MRO, so you typically don't need to worry too much about how the algorithm works. There is one feature of classes, though—the `super()` function—that relies on the MRO extensively.

Using super() to Pass Control to Other Classes

One of the most common reasons to create a subclass is to customize the behavior of some existing method. It could be as simple as logging every time the method is called or as complex as completely replacing its behavior with a different implementation. In the case of the former, where you're simply tweaking existing behavior, it's quite useful to be able to use the original implementation directly, so you don't have to reinvent the wheel just to make some minor changes.

To achieve this, Python supplies the built-in `super()` function, which is all too often misunderstood. The common explanation of `super()` is that it allows you to call a method on a base class within the overridden method on a subclass. That description works to a point, but before explaining it more fully, let's examine how it behaves in the simple case, to see what that even means.

Consider an application that needs to create a dictionary that automatically returns `None` for any keys that don't already have a value associated with them. This is fairly similar to `defaultdict`, but it doesn't have to create a new value each time; it just returns `None`.

```
>>> class NoneDictionary(dict):
...     def __getitem__(self, name):
...         try:
...             return super(NoneDictionary, self).__getitem__(name)
...         except KeyError:
...             return None
...
>>> d = NoneDictionary()
>>> d['example']
>>> d['example'] = True
>>> d['example']
True
```

Before getting too much further, it's important to realize what `super()` is really doing here. In some languages, `super()` is simply a language feature that gets compiled into some special code to access methods from other classes. In Python, though, `super()` returns an actual object, which has a set of attributes and methods that are based on where it was used.

From this simple example, it does seem that `super()` just provides access to a method on the base class, but remember that there can be any number of base classes involved, with more than one specified on each class. Given the complex nature of some inheritance structures, it should be clear by now that Python would use the MRO to determine which method to use. What may not be obvious, though, is which MRO is used when looking up the method.

Just looking at it, you might think that Python uses the MRO of the class where `super()` was used, which would be `NoneDictionary` in the example given here. Since most cases will look very much like that example, that assumption will be accurate enough to account for most cases. However, more complicated class hierarchies raise the question of what happens when the MRO gets changed in subclasses. Consider the following set of classes.

115

```
>>> class A:
...     def test(self):
...         return 'A'
...
>>> class B(A):
...     def test(self):
...         return 'B->' + super(B, self). test()
...
>>> B().test()
'B->A'
```

In this example, using super() inside of B refers to its base class, A, as expected. Its test() method includes a reference to itself, so we'll be able to see along the way if things change. Along with B, we could define another class, C, which also subclasses A. To illustrate things a bit better down the road, C will implement its own test() method, without using super().

```
>>> class C(A):
...     def test(self):
...         return 'C'
...
>>> C().test()
'C'
```

Of course, there's nothing unusual or problematic about this so far, since it doesn't interact with A or B in any way. Where things get interesting is when we create a new class, D, which subclasses both B and C. It doesn't need a test() method, so we just leave its body blank, making it as simple as a class can be. Let's see what happens to test() now.

```
>>> class D(B, C):
...     pass
...
>>> D().test()
'B->C'
```

Now we can finally see what's going on. We can see that test() gets called on B, causing its reference in the output, but when it calls super().test(), it refers to the method of C, rather than the one on A. If Python simply used the MRO of the class where the method was defined, it would reference A, not C. Instead, since it uses C, we can gain some insight into how super() really works.

In the most common case, which includes the usage shown here, super() takes two arguments: a class and an instance of that class. As our example here has shown, the instance object determines which MRO will be used to resolve any attributes on the resulting object. The provided class determines a subset of that MRO, because super() only uses those entries in the MRO that occur after the class provided.

The recommended usage is to provide the class where super() was used as the first argument, and the standard self as the second argument. The resulting object will retain the instance namespace dictionary of self, but it only retrieves attributes that were defined on the classes found later in the MRO than the class provided. Technically, though, you could pass in a different class and get different results.

```
>>> class B(A):
...     def test(self):
...         return 'B->' + super(C, self). test()
```

```
...
>>> class D(B, C):
...     pass
...
>>> D().test()
'B->A'
```

In this example, where B actually references C in its invocation of super(), the resulting MRO skips C, moving straight onto A, which is shown by calling test() again. This is a dangerous thing to do in common practice, though, as shown when trying to use B on its own.

```
>>> B().test()
Traceback (most recent call last):
  ...
TypeError:  super(type, obj):  obj must be an instance or subtype of type
```

Because self isn't a subclass of C in this case, C isn't anywhere in the MRO, so super() can't determine where it should start looking for attributes. Rather than creating a useless object that just throws an AttributeError for everything, super() fails when first called, providing a better error message.

Warning: Be careful with Your Arguments

One common mistake when using super() is to use it on a method that won't always have the same signature across all the various classes. In our examples here, the test() method doesn't take any arguments, so it's easy to make sure it's the same across the board. Many other cases, like __getitem__() shown previously, are standard protocols that should never have their function signatures significantly changed by any subclass. Chapter 5 shows many of these cases in more detail.

Unfortunately, you can't always know what another class will do, so using super() can sometimes cause problems by providing the wrong arguments to the class given. Of course, this really isn't any different than passing in an object that has a different protocol than what another function expects.

The reason it's worth noting with super() is that it's easy to assume you know what function you're actually calling. Without a solid understanding of how MROs work and how super() determines which attributes to use, problems can seem to come up out of nowhere. Even with a thorough knowledge of these topics, though, the only real defense against such problems is an agreement among all the classes involved to not change method signatures.

Introspection

Given all the different inheritance options available, it's appropriate that Python provides a number of tools to identify what structure a class uses. The most obvious introspection task for use with classes is to determine whether an object is an instance of a given class. This behavior is provided using the built-in isinstance() function, which takes any arbitrary object as its first argument and a Python class as its second argument. Only if the given class is anywhere in the inheritance chain of the object's class will isinstance() return True.

```
>>> isinstance(10, int)
True
>>> isinstance('test', tuple)
False
```

A natural complement to `isinstance()` is the ability to determine whether one class has another class somewhere in its inheritance chain. This feature, provided by the built-in is `subclass()` function, works just like is `instance()`, except that it operates on a class rather than an instance of it. If the first class contains the second anywhere in its inheritance chain, `issubclass()` returns `True`.

```
>>> issubclass(int, object)
True
>>> class A:
...     pass
...
>>> class B(A):
...     pass
...
>>> issubclass(B, A)
True
>>> issubclass(B, B)
True
```

That last example may seem odd, since `B` clearly can't be a subclass of itself, but this behavior is to remain consistent with `isinstance()`, which returns `True` if the type of the provided object is the exact class provided along with it. In a nutshell, the relationship between the two can be described using a simple expression, which is always true:

```
isinstance(obj, cls) == issubclass(type(obj), cls)
```

If you'd like more information about the inheritance structure for a particular class, there are a few different tools at your disposal. If you'd like to know what base classes were defined for a particular class, simply access its __bases__ attribute, which will contain those base classes in a tuple. It only provides the immediate base classes, though, without any of the classes that were extended deeper than that.

```
>>> B.__bases__
(<class '__main__.A'>,)
```

On the other side of the coin, every class also has a __subclasses__() method, which returns a list of all the subclasses of the class you're working with. Like __bases__, this only goes one level away from the class you're working with. Any further subclasses need to use some other mechanism to keep track of subclasses, some of which will be shown elsewhere in this book.

```
>>> A.__subclasses__()
[<class '__main__.B'>]
```

If you'd like even more information and control, every class also has an __mro__ attribute, which contains the full MRO for that class, wrapped in a tuple. As mentioned previously, this also includes the actual class you pass in along with any of its parent classes.

```
>>> B.__mro__
(<class '__main__.B'>, <class '__main__.A'>, <class 'object'>)
```

The `__mro__` attribute is only available on new-style classes, so if you need to inspect the MRO of an old-style class, you'll have to use the `getmro()` method of the inspect module. Simply pass in the class and you'll get the full MRO as a list. This method also works for new-style classes, so if you're working with Python prior to 3.0, `inspect.getmro()` is compatible with whatever classes you may encounter.

How Classes Are Created

Defining a class in Python works differently than in many other languages, though the differences are not always apparent. It seems quite simple: you supply a name, possibly a base class to inherit from, some attributes and some methods. But when Python encounters that declaration, the process that takes place actually has more in common with functions than you may realize.

To start with, the body of a class declaration is a code block. Just like if, for and while, the body of a class block can contain any valid Python code, which will execute from top to bottom. It'll follow function calls, perform error handling, read files or anything else you ask it to do. In fact, if blocks can be quite useful inside of a class declaration.

```
>>> try:
...     import custom_library
... except ImportError:
...     custom_library = None
...
>>> class Custom:
...     if custom_library is not None:
...         has_library = True
...     else:
...         has_library = False
...
>>> Custom.has_library
False
```

■ **Tip** This example is useful for demonstration purposes only. If you're looking to achieve the exact effect shown here, it's much more pragmatic to simply assign the expression `custom_library is not None` directly to the `has_library` attribute. It returns a Boolean value anyway, so the end result is identical, but it's a much more common approach to the task at hand.

After Python finishes executing the inner code, you'll notice that **has_library** becomes an attribute of the class object that's made available to the rest of your code. This is possible because Python's class declarations work a little bit like functions. When a new class is found, Python starts by creating a new namespace for the block of code inside it. While executing the code block, any assignments are made to that new namespace. Then, the namespace created is used to populate a new type object, which represents the new class.

Creating Classes at Runtime

The previous section alluded to the fact that Python creates type **objects** while executing code, rather than while interpreting and compiling it. As with nearly everything else that happens at runtime, you can hook into that process yourself and use it to your advantage. Doing so takes advantage of what Python does behind the scenes when encountering a class.

The really important stuff happens just after the contents of the class are processed. At this point, Python takes the class namespace and passes it, along with some other pieces of information, to the built-in **type()**, which creates the new class object. This means that all classes are actually subclasses of type, which sits at the base of all of them. Specifically, there are three pieces of information that **type()** uses to instantiate a class.

- The name of the class that was declared

- The base classes the defined class should inherit from

- The namespace dictionary populated when executing the class body

This information is all that's necessary to represent the entire class, and even though Python obtains this information automatically by inspecting the class declaration, you can create a type by passing in the above values directly.

The name is easiest, since it's just a string with the name of the class. Base classes get slightly more involved, but they're still fairly simple: just supply a sequence containing existing class objects that the new class should inherit from. The namespace dictionary is just that: a dictionary, which happens to contain everything that should be attached to the new class by name. Here's an example of how the same class could be created in two different ways.

```
>>> class Example(int):
...     spam = 'eggs'
...
>>> Example
<class '__main__.Example'>
>>> Example = type('Example', (int,), {'spam': 'eggs'})
>>> Example
<class '__main__.Example'>
```

Don't Repeat Yourself

You'll notice that this example ends up having to write the name Example twice, which may seem to violate the DRY principle. Remember, though, that there are really two things going on here, and the two aren't tied to each other. First, the class is being created, which requires us to supply a name. Second, the new class gets assigned to a name in the namespace.

This example uses the same name for both operations, partly for convenience and partly for compatibility with the native class declaration above it. However, the namespace assignment is completely separate from class creation, so any name could be used. In fact, most of the time, you won't even know the name of the class in advance, so you'll almost always use a different name in practice anyway.

Like most times you have low-level access to a common feature, **type()** gives you more than enough rope to hang yourself. One of the three arguments to **type()** is the name of the class to create, so it's possible to create multiple classes with the same name.

In addition, by passing in the attribute namespace, you can supply a new **__module__** attribute to mimic its presence in a different module. It won't actually put the class in the specified module, but it will fool any code that introspects the module later on. Having two classes with both the same name and module could potentially cause problems with tools that introspect modules to determine their structure and hierarchy.

Of course, it's possible to encounter these problems even without using **type()** directly. If you create a class, assign it to a different name, then create a new class with the same name as the original, you can have the exact same naming problem. Also, Python lets you supply a **__module__** attribute within a standard class declaration, so you can even create clashes in code that's not under your control.

Even though it's possible to run into these problems without resorting to **type()** directly, the warning here is that **type()** makes it much easier to accidentally encounter problems. Without it, you'd have to write code that specifically exploits the above points in order to create naming conflicts. With **type()**, though, the values supplied might come from user input, customization settings or any number of other places, and the code won't look like it has any problems of this nature.

Unfortunately, there are no real safeguards against these types of problems, but there are some things you can do to help reduce the risks a bit. One approach would be to wrap all custom class creation inside of a function that keeps track of which names have been assigned and reacts appropriately when a duplicate is created. A more pragmatic option is simply to make sure any introspecting code is capable of handling a case where duplicates are encountered. Which approach to use will depend on the needs of your code.

Metaclasses

Thus far, classes have been defined as being processed by the built-in type, which accepts the class name, its base classes and a namespace dictionary. But **type** is just a class like anything else; it's only special in that it's a class to create classes—a metaclass. Like any other class, though, it can be subclassed to provide customized behavior for our application. Because the metaclass receives the full class declaration as soon as Python encounters it, you can unlock some pretty powerful features.

By subclassing **type**, you can create your own metaclass, which can customize the behavior of new classes to better suit the needs of your application. Like any class-based customization, this is done by creating a subclass of type and overriding any methods that make sense for the task at hand. In most cases, this is either **__new__()** or **__init__()**. The Magic Methods section later in this chapter will explain the difference between the two, but for this discussion, we'll just use **__init__()** since it's easier to work with.

As mentioned previously, **type()** takes three arguments, all of which must be accounted for in any subclasses. To start off simple, consider the following metaclass, which prints out the name of every class it encounters.

```
>>> class SimpleMetaclass(type):
...     def __init__(cls, name, bases, attrs):
...         print(name)
...         super(SimpleMetaclass, cls).__init__(name, bases, attrs)
...
```

This alone is enough to capture a class declaration. Using **super()** here makes sure that any other necessary initialization also takes place. Even though **type** doesn't do anything in its own **__init__()**, remember from earlier in this chapter that this class could be part of a bigger inheritance structure.

Using super() makes sure that the class gets initialized properly, regardless of what "properly" really means in the given context.

To apply this metaclass to a new class and print out its name, Python allows the class definition to specify a metaclass right alongside its parent classes. It looks like a keyword argument, but technically this isn't a function call, so it's actually part of the syntax of a class declaration. Here's an example of how our SimpleMetaclass would work.

```
>>> class Example(metaclass=SimpleMetaclass):
...     pass
...
Example
```

All that was needed here was to supply the metaclass in the class definition, and Python automatically ships that definition off to the metaclass for processing. The only difference between this and a standard class definition is that it uses SimpleMetaclass instead of the standard type.

■ **Note** The first argument to the __init__() method on a metaclass is typically called cls, though you might think it should be self because __init__() operates an instance object, rather than a class. That's true in general, and this case is actually no exception. The only difference here is that the instance is a class object itself, which is an instance of type, so using self would still be accurate. However, because of the differences between classes and objects, we still refer to class objects as cls, rather than self, so they stay well separated.

Compatibility: Prior to 3.0

In Python 3.0, the metaclass syntax was changed to the form you see here. In earlier versions, metaclasses had to be defined as a special __metaclass__ attribute inside the body of the class. When Python encountered this attribute in the namespace of a new class definition, the attribute's value would determine where to send that class definition for processing.

Metaclasses can be difficult to understand without real-world examples to illustrate their usefulness. Let's take a look at how a simple metaclass can be used to provide a powerful framework for registering and using plugins.

Example: Plugin Framework

As an application grows, flexibility becomes increasingly important, so attention often turns to plugins and whether the application can accommodate that level of modularity. There are many ways to implement plugin systems and individual plugins, but they all have three core features in common.

First, you need a way to define a place where plugins can be used. In order to plug something in, there needs to be a socket for the plug to fit into. In addition, it should be very obvious how to implement individual plugins along the way. Lastly, the framework needs to provide an easy way to access all the plugins that were found, so they can all be used. Other features may be added on top, but these are what make a plugin framework.

There are several approaches that would satisfy these requirements, but because plugins are really a form of extension, it makes sense to have them extend a base class. This makes the first requirement fairly simple to define: the point where plugins can attach themselves would be a class. As a class, it takes advantage of Python's own extension features, not only through the built-in subclass syntax but also by allowing the base class to provide some methods that constitute default functionality or offer help for common plugin needs. Here's how such a plugin mount point might look for an application that validates user input.

```python
class InputValidator:
    """
    A plugin mount for input validation.

    Supported plugins must provide a validate(self, input) method, which receives
    input as a string and raises a ValueError if the input was invalid. If the
    input was properly valid, it should just return without error. Any return
    value will be ignored.
    """

    def validate(self, input):
        # The default implementation raises a NotImplementedError
        # to ensure that any subclasses must override this method.
        raise NotImplementedError
```

Even without any of the framework-level code that makes the plugins work, this example demonstrates one of the most important aspects of an extensible system: documentation. Only by properly documenting a plugin mount can you expect plugin authors to correctly adhere to its expectations. The plugin framework itself doesn't make any assumptions about what requirements your application will have, so it's up to you to document them.

With a mount point written, individual plugins can easily be created simply by writing a subclass of the mount point that's already in place. By providing new or overridden methods to satisfy the documented requirements, they can add their own little slice of functionality to the overall application. Here's an example validator that ensures the provided input only consists of ASCII characters.

```python
class ASCIIValidator(InputValidator):
    """
    Validate that the input only consists of valid ASCII characters.

    >>> v = ASCIIValidator()
    >>> v.validate('sombrero')
    >>> v.validate('jalapeño')
    Traceback (most recent call last):
      ...
    UnicodeDecodeError: 'ascii' codec can't decode character '\xf1' in position
    6: ordinal not in range(128)
    """

    def validate(self, input):
        # If the encoding operation fails, str.encode() raises a
        # UnicodeDecodeError, which is a subclass of ValueError.
        input.encode('ascii')
```

■ **Tip** Notice that this also provides its own documentation. Because plugins are also classes all their own, they can be subclassed by even more specialized plugins down the road. This makes it important to include thorough documentation even at this level, to help ensure proper usage later.

Now that we have two of the three components out of the way, the only thing left before tying it all together is to illustrate how to access any plugins that were defined. Since our code will already know about the plugin mount point, that makes an obvious place to access them, and since there could be anywhere from zero to hundreds of plugins, it's optimal to iterate over them, without caring how many there are. Here's an example function that uses any and all available plugins to determine whether some input provided by a user is valid.

```python
def is_valid(input):
    for plugin in InputValidator.plugins:
        try:
            plugin().validate(input)
        except ValueError:
            # A ValueError means invalidate input
            return False
    # All validators succeeded
    return True
```

Having plugins means you can extend the functionality of even a simple function like this without having to touch its code again later. Simply add a new plugin, make sure it gets imported and the framework does the rest. With that, we finally get around to explaining the framework and how it ties all these pieces together. Since we're working with classes whose definitions specify more than just their behavior, a metaclass would be an ideal technique.

All the metaclass really needs to do is recognize the difference between a plugin mount class and a plugin subclass and register any plugins in a list on the plugin mount, where they can be accessed later. If that sounds too simple, it's really not. In fact, the entire framework can be expressed in just a few lines of code, and it only takes one extra line of code on the plugin mount to activate the whole thing.

```python
class PluginMount(type):
    """
    Place this metaclass on any standard Python class to turn it into a plugin
    mount point. All subclasses will be automatically registered as plugins.
    """
    def __init__(cls, name, bases, attrs):
        if not hasattr(cls, 'plugins'):
            # The class has no plugins list, so it must be a mount point,
            # so we add one for plugins to be registered in later.
            cls.plugins = []
        else:
            # Since the plugins attribute already exists, this is an
            # individual plugin, and it needs to be registered.
            cls.plugins.append(cls)
```

That's all that's necessary to supply the entire plugin framework. When the metaclass is activated on the plugin mount, the __init__() method recognizes that the plugins attribute doesn't yet exist, so it creates one and returns without doing anything else. When a plugin subclass is encountered, the `plugins` attribute is available by virtue of its parent class, so the metaclass adds the new class to the existing list, thus registering it for later use.

Adding this functionality to the `inputValidator` mount point described previously is as simple as adding the metaclass to its class definition.

```
class InputValidator(metaclass=PluginMount):
    ...
```

Individual plugins are still defined as standard plugins, without additional effort required. Since metaclasses are inherited by all subclasses, the plugin behavior is added automatically.

Controlling the Namespace

Metaclasses can also be used to help control how Python processes the class declaration. Rather than waiting for the class to be created before acting on it, another tactic is to process the raw components of the class while Python is going through them. This is made possible by a special metaclass called __prepare__().

By supplying a __prepare__() method on your metaclass, you can get early access to the class declaration. In fact, this happens so early that the body of the class definition hasn't even been processed yet. The __prepare__() method receives just the class name and a tuple of its base classes. Rather than getting the namespace dictionary as an argument, __prepare__() is responsible for returning that dictionary itself.

The dictionary returned by __prepare__() is used as the namespace while Python executes the body of the class definition. This allows you to intercept each attribute as soon as it's assigned to the class, so it can be processed immediately. Ordinarily, this is used to return an ordered dictionary, so that attributes can be stored in the order they were declared within the class. For reference, take a look at how a metaclass would work without using __prepare__().

```
>>> from collections import OrderedDict
>>> class OrderedMeta(type):
...     def __init__(cls, name, bases, attrs):
...         print(attrs)
...
>>> class Example(metaclass=OrderedMeta):
...     b = 1
...     a = 2
...     c = 3
...
{'a': 2, '__module__': '__main__', 'b': 1, 'c': 3}
```

The default behavior returns a standard dictionary, which doesn't keep track of how the keys are added. Adding a simple __prepare__() method provides all that's needed to keep the ordering intact after the class is processed.

```
>>> class OrderedMeta(type):
...     @classmethod
...     def __prepare__(cls, name, bases):
...         return OrderedDict()
```

```
...       def __init__(cls, name, bases, attrs):
...           print(attrs)
...
>>> class Example(metaclass=OrderedMeta):
...       b = 1
...       a = 2
...       c = 3
...
OrderedDict([('__module__', '__main__'), ('B', 1), ('A', 2), ('c', 3)])
```

■ **Note** The __module__ attribute is at the beginning of the attribute list because it gets added just after __prepare__() is called, before Python starts processing the body of the class.

With Great Power Comes Great Responsibility

By controlling the object used for the namespace dictionary, you can have a tremendous amount of control over how the entire class declaration behaves. Every time a line in a class references a variable or assigns an attribute, the custom namespace can intercede and change the standard behavior. One possibility is to provide decorators that can be used when defining methods within the class, without requiring a separate import to provide them to the class definition. Likewise, you can control how attributes are assigned by changing their names, wrapping them in helper objects or removing them from the namespace completely.

This amount of power and flexibility can be easily abused to provide a level of magic not seen elsewhere. To a developer simply using your code without fully understanding how it's implemented, it'll look like Python itself is wildly inconsistent. Worse yet, any significant changes you make to the behavior of the class declaration could impact the behavior of other tools your users might try to combine with yours. Chapter 5 will show how you can enable these features by extending your dictionary, but be very careful when doing so.

Attributes

Once an object is instantiated, any data associated with it is kept within a new namespace dictionary that's specific to that instance. Access to this dictionary is handled by attributes, which make for easier access than using dictionary keys. Just like dictionary keys, attribute values can be retrieved, set and deleted as necessary.

Typically, accessing an attribute requires you to know the name of the attribute in advance. The syntax for attributes doesn't offer the same flexibility as dictionary keys in providing variables instead of literals, so it can seem limited if you need to get or set an attribute with a name that came from somewhere else. Instead of offering a special syntax for working with attributes in this way, Python provides a trio of functions.

The first, **getattr()**, retrieves a value from an attribute, given a variable that contains the name of the attribute. The next, **setattr()**, takes both the name of an attribute and its value and attaches that value to the attribute with the given name. Lastly, **delattr()** allows you to delete an attribute value given the name as its argument. With these functions, you can work with any attribute on any object without knowing the attribute names when writing code.

Properties

Rather than only acting as a proxy to the standard namespace dictionary, properties allow attributes to be powered by methods that can access the full power of Python. Typically, properties are defined using the built-in **@property** decorator function. When applied to a method, it forces the method to be called whenever the function's name is accessed as an attribute name.

```
>>> class Person:
...     def __init__(self, first_name, last_name):
...         self.first_name = first_name
...         self.last_name = last_name
...     @property
...     def name(self):
...         return '%s, %s' % (self.last_name, self.first_name)
...
>>> p = Person('Marty', 'Alchin')
>>> p.name
'Alchin, Marty'
>>> p.name = 'Alchin, Martin'  # Update it to be properly legal
Traceback (most recent call last):
  ...
AttributeError: can't set attribute
```

That last error isn't terribly descriptive, but basically properties defined this way only retrieve attribute values, not set them. Function calls are only one way, so in order to set the value, we'll need to add another method that handles that side of things. This new method would accept another variable: the value that should be set on the attribute.

In order to mark the new method as the setter for a property, it's decorated much like the getter property. Rather than using a built-in decorator, though, the getter gains a **setter** attribute that can be used to decorate the new method. This fits with the typical noun-based naming convention of decorators, while also describing which property will be managed.

```
>>> class Person:
...     def __init__(self, first_name, last_name):
...         self.first_name = first_name
...         self.last_name = last_name
...     @property
...     def name(self):
...         return '%s, %s' % (self.last_name, self.first_name)
...     @name.setter
...     def name(self, value):
...         return '%s, %s' % (self.last_name, self.first_name)
...
>>> p = Person('Marty', 'Alchin')
>>> p.name
'Alchin, Marty'
>>> p.name = 'Alchin, Martin'  # Update it to be properly legal
```

```
>>> p.name
'Alchin, Martin'
```

Just make sure that the setter method is named the same as the original getter method or it won't work property. The reason for this is that `name.setter` doesn't actually update the original property with the setter method. Instead, it copies the getter onto the new property and assigns them both to the name given to the setter method. Exactly what this means behind the scenes will be explained better in the next section on descriptors.

In addition to getting and setting values, a property can also delete the current value, using a decorator similar to the setter. By applying `name.deleter` to a method that only accepts the usual self, you can use that method to delete values from the attribute. For the `Person` class shown here, that means clearing out both `first_name` and `last_name` together.

```
>>> class Person:
...     def __init__(self, first_name, last_name):
...         self.first_name = first_name
...         self.last_name = last_name
...     @property
...     def name(self):
...         return '%s, %s' % (self.last_name, self.first_name)
...     @name.setter
...     def name(self, value):
...         return '%s, %s' % (self.last_name, self.first_name)
...     @name.deleter
...     def name(self):
...         del self.first_name
...         del self.last_name
...
>>> p = Person('Marty', 'Alchin')
>>> p.name
'Alchin, Marty'
>>> p.name = 'Alchin, Martin' # Update it to be properly legal
>>> p.name
'Alchin, Martin'
>>> del p.name
>>> p.name
Traceback (most recent call last):
  ...
AttributeError: 'Person' object has no attribute 'last_name'
```

Compatibility: Prior to 3.0

In earlier versions of Python, properties didn't have setter and deleter methods, so you couldn't use them as new decorators for the related methods. Instead, `property()` can be called directly as a function, after all the property methods have been defined, so they can all be set on the property in one pass. This required the methods to all have different names and the return value of the call to `property()` has to be set on the class.

In the Person example here, we could use such method names as _get_name(), _set_name() and _del_name(). Once they're all defined individually, a single call to property with all of them in turn will do the trick: name = property(_get_name, _set_name, _del_name). You can supply just one, two or all three methods, depending on your needs. This behavior is still present in Python 3.0 and beyond as well, though, if you need compatibility with both sides of the transition.

Descriptors

One potential problem with properties is that they require all the methods to be defined as part of the class definition. It's great for adding functionality to a class if you have control over the class yourself, but when building a framework for inclusion in other code, we'll need another approach. Descriptors allow you to define an object that can behave in the same way as a property on any class it's assigned to.

In fact, properties are implemented as descriptors behind the scenes, as are methods, which will be explained in the next section. This makes descriptors perhaps one of the most fundamental aspects of advanced class behavior. They work by implementing any of three possible methods, dealing with getting, setting and deleting values.

The first, __get__(), manages retrieval of attribute values, but unlike a property, a descriptor can manage attribute access on both the class and its instances. In order to identify the difference, __get__() receives both the object instance and its owner class as arguments. The owner class will always be provided, but if the descriptor is accessed directly on the class instead of an instance, the instance argument will be None.

A simple descriptor using only the __get__() method can be used to always provide an up-to-date value when requested. The obvious example, then, is an object that returns the current date and time without requiring a separate method call.

```
>>> import datetime
>>> class CurrentTime:
...     def __get__(self, instance, owner):
...         return datetime.datetime.now()
...
>>> class Example:
...     time = CurrentTime()
...
>>> Example.time
datetime.datetime(2009, 10, 31, 21, 27, 5, 236000)
>>> import time
>>> time.sleep(5 * 60) # Wait five minutes
>>> Example().time
datetime.datetime(2009, 10, 31, 21, 32, 15, 375000)
```

Compatibility: Old-Style vs. New-Style

Descriptors only work when implemented as new-style classes. In Python 3.0 and beyond, this will always be the case, but in older versions of Python, you'll have to inherit from `object` in order to ensure they work properly. Otherwise, accessing the attribute will just return the descriptor object, rather than calling __get__() or either of the other methods shown in the rest of this section.

The related __set__() method manages setting a value on the attribute managed by the descriptor. Unlike __get__(), this operation can only be performed on instance objects. If you assign a value to the given name on the class instead, you'll actually overwrite the descriptor with the new value, removing all of its functionality from the class. This is intentional, because without it, there would be no way to modify or remove a descriptor once it's been assigned to a class.

Since it doesn't need to accept the owner class, __set__() only receives the instance object and the value being assigned. The class can still be determined by accessing the __class__ attribute on the instance object provided, though, so there's no information lost. With both __get__() and __set__() defined on a descriptor, we can do something more useful. For example, here's a basic descriptor that behaves just like an attribute, except that it logs every time its value is changed.

```
>>> import datetime
>>> class LoggedAttribute:
...     def __init__(self):
...         self.log = []
...         self.value_map = {}
...     def __set__(self, instance, value):
...         self.value_map[instance] = value
...         log_value = (datetime.datetime.now(), instance, value)
...         self.log.append(log_value)
...     def __get__(self, instance, owner):
...         if not instance:
...             return self # This way, the log is accessible
...         return self.value_map[instance]
...
>>> class Example:
...     value = LoggedAttribute()
...
>>> e = Example()
>>> e.value = 'testing'
>>> e.value
'testing'
>>> Example.value.log
[(datetime.datetime(2009, 10, 31, 21, 49, 59, 933000), <__main__.Example object a
t 0x...>, 'testing')]
```

Before going on, there are a few important things to notice here. First, when setting a value on the descriptor, __set__() adds it to a dictionary on itself, using the instance as a key. The reason for this is that the descriptor object is shared among all the instances of the class it's attached to. If you were to set the value to the descriptor's self, that value would be shared among all those instances as well.

■ **Note** Using a dictionary is just one way to make sure that instances are handled, but it's not the best. It's used here because the preferred method, assigning directly to the instance's namespace dictionary, is only an option once you know the name of the attribute. Descriptors, on their own, don't have access to that name, so the dictionary is used here instead. Chapter 11 shows an approach to address this problem based on metaclasses.

Also, notice that __get__() returns self if no instance was passed in. Since the descriptor works based on setting values, it has no additional value to contribute when called on the class. Most of the time, when a descriptor is in this situation, it makes more sense to raise an **AttributeError** to prevent users from trying something that doesn't make sense. Doing so here would mean the value log would never be available, so the descriptor returns itself.

In addition to getting and setting values, descriptors can also delete values from the attribute. The __delete__() method manages this behavior, and since it only works on instances and doesn't care about the value, it receives the instance object as its only argument.

In addition to managing attributes, descriptors are also used to implement one of the most important aspects of object-oriented programming: methods.

Methods

When a function is assigned to a class, it's considered to be a method. Even though it still works like a function in general, it has class information available to it because functions are actually descriptors as well. Within the category of methods, though, there are two distinct types: bound and unbound methods.

Unbound Methods

Since descriptors can be accessed from the class as well as its instances, methods can be accessed from both as well. When accessing a function on a class, it becomes an unbound method. The descriptor receives the class, but methods typically require the instance, so they're referred to as unbound when accessed without one.

Calling it an unbound method is really more of a naming convention than any formal declaration. What you get when you accessing the method on a class is just the function object itself.

```
>>> class Example:
...     def method(self):
...         return 'done!'
...
>>> type(Example.method)
<class 'function'>
>>> Example.method
<function method at 0x...>

# self isn't passed automatically

>>> Example.method()
Traceback (most recent call last):
```

```
...
TypeError: method() takes exactly 1 position argument (0 given)
```

It's still callable just like any other standard function, but it also carries information about what class it's attached to. Note that the `self` argument in an unbound method isn't passed automatically, since there's no instance object available to bind to it.

Compatibility: Prior to 3.0

In recent versions of Python, function descriptors simply return themselves when accessed directly on a class, so they show up as any other function. In older versions, they returned an instancemethod object, which showed up in the interpreter as an unbound method. The original function was still available by accessing the `im_func` attribute on the descriptor. The overall functionality hasn't changed in the switch to 3.0, but the name and type of the returned function has.

Bound Methods

Once the class is instantiated, each method descriptor returns a function that's bound to that instance. It's still backed by the same function, and the original unbound method is still available on the class, but the bound method now automatically receives the instance object as its first argument.

```
>>> ex = Example()
>>> type(ex.method)
<class 'method'>
>>> ex.method
<bound method Example.method of <__main__.Example object at 0x...>>

# self gets passed automatically now

>>> ex.method()
'done!'

# And the underlying function is still the same

>>> Example.method == ex.method.__func__
True
```

As you can see, bound methods are still backed by the same function as unbound methods. The only real difference is that bound methods have an instance to receive as the first argument. It's important to realize also that the instance object is passed as a positional argument, so the argument name doesn't need to be `self` in order to work properly, but it's a well-established standard that you should follow whenever possible.

■ **Tip** Since bound methods accept an instance as the first argument, method binding can be faked by explicitly providing an instance as the first argument to an unbound method. It all looks the same to the method, and it can be a useful approach when passing functions around as callbacks.

Compatibility: Prior to 3.0

Older versions of Python worked much the same as recent versions with regard to bound methods. The only significant difference between the two is how the original function is accessed from the method descriptor. As you can see from these examples, recent versions use the name __func__ to access that function, but previously the name was im_func, just like they used for accessing the function from unbound methods. The change in Python 3.0 brings the name in line with other standard attributes like __doc__ and __module__.

Sometimes, though, the method doesn't need access to the instance object all, regardless of whether the class has been instantiated. These methods fall into two separate types.

Class Methods

When a method only needs access to the class it's attached to, it's considered a class method, which Python supports through the use of a built-in @classmethod decorator. This ensures that the method will always receive the class object as its first positional argument, regardless of whether it's called as an attribute of the class or one of its instances.

```
>>> class Example:
...     @classmethod
...     def method(cls):
...         return cls
...
>>> Example.method()
<class __main__.Example at 0x...>
>>> Example().method()
<class __main__.Example at 0x...>
```

Once the @classmethod decorator has been applied—see the section later in this chapter for information on decorators—the method() method will never receive an instance of Example as its first argument, but will always be the class itself or one of its subclasses. The cls argument will always be whatever class was used to call the method, rather than just the one where the method was defined.

Although it may not be clear from the previous example, class methods are actually bound instance methods, just like those described in the previous sections. Since all classes are actually instances of a built-in type, class methods are bound to the class itself.

```
>>> Example.method
<bound method type.method of <class '__main__.Example'>>
```

Class methods can also be created in another, slightly more indirect way. Because all classes are really just instances of metaclasses, you can define a method on a metaclass. All instance classes will then have access to that method as a standard bound method. There's no need to use the @classmethod decorator because the method is already bound to the class using the standard behavior described previously. Here's how it works.

```
>>> class ExampleMeta(type):
...     def method(cls):
...         return cls
...
>>> class Example(metaclass=ExampleMeta):
...     pass
...
>>> Example.method
<bound method ExampleMeta.method of <class '__main__.Example'>>
>>> Example.method()
<class __main__.Example at 0x...>
```

The actual behavior of a method constructed this way is identical to a regular class method in most respects because they're built the same way internally. They can be called from the class itself, rather than requiring an instance, and they always receive the class object as an implicit first argument. The difference, however, is that class methods can still be called from instances, while a bound class method can only be called from the class itself.

The reason for this behavior is that the method is defined in the metaclass namespace, which only puts it in the MRO of instances of that metaclass. All classes that reference the metaclass will have access to the method, but it's not actually in their definitions. Methods decorated with @classmethod are placed directly in the namespace of the class where they're defined, which makes them available to instances of that class as well.

Even though this difference in visibility seems like metaclass-based class methods are just an inferior version of standard decorated class methods, there are two reasons why they may be beneficial to an application. First, class methods are generally expected to be called as attributes of the class, and are rarely called from instance objects. That's not a universal rule, and it's certainly not enough to justify the use of a metaclass on its own, but it's worth noting.

Perhaps more importantly, many applications that already use a metaclass also need to add class methods to any class that uses that metaclass. In this case, it makes sense to just define the methods on the existing metaclass, rather than using a separate class to hold the class methods. This is especially useful when that extra class wouldn't have anything valuable to add on its own; if the metaclass is the important part, it's best to keep everything there.

Static Methods

Occasionally, even the class is more information than is necessary for a method to do its job. This is the case for static methods, which are often implemented for the sake of establishing a namespace for functions that could otherwise be implemented at the module level. Using the staticmethod decorator, the method won't receive any implicit arguments at any time.

```
>>> class Example:
...     @staticmethod
...     def method():
...         print('static!')
...
```

```
>>> Example.method
<function method at 0x...>
>>> Example.method()
static!
```

As you can see, static methods don't really look like methods at all. They're just standard functions that happen to sit on a class. The next section shows how a similar effect can be achieved on instances by taking advantage of Python's dynamic nature.

Assigning Functions to Classes and Instances

Python allows most attributes to be overwritten simply by assigning a new value, which presents an interesting opportunity for methods.

```
>>> def dynamic(obj):
...     return obj
...
>>> Example.method = dynamic
>>> Example.method()
Traceback (most recent call last):
  ...
TypeError: dynamic() takes exactly 1 positional argument (0 given)
>>> ex = Example()
>>> ex.method()
<__main__.Example object at 0x...>
```

Notice here that the function assigned to the class still needs to be written to accept an instance as its first argument. Once assigned, it works just like a regular instance method, so the argument requirement doesn't change at all. Assigning to instances works similarly in syntax, but since the function never gets assigned to a class, there's no binding involved at all. A function assigned directly to an instance attribute works just like a static method that was attached to the class.

```
>>> def dynamic():
...     print('dynamic!')
...
>>> ex.method = dynamic
>>> ex.method()
dynamic!
>>> ex.method
<function dynamic at 0x...>
```

Magic Methods

Objects in Python can be created, manipulated and destroyed in a number of different ways, and most of the available behaviors can be modified by implementing some extra methods on your own custom classes. Some of the more specialized customizations can be found in Chapter 5, but there are several of these special methods that are common to all types of classes. These methods can be categorized according to what aspect of classes they deal with, so the following sections each cover a few different methods.

Creating Instances

The transition from a class to an object is called instantiation. An instance is little more than a reference to the class that provides behavior and a namespace dictionary that's unique to the instance being created. When creating a new object without overriding any special methods, the instance namespace is just an empty dictionary, waiting for data.

Therefore, the first method most classes implement is __init__(), with the purpose of initializing the namespace with some useful values. Sometimes these are just placeholders until more interesting data arrives, while other times, the interesting data comes into the method directly, in the form of arguments. This happens because any arguments passed in to the class instantiation get passed right along to __init__() along the way.

```
>>> class Example:
...     def __init__(self):
...         self.initialized = True
...
>>> e = Example()
>>> e.initialized = True
>>> class Example2:
...     def __init__(self, name, value=''):
...         self.name = name
...         self.value = value
...
>>> e = Example2()
Traceback (most recent call last):
  ...
TypeError: __init__() takes at least 2 positional arguments (1 given)
>>> e = Example2('testing')
>>> e.name
'testing'
>>> e.value
''
```

Like any Python function, you're free to do whatever you like inside of __init__(), but keep in mind that's intended to initialize the object, nothing more. Once __init__() has finished executing, the object should be ready to be used for more practical purposes, but anything beyond basic setup should be deferred to other, more explicit methods.

Of course, the real definition of initialization could mean different things to different objects. For most objects, you'll only need to set a few attributes to either some default values or to the values passed in to __init__(), as shown in the previous example. Other times, those initial values may require calculations, such as converting different lengths of time into seconds, so everything's normalized.

In some less common cases, initialization may include more complicated tasks, such as data validation, file retrieval or even network traffic. For example, a class for working with a web service might take an API token as its only argument to __init__(). It might then make a call to the web service to convert that token into an authenticated session, which would allow other operations to take place. All of the other operations require separate method calls, but the authentication that underlies all of them could happen in __init__().

The main concern with doing too much in __init__() is that there's no indication that anything's going on, short of documentation. Unfortunately, some users just won't read your documentation, no matter how hard you try, so they may still expect initialization to be a simple operation, and they might be surprised to see errors if they don't have a valid network connection, for example. See the example in the next section for one way to address this.

Even though __init__() is probably the most well-known magic method of all, it's not the first that gets executed when creating a new object. After all, remember that __init__() is about initialization an object, not creating it. For the latter, Python provides the __new__() method, which gets most of the same arguments but is responsible for actually creating the new object, prior to initializing it.

Rather than working the typical instance object self, the first argument to __new__() is actually the class of the object being created. This makes it look a lot like a class method, but you don't need to use any decorators to make it work this way—it's a special case in Python. Technically, though, it's a static method, so if you try to call it directly, you'll always need to supply the class; it'll never be sent implicitly, like it would be if it were a true class method.

After the class—typically named cls, like a regular class method—the __new__() method receives all the same arguments that __init__() would receive. Whatever you pass in to the class when trying to create the object will be passed along to __new__() to help define it. These arguments are often useful when customizing the new object for the needs at hand.

This is often different from initialization, because __new__() is typically used to change the very nature of the object being created, rather than just setting up some initial values. To illustrate, consider an example where the class of an object can change depending on what values are passed in when creating it.

Example: Automatic Subclasses

Some libraries consist of a large variety of classes, most of which share a common set of data, but with perhaps different behaviors or other data customizations. This often requires users of the library to keep track of all the different classes and determine which features of their data correspond to the appropriate classes.

Instead, it can be much more helpful to provide a single class that can be created with the given data and have its class automatically be the one that's most appropriate. Using __new__() to customize the creation of new objects, this can be achieved rather simply. The exact behavior will depend very much on the application at hand, but the basic technique is easy to illustrate with a generic example.

For a simple example, consider a class that picks a subclass randomly whenever it's instantiated into an object. This isn't the most practical use, of course, but it illustrates how the process could work. Using random.choice() to pick from the values available from using __subclasses__(), it then instantiates the subclass it finds, rather than the one defined.

```
>>> import random
>>> class Example:
...     def __new__(cls, *args, **kwargs):
...         cls = random.choice(cls.__subclasses__())
...         return super(Example, cls).__new__(cls, *args, **kwargs)
...
>>> class Spam(Example):
...     pass
...
>>> class Eggs(Example):
...     pass
...
>>> Example()
<__main__.Eggs object at 0x...>
>>> Example()
<__main__.Eggs object at 0x...>
```

```
>>> Example()
<__main__.Spam object at 0x...>
>>> Example()
<__main__.Eggs object at 0x...>
>>> Example()
<__main__.Spam object at 0x...>
>>> Example()
<__main__.Spam object at 0x...>
```

In another real world example, you could pass in the contents of a file to a single File class and have it automatically instantiate a subclass whose attributes and methods are built for the format of the file provided. This can be especially useful for large classes of files, such as music or images, that behave similarly in most respects on the surface but have underlying differences that can be abstracted away.

Dealing with Attributes

With an object in use, one of the more common needs is to interact with its attributes. Ordinarily, this is as simple as just assigning and accessing attributes directly, given their name, such as instance.attribute. There are a few cases where this type of access isn't sufficient on its own, so you need more control.

If you don't know the name of the attribute at the time you write the application, you can supply a variable for the name, if you use the built-in getattr() function instead. For example, instance.attribute would become getattr(instance, attribute_name), where the value for attribute_name can be provided from anywhere, as long as it's a string.

That approach only handles the case where you're given a name as a string and you need to look up the instance attribute referenced by that name. On the other side of the equation, you can also tell a class how to deal with attributes it doesn't explicitly manage. This behavior is controlled by the __getattr__() method.

If you define this method, Python will call it whenever you request an attribute that hasn't already been defined. It receives the name of the attribute that was requested, so your class can decide what should be done with it. One common example is a dictionary that allows you to retrieve values by attribute instead of just using the standard dictionary syntax.

```
>>> class AttributeDict(dict):
...     def __getattr__(self, name):
...         return self[name]
...
>>> d = AttributeDict(spam='eggs')
>>> d['spam']
'eggs'
>>> d.spam
'eggs'
```

Of course, a dictionary that allows attribute access isn't terribly useful if attributes are read-only. In order to complete the picture, we should support storing values in attributes as well. Even beyond this simple dictionary example, there are a variety of needs for customizing what happens when you set a value to an attribute. As expected, Python provides a parallel in the form of the __setattr__() method.

This new method takes an extra argument because there's also a value that needs to be managed. By defining __setattr__(), you can intercept these value assignments and handle them however your application needs. Applying this to `AttributeDict` is just as simple as the previous example.

```
>>> class AttributeDict(dict):
...     def __getattr__(self, name):
...         return self[name]
...     def __setattr__(self, name, value):
...         self[name] = value
...
>>> d = AttributeDict(spam='eggs')
>>> d['spam']
'eggs'
>>> d.spam
'eggs'
>>> d.spam = 'ham'
>>> d.spam
'ham'
```

Even though that might look like a complete picture of attribute access, there's still one component missing. When you no longer have use for an attribute and would like to remove it from the object altogether, Python provides the del statement. When you're working with fake attributes managed by these special methods, though, del on its own doesn't work.

For dealing with this situation, Python hooks into the __delattr__() method, if one is present. Since the value is no longer relevant, this method only accepts the name of the attribute along with the standard self. Adding this to the existing `AttributeDict` is easy.

```
>>> class AttributeDict(dict):
...     def __getattr__(self, name):
```

```
...         return self[name]
...      def __setattr__(self, name, value):
...         self[name] = value
...      def __delattr__(self, name):
...         del self[name]
...
>>> d = AttributeDict(spam='eggs')
>>> d['spam']
'eggs'
>>> d.spam
'eggs'
>>> d.spam = 'ham'
>>> d.spam
'ham'
>>> del d.spam
>>> d.spam
Traceback (most recent call last):
  ...
KeyError: 'spam'
```

Warning: Raise the Right Exception

This error message brings up an important point about working with these types of overridden attributes. It's very easy to overlook how exceptions are handled inside your function, so you may end up raising an exception that doesn't make any sense; if an attribute doesn't exist, you would reasonably expect to see an AttributeError, rather than a KeyError.

This may seem like an arbitrary detail, but remember that most code explicitly catches specific types of exceptions, so if you raise the wrong type, you could cause other code to take the wrong path. Therefore, always make sure to raise AttributeError explicitly when encountering something that's the equivalent of a missing attribute. Depending on what the fake attribute does, it might be a KeyError, IOError or perhaps even a UnicodeDecodeError, for example.

This will come up at various points throughout this book and elsewhere in the real world. Chapter 5 covers a variety of protocols where it's just as important to get the exceptions right as the arguments.

String Representations

Of all the different object types that are possible in Python, easily the most common is the string. From reading and writing files to interacting with web services and printing documents, strings dominate many aspects of software execution. Even though most of our data exists in other forms along the way, sooner or later, most of it gets converted to a string.

In order to make that process as simple as possible, Python provides an extra hook to convert an object to its string representation. The __str__() method, when implemented on a class, allows its instances to be coerced to a string using the built-in str() function, which is also used when using print() or string formatting. Details on those features and more can be found in Chapter 7, but for now, take a look at how __str__() works in a simple class.

```
# First, without __str__()

>>> class Book:
...     def __init__(self, title):
...         self.title = title
...
>>> Book('Pro Python')
<__main__.Book object at 0x...>
>>> str(Book('Pro Python'))
'<__main__.Book object at 0x...>'

# And again, this time with __str__()

>>> class Book:
...     def __init__(self, title):
...         self.title = title
...     def __str__(self):
...         return self.title
...
>>> Book('Pro Python')
<__main__.Book object at 0x...>
>>> str(Book('Pro Python'))
'Pro Python'
```

The addition of __str__() allows the class to specify what aspect of the object should be displayed when representing the object as a string. In this example, it was the title of a book, but it could also be the name of a person, the latitude and longitude of a geographic location or anything else that succinctly identifies the object among a group of its peers. It doesn't have to contain everything about the object, but enough to distinguish one from another.

Compatibility: Prior to 3.0

In Python 3.0, all strings became Unicode by default, so it makes sense that __str__() would always return a Unicode string. In older versions, __str__() was expected to return a bytestring, while the separate __unicode__() method would return a Unicode string. Chapter 7 describes the differences between the two types of strings in much more detail, including how they worked in previous versions.

Notice also that when the expression in the interactive interpreter doesn't include the call to str(), it doesn't use the value returned by __str__(). Instead, the interpreter uses a different representation of the object, which is intended to more accurately represent the code nature of the object. For custom classes, this representation is fairly unhelpful, only showing the name and module of the object's class and its address in memory.

For other types, though, you'll notice that the representations can be quite useful in determining what the object is all about. In fact, the ideal goal for this representation is to present a string that, if typed back into the console, would re-create the object. This is extremely useful for getting a feel for the objects in the interactive console.

```
>>> dict(spam='eggs')
{'spam': 'eggs'}
```

```
>>> list(range(5))
[0, 1, 2, 3, 4]
>>> set(range(5))
{0, 1, 2, 3, 4}

>>> import datetime
>>> datetime.date.today()
datetime.date(2009, 10, 31)
>>> datetime.time(12 + 6, 30)
datetime.time(18, 30)
```

This alternate representation is controlled by the __repr__() method, and is used primarily in cases just like this, to describe an object inside the interactive console. It's automatically triggered when referencing an object on its own in the interpreter and is sometimes used in logging applications where __str__() often doesn't provide enough detail.

For the built-ins like lists and dictionaries, the representation is a literal expression that can reproduce the object easily. For other simple objects that don't contain very much data, the date and time examples show that simply providing an instantiation call will do the trick. Of course, datetime would have to be imported first, but it gets the job done.

In cases where the data represented by the object is too numerous to condense into a simple representation like this, the next best thing is to provide a string, surrounded in angle brackets, which describes the object in a more reasonable amount of detail. This is often a matter of showing the class name and a few pieces of data that would identify it. For the Book example, which in the real world would have many more attributes, it could look like this.

```
>>> class Book:
...     def __init__(self, title, author=None):
...         self.title = title
...         self.author = author
...     def __str__(self):
...         return self.title
...     def __repr__(self):
...         return '<%s by %s>' % (self.title, self.author or '<Unknown Author>')
...
>>> Book('Pro Python', author='Marty Alchin')
<Book: Pro Python by Marty Alchin>
>>> str(Book('Pro Python', author='Marty Alchin'))
'Pro Python'
```

Taking It With You

A thorough understanding of classes unlocks a world of possibilities for your applications, whether they're simple personal projects or large frameworks built for mass distribution. In addition to all this freedom, there is a set of established protocols that can allow your classes to work just like some of Python's most well-known types.

CHAPTER 5

■ ■ ■

Common Protocols

Most of the time, you'll want to define objects that are highly customized to the needs of your application. This often means coming up with your own interfaces and APIs that are unique to your own code. The flexibility to do this is essential to the expansion capabilities of any system, but there is a price. Everything new you invent must be documented and understood by those who need to use it.

Understanding how to use the various classes made available by a framework can be quite a chore for users of that framework, even with proper documentation. A good way to ease the burden on users is to mimic interfaces they're already familiar with. There are many existing types that are standard issue in Python programming, and most of them have interfaces that can be implemented in custom classes.

Methods are the most obvious way to implement an existing interface, but with many of the built-in types, most of the operations are performed with native Python syntax rather than explicit method calls. Naturally, these syntactic features are backed by actual methods behind the scenes, so they can be overridden to provide custom behaviors.

The following sections show how the interfaces for some of the most common types used in Python can be imitated in custom code. This is by no means an exhaustive list of all the types that ship with Python, nor is every method represented. Instead, this chapter is a reference for those methods that aren't so obvious because they're masked by syntactic sugar.

Basic Operations

Even though there is a wide variety of object types available in Python, most of them share a common set of operations. These are considered to be something of a core feature set, representing some of the most common high-level aspects of object manipulation, many of which are just as applicable to simple numbers as they are to many other objects.

One of the simplest and most common needs in all of programming, Python included, is to evaluate an expression to a Boolean value, so that it can be used to make simple decisions. Typically, this is used in `if` blocks, but these decisions also come into play when using `while`, and Boolean operations such as `and` and `or`. When Python encounters one of these situations, it relies on the behavior of the `__bool__()` method to determine the Boolean equivalent of an object.

The `__bool__()` method, if implemented, accepts just the usual `self` and must return either `True` or `False`. This allows any object to determine whether it should be considered to be true or false in a given expression, using whatever methods or attributes are appropriate. For example, a class that represents a rectangle might use its area to determine whether the rectangle is considered true or false. Therefore, `__bool__()` only has to check whether there exists a non-zero width and a non-zero height. Here, we use the built-in `bool()`, which uses `__bool__()` to convert the value to a Boolean.

```
>>> class Rectangle:
...     def __init__(self, width, height):
...         self.width = width
```

```
...             self.height = height
...         def __bool__(self):
...             if self.width and self.height:
...                 return True
...             return False
...
>>> bool(Rectangle(10, 15))
True
>>> bool(Rectangle(0, 0))
False
>>> bool(Rectangle(0, 15))
False
```

■ **Tip** The __bool__() method isn't the only way to customize Python's Boolean behavior. If an object instead provides a __len__() method, which is described in the section on sequences later in this chapter, Python will fall back to that and consider any non-zero lengths to be true, while lengths of zero are false.

Compatibility: Prior to 3.0

The name of this method was changed to __bool__() in Python 3.0. In earlier versions, it was called __nonzero__(), which reflected earlier usage of 1 and 0 in place of True and False. In fact, True was set to 1, False was set to 0 and __nonzero__() could return any integer. Anything that wasn't zero evaluated to True, while 0 itself evaluated to False. Once Python 3.0 changed True and False to true constants, and __nonzero__() changed to require one of them, its name also changed to better reflect its actual behavior and requirements.

Having the wrong method name won't cause any obvious errors, though. Instead, your custom behavior simply won't be used, and Python will revert to whatever implementation is provided in your base classes, falling back to always being True if no valid method was found. In order to ensure compatibility with both versions, you'll need to define both __nonzero__() and __bool__(). This is easiest if you define one and then also assign it to the other name, such as __nonzero__ = __bool__.

With the truthfulness of objects taken into account, you automatically get control over the behavior of such operators as **and**, **or** and **not**. Therefore, there are no separate methods to override in order to customize those operators.

In addition to being able to determine the truthfulness of an object, Python offers a great deal of flexibility in other operations as well. In particular, the standard mathematical operations can be overridden because many of them can apply to a variety of objects beyond just numbers.

Mathematical Operations

Some of the earliest forms of math stemmed from observations about the world around us. Therefore, most of the math we learned in elementary school applies just as easily to other types of objects as it does to numbers. For example, addition could be seen as simply putting two things together, such as tying two strings together to make a single, longer string.

If you only look at it mathematically, you could say that you're really just adding two lengths together, resulting in a single, greater length. But when you look at what really just happened, you now have a brand new string, which is different from the two strings that went into it originally.

This analogy extends easily into Python strings as well, which can be joined using standard addition, rather than requiring a separate, named method. Similarly, if you need to write the same string out multiple times, you can simply multiply it the same way you would a regular number. These types of operations are very common in Python because they can be a simple way to implement common tasks.

```
>>> 2 + 2
4
>>> 'two' + 'two'
'twotwo'
>>> 2 * 2
4
>>> 'two' * 2
'twotwo'
```

Like `__bool__()`, these behaviors are controlled by special methods of their own. Most of them are fairly straightforward, accepting the usual `self` as well as an `other` argument. These methods are bound to the object on the left side of the operator, with the additional `other` being the object on the right side.

The four basic arithmetic operations—addition, subtraction, multiplication and division—are represented in Python using the standard operators `+`, `-`, `*` and `/`. Behind the scenes, the first three are powered by implementations of the `__add__()`, `__sub__()`, `__mul__()` methods. Division is a bit more complicated, so we'll get to that shortly, but for now, let's take a look at how this operator overloading works.

Consider a class that acts as a simple proxy around a value. There's not much use for something like this in the real world, but it's a good starting point to explain a few things.

```
>>> class Example:
...     def __init__(self, value):
...         self.value = value
...     def __add__(self, other):
...         return self.value + other
...
>>> Example(10) + 20
30
```

This is just one example of a few basic arithmetic operations that are available for your code to customize. There are also more advanced operations that will be detailed throughout the remainder of this chapter, but the list of these basic arithmetic operators is as follows:

Operation	Operator	Custom Method
Addition	+	`__add__()`
Subtraction	-	`__sub__()`
Multiplication	*	`__mul__()`
Division	/	`__truediv__()`

Here's where things get interesting because you'll notice that the method for division isn't __div__(), like you might expect. The reason for this is that division comes in two different flavors. The kind of division you get when you use a calculator is called true division in Python, which uses the __truediv__() method, which works as you'd expect.

However, true division is the only arithmetic operation that can take two integers and return a non-integer. In some applications, it's useful to always get an integer back instead. If you're displaying an application's progress as a percentage, for instance, you don't really need to display the full floating point number.

Instead, an alternative operation is available, called floor division. If the result of true division would land between two integers, floor division will simply return the lower of the two, so that it always returns an integer. Floor division, as you might expect, is implemented with a separate __floordiv__() and is accessed using the // operator.

```
>>> 5 / 4
1.25
>>> 5 // 4
1
```

Compatibility: Prior to 3.0

The difference between floor division and true division is especially apparent when moving to Python 3.0 because the default behavior changed at that point. Previously, using the / operator meant using floor division, which was implemented using __div__(). True division was available by importing division from the __future__ package, which would cause the / operator to use __truediv__() instead.

Python 3.0 then defaulted to __truediv__() and dropped support for __div__() entirely. Explicit floor division, using //, had been available for some time, even through all the changes that took place regarding true division.

There's also a modulo operation, which is related to division. In the event that a division operation would result in a remainder, using modulo would return that remainder. This uses the % operator, implemented using __mod__(). This is used by strings to perform standard variable interpretation, even though that has nothing to do with division.

```
>>> 20 // 6
3
>>> 20 % 6
2
>>> 'test%s' % 'ing'
'testing'
```

In effect, you can use floor division and a modulo operation to obtain the integer result of a division operation as well as its remainder, which retains all the information about the result. This is sometimes preferable to true division, which would simply produce a floating point number. For example, consider a function that takes a number of minutes and has to return a string containing the number of hours and minutes.

```
>>> def hours_and_minutes(minutes):
...     return minutes // 60, minutes % 60
...
>>> hours_and_minutes(60)
(1, 0)
>>> hours_and_minutes(137)
(2, 17)
>>> hours_and_minutes(42)
(0, 42)
```

In fact, this basic task is common enough that Python has its own function for it: divmod(). By passing in a base value and a value to divide it by, you can get the results of floor division and a modulo operation at the same time. Rather than simply delegating to those two methods independently, though, Python will try to call a __divmod__() method, which allows a custom implementation to be more efficient.

In lieu of a more efficient implementation, the __divmod__() method can be illustrated using the same technique as the hours_and_minutes() function. All we have to do is accept a second argument in order to take the hard-coded 60 out of the method.

```
>>> class Example:
...     def __init__(self, value):
...         self.value = value
...     def __divmod__(self, divisor):
...         return self.value // divisor, self.value % divisor
...
>>> divmod(Example(20), 6)
(3, 2)
```

There's also an extension of multiplication, called exponentiation, where a value is multiplied by itself a number of times. Given its relationship to multiplication, Python uses a double-asterisk ** notation to perform the operation. It's implemented using a __pow__() method because real-world math typically calls it raising a value to a power of some other value.

```
>>> class Example:
...     def __init__(self, value):
...         self.value = value
...     def __pow__(self, power):
...         val = 1
...         for x in range(power):
...             val *= self.value
...         return val
...
>>> Example(5) ** 3
125
```

Unlike the other operations, exponentiation can be performed in one other way as well, by way of the built-in pow() function. The reason there's a different operator is that it allows for an extra argument to be passed in. This extra argument is a value that should be used to perform a modulo operation after the exponentiation has been performed. This extra behavior allows for a more efficient way to perform such tasks as finding prime numbers, which is commonly used in cryptography.

```
>>> 5 ** 3
125
>>> 125 % 50
25
>>> 5 ** 3 % 50
25
>>> pow(5, 3, 50)
25
```

In order to support this behavior with the __pow__() method, you can optionally accept an extra argument, which will be used to perform the modulo operation. This new argument must be optional in order to support the normal ** operator. There's no reasonable default value that can be used blindly without causing problems with standard exponentiation, so it should default to **None** to determine whether the modulo operation should be performed.

```
>>> class Example:
...     def __init__(self, value):
...         self.value = value
...     def __pow__(self, power, modulo=None):
...         val = 1
...         for x in range(power):
...             val *= self.value
...         if modulo is not None:
...             val %= modulo
...         return val
...
>>> Example(5) ** 3
125
>>> Example(5) ** 3 % 50
25
>>> pow(Example(5), 3, 50)
25
```

■ **Caution** As with the __divmod__() implementation shown previously, this example is not a very efficient approach at solving the problem. It does produce the correct values, but it should be used only for illustration.

Bitwise Operations

A separate group of operations act on values not as numbers directly, but rather as a sequence of individual bits. At that level, there are a few different ways of manipulating values that are applicable to not only numbers but some other types of sequences as well. The simplest bitwise manipulation is a shift, where the bits within a value are moved to the right or to the left, resulting in a new value.

In binary arithmetic, shifting bits one place to the left multiplies the value by two. This is just like in decimal math: if you move all the digits in a number one place to the left and fill in the gap on the right with a zero, you've essentially multiplied the value by ten. This behavior exists for any numbered base, but computers work in binary, so the shifting operations do as well.

Shifting is achieved using the << and >> operators for left and right, respectively. The right-hand side of the operator indicates how many positions the bits should be shifted. Internally, these operations are supported by the __lshift__() and __rshift__() methods, each of which accepts the number of positions to shift as its only additional argument.

```
>>> 10 << 1
20
>>> 10 >> 1
5
```

In addition to shuffling the bits around, there are a few operations that compare the bits in each value to each other, resulting in a new value that represents some combination of the two individual values. The four bitwise comparison operations are &, |, ^ and ~ referred to AND, OR, XOR (exclusive OR) and inversion, respectively.

An AND comparison returns 1 only if both of the individual bits being compared are 1. If it's any other combination, the result is 0. This behavior is often used to create a bitmask, where you can reset all irrelevant values to 0 by applying AND to a value that has 1 for each of the useful bits and 0 for the rest. This will clear out any bits you aren't interested in, allowing for easy comparisons with sets of binary flags. Supporting this behavior in your code requires the presence of an __and__() method.

OR comparisons return 1 if either of the individual bits being compared is 1. It doesn't matter if both of them are 1; as long as at least one of them is 1, the result will be 1. This is often used to join sets of binary flags together, so that all the flags from both sides of the operator are set in the result. The method required to support this functionality is __or__().

The standard OR operator is sometimes called an inclusive OR, to contrast it with its cousin, the exclusive OR, which is typically abbreviated as XOR. In an XOR operation, the result is 1 only if one of the individual bits was 1 but not the other. If both bits are 1 or both bits are 0, the result will be 0. XOR is supported by the __xor__() method.

Lastly, Python also offers bitwise inversion, where each of the bits gets flipped to the opposite value from what it currently is; 1 becomes 0 and vice versa. Numerically, this swaps between negative and positive values, but it doesn't simply change the sign. Here's an example of how numbers react when inverted using the ~ operator.

```
>>> ~42
-43
>>> ~-256
255
```

This behavior is based on the way computers work with signed values. The most significant bit is used to determine whether the value is positive or negative, so flipping that bit changes the sign. The change in the absolute value after inversion is due to a lack of -0. When 0 is inverted, it becomes -1 rather than -0, so all other values follow suit after that.

In custom code, inversion is typically most useful when you have a known set of all possible values, along with individual subsets of those values. Inverting these subsets would remove any existing values and replace them with any values from the master set that weren't previous in the subset.

This behavior can be provided by supplying an __invert__() method on your object. Unlike the other bitwise methods, though, __invert__() is unary, so it doesn't accept any additional arguments beyond the standard self.

■ **Note** The inversion behavior described here is valid for numbers that encoded using the two's-complement method for working with signed numbers. There are other options[1] available that can behave differently to what's shown here if a custom number class provides the __invert__() method to do so. By default, Python works only with the two's-complemented encoding method.

Variations

In addition to the normal behavior of operations, there are a couple different ways they can also be accessed. The most obvious issue is that the methods are typically bound to the value on the left-hand side of the operator. If your custom object gets placed on the right-hand side instead, there's a good chance that the value on the left won't know how to work with it, so you'll end up with a TypeError instead of a usable value.

This behavior is understandable but unfortunate because if the custom object knows how to interact with the other value, it should be able to do so regardless of their positions. To allow for this, Python gives the value on the right-hand side of the operator a chance to return a valid value.

When the left-hand side of the expression fails to yield a value, Python then checks to see if the value on the right is of the same type. If it is, there's no reason to expect that it would be able to do any better than the first time around, so Python simply raises the TypeError. If it's a different type, though, Python will call a method on the right-hand value, passing in the left-hand value as its argument.

This process swaps the arguments around, binding the method to the value on the right-hand side. For some operations, such as subtraction and division, the order of the values is important, so Python uses a different method to indicate the change in ordering. The names of these separate methods are mostly the same as the left-hand methods, but with an **r** added after the first two underscores.

```
>>> class Example:
...     def __init__(self, value):
...         self.value = value
...     def __add__(self, other):
...         return self.value + other
...
>>> Example(20) + 10
30
>>> 10 + Example(20)
Traceback (most recent call last):
  ...
TypeError: unsupported operand type(s) for +: 'int' and 'Example'
>>> class Example:
...     def __init__(self, value):
...         self.value = value
...     def __add__(self, other):
...         return self.value + other
...     def __radd__(self, other):
...         return self.value + other
...
```

---

[1] http://en.wikipedia.org/wiki/Signed_number_representations

```
>>> Example(20) + 10
30
>>> 10 + Example(20)
30
```

■ **Tip** In cases like this, where the order of the values doesn't affect the result, you can actually just assign the left-hand method to the name of the right-hand method. Just remember that not all operations work that way, so you can't blindly copy the method to both sides without ensuring that it makes sense.

Another common way to use these operators is to modify an existing value and assign the result right back to the original value. As has been demonstrated without explanation earlier in this chapter, an alternative form of assignment is catered to these modifications. By simply appending = to the operator you need, you can assign the result of the operation to the value on the left-hand side.

```
>>> value = 5
>>> value *= 3
>>> value
15
```

By default, this form of augmented assignment uses the standard operator methods in the same way as was described previously in this chapter. However, that requires creating a new value after the operation, which is then used to overwrite an existing value. Instead, it can sometimes be advantageous to modify the value in-place, as long as you can identify when this assignment is taking place.

Like the right-hand side methods, in-place operators use essentially the same method names as the standard operators, but this time with an i after the underscores. There's no right-hand side equivalent of this operation, though, because the assignment is always done with the variable on the left-hand side. With everything taken into account, here's the list of available operators, along with the methods required to customize their behavior.

Operation	Operator	Left-hand	Right-hand	In-line
Addition	+	__add__()	__radd__()	__iadd__()
Subtraction	-	__sub__()	__rsub__()	__isub__()
Multiplication	*	__mul__()	__rmul__()	__imul__()
True division	/	__truediv__()	__rtruediv__()	__itruediv__()
Floor division	//	__floordiv__()	__rfloordiv__()	__ifloordiv__()
Modulo	%	__mod__()	__rmod__()	__imod__()
Division & modulo	divmod()	__divmod__()	__rdivmod__()	N/A
Exponentiation	**	__pow__()	__rpow__()	__ipow__()
Left binary shift	<<	__lshift__()	__rlshift__()	__ilshift__()

Right binary shift	>>	__rshift__()	__rrshift__()	__irshift__()
Bitwise AND	&	__and__()	__rand__()	__iand__()
Bitwise OR	|	__or__()	__ror__()	__ior__()
Bitwise XOR	^	__xor__()	__rxor__()	__ixor__()
Bitwise inversion	~	__invert__()	N/A	N/A

■ **Note** There's no in-line method for the division and modulo operation because it's not available as an operator that supports assignment. It's only called as the `divmod()` method, which has no in-line capabilities. Also, bitwise inversion is a unary operation, so there's no right-side or in-line method available.

Even though these operations are primarily focused on numbers, many of them also make sense for other types of objects. There is another set of behaviors, though, that really only makes sense for numbers and objects that can act like numbers.

Numbers

Underneath it all, computers are all about numbers, so it's only natural that they play an important role in most applications. Beyond the operations outlined in the previous section, there are many various behaviors exhibited by numbers that may not be as obvious.

The most basic behavior a custom number can have is to convince Python that it is in fact a number. This is necessary when trying to use an object as an index in a sequence. Python requires that all indexes be integers, so there needs to be a way to coerce an object into an integer for the sake of being used as an index. For this, Python uses an **__index__()** method, raising a **TypeError** if it doesn't exist or it returns something other than an integer.

```
>>> sequence = [1, 2, 3, 4, 5]
>>> sequence[3.14]
Traceback (most recent call last):
  ...
TypeError: list indices must be integers, not float
>>> class FloatIndex(float):
...     def __index__(self):
...         # For the sake of example, return just the integer portion
...         return int(self)
...
>>> sequence[FloatIndex(3.14)]
4
>>> sequence[3]
4
```

In addition to simple index access, __index__() is used to coerce an integer for the sake of slicing and to generate a starting value for conversion using the built-in bin(), hex() and oct() functions. When looking to explicitly force an integer in other situations, you can use the __int__() method, which is used by the built-in int() method. Other type conversions can be performed using __float__() to support float() and __complex__() for complex().

One of the most commonly required operations when converting one number to another is rounding. Unlike int(), which blindly cuts off any part of the value that's not an integer, rounding affords more control over what type of value you end up with and how much precision is retained.

When you pass a decimal or a floating point number into int(), the effect is essentially just a floor operation. Like floor division mentioned previously, a floor operation takes a number between two integers and returns the lower of the two. The math module contains a floor() function to perform this operation.

As you might expect, this relies on a __floor__() method on a custom object to perform the floor operation. It doesn't require any arguments beyond the usual self and should always return an integer. Python doesn't actually enforce any requirements on the return value, though, so if you're working with some subclass of integers, you can return one of those instead.

On the other hand, you may need to go with the higher of the two, which would be a ceiling operation. This is done using math.ceil() and implemented with the __ceil__() method. Like __floor__(), it doesn't take any additional arguments and returns an integer.

More likely, you'll need to round a value to a specific number of digits. This is achieved using the round() function, which is a built-in, rather than being located in the math module. It takes up to two arguments and is implemented using the __round__() method on a custom object.

The first argument to round() is the object that __round__() will be bound to, so it comes through as the standard self. The second argument is a bit more nuanced, though. It's the number of digits to the right of the decimal point that should be considered significant, and thus retained in the result. If it's not provided, round() should assume none of those digits are significant and return an integer.

```
>>> round(3.14, 1)
3.1
>>> round(3.14)
3
>>> round(3.14, 0)
3.0
>>> import decimal
>>> round(decimal.Decimal('3.14'), 1)
Decimal('3.1')
>>> round(decimal.Decimal('3.14'))
3
```

As you can see, there's actually a difference between passing a second argument of 0 and not passing one at all. The return value is essentially the same, but when not passing it in, you should always get an integer. When passing in a 0 instead, you'll get whatever type you pass in, but with only the significant digits included.

In addition to rounding digits to the right of the decimal point, round() can act on the other side as well. By passing in a negative number, you can specify the number of digits to the left of the decimal point that should be rounded away, leaving the other digits remaining.

```
>>> round(256, -1)
260
>>> round(512, -2)
500
```

Sign Operations

There is also a selection of unary operations that can be used to adjust the sign of a value. The first, -, negates the sign, swapping between positive and negative values. Customization of this behavior is made available by providing a __neg__() method, which accepts no extra arguments beyond self.

To complement the negative sign, Python also supports a positive sign, using +. Because numbers are ordinarily assumed to be positive, this operator actually doesn't do anything on its own; it simply returns the number unchanged. In the event that a custom object needs an actual behavior attached to this, however, a __pos__() method can provide it.

Lastly, a number can also have an absolute value, which is generally defined as its distance from zero. Therefore, the sign is irrelevant, and all values become positive. Therefore, applying abs() to a number removes the negative sign if present, but leaves positive values unchanged. This behavior is modified by an __abs__() method.

Comparison Operations

The operations shown thus far have been concerned with returning a modified value, based at least in part on one or more existing values. Comparison operators, on the other hand, return either True or False, based on the relationship between two values.

The most basic comparison operators, is and is not, operate directly on the internal identity of each object. Because the identity is typically implemented as the object's address in memory, which can't be changed by Python code, there's no way to override this behavior. Its use is generally reserved for comparison with known constants, such as None.

The operators that are available represent the standard numerical comparisons, which detect if one value is higher, lower or exactly equal to another. The most versatile is testing for equality, using ==. Its versatility comes from the fact that it's not limited to numerical values because many other types can have objects that are considered equal to each other. This behavior is controlled by an __eq__() method.

Inequality is represented in Python by the != operator, which behaves just as you would expect. What you might not expect, however, is that this functionality is not tied to == in any way. Rather than simply calling __eq__() and inverting its result, Python relies on a separate __ne__() method to handle inequality testing. Therefore, if you implement __eq__(), always remember to supply __ne__() as well to ensure that everything works as expected.

In addition, you can compare one value as less than or greater than another, using < and >, which are implemented using __lt__() and __gt__(), respectively. Equality can also be combined with these, so that one value can be greater than or equal to another, for instance. These operations use <= and >= and are supported by __lte__() and __gte__().

These comparisons are often used for objects that are predominantly represented by a number, even if the object itself is much more than that. Dates and times are notable examples of objects that are easily comparable because they're each essentially a series of numbers that can each be compared individually if needed.

```
>>> import datetime
>>> a = datetime.date(2009, 10, 31)
>>> b = datetime.date(2010, 1, 1)
>>> a == b
False
>>> a < b
True
```

Compatibility: Prior to 3.0

Earlier versions of Python also provided a shortcut: if any of these more specific comparison operators were missing, Python would fall back to a generic __cmp__() method, which returns a positive value if self is greater than other, a negative value if it's the other way around or 0 if the two values are equal. In Python 3.0, support for __cmp__() was removed, so you'll need to specify __lt__() and its friends to get full comparison functionality. Because __cmp__() was only a fallback previously, the __lt__() approach is fully compatible with other versions as well.

Strings are an interesting case with regard to comparisons. Even though a string isn't numeric in an obvious sense, each character in a string is simply another representation of a number, so string comparisons also work. These comparisons drive the sorting features of strings.

Iterables

It may seem like sequences are the obvious next choice, but there's a more generic form to consider first. An object is considered iterable if it can yield objects one at a time, typically within a **for** loop. This definition is intentionally simple, because at a high level, iterables really don't go beyond that. Python does have a more specific definition of iterables, though.

In particular, an object is iterable if passing it into the built-in **iter()** function returns an iterator. Internally, **iter()** inspects the object passed in, looking first for an __iter__() method. If such a method is found, it's called without any arguments and is expected to return an iterator. There's another step that will take place if __iter__() wasn't available, but for now, let's focus on iterators.

Even though the object is considered iterable, it's the iterator that does all the real work, but there's really not that much to it. There's no requirement for what its __init__() method should look like, because it gets instantiated within the __iter__() method of its master object. The required interface consists of just two methods.

The first method, perhaps surprisingly, is __iter__(). Iterators should always be iterable on their own as well, so they must provide an __iter__() method. There's usually no reason to do anything special in this method, though, so it's typically implemented to just return **self**. If you don't supply __iter__() on the iterator, the main object will still be iterable in most cases, but some code will expect its iterator to be usable on its own as well.

More importantly, an iterator must always provide a __next__() method, where all the real work happens. Python will call __next__() to retrieve a single value from the iterator, with that value being used in the body of whatever code called the iterator. When that code needs a new value, typically for the next pass in a loop, it calls __next__() again to get a new value. This process continues until one of a few things happens.

If Python encounters anything that causes the loop to complete while the iterator still has items it could yield, the iterator just stands by, waiting for some other code to ask for another item. If that never happens, eventually there will be no more code that knows about the iterator at all, so Python will remove it from memory. Chapter 6 covers this garbage collection process in greater detail.

There are a few different cases where an iterator might not be given a chance to finish. The most obvious is a **break** statement, which would stop the loop and continue on afterward. Additionally, a **return** or a **raise** statement would implicitly break out of any loop it's part of, so the iterator is left in the same state as when a **break** occurs.

More commonly, though, the loop will just let the iterator run until it doesn't have any more items to produce. When using a generator, this case is handled automatically when the function returns without yielding a new value. With an iterator, this behavior must be provided explicitly.

Because **None** is a perfectly valid object that could reasonably be yielded from an iterator, Python can't just react to __next__() failing to return a value. Instead, the **StopIteration** exception provides a way for __next__() to indicate that there are no more items. When this is raised, the loop is considered complete, and execution resumes on the next line after the end of the loop.

Compatibility: Prior to 3.0

Prior to Python 3.0, iterators were expected to have a method named next(), rather than __next__(). The behavior of next() is identical to what's described here, but the name was changed to better reflect the other hooks that Python uses to provide custom functionality. In order to support versions of Python on both sides of the transition, simply provide both next() and __next__() with identical behavior. You can typically just define __next__() and assign it to next so you don't have to duplicate the code.

To illustrate how all of this fits together, let's take a look at the behavior of the built-in **range()** function. It's not a generator because you can iterate over it multiple times. To provide similar functionality, we need to return an iterable object instead, which can then be iterated as many times as necessary.

```python
class Range:
    def __init__(self, count):
        self.count = count

    def __iter__(self):
        return RangeIter(self.count)

class RangeIter:
    def __init__(self, count):
        self.count = count
        self.current = 0

    def __iter__(self):
        return self


    def __next__(self):
        value = self.current
        self.current += 1
        if self.current > self.count:
```

```
            raise StopIteration
        return value

>>> def range_gen(count):
...     for x in range(count):
...         yield x
...
>>> r = range_gen(5)
>>> list(r)
[0, 1, 2, 3, 4]
>>> list(r)
[]
>>> r = Range(5)
>>> list(r)
[0, 1, 2, 3, 4]
>>> list(r)
[0, 1, 2, 3, 4]
```

Iterators are the most powerful and flexible way to implement an iterable, so they're generally preferred, but there's also another way to achieve a similar effect. What makes an object iterable is the fact that iter() returns an iterator, so it's worth noting that iter() supports a certain kind of special case.

If an object doesn't have an __iter__() method, but contains a __getitem__() method instead, Python can use that in a special iterator that exists just to handle that case. We'll get to more details in the next section on sequences, but the basic idea is that __getitem__() accepts an index and is expected to the return the item in that position.

If Python finds __getitem__() instead of __iter__(), it will automatically create an iterator designed to work with it. This new iterator calls __getitem__() several times, each with a value from a series of numbers, beginning with zero, until __getitem__() raises an IndexError. Therefore, our custom Range iterable can be rewritten quite simply.

```
class Range:
    def __init__(self, count):
        self.count = count

    def __getitem__(self, index):
        if index < self.count:
            return index
        raise IndexError

>>> r = Range(5)
>>> list(r)
[0, 1, 2, 3, 4]
>>> list(r)
[0, 1, 2, 3, 4]
```

■ **Note** Python will only use this __getitem__() behavior if __iter__() is not present. If both are provided on a class, the __iter__() method will be used to control the iteration behavior.

Example: Repeatable Generators

The ability to iterate over an object multiple times is very common among explicitly iterable object types, but generators are often more convenient to work with. If you need to have a generator that can restart itself each different time the iterator is accessed, it may seem like you're stuck either losing out on that functionality or adding a bunch of otherwise unnecessary code that exists solely to allow for proper iteration.

Instead, like many other behaviors, we can rely on Python's standard way to augment a function and factor it out into a decorator. When applied to a generator function, this new decorator can handle everything necessary to create an iterable that triggers the generator from the beginning each time a new iterator is requested.

```
def repeatable(generator):
    """
    A decorator to turn a generator into an object that can be
    iterated multiple times, restarting the generator each time.
    """
    class RepeatableGenerator:
        def __init__(self, *args, **kwargs):
            self.args = args
            self.kwargs = kwargs

        def __iter__(self):
            return iter(generator(*self.args, **self.kwargs))

    return RepeatableGenerator

>>> @repeatable
... def generator(max):
...     for x in range(max):
...         yield x
...
>>> g = generator(5)
>>> list(g)
[0, 1, 2, 3, 4]
>>> list(g)
[0, 1, 2, 3, 4]
```

By creating a new class that can be instantiated when the generator function is called, its __iter__() method will get called instead of the generator's. This way, the generator can be called from scratch each time a new loop begins, yielding a new sequence rather than trying to pick up where it left off, which would often mean returning an empty sequence.

■ **Caution** Even though most generators return a similar sequence each time through and can be restarted without worry, not all of them behave that way. If a generator changes its output based on when it's called, picks up where it left off on subsequent calls or produces side-effects, this decorator is not recommended. By changing the behavior to explicitly restart the decorator each time, the new generator could yield unpredictable results.

There's one problem with the code as it stands, though. The `@repeatable` decorator receives a function but returns a class, which works fine in the example provided, but has some very troubling implications. To start, remember from Chapter 3 that wrapper functions have new properties, a problem that can be fixed using the `@functools.wraps` decorator.

Before we can even consider using another decorator, though, we have to solve the bigger problem: we're returning a completely different type than the original function. By returning a class instead of a function, we'll cause problems with any code that expects it to be a function, including other decorators. Worse yet, the class returned can't be used as a method because it doesn't have a __get__() method to bind it to its owner class or an instance of it.

To solve these issues, we have to introduce a wrapper function around the class, which will instantiate the object and return it. This way, we can use `@functools.wraps` to retain as much of the original decorator as possible. Better yet, we can then also return a function, which can be bound to classes and instances without any trouble.

```python
import functools

def repeatable(generator):
    """
    A decorator to turn a generator into an object that can be
    iterated multiple times, restarting the generator each time.
    """
    class RepeatableGenerator:
        def __init__(self, *args, **kwargs):
            self.args = args
            self.kwargs = kwargs

        def __iter__(self):
            return iter(generator(*self.args, **self.kwargs))

    @functools.wraps(generator)
    def wrapper(*args, **kwargs):
        return RepeatableGenerator(*args, **kwargs)

    return wrapper
```

Sequences

After numbers, sequences are perhaps some of most commonly used data structures in all of programming, including Python. Lists, tuples, sets and even strings are sequences that share a common set of features, which are actually a specialized type of iterator. In addition to being able to yield a series of items individually, sequences have additional attributes and behaviors supporting the fact that they know about the entire set of items all at once.

These extra behaviors don't necessarily require that all the items be loaded into memory at the same time. The efficiency gains achieved through iteration are just as valid with sequences as with any other iterable, so that behavior doesn't change. Instead, the added options simply refer to collection as a whole, including its length and the ability to get a subset of it, as well as accessing individual items without getting the whole sequence.

The most obvious feature of a sequence is the ability to determine its length. For objects that can contain any arbitrary items, this requires knowing—or perhaps counting—all those items. For others, the object can use some other information to reach the same result. Customization of this behavior is achieved by providing a __len__() method, which is called internally when the object is passed into the built-in len() function.

To continue along the same lines as previous examples, here's how a simple replacement Range class could use knowledge of its configuration to return the length without having to yield a single value.

```python
class Range:
    def __init__(self, max):
        self.max = max

    def __iter__(self):
        for x in range(self.max):
            yield x

    def __len__(self):
        return self.max
```

Because sequences contain a fixed collection of items, they can be iterated not only from start to finish, but also in reverse. Python provides the reversed() function, which takes a sequence as its only argument and returns an iterable that yields items from the sequence in reverse. There may be particular efficiency gains to be had, so a custom sequence object can provide a __reversed__() method to customize the internal behavior of reversed().

Taking this notion to the Range class again, it's possible to provide a reversed range using an alternative form of the built-in range().

```python
class Range:
    def __init__(self, max):
        self.max = max

    def __iter__(self):
        for x in range(self.max):
            yield x

    def __reversed__(self):
        for x in range(self.max - 1, -1, -1):
            yield x
```

Now that we have the ability to iterate over a sequence both forward and backward as well as report its length, the next step is to provide access to individual items. In a plain iterable, you can only access items by retrieving them one at a time as part of a loop. With all the values in the sequence known in advance, a custom class can provide access to any item at any time.

The most obvious task is to retrieve an item given an index that's known in advance. For example, if a custom object contained the arguments passed in on the command line, the application would know the specific meaning of each argument and would typically access them by index rather than simply iterating over the whole sequence. This uses the standard sequence[index] syntax, with its behavior controlled by the __getitem__() method.

With __getitem__(), individual items can be picked out of the sequence or retrieved from some other data structure if necessary. Continuing on the Range theme again, __getitem__() can calculate what the appropriate value should be without cycling through the sequence. In fact, it can even support the full range of arguments that are available to the built-in range().

```python
class Range:
    def __init__(self, a, b=None, step=1):
```

```
        """
        Define a range according to a starting value, an end value and a step.

        If only one argument is provided, it's taken to be the end value. If
        two arguments are passed in, the first becomes a start value, while the
        second is the end value. An optional step can be provided to control
        how far apart each value is from the next.
        """
        if b is not None:
            self.start = a
            self.end = b
        else:
            self.start = 0
            self.end = a
        self.step = step

    def __getitem__(self, key):
        value = self.step * key + self.start
        if value < self.end:
            return value
        else:
            raise IndexError("key outside of the given range")
```

```
>>> r = Range(5)
>>> list(r)
[0, 1, 2, 3, 4]
>>> r[3]
3
>>> r = Range(3, 17, step=4)
>>> list(r)
[3, 7, 11, 15]
>>> r[2]
11
>>> r[4]
Traceback (most recent call last):
  ...
IndexError: indexed value outside of the given range
```

In the event that the index passed in is beyond the range of available items, __getitem__() should raise an IndexError. Highly specialized applications could define a more specific subclass and raise that instead, but most use cases will simply catch IndexError on its own.

In addition to matching the expectations of most Python programmers, properly raising IndexError is essential to allow a sequence to be used as an iterable without implementing __iter__(). Python will simply pass in integer indexes until the __getitem__() method raises an IndexError, at which point it'll stop iterating over the sequence.

Beyond just accessing a single item at a time, a sequence can provide access to subsets of its contents by way of slicing. When using the slicing syntax, __getitem__() receives a special slice object instead of an integer index. A slice object has dedicated attributes for the start, stop and and step portions of the slice, which can be used to determine which items to return. Here's how this affects the Range object we've been examining.

```
class Range:
    def __init__(self, a, b=None, step=1):
        """
        Define a range according to a starting value, an end value and a step.

        If only one argument is provided, it's taken to be the end value. If
        two arguments are passed in, the first becomes a start value, while the
        second is the end value. An optional step can be provided to control
        how far apart each value is from the next.
        """
        if b is not None:
            self.start = a
            self.end = b
        else:
            self.start = 0
            self.end = a
        self.step = step

    def __getitem__(self, key):
        if isinstance(key, slice):
            r = range(key.start or 0, key.stop, key.step or 1)
            return [self.step * val + self.start for val in r]
        value = self.step * key + self.start
        if value < self.end:
            return value
        else:
            raise IndexError("key outside of the given range")
```

The next logical step is to allow an individual item in the sequence to be set according to its index. This in-place assignment uses essentially the same sequence[index] syntax but as the target of an assignment operation. It's supported by a custom object in its __setitem__() method, which accepts both the index to access and the value to store at that index.

Like __getitem__(), though, __setitem__() can also accept a slice object as its index, rather than an integer. Because a slice defines a subset of the sequence, though, the value that's passed is expected to be another sequence. The values in this new sequence will then take the place of those in the subset referenced by the slice.

Things aren't exactly as they seem, though, because the sequence being assigned to the slice doesn't actually need to have the same number of items as the slice itself. In fact, it can be of any size, whether larger or smaller than the slice it's being assigned to. The expected behavior of __setitem__() is to simply remove the items referenced by the slice, then place the new items in that gap, expanding or contracting the size of the total list as necessary to accommodate the new values.

■ **Note** The __setitem__() method is only intended for replacing existing values in the sequence, not for strictly adding new items. To do that, you'll need to also implement append() and insert(), using the same interfaces as standard lists.

Removing an item from a list can be achieved in one of two different ways. The explicit method for this is remove(), which takes the index of the item that should be removed. The remaining items that were positioned after the removed item are then shifted to the left to fill in the gap. This same behavior is also available using a del sequence[index] statement.

Implementing remove() is straightforward enough, given that it's an explicit method call. The simple case for del works just like remove(), but using a __delitem__() method instead. In fact, if deleting a single item was all that mattered, you could simply assign an existing remove() method to the __delitem__ attribute, and it would work as expected. Unfortunately, slicing complicates matters slightly.

Deleting items from a slice works just like the first portion of the slicing behavior of __setitem__(). Instead of replacing the items in the slice with a new sequence, though, the sequence should simply shift its items to close up the gap.

With all the different ways to make changes to the contents of a sequence, the last—but not least—important feature is to test whether an item is a part of the given sequence. By default, Python will simply iterate over the sequence—using the techniques listed previously in the section on iterables—until it either finds the item being tested or exhausts all the values provided by the iterator. This allows a membership test to be performed on iterables of any type, without being limited to full sequences.

In order to be more efficient, sequences can override this behavior as well, by providing a __contains__() method. Its signature looks like __getitem__(), but rather than accepting an index, it accepts an object and returns True if the given object is present in the sequence or False otherwise. In the Range example examined previously, the result of __contains__() can be calculated on the fly, based on the configuration of the object.

```python
class Range:
    def __init__(self, a, b=None, step=1):
        """
        Define a range according to a starting value, an end value and a step.

        If only one argument is provided, it's taken to be the end value. If
        two arguments are passed in, the first becomes a start value, while the
        second is the end value. An optional step can be provided to control
        how far apart each value is from the next.
        """
        if b is not None:
            self.start = a
            self.end = b
        else:
            self.start = 0
            self.end = a
        self.step = step

    def __contains__(self, num):
        return self.start <= num < self.end and \
               not (num - self.start) % self.step

>>> list(range(5, 30, 7))
[5, 12, 19, 26]
>>> 5 in Range(5, 30, 7)
True
>>> 10 in Range(5, 30, 7)
False
```

```
>>> 33 in Range(5, 30, 7)
False
```

Many of the methods presented here for sequences are also valid for the next container type, which maps a collection of keys to associated values.

Mappings

While sequences are contiguous collections of objects, mappings work a bit differently. In a mapping, the individual items are actually a pair, consisting of both a key and a value. Keys don't have to be ordered because iterating over them isn't generally the point. Instead, the goal is to provide immediate access to the value referenced by a given key. The key is typically known in advance, and most common usage expects it.

Accessing a value by its key uses the same syntax as using indexes in sequences. In fact, Python doesn't know or care if you're implementing a sequence, a mapping or something completely different. The same methods, __getitem__(), __setitem__() and __delitem__() are reused to support the obj[key] syntax, regardless of which type of object is used. That doesn't mean the implementations of these methods can be identical, though.

For a mapping, a key is used in place of an index. Even though there's no difference in syntax between the two, keys support a wider range of allowed objects. In addition to plain integers, a key may be any hashable Python object, such as dates, times or strings; of these, strings are by far the most common. It's up to your application, though, to decide whether there should be any limitations on what keys to accept.

Python supports so much flexibility, in fact, that you can even use the standard slicing syntax without regard to what values are involved in the slice. Python simply passes along whatever objects were referenced in the slice, so it's up to the mapping to decide how to deal with them. By default, lists handle slices by explicitly looking for integers, using __index__() if necessary to coerce objects into integers. For dictionaries, on the other hand, slice objects aren't hashable, so dictionaries don't allow them to be used as keys.

■ **Tip** For the most part, you can accept anything in a custom dictionary, even if you intend to use only a specific type, such as strings, as your keys. As long as it only gets used in your own code, it won't make any difference because you're in control of all its uses. If you make modifications that prove to be useful outside of your application, other developers will make use of it for their own needs. Therefore, you should restrict the available keys and values only if you really need to; otherwise, it's best to leave options open, even for yourself.

Even though this chapter hasn't generally covered any methods that are called directly as part of the public interface, mappings have three methods that provide particularly useful access to internal components, which should always be implemented. These methods are necessary because mappings essentially contain two separate collections—keys and values—which are then joined together by association, while sequences only contain a single collection.

The first of these extra methods, keys(), iterates over all the keys in the mapping, without regard to their values. By default, the keys can be returned in any order, but some more specialized classes could choose to provide an explicit order for these keys. This same behavior is provided by iteration over the mapping object itself, so be sure to always supply an __iter__() method that does the same thing as keys().

The next method, values(), is complementary, iterating over the values side of the mapping instead. Like the keys, these values generally aren't assumed to be in any sort of order. In practice, the C implementation of Python uses the same order as it does for the keys, but order is never guaranteed, even between the keys and values of the same object.

In order to reliably get all the keys and values in their associated pairs, mappings provide an items() method. This iterates over the entire collection, yielding each pair as a tuple in the form of (key, value). Because this is often more efficient than iterating over the keys and using mapping[key] to get the associated value, all mappings should provide an items() method and make it as efficient as possible.

Compatibility: Prior to 3.0

In older versions of Python, the keys(), values() and items() methods were expected to return lists of values rather than an iterable that would yield them. The iterable behavior was instead provided by alternate methods, prefixed with iter—iterkeys(), itervalues() and iteritems(). Python 3.0 changed the focus of most methods to iterate over values wherever possible, so these mapping methods now iterate directly, and the iter companion methods are no longer available.

Callables

In Python, both functions and classes can be called to execute code at any time, but those aren't the only objects that can do so. In fact, any Python class can be made callable by simply attaching a single extra method to the class definition. This method, appropriately named __call__(), accepts the usual self along with any arguments that should be passed along in the function call.

There are no special requirements for what arguments __call__() can accept because it works like any other function when it's being called. The only difference is that it also receives the object it's attached to as the first argument.

```
>>> class CallCounter:
...     def __init__(self):
...         self.count = 0
...     def __call__(self, *args, **kwargs):
...         self.count += 1
...         return 'Number of calls so far: %s' % self.count
...     def reset(self):
...         self.count = 0
...
>>> counter = CallCounter()
>>> counter()
'Number of calls so far: 1'
>>> counter()
'Number of calls so far: 2'
>>> counter()
'Number of calls so far: 3'
>>> counter.reset()
>>> counter()
'Number of calls so far: 1'
```

■ **Caution** As a function itself, __call__() can also be decorated any number of times, but remember that it's still a method, even though it gets used by calling the object directly. As a method, any decorators applied to it must be able to deal with the first argument being an instance of the object.

As for what __call__() can do, the sky is the limit. Its purpose is solely to allow an object to be callable; what happens during that call depends entirely on the needs at hand. This example shows that it can also take any additional arguments you may need, like any other function. Its greatest strength, though, is that it allows you to essentially provide a function that can be customized on its own, without the need for any decorators.

Context Managers

As mentioned briefly in Chapter 2, objects can also be used as context managers for use in a with statement. This allows an object to define what it means to work within the context of that object, setting things up prior to executing the contained code and cleaning up after execution has finished.

One common example is file handling, because a file must be opened for a specific type of access before it can be used. Then it also needs to be closed when it's no longer in use, to flush any pending changes to disk. This makes sure other code can open the same file later on, without conflicting with any open references. What happens between those two operations is said to be executed within the context of the open file.

As mentioned, there are two distinct steps to be performed by a context manager. First, the context needs to be initialized, so that the code that executes inside the with block can make use of the features provided by the context. Just prior to execution of the interior code block, Python will call the __enter__() method on the object. This method doesn't receive any additional arguments, just the instance object itself. Its responsibility is then to provide the necessary initialization for the code block, whether that means modifying the object itself or making global changes.

If the with statement includes an as clause, the return value of the __enter__() method will be used to populate the variable referenced in that clause. It's important to realize that the object itself won't necessarily be that value, even though it may seem that way looking at the syntax for the with statement. Using the return value of __enter__() allows the context object to be more flexible, though that behavior can be achieved by simply returning self.

Once the code inside the with block finishes executing, Python will call the __exit__() method on the object. This method is then responsible for cleaning up any changes that were made during __enter__(), returning the context to whatever it was prior to processing the with statement. In the case of files, this would mean closing the file automatically, but it could be virtually anything.

Of course, there are a few ways that execution within the with block can complete. The most obvious is if the code simply finishes on its own, without any problems or other flow control. Statements such as return, yield, continue and break can also interrupt execution of the code block, in which case __exit__() will still be called because the cleanup is still necessary. In fact, even if an exception is raised, __exit__() is still given a chance to reverse any changes that were applied during __enter__().

In order to identify whether the code finished normally or stopped early by way of an exception, the __exit__() method will be given three additional arguments. The first is the class object for the exception that was raised, followed by the instance of that class, which is what was actually raised in the code. Lastly, __exit__() will also receive a traceback object, representing the state of execution as of when the exception was raised.

All three of those arguments are always passed in, so any implementations of __exit__() must accept them all. If execution completed without raising any exceptions, the arguments will still be provided, but their values will simply be **None**. Having access to both the exception and a traceback allows your implementation of __exit__() to intelligently react to whatever went wrong and what led to the problem.

■ **Tip** The __exit__() method doesn't suppress any exceptions on its own. If __exit__() completes without a return value, the original exception, if any, will be re-raised automatically. If you need to explicitly catch any errors that occur within the **with** block, simply return **True** from __exit__() instead of letting it fall off the end, which would return an implicit **None**.

To show one simple example, consider a class that uses context management to silence any exceptions that are raised within the with block. In this case, __enter__() doesn't need to do anything because the exception handling will be done in __exit__().

```
>>> class SuppressErrors:
...     def __init__(self, *exceptions):
...         if not exceptions:
...             exceptions = (Exception,)
...         self.exceptions = exceptions
...     def __enter__(self):
...         pass
...     def __exit__(self, exc_class, exc_instance, traceback):
...         if isinstance(exc_instance, self.exceptions):
...             return True
...         return False
...
>>> with SuppressErrors():
...     1 / 0  # Raises a ZeroDivisionError
...
>>> with SuppressErrors(IndexError):
...     a = [1, 2, 3]
...     print(a[4])
...
>>> with SuppressErrors(KeyError):
...     a = [1, 2, 3]
...     print(a[4])
...
Traceback (most recent call last):
  ...
IndexError: list index out of range
```

Taking It With You

There is perhaps one thing that is most important to understand about all the protocols listed in this chapter: they aren't mutually exclusive. It's possible—and sometimes very advantageous—to implement multiple protocols on a single object. For example, a sequence can also be used as a callable and a context manager if each of those behaviors makes sense for a given class.

While this chapter deals primarily with the behaviors of objects, as provided by their classes, the next will cover how you can manage those objects and their data once they've been instantiated in working code.

CHAPTER 6

■ ■ ■

Object Management

Creating an instance of a class is only the beginning; once you have an object, there are a number of things you can do with it. This is obvious, of course, because objects have methods and attributes that are intended to control their behavior, but those are defined by each class. Objects, as a whole, have an additional set of features that allow you to manage them in a number of different ways.

In order to understand these features, it's first necessary to understand what actually constitutes an object. At a high level, an object is simply the product of data and behavior, but internally, Python considers an object to be a combination of three specific things:

- Identity—Each object is unique, with an identity that can be used to compare objects to each other without having to look at any other details. This comparison, using the is operator, is very strict, though, without access to any of the subtleties outlined in Chapter 5. In actual implementations, an object's identity is simply its address in memory, so no two objects can ever have the same identity.

- Type—The subject of the previous two chapters, an object's type is defined by its class and any base classes that support it. Unlike identity, a type is shared among all of its instances; each object simply contains a references to its class.

- Value—With a shared type to provide behavior, each object also has a value that makes it distinct among its peers. This value is provided by a namespace dictionary that's specific to a given object, where any aspect of its individuality can be stored and retrieved. This is different from the identity, though, because the value is designed to work with the type to do useful things; identity is unrelated to the type at all, so it doesn't have anything to do with the behaviors specified for the class.

These three pieces can be referenced and, in some cases, changed to suit the needs of an application. An object's identity can't be modified at any time, so its value is constant for the life of the object. The identity is also unique throughout the life of the object, but once the object is destroyed, its identity can—and often will—be reused for a future object, which then retains that identity until the object is destroyed.

If you want to retrieve an identity at any time, you can pass the object into the built-in id() function because the object itself doesn't know anything about its identity. In fact, the identity isn't related to anything specific to the object; none of its attributes have any bearing on its identity. Therefore, you won't get the same identity if you instantiate what would otherwise be an identical object.

Types have been covered thoroughly in the previous two chapters, so the next obvious component is the value, which is implemented by way of a namespace dictionary.

Namespace Dictionary

As hinted at previously, an object's namespace is implemented as a dictionary that's created for each new object as it's being instantiated. This is then used to store values for all the attributes on the object, thus comprising the value for the object as a whole.

Unlike the identity, though, this namespace dictionary can be accessed and modified at run-time, as it's available as the __dict__ attribute on an object. In fact, since it's an attribute, it can even be replaced with a new dictionary altogether. This is the basis of what's commonly referred to as the Borg pattern, named after the collective consciousness from the Star Trek universe.

Example: Borg Pattern

Like its namesake, the Borg pattern allows a large number of instances to share a single namespace. In this way, the identity for each object remains distinct, but its attributes—and thus, its behaviors—are always the same as all of its peers. This primarily allows a class to be used in applications where it could be instantiated several times, with potential modifications made to it each time. By using the Borg pattern, these changes can be accumulated in a single namespace, so each instance reflects all the changes that have been made to each object.

This is achieved by attaching a dictionary to the class, then assigning that dictionary to the namespace of each object as it's being instantiated. As Chapter 4 demonstrated, there are two opportunities available for behaviors like this: __init__() and __new__(). Since both methods execute during instantiation of the object, they seem to be equally viable options, but let's take a look at how they would each work.

The __init__() method is the usual place to start because it's much better understood and more widely adopted. This method typically initializes instance attributes, so the dictionary assignment would need to take place prior to any other initialization. That's easy enough to do, though, by simply placing it at the beginning of the method. Here's how this would work.

```
>>> class Borg:
...     _namespace = {}
...     def __init__(self):
...         self.__dict__ = Borg._namespace
...         # Do more interesting stuff here.
...
>>> a = Borg()
>>> b = Borg()
>>> hasattr(a, 'attribute')
False
>>> b.attribute = 'value'
>>> hasattr(a, 'attribute')
True
>>> a.attribute
'value'
>>> Borg._namespace
{'attribute': 'value'}
```

This certainly does the job, but there are a few pitfalls with the approach, particularly when you start working with inheritance. All subclasses would need to make sure they use super() in order to call the initialization procedures from the Borg class. If any subclass fails to do so, it won't use the shared namespace, nor will any of its subclasses, even if they do use super(). Further, subclasses should use `super()` before doing any attribute assignments of their own. Otherwise, those assignments will get overwritten by the shared namespace.

That only applies when Borg is applied to other classes that know about it, though. The problem is even more pronounced when working with **Borg** as a mixin, because it would get applied alongside classes that don't know about it—and they shouldn't have to. But since they can get combined anyway, it's worth examining what would happen.

```
>>> class Base:
...     def __init__(self):
...         print('Base')
...
>>> class Borg:
...     _namespace = {}
...     def __init__(self, *args, **kwargs):
...         self.__dict__ = Borg._namespace
...         print('Borg')
...
>>> class Testing(Borg, Base):
...     pass
...
>>> Testing()
Borg
<__main__.Testing object at 0x...>
>>> class Testing(Base, Borg):
...     pass
...
>>> Testing()
Base
<__main__.Testing object at 0x...>
```

As you can see, this exhibits the typical problem when not using **super()**, where the order of base classes can completely exclude the behaviors of one or more of them. The solution, of course, is to just use **super()**, but in the case of mixins, you typically don't have control over both the classes involved. Adding **super()** would suffice in the case of **Borg** coming before its peer, but mixins are usually applied after their peers, so it doesn't really help much.

With all this in mind, it's worth considering the alternative __new__() method. All methods are vulnerable to the same types of problems that were shown for __init__(), but at least we can reduce the chance of collisions that would cause those problems. Since the __new__() method is less commonly implemented, the odds of running into conflicting implementations are much smaller.

When implementing the **Borg** pattern with __new__(), the object must be created along the way, usually by calling __new__() on the base **object**. In order to play nicely with other classes as a mixin, though, it's still better to use **super()** here as well. Once the object is created, we can replace its namespace dictionary with one for the entire class.

```
>>> class Base:
...     def __init__(self):
...         print('Base')
...
>>> class Borg:
...     _namespace = {}
...     def __new__(cls, *args, **kwargs):
```

```
...            print('Borg')
...            obj = super(Borg, cls).__new__(cls, *args, **kwargs)
...            obj.__dict__ = cls._namespace
...            return obj
...
>>> class Testing(Borg, Base):
...     pass
...
>>> Testing()
Borg
Base
<__main__.Testing object at 0x...>
>>> class Testing(Base, Borg):
...     pass
...
>>> Testing()
Borg
Base
<__main__.Testing object at 0x...>
>>> a = Testing()
Borg
Base
>>> b = Testing()
Borg
Base
>>> a.attribute = 'value'
>>> b.attribute
'value'
```

Now **Borg** comes first in the most common situations, without any unusual requirements on any classes that operate alongside them. There's still one problem with this implementation, though, and it's not very obvious from this example. As a mixin, **Borg** could be applied in any class definition, and you might expect that its namespace behavior would be limited to that defined class and its subclasses.

Unfortunately, that's not what would happen. Because the **_namespace** dictionary is on **Borg** itself, it'll be shared among all the classes that inherit from **Borg** at all. In order to break that out and apply it only to those classes where **Borg** is applied, a slightly different technique is necessary.

Since the **__new__()** method receives the class as its first positional argument, the Borg mixin can use that object as a namespace on its own, thereby splitting up the managed dictionary into individual namespaces, with one for each class that's used. In a nutshell, **Borg.__new__()** must create a new dictionary for each new class it encounters, assigning it to a value in the existing **_namespace** dictionary, using the class object as its key.

```
>>> class Borg:
...     _namespace = {}
...     def __new__(cls, *args, **kwargs):
...         obj = super(Borg, cls).__new__(cls, *args, **kwargs)
...         obj.__dict__ = cls._namespace.setdefault(cls, {})
...         return obj
...
>>> class TestOne(Borg):
...     pass
```

```
...
>>> class TestTwo(Borg):
...     pass
...
>>> a = TestOne()
>>> b = TestOne()
>>> a.spam = 'eggs'
>>> b.spam
'eggs'
>>> c = TestTwo()
>>> c.spam
Traceback (most recent call last):
  ...
AttributeError: 'TestTwo' object has no attribute 'spam'
>>> c.spam = 'burger'
>>> d = TestTwo()
>>> d.spam
'burger'
>>> a.spam
'eggs'
```

As you can see, by using cls a kind of namespace of its own, we can compartmentalize the managed values on a per-class basis. All instances of TestOne share the same namespace, while all instances of TestTwo share a separate namespace, so there's never any overlap between the two.

Example: Self-caching properties

Even though attributes are the primary means of accessing an object's namespace dictionary, remember from Chapter 4 that attribute access can be customized using special methods, such as __getattr__() and __setattr__(). Those methods are what Python actually uses when accessing an attribute, and it's up to those methods to look things up in the namespace dictionary internally. If you were to define them in pure Python, they'd look a lot like this:

```python
class object:
    def __getattr__(self, name):
        try:
            return self.__dict__[name]
        except KeyError:
            raise AttributeError('%s object has no attribute named %s' % (
                self.__class__.__module__, name))

    def __setattr__(self, name, value):
        self.__dict__[name] = value

    def __delattr__(self, name):
        try:
            del self.__dict__[name]
        except KeyError:
            raise AttributeError('%s object has no attribute named %s' % (
                self.__class__.__module__, name))
```

As you can see, every access to the attribute performs a lookup in the namespace, raising an error if it wasn't there. This means that in order to retrieve an attribute, its value must have been created and stored previously. For most cases, this behavior is appropriate, but in some cases, the attribute's value can be a complex object that's expensive to create, and it might not get used very often, so it's not very advantageous to create it along with its host object.

One common example of this situation is an Object-Relational Mapper (ORM) sitting between application code and a relational database. When retrieving information about a person, for instance, you'd get a Person object in Python. That person might also have a spouse, children, a house, an employer or even a wardrobe filled with clothing, all of which could also be represented in the database as related to the person you've retrieved.

If we were to access all of that information as attributes, the simple approach described previously would require all of that data to be pulled out of the database every time a person is retrieved. Then, all of that data must be collected into separate objects for each of the types of data: Person, House, Company, Clothing and probably a host of others. Worse yet, each of those related objects has other relationships that would be accessible as attributes, which can quickly seem like you need to load up the entire database every time a query is made.

Instead, the obvious solution is to load that information only when requested. By keeping track of a unique identifier for the person, along with a set of queries that know how to retrieve the related information, methods can be added that will be able to retrieve that information when necessary.

Unfortunately, methods are expected to perform their task every time they're called. If you need the person's employer, for example, you'd have to call a Person.get_employer() method, which would make a query in the database and return the result. If you call the method again, another query is made, even though it's often unnecessary. This could be avoided by storing the employer as a separate variable, which could be reused instead of calling the method again, but that doesn't hold up once you start passing the Person object around to different functions that might have different needs.

Instead, a more preferable solution would be to make an attribute that starts out with as little information as possible—perhaps even none at all. Then, when that attribute is accessed, the database query is made, returning the appropriate object. This related object can then be stored in the main object's namespace dictionary, where it can be accessed directly later on, without having to hit the database again.

Querying a database when accessing an attribute is a fairly easy task, actually. Applying the @property decorator to a method will produce the desired effect, calling the function whenever the attribute is accessed. Caching its return value requires a bit more finesse, though, but it's really fairly simple: simply overwrite the existing value if there's already one in the object's namespace or create a new one otherwise.

This could be simply added into the behavior of an existing property, as it only requires a few extra lines of code to support. Here's all it would take:

```python
class Example:
    @property
    def attribute(self):
        if 'attribute' not in self.__dict__:
            # Do the real work of retrieving the value
            self.__dict__['attribute'] = value
        return self.__dict__['attribute']
```

■ **Caution** When caching property values like this, be careful to check that the computed value shouldn't change based on the value of other attributes. Computing a full name based on first and last names, for example, is a poor candidate for caching because changing the first name or last name should change the value of the full name as well; caching would prevent that behavior.

Notice, though, that this really just performs a little work before the real code and a little bit afterward, making it an ideal task for a decorator. Here's what that decorator could look like:

```
import functools

def cachedproperty(name):
    def decorator(func):
        @property
        @functools.wraps(func)
        def wrapper(self):
            if name not in self.__dict__:
                self.__dict__[name] = func(self)
            return self.__dict__[name]
        return wrapper
    return decorator
```

Once applied to a function, `cachedproperty()` will work like a standard property, but with the caching behavior applied automatically. The one difference you'll notice, though, is that you must supply the name of the attribute as an argument to `cachedproperty()` in addition to naming the function that you're decorating. Here's how it would look:

```
>>> class Example:
...     @cachedproperty('attr')
...     def attr(self):
...         print('Getting the value!')
...         return 42
...
>>> e = Example()
>>> e.attr
Getting the value!
42
>>> e.attr
42
```

Why must the name be supplied twice? The problem, as mentioned in previous chapters, is that descriptors, including properties, don't get access to the names they're given. Since the cached value is stored in the object namespace according to the name of the attribute, we need a way to pass that name into the property itself. This is a clear violation of DRY, though, so let's see what other techniques are available and what their pitfalls would be.

One option would be to store a dictionary on the cached property descriptor directly, using object instances as keys. Each descriptor would get a unique dictionary, and each key would be a unique object, so you'd be able to store as many values as you have objects that have the attribute attached.

```python
def cachedproperty(func):
    values = {}

    @property
    @functools.wraps(func)
    def wrapper(self):
        if self not in values:
            values[self] = func(self)
        return values[self]
    return wrapper
```

This new decorator allows you to cache an attribute without having to specify the name. If you're skeptical about it, though, you might wonder about storing those values in a single dictionary for all objects, without referencing the name of the attribute. After all, that would seem to mean that if you had more than one cached property on a single object, their values would overwrite each other and you'd have all sorts of confusion.

That's not a problem in this situation, though, because the dictionary is created inside of the cachedproperty() function, which means each property gets its own private namespace. This way, there's no chance of collision, no matter how many cached properties you place on an object. The dictionary will be shared only if you assign an existing property to a new name without redefining it. In that case, the second name should always behave exactly like the first, and the cache described here will still maintain that behavior.

However, there is one other problem with this property that may not be so obvious. Believe it or not, this contains a memory leak, which could be severely harmful if it gets used in a large part of an application without being fixed.

In some cases, the best fix will be to simply go back to the first form described in this chapter, where the attribute's name is provided explicitly. Since the name isn't provided to a descriptor, this approach would require the use of a metaclass. Of course, metaclasses are overkill for simple situations like this, but in cases where a metaclass is used for other reasons anyway, having the name available can be quite useful. Chapter 11 showcases a framework that uses the metaclass approach to great effect.

In order to avoid using a metaclass, it's first necessary to understand what the memory leak is, why it's happening and how we can avoid it. It all has to do with how Python removes objects from memory when they're no longer in use, a process called garbage collection.

Garbage Collection

Unlike lower-level languages like C, Python doesn't require you to manage your own memory usage. You don't have to claim a certain amount of memory for an object or remove your claim on that memory when the object is no longer needed. In fact, you often don't even need to worry about how much memory an object will take up or how to determine when it's no longer needed. Python handles those gritty details behind the scenes.

Collection is easy to understand: Python deletes any objects that are identified as garbage, clearing whatever memory they were using so that memory is available for other objects. Without this process, every object created would stay in memory forever, and you'd slowly—or quickly—run out of memory, at which point everything comes to a grinding halt.

As you probably noticed, effective garbage collection first requires the ability to reliably identify an object as garbage. Even with the ability to remove garbage from memory, failing to recognize garbage will cause memory leaks to creep into an application. The last example in the previous section contains a simple situation that can cause Python to not notice when an object becomes garbage, so we need to examine how that gets determined.

Reference Counting

At a high level, an object is considered garbage when it's no longer accessible by any code. In order to determine whether an object is accessible, Python counts how many data structures refer to the object at any given time.

The most obvious way to reference an object is to assign it to any namespace, including modules, classes, objects and even dictionaries. Other types of references include any kind of container object, such as a list, tuple or set. Even less obvious is that every function has its own namespace, which can contain references to objects, even in the case of closures. Essentially, anything that provides access to an object increases its reference count. In turn, removing an object from such a container decreases its reference count.

To illustrate, here are a few examples of situations that would create new references:

```
>>> a = [1, 2, 3]
>>> b = {'example': a}
>>> c = a
```

After executing these three lines of code, there are now three references to the list [1, 2, 3]. Two of them are fairly obvious, when it was assigned to a and later reassigned to c. The dictionary at b also has a reference to that list, though, as the value of its 'example' key. That dictionary, in turn, has just one reference, having been assigned as the value of b.

The del statement is perhaps the most obvious way to remove a reference to an object, but it's not the only option. If you replace a reference to one object with a reference to another, you'll also implicitly remove the reference to the first object. For example, if we were to run these two lines of code, we end with just one reference to the list shown as a.

```
>>> del c
>>> a = None
```

Even though it's no longer available in the root namespace, that list is still available as part of the dictionary, which itself is still accessible as b. Therefore, they each have just one reference, and neither will be garbage collected. If you were to del b right now, the reference count for the dictionary becomes zero and will be eligible for garbage collection. Once that's been collected, the reference count for the list is reduced to zero and is collected as garbage.

■ **Tip** By default, Python simply clears out the memory that was occupied by the object. You don't need to do anything in order to support that behavior and it works just fine for most cases. In the rare event that an object has some special needs to address when it's deleted, the __del__() method can provide this customization.

Instead of deleting objects, there are a number of other things you can do with them as well. Here's a look at a very different situation that can alter the way reference counting works.

Cyclical References

Consider the scenario where you have a dictionary that refers to a list as one of its values. Because lists are containers as well, you could actually append the dictionary as a value to the list. What you end up with is a cyclical reference, where each object refers to the other. To extend the previous examples, let's examine what would happen with this line of code:

```
>>> b['example'].append(b)
```

Prior to this, the dictionary and the list had one reference each, but now the dictionary gains another reference by being included as a member of the inner list. This situation will work just fine in normal operation, but it does present an interesting problem when it comes to garbage collection.

Remember that using `del b` would decrease the reference count of the dictionary by one, but now that the list also contains a reference to that same dictionary, its reference count goes from two to one, rather than dropping to zero. With a reference count above zero, the dictionary wouldn't be considered garbage and it would stay in memory, along with its reference to the list. Therefore, the list also has a reference count of one, keeping it in memory.

What's the problem here? Well, after you delete the reference at the variable **b**, the references those two objects have to each other are now the only references they have in the entire Python interpreter. They're completely cut off from any code that will continue executing, but because garbage collection uses reference counts, they'll stay in memory forever unless something else is done.

To address this, Python's garbage collection comes with code designed to spot these structures when they occur, so they can be removed from memory as well. Any time a set of objects is referenced only by other objects in that set—and not from anywhere else in memory—it's flagged as a reference cycle. This allows the garbage collection system to reclaim the memory it was using.

Things start to get really tricky when you implement `__del__()`, though. Ordinarily, `__del__()` works just fine because Python can intelligently figure out when to delete the object. Therefore, `__del__()` can be executed in a predictable manner, even when multiple objects are deleted within a short span.

When Python encounters a reference cycle that's inaccessible from any other code, it doesn't know the order to delete the objects in that cycle. This becomes a problem with the custom `__del__()` method because it could act on related objects as well. If one object is part of an orphaned reference cycle, any related objects are all also scheduled for deletion, so which one should fire first?

After all, each object in the cycle could reference one or more of the other objects in that same cycle. Without an object to definitively be considered first, Python would have to simply guess which one should be first. Unfortunately, that leads to behavior that is not only unpredictable but also unreliable across the many times it could occur.

Therefore, Python has to take one of only two predictable, reliable courses of action. One option would be to simply ignore the `__del__()` method and delete the object just as it would if the `__del__()` method wasn't found. Unfortunately, that changes the behavior of the object based on things outside that object's control.

The other option, which Python does take, is to leave the object in memory. This avoids the problem of trying to order a variety of `__del__()` methods while maintaining the behavior of the object itself. The problem, though, is that this is in fact a memory leak, and it's only there because Python can't make a reliable assumption about your intentions.

In the face of ambiguity, refuse the temptation to guess

This situation with __del__() in a cyclical reference is a perfect example of ambiguity because there's no clear way to handle the situation. Rather than guess, Python sidesteps it by simply leaving the objects in memory. It's not the most memory-efficient way to address the problem, but consistency is far more important in situations like this. Even though it potentially means more work for the programmer, that extra work results in much more explicit, reliable behavior.

There are three ways you can avoid this problem. First, you can avoid having any objects with __del__() methods involved in any cyclical references. The easiest way to accomplish that is to avoid the __del__() method entirely. Most of the common reasons to customize an object's teardown are more appropriately handled using a context manager.

In those rare cases where __del__() proves necessary, the second option is to simply avoid having the objects appear in reference cycles. That's not always easy to do, though, because it requires you to have complete control over all the ways the object might be used. That might work for some highly internalized implementation details, but if it's part of a public interface, it's probably not an option.

Lastly, if you can't prevent the cycles from being orphaned, Python does provide a way that you can still detect them and have a chance to clean them up on a regular basis. Once all other references are removed and the garbage collection cycle runs, Python keeps the entire cycle alive by placing each object involved into a special list, available in the gc module.

The gc module provides a few options that are useful for getting into the guts of the garbage collection system, but the factor at hand here is the garbage attribute. This attribute contains objects that are otherwise unreachable but are part of a cycle that includes __del__() somewhere along the line. Accessing them as part of gc.garbage allows you to try to break the cycle after the fact, which will allow their memory to be relinquished.

Consider the following example, which also shows the usage of gc.collect(), a module-level function that manually runs the garbage collector, so that cyclical references are detected and placed in gc.garbage accordingly.

```
>>> import gc
>>> class Example:
...     def __init__(self, value):
...         self.value = value
...     def __repr__(self):
...         return 'Example %s' % self.value
...     def __del__(self):
...         print('Deleting %r' % self)
...
>>> e = Example(1)
>>> e
Example 1
>>> del e
>>> gc.collect()
Deleting Example 1
0

# Now let's try it with a cyclical reference
```

```
>>> e = Example(2)
>>> e.attr = e
>>> del e
>>> gc.collect()
2
>>> gc.garbage
[Example 2]

# From here, we can break the cycle and remove it from memory

>>> e = gc.garbage[0]
>>> del e.attr
>>> del e
>>> gc.collect()
0
>>> gc.garbage
[Example 2]

# Don't forget to clear out gc.garbage as well

>>> gc.garbage[:] = []
Deleting Example 2
>>> gc.garbage
[]
```

In the real world, though, __del__() is rarely needed, and it's even more rare to run into very severe problems with cyclical references. Far more common, however, is the need to adjust how references themselves are created and what to do when you don't really need a reference all your own.

Weak References

As we've seen, assigning an object creates a reference to it, and those references keep that object alive in memory. But what happens when you need to access an object but you don't care to keep it alive? For this, Python provides the concept of a weak reference: you get a reference to the object without increasing its reference count.

By getting a reference without increasing the object's reference count, you can perform operations on that object without getting in the way of how it would ordinarily be deleted. This can be very important for applications that register objects for use later. The registry itself keeps references to all the registered objects, which ordinarily wouldn't get deleted, because the application that knows about the object typically doesn't know anything about the registration system.

Creating a weak reference is fairly simple, thanks to the weakref module in the standard library. The ref() class within that module creates a weak reference to whatever object is passed into it, allowing that reference to be used later. To provide access to the original object, a weak reference is a callable object that takes no arguments and returns the object.

In order to see what was supposed to happen, we have to first store a reference to that object outside the weak reference. That way, we can not only create a weak reference that has access to the object but we can then delete the additional reference to see how the weak reference behaves.

```
>>> import weakref
>>> class Example:
...     pass
```

```
...
>>> e = Example()
>>> e
<__main__.Example object at 0x...>
>>> ref = weakref.ref(e)
>>> ref
<weakref at ...; to 'Example' at ...>
>>> ref()
<__main__.Example object at 0x...>

>>> del e

>>> ref
<weakref at ...; dead>
>>> ref()
>>>
```

As you can see, as long as there's at least one other reference keeping the object alive, the weak reference has easy access to it. Once the object is deleted elsewhere, the weak reference object itself is still available, but it simply returns **None** when called. We could make the example even simpler as well, by passing a new object directly into the weak reference.

```
>>> ref = weakref.ref(Example())
>>> ref
<weakref at ...; dead>
>>> ref()
>>>
```

Wait, what just happened? Where did the **Example** object go? This simple example illustrates one of the most common problems you're likely to encounter with weak references. Because you're instantiating the object as part of the call to **ref()**, the only reference that gets created for that object is inside of **ref()**.

Ordinarily, that would be fine, but that particular reference doesn't help keep the object alive, so the object is immediately marked for garbage collection. The weak reference provides access to the object only if there's something else to keep it alive, so in this case, the reference simply returns **None** when called. That situation may seem obvious, but there are a few others that may come up when you least expect them.

One such situation that can come up involves creating a weak reference inside of a function.

```
>>> def example():
...     e = Example()
...     ref = weakref.ref(e)
...     return ref
...
>>> e = example()
>>> e
<weakref at ...; dead>
>>> e()
>>>
```

As you can see, even though the **example()** function stores a strong reference inside itself, the weak reference goes dead immediately. The problem here is that every function gets a brand new namespace every time it executes, and it's deleted when the function finishes, because execution is the only thing keeping it alive.

By default, all assignments in the function take place in that namespace, so once it's destroyed, any objects assigned are destroyed as well unless they have references stored elsewhere. In this case, the only other reference to the **Example** object is weak, so the object gets destroyed once the **example()** function returns.

The recurring theme here is that weak references can cause problems when used along with any kind of implicit reference removal. We've discussed two already, but there are other similar situations as well. For example, a **for** loop automatically assigns at least one variable each time the loop begins, overwriting any values that were previously assigned to the same name. Because that also destroys the reference to whatever object was used in the previous iteration, a weak reference created inside the loop isn't enough to keep that object alive.

Pickling

So far, we've only discussed how objects are handled inside of Python, but it's often necessary to exchange data with external processes, such as files, databases and network protocols. Most of the time, the structure of that data outside of Python is already established, so your application will need to adhere to that structure. Other times, though, the only reason to send the data into something else is to store it for a while and read it back into Python later.

In this case, the external system really doesn't care what your data is or how it's structured. As long as it's a data type that system can understand, it should be usable. Since the most flexible and widely supported data type is a string, it's necessary to export Python's data structures to strings. For this, Python provides the **pickle** module.

In the real world, pickling is a way of preserving food, so it can be stored for long periods of time and consumed much later. Without preservation techniques like pickling, food would have to be consumed almost immediately after it's produced. The same is true for data: it's easy to consume shortly after it's produced, but saving it for later requires some extra work.

The action of pickling is performed by using the **pickle** module's **dump()** or **dumps()** functions. Both of these functions can take any object as the first argument, but they differ in where they output the string representing that object. In the case of **dump()**, a second required argument specifies a writable file-like object, which the function will use as the destination for the pickled value. The **dumps()** function, on the other hand, simply returns the string directly, allowing the code that called the function to decide where to put it. Beyond that, the two functions are identical, and the examples throughout the rest of this section will use **dumps()**, as it shows the output much more easily.

```
>>> import pickle
>>> pickle.dumps(1)
b'\x80\x03K\x01.'
>>> pickle.dumps(42)
b'\x80\x03K*.'
>>> pickle.dumps('42')
b'\x80\x03X\x02\x00\x00\x0042q\x00.'
```

As you can see, the pickled output can contain more information than the original value, because it also needs to store the type, so the object can be reconstituted later.

Compatibility: Prior to 3.0

Regardless of the value passed in, the pickled string always contains two bytes that tell Python which version of the pickling protocol to use. Because the protocol can change over time, this is a necessary step to ensure compatibility with future versions of Python. In the rare case that you need to pickle an object in one version and need to retrieve that object in a previous version, you can control the version of the protocol Python uses to generate the string.

By passing in a version number as the `protocol` keyword argument, you can help control the compatibility of the output string. The current value of 3 was introduced in Python 3.0; 2 came with Python 2.3 to better support new-style classes; 1 and 0 are from much older versions of Python than you're likely to encounter. By using `protocol=2`, you can exchange data with older versions of Python.

One important thing to remember, though, is that not all object types are available in all Python installations. Each version of Python typically introduces at least a few new types, and third-party libraries account for many more that you need to be aware of. If you pickle an object in one Python setup, an equivalent type needs to be available wherever you hope to unpickle it later.

Once a value has been pickled, the resulting string can be stored or passed around however your application requires. Once it's time to retrieve the object back into Python, the `pickle` module provides two addition functions, `load()` and `loads()`. The difference between the two is similar to the dump functions: `load()` accepts a readable file-like object, while `loads()` accepts a string.

```
>>> pickled = pickle.dumps(42)
>>> pickled
b'\x80\x03K*.'
>>> pickle.loads(pickled)
42
```

Dumping objects into pickled strings and loading them back again are just the external tasks, though. Like in the many protocols described previously, Python allows individual objects to control how they're pickled and restored. Because pickling represents a sort of snapshot of the object at the time it was pickled, these functions are named to refer to the state of the object at a given time.

The first method to consider is `__getstate__()`, which controls what gets included in the pickled value. It doesn't take any additional arguments and returns whatever value Python should include in the pickled output. For complex objects, the value will typically be a dictionary or perhaps a tuple, but it's completely up to each class to define what values are pertinent to the object.

For example, a currency conversion class might contain a number to use as the current amount as well as a string to indicate the currency being represented. In addition, it would likely have access to a dictionary of current exchange rates, so that it can convert the amount to a different currency. If a reference to that dictionary were placed on the object itself, Python would pickle it all together.

```
>>> class Money:
...     def __init__(self, amount, currency):
...         self.amount = amount
...         self.currency = currency
...         self.conversion = {'USD': 1, 'CAD': .95}
...     def __str__(self):
...         return '%.2f %s' % (self.amount, self.currency)
```

```
...     def __repr__(self):
...         return 'Money(%r, %r)' % (self.amount, self.currency)
...     def in_currency(self, currency):
...         ratio = self.conversion[currency] / self.conversion[self.currency]
...         return Money(self.amount * ratio, currency)
...
>>> us_dollar = Money(250, 'USD')
>>> us_dollar
Money(250, 'USD')
>>> us_dollar.in_currency('CAD')
Money(237.5, 'CAD')
>>> pickled = pickle.dumps(us_dollar)
>>> pickled
b'\x80\x03c__main__\nMoney\nq\x00)\x81q\x01}q\x02(X\x08\x00\x00\x00currencyq\x03
X\x03\x00\x00\x00USDq\x04X\x06\x00\x00\x00amountq\x05K\xfaX\n\x00\x00\x00convers
ionq\x06}q]\x07(h\x04Kx01X\x03\x00\x00\x00CADq\x08G?\xeeffffffuub.'
```

As you can see, this is already quite an expansive pickled value, and that's with just having two currencies stored in the dictionary. Since the currency conversion values aren't specific to the instance at hand—and they'll change over time anyway—there's no reason to store them in the pickled string, so we can use __getstate__() to provide just those values that are actually important.

If you look closely at the pickled output of the existing **Money** object, you'll notice that the attribute names are also included because Python doesn't know if they're important. In lieu of any explicit instructions from __getstate__(), it includes as much information as possible, to be sure the object can be re-created later. Because we already know that there are just two values that are necessary, we can return just those two values as a tuple.

```
>>> class Money:
...     def __init__(self, amount, currency):
...         self.amount = amount
...         self.currency = currency
...         self.conversion = {'USD': 1, 'CAD': .95}
...     def __str__(self):
...         return '%.2f %s' % (self.amount, self.currency)
...     def __repr__(self):
...         return 'Money(%r, %r)' % (self.amount, self.currency)
...     def __getstate__(self):
...         return self.amount, self.currency
...     def in_currency(self, currency):
...         ratio = self.conversion[currency] / self.conversion[self.currency]
...         return Money(self.amount * ratio, currency)
...
>>> us_dollar = Money(250, 'USD')
>>> us_dollar
Money(250, 'USD')
>>> us_dollar.in_currency('CAD')
Money(237.5, 'CAD')
>>> pickled = pickle.dumps(us_dollar)
>>> pickled
b'\x80\x03c__main__\nMoney\nq\x00)\x81q\x01K\xfaX\x03\x00\x00\x00USDq\x02\x86q\x
03b.'
```

As you can see, this cuts the size of the pickled output to just over a third of what it was before. In addition to being more efficient, it's more practical because it doesn't contain unnecessary information. Other attributes that should avoid being pickled are initialization values, system-specific details and other transient information that's simply related to the object's value, rather than being part of that value directly.

That's only half of the equation, though. Once you have customized the pickled output of an object, it can't be retrieved back into a Python object without also customizing that side of things. After all, by storing the value as a tuple, we've removed some of the hints Python used to rebuild the object, so we have to provide an alternative.

As you might have guessed, the complement to __getstate__() is __setstate__(). The __setstate__() method accepts just one additional argument: the state of the object to restore. Since __getstate__() can return any object to represent state, there's no specific type that will also be passed into __setstate__(). It's not at all random, though; the value passed into __setstate__() will be exactly the same value that was returned from __getstate__().

In the case of our currency converter, the state is represented by a 2-tuple containing the amount and currency.

```
>>> class Money:
...     def __init__(self, amount, currency):
...         self.amount = amount
...         self.currency = currency
...         self.conversion = {'USD': 1, 'CAD': .95}
...     def __str__(self):
...         return '%.2f %s' % (self.amount, self.currency)
...     def __repr__(self):
...         return 'Money(%r, %r)' % (self.amount, self.currency)
...     def __getstate__(self):
...         return self.amount, self.currency
...     def __setstate__(self, state):
...         self.amount = state[0]
...         self.currency = state[1]
...     def in_currency(self, currency):
...         ratio = self.conversion[currency] / self.conversion[self.currency]
...         return Money(self.amount * ratio, currency)
...
>>> us_dollar = Money(250, 'USD')
>>> pickled = pickle.dumps(us_dollar)
>>> pickle.loads(pickled)
Money(250, 'USD')
```

And with that, the Money class now fully controls how its value gets pickled and unpickled. That should be the end of it, right? Well, just to be sure, let's test that in_currency() method again because that's an important aspect of its behavior.

```
>>> us_dollar = pickle.loads(pickled)
>>> us_dollar
Money(250, 'USD')
>>> us_dollar.in_currency('CAD')
Traceback (most recent call last):
  ...
AttributeError: 'Money' object has no attribute 'conversion'
```

So why didn't this work? When unpickling an object, Python doesn't call **__init__()** along the way because that step is only supposed to take place when setting up new objects. Since the pickled object was already initialized once before the state was saved, it would usually be wrong to try to initialize it again. Instead, you can include initialization behaviors like that inside of **__setstate__()** to ensure that everything's still in place properly.

```
>>> class Money:
...     def __init__(self, amount, currency):
...         self.amount = amount
...         self.currency = currency
...         self.conversion = self.get_conversions()
...     def __str__(self):
...         return '%.2f %s' % (self.amount, self.currency)
...     def __repr__(self):
...         return 'Money(%r, %r)' % (self.amount, self.currency)
...     def __getstate__(self):
...         return self.amount, self.currency
...     def __setstate__(self, state):
...         self.amount = state[0]
...         self.currency = state[1]
...         self.conversion = self.get_conversions()
...     def get_conversions(self):
...         return {'USD': 1, 'CAD': .95}
...     def in_currency(self, currency):
...         ratio = self.conversion[currency] / self.conversion[self.currency]
...         return Money(self.amount * ratio, currency)
...
>>> us_dollar = Money(250, 'USD')
>>> pickled = pickle.dumps(us_dollar)
>>> pickle.loads(pickled)
Money(250, 'USD')
>>> us_dollar.in_currency('CAD')
Money(237.5, 'CAD')
```

Of course, all of this is only useful if you're copying an object to be stored or sent outside of Python. If all you'll need to do is work with it inside of Python itself, you can simply copy the object internally.

Copying

Mutable objects come with one potentially prominent drawback: changes made to an object are visible from every reference to that object. All mutable objects work this way because of how Python references objects, but that behavior isn't always the most useful. In particular, when working with objects passed in as arguments to a function, the code that called the function will often expect the object to be left unchanged. If the function needs to make modifications in the course of its work, you'll need to take some extra care.

In order to make changes to an object without those changes showing up elsewhere, you'll need to copy the object first. Some objects provide a mechanism for this right out of the box. Lists, for instance, support slicing to retrieve items from the list into a new list. That behavior can be used to get all the items at once, creating a new list with those same items. Simply leave out the start and end values, and the slice will copy the list automatically.

```
>>> a = [1, 2, 3]
>>> b = a[:]
>>> b
[1, 2, 3]
>>> b.append(4)
>>> b
[1, 2, 3, 4]
>>> a
[1, 2, 3]
```

Similarly, dictionaries have their own way to copy their contents, though not using a syntax like lists use. Instead, dictionaries provide a **copy()** method, which returns a new dictionary with all the same keys and values.

```
>>> a = {1: 2, 3: 4}
>>> b = a.copy()
>>> b[5] = 6
>>> b
{1: 2, 3: 4, 5: 6}
>>> a
{1: 2, 3: 4}
```

Not all objects include this type of copying behavior internally, but Python allows you to copy any object, even if it doesn't have its own copying mechanism.

Shallow Copies

To get a copy of any arbitrary object, Python provides a **copy** module. The simplest function available in that module is also named **copy()**, and it provides the same basic behavior as the techniques shown in the previous section. The difference is that, rather than being a method on the object you want to copy, **copy.copy()** allows you to pass in any object and get a shallow copy of it. Not only can you copy a wider variety of objects, you can do so without needing to know anything about the objects themselves.

```
>>> import copy
>>> class Example:
...     def __init__(self, value):
...         self.value = value
...
>>> a = Example('spam')
>>> b = copy.copy(a)
>>> b.value = 'eggs'
>>> a.value
'spam'
>>> b.value
'eggs'
```

Of course, this is just a shallow copy. Remember from the beginning of this chapter that an object is really the combination of three components: an identity, a type and a value. When you make a copy of an object, what you're really doing is creating a new object with the same type, but with a new identity and a new—but identical—value.

For mutable objects, that value typically contains references to other objects, such as the items in a list or the keys and values in a dictionary. The value for the copied object may have a new namespace, but it contains all the same references. Therefore, when you make changes to a member of the copied object, those changes get reflected in all other references to that same object, just like any other namespace. To illustrate, consider a dictionary that contains lists as its values.

```
>>> a = {'a': [1, 2, 3], 'b': [4, 5, 6]}
>>> b = a.copy()
>>> a['a'].append(4)
>>> b['b'].append(7)
>>> a
{'a': [1, 2, 3, 4], 'b': [4, 5, 6, 7]}
>>> b
{'a': [1, 2, 3, 4], 'b': [4, 5, 6, 7]}
```

As you can see, the copy only goes one level deep, so it's considered to be "shallow." Beyond the object's own namespace, only references get copied, not the objects themselves. This is true for all types of objects, not just the lists and dictionaries shown here. In fact, custom objects can even customize this behavior by providing a __copy__() method. The **copy()** function will call __copy__() with no arguments if it exists, so that method can determine which values get copied and how they're handled.

Typically, shallow copies are useful when the first layer is the only part of a value you need to change, particularly when it makes more sense to specifically keep the rest of the objects intact. The basic example case for this is sorting a list, where a new list must be created in order to sort the items, but those items themselves should remain as they were.

To illustrate, consider a custom implementation of Python's built-in **sorted()** method, which sorts the items into a new list, while keeping the original unchanged.

```
>>> def sorted(original_list, key=None):
...     copied_list = copy.copy(original_list)
...     copied_list.sort(key=key)
...     return copied_list
...
>>> a = [3, 2, 1]
>>> b = sorted(a)
>>> a
[3, 2, 1]
>>> b
[1, 2, 3]
```

Of course, this still relies on the object passed in being a list, but it illustrates how shallow copies can be useful. In other situations, you may need to modify the whole structure as deep as you can get.

Deep Copies

It's often necessary for algorithms to need to reorganize data in large structures in order to solve a particular problem. Sorting, indexing, aggregating and rearranging data are all common tasks to perform in these more complex operations. Since the goal is simply to return some analysis of that data, the original structure needs to remain intact. We need a deeper copy than what we've examined so far.

For these situations, Python's **copy** module also contains a **deepcopy()** method, which copies not only the original structure but also the objects that are referenced by it. In fact, it looks recursively through all those objects for any other objects, copying each in turn. This way, you're free to modify the copy however you like, without fear of modifying the original or any modifications to the original being reflected in the copy.

```
>>> original = [[1, 2, 3], [1, 2, 3]]
>>> shallow_copy = copy.copy(original)
>>> deep_copy = copy.deepcopy(original)
>>> original[0].append(4)
>>> shallow_copy
[[1, 2, 3, 4], [1, 2, 3]]
>>> deep_copy
[[1, 2, 3], [1, 2, 3]]
```

It's not truly recursive, though, because full recursion would sometimes make for infinite loops if the data structure had a reference to itself at any time. Once a particular object is copied, Python makes a note of it, so that any future references to that same object can simply be changed to refer to the new object, rather than create a brand new one every time.

Not only does that avoid recursively copying the same object if it's somehow a member of itself, it also means that any time the same object is found more than once in the structure, it'll only be copied once and referenced as many times as necessary. That means the copied structure will have the same behavior as the original with regard to how changes are reflected in referenced objects.

```
>>> a = [1, 2, 3]
>>> b = [a, a]
>>> b
[[1, 2, 3], [1, 2, 3]]
>>> b[0].append(4)
>>> b
[[1, 2, 3, 4], [1, 2, 3, 4]]
>>> c = copy.deepcopy(b)
>>> c
[[1, 2, 3, 4], [1, 2, 3, 4]]
>>> c[0].append(5)
>>> c
[[1, 2, 3, 4, 5], [1, 2, 3, 4, 5]]
```

This is a must for algorithms that rely on objects being present in multiple places of a structure. Each copy will behave the same as the original in that regard, so there's no worry about how many times it gets copied before an algorithm starts working with it.

One other problem that can come up with deep copies is that Python doesn't know what might or might not be important, so it copies everything, which might end up being far more than you need. In order to control that behavior, custom objects can specify the deep copying behavior separately from shallow copies.

By supplying a __deepcopy__() method, an object can specify which values are pertinent to the copy, much like how __getstate__() works for pickling. The biggest difference from __getstate__(), and from __copy__() as well, is that __deepcopy__() also accepts a second argument, which will be a dictionary used to manage the identity of objects during copies. Because the deep copy should only copy each object once and use references any other time that object is used, this identity namespace provides a way to keep track of which objects are indeed the same because it maps their identities to the objects themselves.

Taking It With You

Every application knows how to deal with objects at a basic level, but with the techniques shown in this chapter, you'll be able to move on to managing large collections of objects, spanning a wide variety of different types. In the next chapter, we'll shift from a macro-level view of objects to a micro-level examination of one specific type of object: the humble string.

CHAPTER 7

■ ■ ■

Strings

Given the fundamental nature of strings in all forms of programming, it should come as no surprise that Python's string features can fill an entire chapter. Whether it's interacting with users by way of keyboard input, sending content over the Web, analyzing the great American novel or participating in a Turing test,[1] strings can be used for just about anything.

With all this emphasis on strings, Python makes sure to include a wide variety of features to support them. Some of these features are built right into the string objects themselves, while others are provided by modules in the standard library and many third-party libraries offer even more options. This chapter will focus on strings themselves and the tools in the standard library, rather than investigating third-party applications.

The first thing to understand about Python strings is that there are actually two different types: bytes and Unicode strings.

Bytes

At a very basic level, a string is really just a sequence of individual bytes. In this general sense, bytes are used for every piece of data a computer processes. Numbers, strings and more complex objects are all stored as bytes at some point, and anything more structured is built on top of a sequence of bytes. In a byte string, represented in Python by a bytes object, each character represents exactly one byte, so it's easy to interact with files and other interfaces to the outside world.

While standard strings—described later in the section on text—are identified as literals simply with a pair of straight single quotes ('example'), byte string literals include a b before the first quote. This is used in the source code as well as the repr() output for these values.

```
>>> b'example'
b'example'
```

Compatibility: Prior to 3.0

Originally, Python strings only supported sequences of bytes. Once it gained Unicode support, as described in the next section, the existing basic string started being called a "byte string" because it could only support one byte per character. This left it well-suited for non-textual data, like numbers and complex structures, particularly when working with files.

---

[1] http://propython.com/turing_test/

In Python 3.0, this distinction was made official with the new `bytes` type, which is equivalent to the standard `str` type in older versions. Therefore, to be compatible with older Python installations, you should use regular strings when working with non-textual data. Python 2.6 did add support for the `b''` syntax mentioned here, but only for the sake of migrating source code; there is no actual `bytes` type. If you create a string using this syntax prior to 3.0, you'll just get a standard `str` object out of it.

Unfortunately, this is one area where it's impossible to be fully compatible with both the Python 2 line and the Python 3 line in the same code. There's simply no syntax or type that will reliably get the same behavior in both. For easiest maintenance, you can write code using the Python 2 syntax—perhaps even marking strings with `b` if you don't need compatibility with Python 2.5 or below—and use the `2to3` tool to convert those files to be compatible with Python 3.

The primary use of bytes is to convey non-textual information, such as numbers, dates, sets of flags and a number of other things. Even though Python doesn't directly know how to deal with those particular values, a bytes object will make sure that they pass through unchanged, so that your own code can handle each situation appropriately. Without any assumptions about the intentions of the data, bytes offer you maximum flexibility, but that means you'll need some way to convert data back and forth between bytes and something with more meaning to your application.

Simple Conversion: chr() and ord()

At a basic level, a byte is really just a number, which happens to be represented by a character of some kind. Python considers numbers and characters to be two different things, but their values are equivalent, so it's fairly easy to convert between them. Given a single byte, you can pass it into the built-in ord() function, which will return its equivalent integer value.

```
>>> ord(b'A')
65
>>> ord(b'!')
33
>>> list(b'Example')
[69, 120, 97, 109, 112, 108, 101]
```

Notice what happens when iterating over a sequence of bytes. Rather than one-character byte strings, you actually get the raw integers immediately, removing the need for ord() at all. This works well when converting single-byte values from bytes to numbers, but going in the other direction requires the built-in chr() function. As an inverse to ord(), it returns a single character based on the integer value you pass in.

```
>>> chr(65)
'A'
>>> chr(33)
'!'
>>> [chr(o) for o in [69, 120, 97, 109, 112, 108, 101]]
['E', 'x', 'a', 'm', 'p', 'l', 'e']
>>> ''.join(chr(o) for o in [69, 120, 97, 109, 112, 108, 101])
'Example'
```

There's one important thing to notice here: the string returned by chr() is a standard string, rather than a byte string, as evidenced by the lack of a b prefix. As you'll see in the section on text later in this chapter, standard strings work a bit differently from byte strings. The biggest problem for our purposes here, though, is that a standard string doesn't always equate directly to a single byte, so it's possible to get things wrong. In order to get things to work more reliably and get some extra features on top of it, we can use the struct module.

Complex Conversion: The Struct Module

In addition to the problem with chr() returning standard strings, a big problem with the ord()/chr() combination is that it can only be reliably used when working with individual bytes. When converting numbers to bytes, that limits it to values from 0 to 255. In order to support a wider range of values and some other interesting features, Python provides the struct module.

Similarly to how chr() and ord() represent a pair to convert values between byte strings and native Python values, struct.pack() writes out byte strings, while struct.unpack() reads those values back into Python. Unlike those simpler functions, though, the struct module uses a format string to specify how values should get converted. This format has its own sort of simple syntax to control what types of values to use and how they work.

Since we came by struct to overcome some difficulties with chr(), we'll start by looking at how struct.pack() can provided the intended functionality. The format to use for a single, unsigned byte is B, and here's how you'd use it in practice.

```
>>> import struct
>>> struct.pack(b'B', 65)
b'A'
>>> struct.pack(b'B', 33)
b'!'
>>> struct.pack(b'BBBBBBB', 69, 120, 97, 109, 112, 108, 101)
b'Example'
```

As you can see, the first argument is the format string itself, with one character for each argument that should get converted into the byte string. All additional arguments are used to provide the values that should be converted. Therefore, for each format specifier, you'll need to include an argument at the equivalent position.

As mentioned, B specifies an unsigned value, which means there can be no negative values. With this, you could provide values from 0 to 255, but nothing below zero. A signed value, on the other hand, allows negative values by using one of the eight bits in the byte to identify whether the value is positive or negative. There are still 256 unique values, but the range is shifted a bit so that half the values are on each side of the sign. With 0 being considered a positive value, a signed byte can contain values from -128 to 127. To complement unsigned bytes, the format specifier for signed bytes is b.

```
>>> struct.pack(b'b', 65)
b'A'
>>> struct.pack(b'Bb', 65, -23)
b'A\xe9'
>>> struct.pack(b'B', 130)
b'\x82'
>>> struct.pack(b'b', 130)
Traceback (most recent call last):
  ...
struct.error: byte format requires -128 <= number <= 127
```

Of course, B and b are only valid for single byte values, limited to 256 total values. To support larger numbers, you can use H and h for 2-byte numbers, allowing up to 65,536 values. Just like the single-byte option, the uppercase format assumes an unsigned value, while the lowercase format assumes a signed value.

```
>>> struct.pack(b'Hh', 42, -137)
b'*\x00w\xff'
```

Now that a single value can span multiple bytes, there comes the question of which byte comes first. One of the two bytes contains the 256 smallest values, while the other contains the values 0 to 256, but multiplied by 256. Therefore, getting the two mixed up can greatly affect the value that gets stored or retrieved. This is easy enough to see by taking a quick look at the inverse function, struct.unpack().

```
>>> struct.unpack(b'H', b'*\x00')
(42,)
>>> struct.unpack(b'H', b'\x00*')
(10752,)
```

As you can see, the function call for struct.unpack() looks very similar to struct.pack(), but there are a couple notable differences. First, there are always only two arguments to unpack() because the second argument is the raw byte string. This string can contain multiple values to be pulled out, but it's still passed as just one argument, unlike pack().

Instead, the return value is a tuple, which could contain multiple values. Therefore, struct.unpack() is a true inverse of struct.pack(); that is, you can pass the result from one into the call to the other and get the same value you passed in the first time. All you need is to ensure you use the same format string in each of the individual function calls.

```
>>> struct.unpack(b'Hh', struct.pack(b'Hh', 42, -42))
(42, -42)
>>> struct.pack(b'Hh', *struct.unpack(b'Hh', b'*\x00\x00*'))
b'*\x00\x00*'
```

So what's the problem with values spanning multiple bytes? After all, these examples show that values can be converted to a string and back without worrying about how those strings are created or parsed. Unfortunately, it's only easy because we're currently working only within Python, which has an implementation that's consistent with itself. If you have to work with strings, such as file contents, that need to be used with other applications, you'll need to make sure you match up with what those applications expect.

Therefore, struct formats also allow you to explicitly specify the endianness of a value. Endianness is the term for how the bytes of a value are ordered; in a big-endian value, the most significant byte—the byte that provides the largest part of the number—gets stored first. For little-endian values, the least significant byte is stored first.

To distinguish between the two, the format specification can take a prefix. If you place a < before the format, you can explicitly declare it to be little-endian. Conversely, using > will mark it as big-endian. If neither options is supplied, as in the previous examples, the default behavior is to use the same endianness as the system where Python is executing, which is typically little-endian on modern systems. This allows you to control the way values are treated for both pack() and unpack(), covering both sides of the conversion process.

```
>>> struct.pack(b'<H', 42)
b'*\x00'
```

```
>>> struct.pack(b'>H', 42)
b'\x00*'
>>> struct.unpack(b'<H', b'*\x00')
(42,)
>>> struct.unpack(b'>H', b'*\x00')
(10752,)
```

Now that it's possible to control the ordering of multiple-byte numbers, it's easier to work with larger values. In addition to the one- and two-byte integers discussed previously, struct supports four-byte values using I and i, while eight-byte values can be specified using Q and q. Like the others, uppercase letters indicate unsigned values, while lowercase letters indicate signed values.

The struct module goes beyond just conversion of integers, though. You can also convert floating point values using the f format, or perhaps even the b format for greater precision. In fact, you can use struct to work with strings inside strings as well, giving you some extra flexibility. The s format code, combined with a numeric prefix to indicate the size of the string to read or write.

```
>>> struct.pack(b'7s', b'example')
b'example'
>>> struct.unpack(b'7s', b'example')
(b'example',)
>>> struct.pack(b'10s', b'example')
b'example\x00\x00\x00'
```

As you can see, pack() will add in null bytes to fill in as many bytes as necessary to match the prefix supplied in the format. But why would you want to use struct to turn a string into a string? The benefit is that you can pack and unpack multiple values at a time, so the string might just be part of the structure. Consider a simple byte string that contains a person's contact information.

```
>>> first_name = 'Marty'
>>> last_name = 'Alchin'
>>> age = 28
>>> data = struct.pack(b'10s10sB', last_name, first_name, age)
>>> data
b'Alchin\x00\x00\x00\x00Marty\x00\x00\x00\x00\x00\x1c'
```

If you're looking to work with strings in this manner, though, you're more likely working with text, where the string has meaning as a whole, rather than its characters being conversions of some other types of values.

Text

Conceptually, text is a collection of written words. It's a linguistic concept that existed long before computing, but once it became clear that computers would need to work with text, it was necessary to determine how to represent text in a system designed for numbers. When programming was still young, text was limited to a set of characters known as the American Standard Code for Information Interchange (ASCII).

Notice the "American" part in there; this set of 127 characters—only 95 of them printable—is designed to address only the needs of the English language. ASCII only covered 7 bits of each byte, so there was some room for potential future expansion, but even another 128 values weren't enough. Some applications employed special tricks to convey additional letters by adding accents and other marks, but the standard was still very limited in scope.

Unicode

Later, the Unicode standard emerged as an alternative that could contain most of the characters used in the vast majority of the world's languages. In order for Unicode to support as many code points as it needs, each code point takes up more than one byte, unlike in ASCII. When loaded in memory, this isn't a problem because it's only used within Python, which only has one way of managing those multiple-byte values.

■ **Note** The Unicode standard is actually made up of more than a million individual "code points" rather than characters. A code point is a number that represents some facet of written text, which can be a regular character, a symbol or a modifier, such as an accent. Some characters are even present at multiple code points for compatibility with systems in use prior to the introduction of Unicode.

By default, all standard strings in Python are Unicode, supporting a wide array of languages in the process. The byte strings shown in the previous section all required the use of a b prefix to distinguish them as different from standard Unicode strings.

Compatibility: Prior to 3.0

Much like other programming languages, strings in Python used to be byte strings by default, with Unicode represented by a separate type. While byte strings were quoted without a prefix, Unicode strings used the u prefix to indicate that they support the full Unicode character set. In the switch to Python 3, Unicode strings were made the default, and the u prefix is no longer supported.

Unfortunately, like the byte strings mentioned earlier in this chapter, there's no syntax that will be compatible with both versions of Python. Instead, any strings marked with the u prefix in your Python 2.x code will be converted to the new syntax with the 2to3 conversion tool.

The trouble comes when writing those values out to strings that can be read by other systems because not all systems use the same internal representation of Unicode strings. Instead, there are several different encodings that can be used to collapse a Unicode string into a series of bytes for storage or distribution.

Encodings

Much like how multiple bytes can be used to store a number larger than one byte would allow, Unicode text can be stored in a multiple-byte format. Unlike numbers, though, text generally contains a large number of individual characters, so storing each as up to four bytes would mean a long passage of text could end up much larger than it may seem.

To support text as efficiently as possible, it quickly became clear that not all text requires the full range of available characters. This book, for example, is written in English, which means the vast majority of its content lies within the ASCII range. As such, most of it could go from four bytes per character down to just one.

ASCII is one example of a text encoding. In this particular case, a small set of available characters are mapped to specific values from 0 to 255. The characters chosen are intended to support English, so it contains all the available letters in uppercase and lowercase variants, all ten numerals and a variety of punctuation options. Any text that contains just these values can be converted to bytes using the ASCII encoding.

The encoding process itself is managed using a string's encode() method. Simply pass in the name of an encoding and it will return a byte string representing the text in the given encoding. In the case of ASCII, the representation of the byte string looks just like the input text, because each byte maps to exactly one character.

```
>>> 'This is an example, with punctuation and UPPERCASE.'.encode('ascii')
b'This is an example, with punctuation and UPPERCASE.'
```

By mapping each byte to a single character, ASCII is very efficient, but only if the source text only contains those characters specified in the encoding. Certain assumptions had to be made about what characters were important enough to include in such a small range. Other languages will have their own characters that take priority, so they use different encodings in order to be as efficient as ASCII is for English.

Some languages, including Chinese and Japanese, have so many characters that there's no way a single byte could hope to represent them. The encodings for these languages use two bytes for every character, further highlighting how different the various text encodings can be. Because of this, an encoding designed for a particular language often can't be used for text outside of that language.

To address this, there are some more generic Unicode-focused encodings. Because of the sheer number of available characters, these encodings use a variable-length approach. In UTF-8, the most common of these, characters within a certain range can be represented in a single byte. Other characters require two bytes, while still others can use three or even four bytes. UTF-8 is desirable because of a few particular traits it exhibits.

- It can support any available Unicode code point, even if it isn't commonly in actual text. That feature isn't unique to UTF-8, but it definitely sets it apart from other language-specific encodings, such as ASCII.

- The more common the character is in actual use, the less space its code point takes. In a collection of mostly English documents, for example, UTF-8 can be nearly as efficient as ASCII. Even when encoding non-English text, most languages share certain common characters, such as spaces and punctuation, which can be encoded with a single byte. When it has to use two bytes, it's still more efficient than an in-memory Unicode object.

- The single-byte range precisely coincides with the ASCII standard, making UTF-8 completely backward compatible with ASCII text. All ASCII text can be read as UTF-8, without modification. Likewise, text that only contains characters that are also available in ASCII can be encoded using UTF-8 and still be accessed by applications that only understand ASCII.

For these reasons, among others, UTF-8 has emerged as a very common encoding for applications that need to support multiple languages or where the language of the application isn't known at the time it's being designed. That may seem like an odd situation to be in, but it comes up fairly frequently when looking at frameworks, libraries and other large-scale applications. They could be deployed in any environment on the planet, so they should do as much as possible to support other languages. The next chapter will describe, in more detail, the steps an application can take to support multiple languages.

The consequences of using the wrong encoding can vary, depending on the needs of the application, the encoding used and the text passed in. For example, ASCII text can be decoded using UTF-8 without a problem, yielding a perfectly valid Unicode string. Reversing that process is not always as forgiving because a Unicode string can contain code points outside the valid ASCII range.

```
>>> ascii = 'This is a test'.encode('ascii')
>>> ascii
b'This is a test'
>>> ascii.decode('utf-8')
'This is a test'
>>> unicode = 'This is a test: \u20ac'  # A manually encoded Euro symbol
>>> unicode.encode('utf-8')
b'This is a test: \xe2\x82\xac'
>>> unicode.encode('ascii')
Traceback (most recent call last):
    ...
UnicodeEncodeError: 'ascii' codec can't encode character '\u20ac' in position 16
: ordinal not in range(128)
```

Other times, text can seem to be encoded or decoded properly, only to have the resulting text be gibberish. Typically, though, problems like that arise when upgrading an application to include proper Unicode support, but existing data wasn't encoded consistently. Building an application for Unicode from the ground up doesn't completely eliminate the possibility of these problems, but it greatly helps avoid them.

Compatibility: Prior to 3.0

One of the main reasons all of this seems confusing is that Python 2 was fairly vague on how encoding and decoding were supposed to work. Both byte strings and Unicode strings had an encode() and a decode() method, and the two types could often be used interchangeably. Python 3 clarifies the situation by only putting encode() on standard Unicode strings, while decode() is only available from byte strings. This, along with a few other differences, means the two can no longer be used interchangeably.

Most applications do well using UTF-8, but there are a number of other encodings available. Feel free to consult the full list,[2] in case something else is more appropriate for your needs.

Simple Substitution

There are a few different ways to produce a string with information that's only available at run-time. Perhaps the most obvious is to concatenate multiple strings together using the + operator, but that only works if all the values are strings. Python won't implicitly convert other values to strings to be

---

[2] http://propython.com/standard-encodings/

concatenated, so you'd have to convert them explicitly, by first passing them into the str() function, for example.

As an alternative, Python strings also support a way to inject objects into a string. This uses placeholders inside a string to denote where objects should go, along with a collection of objects that should fill them in. This is called string substitution, and is performed using the % operator, using a custom __mod__() method, as described in Chapter 5.

Placeholders consist of a percent sign and a conversion format, optionally with some modifiers between them to specify how the conversion should take place. This scheme allows the string to specify how objects should get converted, rather than having to call separate function explicitly. The most common of these formats is %s, which is equivalent to using the str() function directly.

```
>>> 'This object is %s' % 1
'This object is 1'
>>> 'This object is %s' % object()
'This object is <object object at 0x...>'
```

Because this is equivalent to calling str() directly, the value placed into the string is the result of calling the object's __str__() method. Similarly, if you use the %r placeholder inside the substitution string, Python will call the object's __repr__() method instead. This can be useful for logging arguments to a function, for example.

```
>>> def func(*args):
...     for i, arg in enumerate(args):
...         print('Argument %s: %r' % (i, arg))
...
>>> func('example', {}, [1, 2, 3], object())
Argument 0: 'example'
Argument 1: {}
Argument 2: [1, 2, 3]
Argument 3: <object object at 0x...>
```

This example also illustrates how multiple values can be placed into the string at once, by wrapping them in a tuple. They're matched up with their counterparts in the string according to their position, so the first object goes in the first placeholder and so on. Unfortunately, this feature can also be a stumbling block at times, if you're not careful. The most common error occurs when attempting to inject a tuple into the substitution string.

```
>>> def log(*args):
...     print('Logging arguments: %r' % args)
...
>>> log('test')
"Logging arguments: 'test'"
>>> log('test', 'ing')
Traceback (most recent call last):
  ...
TypeError: not all arguments converted during string formatting
```

What's going on here is that Python makes no distinction between a tuple that was written as such in the source code and one that was merely passed from somewhere else. Therefore, string substitution has no way of knowing what your intention is. In this example, the substitution works fine as long as only one argument is passed in because there's exactly one placeholder in the string. As soon as you pass in more than one argument, it breaks.

In order to resolve this, you'll need to build a one-item tuple to contain the tuple you want to place in the string. This way, the string substitution always gets a single tuple, which contains one tuple to be placed into a single placeholder.

```
>>> def log(*args):
...     print('Logging arguments: %r' % (args,))
...
>>> log('test')
"Logging arguments: ('test',)"
>>> log('test', 'ing')
"Logging arguments: ('test', 'ing')"
```

With the tuple situation sorted out, it's worth noting that objects can be inserted by keyword as well. Doing so requires the substitution string to contain the keywords in parentheses, immediately following the percent sign. Then, to pass in values to inject, simply pass in a dictionary of objects, rather than a tuple.

```
>>> def log(*args):
...     for i, arg in enumerate(args):
...         print('Argument %(i)s: %(arg)r' % {'i': i, 'arg': arg})
...
>>> log('test')
Argument 0: 'test'
>>> log('test', 'ing')
Argument 0: 'test'
Argument 1: 'ing'
```

In addition to being able to more easily rearrange placeholders in the substitution string, this feature allows you to include just those values that are important. If you have a dictionary with more values than you need in the string, you can reference only the ones you need. Python will simply ignore any values that aren't mentioned by name in the string. This is in contrast to the positional option, where supplying more values than you've marked in the string will result in a TypeError.

Compatibility: Going Forward

The string formatting described in this section is a bit of an interesting case with regard to compatibility. It's considered to be obsolete, having been replaced by the more robust string formatting system described in the next section. However, it was not removed from Python during the switch to version 3, so strings that use this system will work in all versions of Python covered by this book, including 3.1.

The long-term plan, though, is to remove this feature in a future version of Python, once the new formatting option takes hold. Therefore, this section exists to document something that will work in all current versions of Python as of this book's publish date, but it will be removed at some point in the future. Please use this section, along with the next one, as a guide to understanding how existing string substitution works, so that any strings using it can be converted to the newer formatting feature.

Formatting

For a more powerful alternative to the simple string substitution described in the previous section, Python also includes a robust formatting system for strings. Rather than relying on a less obvious operator, string formatting uses an explicit format() method on strings. In addition, the syntax used for the formatting string is considerably different from what was used in simple substitution previously.

Instead of using a percent sign and a format code, format() expects its placeholders to be surrounded by curly braces. What goes inside those braces depends on how you plan to pass in the values and how they should be formatted. The first portion of the placeholder determines whether it should look for a positional argument or a keyword argument. For positional arguments, the content is a number, indicating the index of the value to work with, while for keyword arguments, you supply the key that references the appropriate value.

```
>>> 'This is argument 0: {0}'.format('test')
'This is argument 0: test'
>>> 'This is argument key: {key}'.format(key='value')
'This is argument key: value'
```

This may look a lot like the older substitution technique, but it has one major advantage already. Because formatting is initiated with a method call, rather than an operator, you can specify both positional and keyword arguments together. That way, you can mix and match indexes and keys in the format string if necessary, referencing them in any order.

As an added bonus, that also means that not all positional arguments need to be referenced in the string in order to work properly. If you supply more than you need, format() will just ignore anything it doesn't have a placeholder for. This makes it much easier to pass a format string into an application that will call format() on it later, with arguments that may come from another source. One such example is a customizable validation function that accepts an error message during customization.

```
>>> def exact_match(expected, error):
...     def validator(value):
...         if value != expected:
...             raise ValueError(error.format(value, expected))
...     return validator
...
>>> validate_zero = exact_match(0, 'Expected {1}, got {0}')
>>> validate_zero(0)
>>> validate_zero(1)
Traceback (most recent call last):
  ...
ValueError: Expected 0, got 1
>>> validate_zero = exact_match(0, '{0} != {1}')
>>> validate_zero(1)
Traceback (most recent call last):
  ...
ValueError: 1 != 0
>>> validate_zero = exact_match(0, '{0} is not the right value')
>>> validate_zero(1)
Traceback (most recent call last):
  ...
ValueError: 1 is not the right value
```

As you can see, this feature lets the validator function call format() using all the information it has available at the time, leaving it up to the format string to determine how to lay it out. With the other string substitution, you'd be forced to use keywords to achieve the same effect because positional arguments just didn't work the same way.

Compatibility: Converting Strings

If you prefer the previous behavior of looking up positional arguments without having to number them explicitly—or if you're looking for an easy way to convert all your strings over at once—this new feature can work the same way. Simply leave out the index altogether and it'll pick up arguments according to the order in which the placeholders appear in the string. So if you used a string like '%s: %r' with the older substitution technique, the direct equivalent in the newer formatting would be '{!s}: {!r}'.

You can't use this alongside explicitly numbered placeholders, though, so you'll have to choose one style for the whole string. That works out for an automated conversion to the new style, but it requires some attention if you have complicated strings that need to reorder arguments later on. Of course, keyword arguments don't have any ambiguity in either case, so they work fine alongside either style.

Looking Up Values Within Objects

In addition to being able to reference the objects being passed in, the format string syntax allows you to refer to portions of those objects specifically. The syntax for this looks much like it would in regular Python code. To reference an attribute, separate its name from the object reference with a period. To use an indexed or keyword value, supply the index or keyword inside square brackets; just don't use quotes around the keyword.

```
>>> import datetime
>>> def format_time(time):
...     return '{0.minute} past {0.hour}'.format(time)
...
>>> format_time(datetime.time(8, 10))
'10 past 8'
>>> '{0[spam]}'.format({'spam': 'eggs'})
'eggs'
```

Distinguishing Types of Strings

You may remember that simple substitution required you to specify either %s or %r to indicate whether the __str__() method or the __repr__() method should be used to convert an object to a string, while the examples given thus far haven't included such a hint. By default, format() will use __str__(), but that behavior can still be controlled as part of the format string. Immediately following the object reference, simply include an exclamation point, followed by either s or r.

```
>>> validate_test = exact_match('test', 'Expected {1!r}, got {0!r}')
>>> validate_test('invalid')
Traceback (most recent call last):
  ...
```

```
ValueError: Expected 'test', got 'invalid'
```

Standard Format Specification

Where this new string formatting really differs from the previous substitution feature is in the amount of flexibility available to format the output of objects. After the field reference and the string type mentioned in previous sections, you can include a colon, followed by a string that controls the formatting of the referenced object. There's a standard syntax for this format specification, which is generally applicable to most objects.

The first option controls the alignment of the output string, which is used when you need to specify a minimum number of characters to output. Supplying a left angle bracket (<) produces a left-aligned value, a right angle bracket (>) aligns to the right and a caret (^) centers the value. The total width can be specified as a number afterward.

```
>>> import os.path
>>> '{0:>20}{1}'.format(*os.path.splitext('contents.txt'))
'           contents.txt'
>>> for filename in ['contents.txt', 'chapter.txt', 'index.txt']:
...     print('{0:<10}{1}'.format(*os.path.splitext(filename)))
...
contents  .txt
chapter   .txt
index     .txt
```

Notice here that the default behavior of the length specification is to pad the output with spaces to reach the necessary length. That too can be controlled by inserting a different character before the alignment specifier. For example, some plain-text document formats expect headings to be centered within a length of equal signs or hyphens. This is easy to accomplish using string formatting.

```
>>> def heading(text):
...     return '{0:=^40}'.format(text)
...
>>> heading('Standard Format Specification')
'=====Standard Format Specification======'
>>> heading('This is a longer heading, beyond 40 characters')
'This is a longer heading, beyond 40 characters'
```

The second call here demonstrates an important property of the length format; if the argument string is longer than the length specified, format() will lengthen the output to match, rather than truncating the text. That creates a bit of a problem with the heading example, though, because if the input was too long, the output doesn't contain any of the padding characters at all. This can be fixed by explicitly adding in one character each at the beginning and end of the string and reducing the placeholder's length by two to compensate.

```
>>> def heading(text):
...     return '={0:=^38}='.format(text)
...
>>> heading('Standard Format Specification')
'=====Standard Format Specification======'
>>> heading('This is a longer heading, beyond 40 characters')
'=This is a longer heading, beyond 40 characters='
```

Now the heading will always be at least 40 characters wide but also always have at least one equal sign on each side of the text, even if it runs long. Unfortunately, doing so now requires writing the equal sign three times in the format string, which becomes a bit of a maintenance hassle once we consider that sometimes the padding character will be a hyphen.

Solving one part of this problem is simple: because we're explicitly numbering the placeholders, we can pass in the padding character as an argument and just reference that argument twice in the format string; once at the beginning and once at the end. That alone doesn't really solve the problem, though, because it leaves the core problem untouched: how to replace just part of the argument reference for the text.

To solve that problem, the format specification also allows argument references to be nested. Inside the placeholder for the text portion, we can add another placeholder at the position reserved for the padding character, and Python will evaluate that one first, before trying to evaluate the other. While we're at it, this also allows us to control how many characters the output will fill up.

```
>>> def heading(text, padding='=', width=40):
...     return '{1}{0:{1}^{2}}{1}'.format(text, padding, width - 2)
...
>>> heading('Standard Format Specification')
'=====Standard Format Specification======'
>>> heading('This is a longer heading, beyond 40 characters')
'=This is a longer heading, beyond 40 characters='
>>> heading('Standard Format Specification', padding='-', width=60)
'---------------Standard Format Specification----------------'
```

Example: Plain Text Table of Contents

Though there are many forms of documentation, plain text is perhaps the most common, as it doesn't require any additional software to view. Navigating large chunks of documentation can be difficult, though, because of the lack of links or page numbers for a table of contents. Line numbers could be used instead of page numbers, but a properly formatted table of contents can still be tedious to maintain.

Consider a typical table of contents, where the title of a section is left-aligned and the page or line number is right-aligned, and the two are joined by a line of periods to help guide the eye from one to the other. Adding or removing lines from such a format is simple, but every time you change the name or location of a section, you not only have to change the relevant information; you also need to update the line of periods in-between, which is less than ideal.

String formatting can come in handy here because you can specify both alignment and padding options for multiple values within a string. With this, you can set up a simple script that formats the table of contents for you automatically. The key to doing this, though, is to realize what you're working with.

On the surface, it seems like the goal is just as mentioned: to left-align the section title, right-align the line number and place a line of periods in-between. Unfortunately, there's no option to do exactly that, so we'll need to look at it a bit differently. By having each part of the string be responsible for part of the padding, it's fairly easy to achieve the desired effect.

```
>>> '{0:.<50}'.format('Example')
'Example...........................................'
>>> '{0:.<50}'.format('Longer Example')
'Longer Example....................................'
>>> '{0:.>10}'.format(20)
'........20'
>>> '{0:.>10}'.format(1138)
'......1138'
```

With these two parts in place, they just need to be combined in order to create a full line in the table of contents. Most plain text documents are limited to 80 characters in a single line, so we can expand it a bit to give some breathing room for longer titles. In addition, 10 digits is a bit much to expect for line numbers even in extremely long documents, so that can be reduced in order to yield more space for the titles as well.

```
>>> def contents_line(title, line_number=1):
...     return '{0:.<70}{1:.>5}'.format(title, line_number)
...
>>> contents_line('Installation', 20)
'Installation..........................................................20'
>>> contents_line('Usage', 112)
'Usage................................................................112'
```

Calling this function one line at a time isn't a realistic solution in the long run, though, so we'll create a new function that can accept a more useful data structure to work with. It doesn't need to be complicated, so we'll just use a sequence of 2-tuples, each consisting of a section title and its corresponding line number.

```
>>> contents = (('Installation', 20), ('Usage', 112))
>>> def format_contents(contents):
...     for title, line_number in contents:
...         yield '{0:.<70}{1:.>5}'.format(title, line_number)
...
>>> for line in format_contents(contents):
...     print(line)
...
Installation..........................................................20
Usage................................................................112
```

Custom Format Specification

The true strength of the new formatting system, though, is that format() isn't actually in control of the formatting syntax described in the previous section. Like many of the features described in Chapter 4, it instead delegates that control to a method on the objects passed in as arguments.

This method, __format__(), accepts one argument, which is the format specification that was written into the format string where the object is being placed. It doesn't get the entire bracketed expression, though, just the bit after the colon. This is true for all objects, as you can see by calling it directly on a brand new instance of object.

```
>>> object().__format__('=^40')
'=====<object object at 0x0209F158>======'
```

Because of this, the standard format specification options described in the previous section aren't the only way to do things. If you have a custom need, you can override that behavior by replacing that method on the class you're working with. You can either extend the existing behavior or write a completely new one.

For example, you could have a class to represent a verb, which can have a present or a past tense. This Verb class could be instantiated with a word to use for each tense, then be used in expressions to form complete sentences.

```
>>> class Verb:
...     def __init__(self, present, past=None):
...         self.present = present
...         self.past = past
...     def __format__(self, tense):
...         if tense == 'past':
...             return self.past
...         else:
...             return self.present
...
>>> format = Verb('format', past='formatted')
>>> message = 'You can {0:present} strings with {0:past} objects.'
>>> message.format(format)
'You can format strings with formatted objects.'
>>> save = Verb('save', past='saved')
>>> message.format(save)
'You can save strings with saved objects.'
```

In this example, there's no way for the placeholder string to know how to format a past tense verb, so it delegates that responsibility to the verb passed in. This way, the string can be written once and used many times with different verbs, without skipping a beat.

Taking It With You

Because strings are so common throughout all kinds of programming, you'll find yourself with a wide range of needs. The features shown in this chapter will help you make better use of your strings, but the proper combination of techniques is something that can't be written for you. As you go forward with your code, you'll need to keep an open mind about which techniques to use, so that you can choose what's best for your needs.

So far, these chapters have focused on how to use various aspects of Python to perform complex and useful tasks so that your applications can be that much more powerful. The next chapter will show you how to verify that those tasks are being performed properly.

CHAPTER 8

■ ■ ■

Documentation

Documentation is arguably the most difficult part of any project. Code tends to come fairly easy to programmers, but documentation requires a different set of skills because the audience is strictly human. The magnitude of the differences can vary greatly between projects and audiences. Sometimes all that's necessary is some example code, while other topics can fill entire books and still have plenty left to cover.

The language of documentation is very different from that of code, so it can be difficult to excel at both. This causes many programmers to take the path of least resistance, opting for tools that automatically generate some minimal form of documentation from the code itself, so the extra work is kept to a minimum. Though that can seem sufficient, such tools can only do so much because they're limited by what the code alone can tell them.

This chapter will show the tools available to help describe your code and its features for human understanding. There are several options available, some of which go alongside the code itself, while others accompany it on the outside. These can be used individually or in combination to form a full set of documentation for any project. How much of each is necessary will differ based on the needs of each application, but each has its place.

Each section in this chapter will highlight how to document your code with the available tools, along with the benefits and drawbacks of each approach. The most important thing to remember about documentation, though, is that it's all about presenting what people need to know about your application and how to use it. You must always consider how your code works and what your users will need to know to interact with it. Only then can you pick the approaches that are best for your needs.

Proper Naming

The simplest form of documentation is to properly name the various aspects of your code. With very few exceptions, every single class, function and variable is given a name when it's defined. Because these names are already required, all it takes is a little extra thought to make sure they're accurate and easy to understand. To illustrate how valuable this can be, take a look at a function signature with vague, generic names and see if you can guess what it does.

```
def action(var1, var2):
```

Given some code inside the body of the function, you might be able to get a good idea of its purpose, but the signature itself does nothing to help. In fact, the only reason the code in the body would be more helpful is that it would typically use more standardized features available from elsewhere. For instance, loops and slicing are easily recognizable, as are methods from commonly used objects, like a string's `format()` method. These are just clues to help make an educated guess, though; the naming should make it obvious.

```
def find_words(text, word):
```

Just picking some more descriptive names makes the purpose of the function and its arguments much clearer. As a rule of thumb, classes and variables should be named as singular nouns, such as Book, Person, Restaurant, index and first_name. Functions, on the other hand, should be given verbs as names, such as find(), insert() and process_user().

PEP-8[1] also included as an appendix in this book, offers some more specific guidelines for naming various types of objects. See its Naming Conventions section for details. Once you get inside a block of code, things aren't always as easy to follow, so comments can help clarify.

Comments

In classes and functions that are very long or complex, the name alone is often not sufficient to convey all the things the code is doing. Variable names can certainly help, but that usually only explains *what* the code does; it's typically more useful to explain *why* the code does what it does. Both of these can be addressed by placing comments in your code.

Comments are one of the most basic forms of documentation a programmer can use, yet they're also among the most powerful. Comments are placed directly alongside the rest of your code, where it's easiest to write and is often most helpful. Comments offer a convenient way to make small notes where they're most relevant, which can help make complex code easier to understand later on.

Python's comments are separated from code by the # symbol. All of the text that follows that symbol is treated as a comment, all the way to the end of the line. This allows comments to either take up a whole line or attach to the end of a line of code. Unlike some other languages, Python doesn't have any syntax for multi-line comments. Instead, each line of a longer comment must be preceded by a # symbol.

```
# This function doesn't really do anything useful. It's only here to show
# how multi-line comments work in Python. Notice how each line has to have
# a separate # to indicate that it's a comment.

def example():
    pass
```

Like naming conventions, the Python Style Guide has a lot to say on how comments should be formatted. See the Comments heading of PEP-8 for details.

Perhaps the biggest limitation of comments is that they're only available when viewing the source file directly. Because comments don't have any impact on the execution of the code, there are no introspection tools available to read them at run-time. For that, we turn to docstrings.

Docstrings

Chapters 3 and 4 briefly alluded to docstrings and how they're used in code. Essentially, a docstring is placed at the beginning of a module, function or class; but rather than assigning it to a variable, you can just leave the string as its own statement. As long as it's the first thing in the code block, Python will interpret it as a docstring.

```
def find_words(text, word):
    """
```

---

[1] http://www.python.org/dev/peps/pep-0008/

```
Locate all instances of a word in a given piece of text.
Return a list of indexes where the words were found.
If no instances of the word were found, return an empty list.

text -- a block of text to search
word -- an individual word to search for
"""
```

This information could be presented in a set of comments, but there's one major advantage of using docstrings instead: Python makes them available in code. In keeping with the spirit of transparency, docstrings can be accessed at runtime through the __doc__ attribute of modules, classes and functions. Perhaps the most obvious benefit this brings is that the various automatic documentation generators get a lot more information to work with. Better yet, that information is written specifically for humans, which can greatly improve the quality of the final output.

Exactly how it's written, though, is entirely up to you. Aside from where docstrings can be placed in your code, Python makes no assumptions or requirements about the format or structure of their contents. PEP 257,[2] also provided as an appendix, provides a number of recommendations, but the final decision is left up to you. The goal is to help people understand how to use your code, though, so there are a few particulars that everyone should follow.

Describe What the Function Does

As simple as it sounds, it can sometimes be difficult to step back from how the code works and simply describe what it does. For most functions, you should be able to describe it in one sentence, preferably on a single line. Common examples are, "Add an item to the collection," and, "Cache an object for later use." The details of how the code achieves that goal are best left out of the docstring.

Explain the Arguments

Argument names are limited to one or two words. This works well as a simple reminder of their purpose but more information is usually needed to understand their purposes in the first place. This is particularly important for optional arguments, which often help control how the function works. Even if the argument names are self-explanatory, including a brief description helps maintain consistency across your documentation.

Don't Forget the Return Value

Any time a function returns a value, the nature of that value should be documented. It should include the return value's type as well as any relevant details about how the object will be formed. For example, find_words() returns a list, but that list contains indexes where the words were found, rather than returning the words themselves, so that behavior is documented.

Also, make sure that if the return value differs slightly based on what input was given or what other conditions the function works with, the different forms of return values are given. For example, a function to retrieve an object by name might be given a name that doesn't match any existing objects. In that case, it's important to document whether the function will create a new object or raise an exception.

---

[2] http://www.python.org/dev/peps/pep-0257/

Include Any Expected Exceptions

Every piece of code contains opportunities for exceptions to be raised. Sometimes those exceptions are actually part of the code's expected functionality, such as when looking for an object by a name that doesn't match anything. In these cases, the exceptions should be documented right alongside the return values. These explicit exceptions are frequently caught by the code that calls your function, so it's necessary to indicate which ones will be raised, as well as the circumstances under which they'll be raised.

Documentation Outside the Code

One thing you'll notice about the recommendations in the previous section is that they aren't specific to docstrings. You should also document your application outside of the code, and that documentation needs to include all the same details. What makes this external documentation different is how the information is presented, and it'll also include additional information not covered inside the code itself.

This general class of documentation can cover a wide variety of topics, many of which wouldn't make any sense inside the code. After all, someone who's reading your code is likely to have something already in mind to look for. They'll be looking for more information about a specific module, class or function that they already know how to find. Other users will have a broader range of needs, from installation and tutorials to more topical references that show how to combine multiple features toward a certain goal.

Installation and Configuration

Before anyone can use your software, they need to obtain it and get it working. This almost goes without saying, but not quite. There are a number of issues that users need to tackle before they can use your code, and you need to make sure that those issues are addressed as thoroughly as possible.

Obtaining the code is the first step. However you choose to distribute your code, you'll need to make sure your users know how to get it. Sometimes it'll be a simple one-line command, but in other cases, it may require first obtaining other applications such as version control software to get the latest code without waiting for a release. Chapter 10 will describe some of the more common ways to distribute your code, along with what your choices will mean for the users who need to retrieve it.

Tutorials

After getting an application, many users want to immediately get an idea of how to use it. Everybody appreciates immediate gratification, so you can use their first experience with your software as an opportunity to accomplish something quickly. Tutorials are a great way to walk your users through the most common features of your application.

A tutorial can often showcase the greatest strengths of an application, so it can also be your first chance to convince someone to try it out in the first place. This is particularly true with libraries and frameworks, which are designed to be integrated into other code rather than be used independently. If your audience can get a quick feel for how your approach can help them work with their own code, it'll make a lasting impression.

Reference Documents

Once your users have a good idea of how your application can help them and have gotten a bit of experience under their belts, their needs change again. At this point, they no longer need to be convinced to use your software, and they're ready to move beyond learning how to use it. Now they need reminders of how all the features work, how those features work together and how they can integrate with the tasks they're really trying to perform.

Different readers will look for different forms of reference documentation. Some may prefer method-level arguments and return values, like those contained in docstrings, while others may get more out of a broader overview, written in plain language. Readers like you even enjoy a physical book, easy to pick up and flip through at a moment's notice.

With all these different preferences, it's unlikely that you'll be able to write reference documentation in a way that will suit all tastes. As author, it's your job to determine what type of documentation best suits your application. Look to your own preferences for the type of documentation you like to read most, as that's likely to be in the same spirit of the software you create. Just write the way you'd like to read. The users who like your documentation are likely to be the very same ones who will like your software.

■ **Note** One important thing to remember is that you may not need reference documentation at all. For very simple applications, a tutorial alone may be enough to illustrate and explain all the available features.

Documentation Utilities

Some of the most challenging aspects of documentation have nothing to do with your application or how you plan to write about it. Beyond those concerns, tasks such as formatting, referencing and presenting documentation can consume quite a bit of time and energy. The more documents you need to write, the harder these tasks become. The third-party docutils package[3] provides a comprehensive set of tools to make this process more manageable.

The crown jewel of the docutils package is reStructuredText, more often referred to as ReST or simply RST. reStructuredText is a markup language designed for writing technical documents, taking what its developers call a What You See Is What You Mean (WYSIWYM) approach. This is in contrast with the more traditional What You See Is What You Get (WYSIWYG), where editing based on the visual layout and formatting of the document.

In WYSIWYM, the goal is to indicate the structure and intentions of the document, without regard to exactly how it will be presented. Much like HTML, separating content from its presentation allows you to focus on what's really important about your documentation and leave the details of visual style for later. reStructuredText uses a more text-friendly approach than HTML, though, so that even unformatted documents are easily readable.

Readability Counts

In keeping with Python philosophy, reStructuredText focuses on readability at all times, even before the document gets formatted into its final format. The structure of a document and the instructions are designed to be understandable and easy to remember and format.

---

[3] http://docutils.sourceforge.net/

Formatting

The most basic unit of any type of document is the paragraph, so reStructuredText makes them the easiest to work with. All you need to do is write a block of text with each line of text starting immediately below the one before it. The number of lines and the length of each line are irrelevant, as long as there are no completely blank lines between any lines of text in a given paragraph.

Blank lines are reserved for separating paragraphs from each other and from other types of content. This forms a simple way to distinguish one paragraph from another. You can use multiple blank lines if you'd like, but only one is required. Indenting a paragraph indicates a quoted passage from another document, which will typically also be indented in the output. To illustrate, here are a couple of simple paragraphs written for reStructuredText.

```
The reStructuredText format is very simple when it comes down to it. It's all
about readability and flexibility. Common needs, such as paragraphs and inline
formatting, are simple to write, read and maintain. More complex features are
possible, and they use a simple, standardized syntax.
After all, the Zen of Python says:

    Simple is better than complex.
    Complex is better than complicated.
```

Most application documentation will also include blocks of code along with regular text. This is particularly useful for tutorials, where a block of code can be built up in pieces, with explanations in between. Distinguishing between a paragraph and a block of code is based on a double colon at the end of a normal paragraph, followed by an indented block of code. This will end the first paragraph with a colon and format the indented text as code.

```
The reStructuredText format is very simple when it comes down to it. It's all
about readability and flexibility. Common needs, such as paragraphs and inline
formatting, are simple to write, read and maintain. More complex features are
possible, and they use a simple, standardized syntax.
After all, the Zen of Python says::

    Simple is better than complex.
    Complex is better than complicated.
```

■ **Note** You'll notice that the example shown here isn't actually code. The double-colon format technically distinguishes a block of text as preformatted. This prevents the reStructuredText parser from doing any additional processing on that block. Therefore, even though it's most useful for including code in your documentation, it can be used for anything that already has its own formatting that should remain intact.

Inside an individual paragraph, you can also format text in all the ways you'd expect. Rather than directly marking things for italics or bold, this formatting requires the use of additional punctuation before and after the text you'd like to format. Surrounding a word or phrase with asterisks marks it as emphasized, which will typically render in italics. Using an extra pair of asterisks beyond that will indicate strong emphasis, often rendering as bold.

Links

When working with large amounts of documentation, one of the most important features you can offer is linking multiple documents together. The reStructuredText format offers several different ways to link to additional information, whether footnotes, other sections in the same document or completely different documents. The simplest form of link you can include is a URL, which will get converted into a link when rendering the document. Other types of links require a bit more formatting.

Links take the form of an underscore following the text that should be used as the link. The target of the link is specified differently, depending on where that target is located. In the most common case, where a document links to some external web page, the link target is placed in what might appear to be its own paragraph, with a structure that tells the parser that it's a link instead of an actual paragraph.

```
This paragraph shows the basics of how a link is formed in reStructuredText.
You can find additional information in the official documentation_.

.. _documentation: http://docutils.sf.net/docs/
```

This will cause the word "documentation" to be used as the link itself, referencing the target given on the bottom line. You'll usually need to use more than one word for the text of a link, but this doesn't provide a way to specify how much text should be included. To do that, you'll need to enclose the text in backticks (`). The underscore then goes outside the enclosure, immediately following the second backtick.

```
This paragraph shows the basics of how a link is formed in reStructuredText.
You can find additional information in the `official documentation`_.

.. _official documentation: http://docutils.sf.net/docs/
```

In this case, the link target is specified immediately below the paragraph where the link should be placed. This particular case can be simplified a bit by creating an anonymous link, which no longer requires rewriting the link text underneath. In order to distinguish it from a regular link, you'll need to use two underscores after the link text instead of just one. Then, the link target is specified with only two underscores at the beginning of the line.

```
This paragraph shows the basics of how a link is formed in reStructuredText.
You can find additional information in the `official documentation`__.

__ http://docutils.sf.net/docs/
```

Readability Counts

There's also another way to specify external links that's even more space-efficient: place the link target directly alongside the link text, inside the paragraph itself. Links formatted this way still use backticks to set the link apart from the rest of the text, but the link target goes inside the backticks as well, after being enclosed in angle brackets. To distinguish it as a link, two underscores are still used, so it gets parsed as an anonymous link. For example, `` `Pro Python <http://propython.com/>`__ ``.

The problem with this approach is that having the URL inside the paragraph can be very distracting when reading the source code for the document, even though the target will be hidden from view from the final output. Furthermore, named link targets can all be placed at the end of the document, so they don't even have to interrupt the flow from one paragraph to another.

Rather than referencing external documents, you can also include footnotes to be placed at the end of the same document or in an attached bibliography. Defining this type of link works much like standard links except that the link text is set apart by square brackets. Between the brackets, the text can either be just a number or a small piece of text, which will be used to reference the related information elsewhere.

Then, at the end of the document, the referenced information can be included in a format similar to named link targets. Rather than using an underscore to signify it, the reference text from earlier in the document is enclosed in square brackets again. After that, simply write the related text in the paragraph. This can be used for references to traditional publications, such as books, as well as for minor additions to further clarify the main text.

```
The reStructuredText format isn't part of Python itself, but it's popular enough
that even published books [1]_ reference it as an integral part of the Python
development process.
```

```
.. [1] Alchin, Marty. *Pro Python*. Apress, 2010.
```

In addition to these options, docutils allows reStructuredText to be expanded to provide other features. One application that provides some additional features is Sphinx.

Sphinx

The base features provided by reStructuredText are designed to work with individual documents. Even though it's easy to reference other documents, those references must be explicitly included in each document. If you write a complex application that requires multiple documents, each one will need to know the full structure of all the documents in order to reference them.

Sphinx[4] is an application that attempts to address that problem by working with the documents as a whole collection. In this way, it's somewhat similar to other, more popular automated systems like Javadoc and Doxygen, but Sphinx is designed to get its content from dedicated files rather than directly from the code itself. It can also include content based on code, but the main goal is to write documentation on its own.

By managing references across documents more effectively, Sphinx can generate an entire documentation package at once. This can be a web site full of linked HTML documents or even a single

---

[4] http://sphinx.pocoo.org/

PDF document that includes all the documents as individual sections. In addition, Sphinx offers a variety of styling options, with many already supplied by a growing community.

Taking It With You

The tools shown here serve only as a base for the real work of documenting your code. The real work of documentation requires taking a step back from the code itself, so you can see your application the way your users and other developers would see it. Keeping that in mind, it's often useful to read documentation for other similar applications. That will give you a good idea of what your users are used to seeing, the types of questions they need answered and how to distinguish your application as a superior alternative to the existing options.

On other side of the spectrum, you can also help your users by taking a very close look at your code. Putting your code under the tightest scrutiny will allow you to write tests. The next chapter will show how tests can verify that your application works the way it should, and that your documentation stays as accurate as possible.

CHAPTER 9

■■■

Testing

Writing an application is only part of the process; it's also important to check that all the code works as it should. You can visually inspect the code, but it's better to execute it in a variety of situations that may arise in the real world to make sure it behaves properly in all situations. This process is called unit testing because the goal is to test the smallest available units of execution.

Typically, the smallest unit is a function or method, many of which combine to form a full application. By breaking it down into individual units, you can minimize how much each test is responsible for. This way, a failure of any particular unit doesn't involve hundreds of lines of code, so it's easier to track down exactly what's going wrong.

Testing each individual unit can be a lengthy process for large applications, though, given how many scenarios you may need to take into account. Rather than try to get through all of it manually, you can automate the process by letting your code do the heavy lifting. Writing a test suite allows you to easily try all the different paths your code might take, verifying that each behaves as it should.

Test-Driven Development (TDD)

One of the more extreme examples of automated testing is the practice of test-driven development, often referred to simply as TDD. As the name implies, this practice uses automated testing to drive the development process. Whenever a new feature is written, tests for that feature are written first—tests that will fail right away. Once the tests are in place, you would write code to make sure those tests pass.

One value of this approach is that it encourages you to understand the desired behavior more thoroughly before setting out to write the code. For example, a function that processes text might have a number of common input strings, each with a desired output. Writing the test first encourages you to think about the output string for each available input string, without regard to how the string is processed internally. By shifting the focus away from code at the outset, it's easier to see the big picture.

The more obvious advantage, though, is that it ensures that every piece of code in an application has a set of tests associated with it. When code comes first, it's all too easy to run a few basic scenarios manually, then move on to coding the next feature. Tests can get lost in the shuffle, even though they're essential to the long-term health of the project. Getting in the habit of writing tests first is a good way to make sure they do get written.

Unfortunately, many developers find test-driven development far too strict for practical work. As long as the tests get written as comprehensively as possible, though, your code will reap the benefits. One of the easiest ways to do this is to write doctests.

Doctests

The topic of documentation was well covered in the previous chapter, but one particular aspect of it can be useful for testing. Since Python supports docstrings that can be processed by code, rather than just by people, the content within those strings can be used to perform basic tests as well.

In order to play double-duty alongside regular documentation, doctests must look like documentation, while still being something that can be parsed, executed and verified for correctness. One format fits that bill very conveniently, and it's been in use throughout this book. Doctests are formatted as interactive interpreter sessions, which already contain both input and output in an easily identifiable format.

Formatting Code

Even though the overall format of a doctest is identical to the interpreter sessions shown throughout this book, there are some specific details that are important to identify. Each line of code to execute begins with three right angle brackets (>>>) and a single space, followed by the code itself.

```
>>> a = 2
```

Just like the interactive interpreter, any code that extends beyond one line is indicated by new lines beginning with three periods (...) rather than brackets. You can include as many of these as necessary to complete multi-line structures, such as lists and dictionaries, as well as function and class definitions.

```
>>> b = ('example',
... 'value')
>>> def test():
...     return b * a
```

All the lines that start with periods like this are combined with the last line that started with angle brackets, and they're all evaluated together. That means you can leave extra lines if necessary, anywhere in the structure or even after it. This is useful for mimicking the output of an actual interpreter session, which requires a blank line to indicate when indented structures, such as functions or classes, are completed.

```
>>> b = ('example',
...
... 'value')
>>> def test():
...     return b * a
...
```

Representing Output

With the code in place, we just need to verify that its output matches what's expected. In keeping with the interpreter format, output is presented beneath one or more lines of input code. The exact formatting of the output will depend on the code being executed, but it's the same as you'd see when typing the code into the interpreter directly.

```
>>> a
2
>>> b
```

```
('example', 'value')
>>> test()
('example', 'value', 'example', 'value')
```

In these examples, the output string is equivalent to passing the return value from the expression into the built-in repr() function. Therefore, strings will always be quoted, and many specific types will have a different format than if you print them directly. Testing the output of str() can be achieved simply by calling str() in the line of code. Alternatively, the print() function is also supported and works just as you'd expect.

```
>>> for value in test():
...     print(value)
example
value
example
value
```

In examples like this, all lines of the output are checked against what was actually returned or printed by the code provided. This provides a very readable way to deal with sequences, as shown here. For longer sequences, as well as situations where output is allowed to change from one run to another, output may also include three periods as ellipses, indicating a place where additional content should be ignored.

```
>>> for value in test():
...     print(value)
example
...
value
```

This form is particularly useful when testing exceptions, because the interpreter output includes file paths, which will nearly always change from one system to another, and aren't relevant to most tests. In these cases, what's important to test is that the exception is raised, that it's the correct type and that its value, if any, is correct.

```
>>> for value in test:
...     print(value)
Traceback (most recent call last):
    ...
TypeError: 'function' object is not iterable
```

As the output format here suggests, the doctest will verify the first and last lines of the exception output, while ignoring the entire traceback in between. Since the traceback details are typically irrelevant to the documentation as well, this format is also much more readable.

Integrating With Documentation

Since the tests are meant to be built into documentation, there needs to be a way to make sure that only the tests get executed. In order to distinguish between the two without interrupting the flow of documentation, tests are set aside by nothing more than an extra newline. You'd always have to use one newline to avoid them all running together on a single line, so adding an extra simply leaves one blank line between the two.

```
"""
This is an example of placing documentation alongside tests in a single string.

>>> print 'Hello, world!'
'Hello, world!'

Additional documentation can be placed between snippets of code, and it won't
disturb the behavior or validity of the tests.
"""
```

Running Tests

The actual execution of doctests is provided by the doctest module. In the simplest form, you can run a single function to test an entire module. This is useful when writing a set of tests for a file that was already written because you can easily test the file individually after writing new tests. Simply import doctest and run its testmod() function to test the module. Here's an example module that contains a couple types of doctests.

```
def times2(value):
    """
    Multiplies the provided value by two. Because input objects can override
    the behavior of multiplication, the result can be different depending on
    the type of object passed in.

    >>> times2(5)
    10
    >>> times2('test')
    'testtest'
    >>> times2(('a', 1))
    ('a', 1, 'a', 1)
    """
    return value * 2

if __name__ == '__main__':
    import doctest
    doctest.testmod()
```

The docstring in times2() function includes tests and, because it's available as a module-level function, the testmod() can see it and execute the tests. This simple construct allows you to call the module directly from the command line and see the results of all doctests in the module. For example, if this module was called times2.py, you could invoke it from the command line as follows.

```
$ python times2.py
$
```

By default, the output only contains errors and failures, so if all the tests pass, there won't be any output at all. Failures are reported on individual tests, with each input/output combination being considered a unique test. This provides fine-grained details about the nature of the tests that were attempted and how they failed. If the final line in the example doctest were to read just ('a', 1) instead, here's what would happen.

```
$ python times2.py
**********************************************************************
File "...", line 11, in __main__.times2
Failed example:
    times2((a, '1'))
Expected:
    (a, '1')
Got:
    (a, '1', a, '1')
**********************************************************************
1 items had failures:
   1 of   3 in __main__.times2
***Test Failed*** 1 failures.
$
```

When working with more complicated applications and frameworks, though, the simple input/output paradigm of doctests breaks down fairly quickly. In those situations, Python provides a more powerful alternative, the unittest module.

The unittest module

Unlike doctests, which require your tests be formatted in a very specific way, unittest offers much more flexibility by allowing you to write your tests in real Python code. As is often the case, this extra power requires more control over how your tests are defined. In the case of unit tests, this control is provided by way of an object-oriented API for defining individual tests, test suites and data fixtures for use with tests.

After importing the unittest module, the first place to start is the TestCase class, which forms the base of most of the module's features. It doesn't do much on its own, but when subclassed, it offers a rich set of tools to help define and control your tests. These tools are a combination of existing methods that you can use to perform individual tests and new methods you can define to control how your tests work. It all starts by creating a subclass of the TestCase class.

```
import unittest

class MultiplicationTestCase(unittest.TestCase):
    pass
```

Setting Up

The starting point for most test cases is the setUp() method, which you can define to perform some tasks at the start of all the tests that will be defined on the class. Common setup tasks include defining static values that will be compared later, opening connections to databases, opening files and loading data to analyze.

This method takes no arguments and doesn't return anything. If you need to control its behavior with any parameters, you'll need to define those in a way that setUp() can access without them being passed in as arguments. A common technique is to check os.environ for specific values that affect the behavior of the tests. Another option is to have a customizable settings modules that can be imported in setUp(), which can then modify the test behavior.

Likewise, any values that setUp() defines for later use can't be returned using the standard value. Instead, they can be stored on the TestCase object itself, which will be instantiated prior to running setUp(). The next section will show that individual tests are defined as methods on that same object, so any attributes stored during setup will be available for use by the tests when they execute.

```python
import unittest

class MultiplicationTestCase(unittest.TestCase):
    def setUp(self):
        self.factor = 2
```

■ **Note** If you look at PEP-8, you'll notice that the name setUp() doesn't follow standard Python naming conventions. The capitalization style here is based on the Java testing framework, JUnit. Python's unit testing system was ported from Java, and some of its style carried over as well.

Writing Tests

With the setup in place, you can write some tests to verify whatever behavior you're working with. Like setUp(), these are implemented as custom methods on your test case class. Unlike setUp(), though, there's no single specific method that must implement all the tests. Instead, the test framework will look at your test case class for any methods whose names begin with the word test.

For each method that it finds, the test framework executes setUp() before executing the test method. This helps ensure that each method can rely on a consistent environment, regardless of how many methods there are, what they each do or in what order they're executed. Completely ensuring consistency requires one other step, but that will be covered in the next section.

When writing the body of a test method, the TestCase class offers some utility methods to describe how your code is supposed to work. These are designed in such a way that each represents a condition that must be true in order to continue. There are several of these methods, with each covering a specific type of assertion. If the given assertion passes, the test will continue to the next line of code; otherwise, the test halts immediately and a failure message will be generated. Each method provides a default message to use in case of a failure but also accepts an argument to customize that message.

- assertTrue(expr, msg=None)—This method tests that the given expression evaluates to True. This is the simplest assertion available, mirroring the built-in assert keyword. Using this method ties failures into the test framework, though, so it should be used instead. If you prefer the assert keyword, this method is also available as assert_().

- assertFalse(expr, msg=None)—The inverse of assertTrue(), this test will only pass if the provided expression evaluates to False.

- fail(msg=None)—This method generates a failure message explicitly. This is useful if the conditions of the failure are more complex than the built-in methods provide for on their own. Generating a failure is preferable to raising an exception because it indicates that the code failed in a way that the test understands, rather than being unknown.

These functions alone provide a basic palette for the rest of your tests. To start converting the earlier doctest to a unit test, we can start by providing a testNumber() method to simulate the first test that was performed previously. Like doctests, the unittest module also provides a simple function to run all the tests found in the given module; this time, it's called main().

```
import unittest
import times2

class MultiplicationTestCase(unittest.TestCase):
    def setUp(self):
        self.factor = 2

    def testNumber(self):
        self.assertTrue(times2.times2(5) == 10)

if __name__ == '__main__':
    unittest.main()
```

Tests are typically stored in a module called tests.py. After saving this file, we can execute it just like the doctest example shown previously.

```
$ python tests.py
.
----------------------------------------------------------------------
Ran 1 test in 0.001s
```

Unlike doctests, unit testing does show some statistics by default. Each period represents a single test that was run, so complex applications with dozens, hundreds or even thousands of tests can easily fill several screens with results. Failures and errors are also represented here, using E for errors and F for failures. In addition, each failure will produce a block of text to describe what went wrong. Look what happens when we change the test expression.

```
import unittest
import times2

class MultiplicationTestCase(unittest.TestCase):
    def setUp(self):
        self.factor = 2

    def testNumber(self):
        self.assertTrue(times2.times2(5) == 42)

if __name__ == '__main__':
    unittest.main()

$ python tests.py
F
======================================================================
FAIL: testNumber (__main__.MultiplicationTests)
----------------------------------------------------------------------
Traceback (most recent call last):
```

```
    File "tests.py", line 9, in testNumber
      self.assertTrue(times2(5) == 42)
AssertionError: False is not True
----------------------------------------------------------------------
Ran 1 test in 0.001s
```

FAILED (failures=1)

As you can see, it shows exactly which test method generated the failure, with a traceback to help track down the code flow that led to the failure. In addition, the failure itself is shown as an AssertionError, with the assertion shown plainly.

In this case, though, the failure message isn't as useful as it could be. All it reports is that False is not True. That's a correct report, of course, but it doesn't really tell the whole story. In order to better track down what went wrong, it'd be useful to know what the function actually returned.

To provide more information about the values involved, we'll need to use a test method that can identify the different values individually. If they're not equal, the test fails just like the standard assertion, but the failure message can now include the two distinct values so you can see how they're different. That can be a valuable tool in determining how and where the code went wrong—which is, after all, the whole point of testing.

- assertEqual(obj1, obj2, msg=None)—This checks that both objects that were passed in evaluate as equal, utilizing the comparison features shown in Chapter 5 if applicable.

- assertNotEqual(obj1, obj2, msg=None)—This is similar to assertEqual() except that this method will fail if the two objects are equal.

- assertAlmostEqual(obj1, obj2, *, places=7, msg=None)—Specifically for numeric values, this method rounds the value to the given number of decimal places before checking for equality. This helps account for rounding errors and other problems due to floating point arithmetic.

- assertNotAlmostEqual(obj1, obj2, *, places=7, msg=None)—The inverse of the previous method, this test fails if the two numbers are equal when rounded to the specified number of digits.

With assertEqual() available, we can change testNumber() to produce a more useful message in the event that the assertion fails.

```
import unittest
import times2

class MultiplicationTestCase(unittest.TestCase):
    def setUp(self):
        self.factor = 2

    def testNumber(self):
        self.assertEqual(times2.times2(5), 42)

if __name__ == '__main__':
    unittest.main()
```

```
$ python tests.py
F
======================================================================
FAIL: testNumber (__main__.MultiplicationTests)
----------------------------------------------------------------------
Traceback (most recent call last):
  File "tests.py", line 9, in testNumber
    self.assertEqual(times2(5), 42)
AssertionError: 10 != 42
----------------------------------------------------------------------
Ran 1 test in 0.001s

FAILED (failures=1)
```

Behind the scenes, assertEqual() does a couple interesting things to be as flexible and powerful as possible. First, by using the == operator, it can compare the two objects using whatever more efficient method the objects themselves may define. Second, the formatting of the output can be configured by supplying a custom comparison method. Several of these customized methods are provided in the unittest module.

- assertSetEqual(set1, set2, msg=None)—Because unordered sequences are typically implemented as sets, this method is designed specifically for sets, using the first set's difference() method to determine whether any items are different between the two.

- assertDictEqual(dict1, dict2, msg=None)—This method is designed specifically for dictionaries, in order to take their values into account as well as their keys.

- assertListEqual(list1, list2, msg=None)—Similar to assertEqual(), this method is targeted specifically at lists.

- assertTupleEqual(tuple1, tuple2, msg=None)—Like assertListEqual(), this is a customized equality check, but this time tailored for use with tuples.

- assertSequenceEqual(seq1, seq2, msg=None)—If you're not working with a list, tuple or a subclass of one of them, this method can be used to do the same job on any object that acts as a sequence.

In addition to these methods provided out of the box, you can add your own to the test framework, so that assertEqual() can more effectively work with your own types. By passing a type and a comparison function into the addTypeEqualityFunc() method, you can register it for use with assertEqual() later on.

Using addTypeEqualityFunc() effectively can be tricky, because it's valid for the entire test case class, no matter how many tests there may be inside it. It may be tempting to add the equality function in the setUp() method, but remember that setUp() gets called once for each test method that was found on the TestCase class. If the equality function will be registered for all tests on that class, there's no point registering it before each one.

A better solution would be to add the addTypeEqualityFunc() call to the __init__() method of the test case class. This also has the additional benefit that you can subclass your own test case class to provide a more suitable base for other tests to work with. That process is explained in more detail later in this chapter.

Compatibility: Prior to 3.1/2.7

The ability to specify custom equality comparison methods was added in Python 3.1 and backported to Python 2.7. Prior to those versions, the only equality features available were `assertEqual()`, `assertAlmostEqual()` and their counterparts. As long as you write your tests to simply reference `assertEqual()` instead of the more specific methods, they'll pass or fail the same way both before and after this change.

The potential problem comes in adding type-specific equality methods for custom classes provided by your application. The `addTypeEqualityFunc()` method was also added in Python 3.1/2.7, so in order to support both options, you'll have to test for its existence. A simple attribute test such as `hasattr(self, 'addTypeEqualityFunc')` will suffice. Just make sure that your custom type provides an `__eq__()` method that performs the same comparison as your test-specific function, so that the tests will still pass and fail equally across all versions.

Other Comparisons

Beyond simple equality, `unittest.TestCase` includes a few other methods that can be used to compare two values. Aimed primarily at numbers, these address the question of whether a tested value is less than or greater than what was expected.

- `assertGreater(obj1, obj2, msg=None)`—Similar to the tests for equality, this tests whether the first object is greater than the second. Like equality, this also delegates to methods on the two objects, if applicable.

- `assertGreaterEqual(obj1, obj2, msg=None)`—This works just like `assertGreater()`, except that the test also passes if the two objects compare as equal.

- `assertLess(obj1, obj2, msg=None)`—This test passes if the first object compares as less than the second object.

- `assertLessEqual(obj1, obj2, msg=None)`—Like `assertLess()`, this tests whether the first object is less than the second but also passes if both are equal.

Compatibility: Prior to 3.1

All of these comparison methods were added to Python in versions 3.1 and 2.7. There is no direct equivalent to this functionality in earlier versions, but the same behavior can be simulated by performing the test directly in your test method and using `fail()` explicitly to generate a useful failure message.

Testing Strings and Other Sequence Content

Sequences present an interesting challenge because they're made up of multiple individual values. Any value in a sequence could determine the success or failure of a given test, so it's necessary to have tools to work with them specifically. First, there are two methods designed for strings, where simple equality may not always be sufficient.

- `assertMultiLineEqual(obj1, obj2, msg=None)`—This is a specialized form of `assertEqual()`, designed for multi-line strings. Equality works like any other string, but the default failure message is optimized to show the differences between the values.

- `assertRegexpMatches(text, regexp, msg=None)`—This tests whether the given regular expression matches the text provided.

More generally, tests for sequences need to make sure that certain items are present in the sequence in order to pass. The equality methods shown previously will only work if the entire sequence must be equal. In the event that some items in the sequence are important but the rest can be different, we'll need to use some other methods to verify that.

- `assertIn(obj, seq, msg=None)`—This tests whether the object is present in the given sequence.

- `assertNotIn(obj, seq, msg=None)`—This works like `assertIn()` except that it fails if the object exists as part of the given sequence.

- `assertDictContainsSubset(dict1, dict2, msg=None)`—This method takes the functionality of `assertIn()` and applies it specifically to dictionaries. Like the `assertDictEqual()` method, this specialization allows it to also take the values into account instead of just the keys.

- `assertSameElements(seq1, seq2, msg=None)`—This tests all the items in two sequences and passes only if the items in both sequences are identical. This only tests for the presence of individual items, not their order within each sequence. This will also accept two dictionaries but will treat it as any other sequence, so it will only look at the keys in the dictionary, not their associated values.

Compatibility: Prior to 3.1/2.7

All of the sequence-specific methods in this section were added in Python 3.1 and backported for inclusion in Python 2.7. Most of these methods can be simulated by writing your own code to perform the test and call `fail()` as necessary. One exception is the `assertMultiLineEqual()` method, which is only customized for the output of the failure message. If you're only interested in the pass/fail functionality, you can simply use `assertEqual()` to achieve the same result.

Testing Exceptions

So far, all the test methods have taken a positive approach, where the test verifies that a successful outcome really is successful. It's just as important to verify unsuccessful outcomes, though, because they still need to be reliable. Many functions are expected to raise exceptions in certain situations, and unit testing is just as useful in verifying that behavior.

- `assertRaises(exception, callable, *args, **kwargs)`—Rather than checking a specific value, this method tests a callable to see that it raises a particular exception. In addition to the exception type and the callable to test, it also accepts any number of positional and keyword arguments. These extra arguments will be passed to the callable that was supplied, so that multiple flows can be tested.

- assertRaisesRegexp(exception, regex, callable, *args, **kwargs)—This method is slightly more specific than assertRaises() because it also accepts a regular expression that must match the exception's string value in order to pass. The expression can be passed in as a string or as a compiled regular expression object.

In our times2 example, there are many types of values that can't be multiplied by an integer. Those situations can be part of the explicit behavior of the function, as long as they're handled consistently. The typical response would be to raise a TypeError, as Python does by default. Using the assertRaises() method, we can test for this as well.

```
import unittest
import times2

class MultiplicationTestCase(unittest.TestCase):
    def setUp(self):
        self.factor = 2

    def testNumber(self):
        self.assertEqual(times2.times2(5), 42)

    def testInvalidType(self):
        self.assertRaises(TypeError, times2.times2, {})
```

Some situations are a bit more complicated, which can cause difficulties with testing. One common example is an object that overrides one of the standard operators. You could call the overridden method by name, but it would be more readable to simply use the operator itself. Unfortunately, the normal form of assertRaises() requires a callable, rather than just an expression.

To address this, both of these methods can act as context managers using a with block. In this form, you don't supply a callable or arguments, but rather just pass in the exception type and, if using assertRaisesRegexp(), a regular expression. Then, in the body of the with block, you can add the code that must raise the given exception. This can also be more readable than the standard version, even for situations that wouldn't otherwise require it.

```
import unittest
import times2

class MultiplicationTestCase(unittest.TestCase):
    def setUp(self):
        self.factor = 2

    def testNumber(self):
        self.assertEqual(times2.times2(5), 42)

    def testInvalidType(self):
        with self.assertRaises(TypeError):
            times2.times2({})
```

The `assertRaises()` method was around before Python 2.5, so it will be available in most Python versions in use today. The regular expression variant, however, was added in Python 3.1 and backported to Python 2.7. The same functionality could be simulated using a `try/except` combination to get access to the error message directly, where its string value can be verified using a regular expression.

Even though the `with` statement and context managers were both introduced in Python 2.5, `assertRaises()` didn't support the context management protocol until version 3.1. Since the `assertRaisesRegexp()` method didn't exist until that version either, there was no support for context managers in earlier versions. To achieve the same effect without context managers, you'll need to create a new callable—often a lambda function—to pass into the test method.

Testing Identity

The last group contains methods for testing the identity of objects. Rather than just checking to see if their values are equivalent, these methods check to see if two objects are in fact the same. One common scenario for this test is when your code caches values for use later. By testing for identity, you can verify that a value returned from cache is the same value that was placed in the cache to begin with, rather than simply an equivalent copy.

- `assertIs(ob1, obj2, msg=None)`—This method checks to see if the two arguments both refer to the same object. The test is performed using the identity of the objects, so objects that might compare as equal will still fail if they're not actually the same object.

- `assertIsNot(obj1, obj2, msg=None)`—This inversion of `assertIs()` will only pass if the two arguments refer to two different objects. Even if they would otherwise compare as equal, this test requires them to have different identities.

- `assertIsNone(obj, msg=None)`—This is a simple shortcut for a common case of `assertIs()`, where an object is compared to the built-in `None` object.

- `assertIsNotNone(obj, msg=None)`—The inversion of `assertIsNone()` will pass only if the object provided is not the built-in `None` object.

None of these methods in this section existed prior to Python 3.1. At that time, they were also backported to Python 2.7, but they won't be present in any default installation of Python 3.0 or Python 2.6 and below. You can still use the `is` keyword in a simple `assertTrue()` test, but you'll probably want to test it in an `if` block, so that you can use `fail()` to generate a more useful failure message, containing both values.

Tearing Down

Just as `setUp()` gets called before each individual test is carried out, the `TestCase` object also calls a `tearDown()` method to clean up any initialized values after testing is carried out. This is used quite often in tests that need to create and store information outside of Python during testing. Examples of such information are database rows and temporary files. Once the tests are complete, that information is no longer necessary, so it makes good sense to clean up after they've completed.

Typically, a set of tests that works with files will have to create temporary files along the way, to verify that they get accessed and modified properly. These files can be created in setUp() and deleted in tearDown(), ensuring that each test has a fresh copy when it runs. The same can be done with databases or other data structures.

■ **Note** The key value of setUp() and tearDown() is that they can prepare a clean environment for each individual test. If you need to set up an environment for all the tests to share or revert some changes after all tests have completed, you'll need to do so before or after starting the testing process.

Providing a Custom Test Class

Because the unittest module is designed as a class to be overridden, you can write your own class on top of it for your tests to use instead. This is a different process than writing tests because you're providing more tools for your tests to use. You can override any of the existing methods that are available on TestCase itself or add any others that are useful to your code.

The most common way to extend the usefulness of TestCase is to add new methods to test different functionality than the original class was designed for. A file-handling framework might include extra methods for testing the size of a given file or perhaps some details about its contents. A framework for retrieving web content could include methods to check HTTP status codes or look for individual tags in HTML documents. The possibilities are endless.

Changing Test Behavior

Another powerful technique available when creating a testing class is the ability to change how the tests themselves are performed. The most obvious way to do this is to override the existing assertion methods, which can change how those tests are performed. There are a few other ways to alter the standard behavior, without overriding the assertion methods.

These additional overrides can be managed in the __init__() method of your custom class because, unlike setUp(), the __init__() method will only be called once per TestCase object. That makes it good for those customizations that need to affect all tests but won't be affected by any of the tests as they run. One such example, mentioned previously in this chapter, is the ability to add custom equality comparison methods, which are registered with the addTypeEqualityFunc() method.

Another modification you can make to the test class is to define what type of exception is used to identify failures. Normally, all test failures raise an AssertionError behind the scenes—the same exception used when an assert statement fails. If you need to change that for any reason, such as to better integrate with a higher-level testing framework, you can assign a new exception type to the failureException class attribute.

As a side-effect of using the failureException attribute to generate failures, you can raise it explicitly using self.failureException to generate a test failure. This is essentially the same as simply calling self.fail(), but it can be more readable in some cases to raise an exception rather than call a method.

Taking It With You

The tools described in this chapter are just the basis of a functional test suite. As you write an application, you'll need to fill in the gaps with the important facets of how your code should work. Always remember, though, that tests aren't just for you. By making sure that new code doesn't break existing code, you can provide a much better guarantee for your users once you distribute your code to the public. The next chapter will show how you can get your code to the masses.

■ ■ ■

## CHAPTER 10

Distribution

Once you have a working application, the next step is to decide how and where to distribute it. You might be writing it for yourself, but you may instead have a wider audience and have a schedule for releasing it to them. There are a number of decisions to be made and tasks to be performed before you can do that, though. This process consists primarily of packaging and distribution, but it begins with licensing.

Licensing

Before releasing any code to the public, you must decide on a license that will govern its use. A license will allow you to convey to your users how you intend your code to be used, how you expect others to use it, what you ask from them in return and what rights you expect them to confer on users of their own code after integrating with yours. These are complex questions that can't be answered in a universal way for every project. Instead, you'll need to consider a number of issues.

Your own philosophy plays a key role, as it affects many other decisions. Some people intend to earn a living from their code, which could mean the source code won't be released at all. Instead, your work could be offered as a service that customers can pay to use. On the other hand, you may be interested in helping people learn to do things better, faster, easier or more reliably. Perhaps the most common license is the GPL.

GNU General Public License (GPL)

When people think of open source, the GPL[1] is often the first thing to come to mind. As one of the vanguards of the Free Software movement, its primary goal is to preserve a certain group of freedoms to the users of software. The GPL requires that if you distribute your program to others, you must also make the source code of that program available to them. That way, they're free to make modifications to your code as they see fit, in order to better support their own needs.

Further, the promise of the GPL is that any users who do alter your code can only distribute their modifications under the GPL or a license that ensures at least the same freedoms. This way, users of the software can be confident that if it doesn't work to their satisfaction, they have a way to make it better, no matter how far removed it may be from the original author.

Because the GPL places requirements on any modifications made to the original code and code that links to it, it's sometimes referred to as "viral." That's not necessarily an insult; it simply refers to the fact that the GPL forces the same license on anything that uses it. In that way, it spreads through software in much the same way as a traditional virus. This isn't unique to the GPL, but it's the feature many in the business world think of first when they think of the GPL and open source in general.

---

[1] http://propython.com/gpl/

Because the goal of the GPL is to preserve freedoms for computer users, it can be seen as restricting the freedom of programmers. The freedom of a programmer to distribute an application without divulging the source code restricts the freedom of a user to modify that code. Of those two opposing forces, the GPL is designed to preserve the user's freedoms by placing a number of restrictions on the behavior of programmers.

The GPL and Python

The GPL was written primarily for statically compiled languages, such as C and C++, so it often speaks in terms of code in "object form" that may be "statically linked" to other code. These terms are central to its vocabulary, but aren't as clearly understood when applied to dynamic languages like Python. Many Python applications use the GPL because of its overall philosophy, but its terms have yet to be tested in court in the context of a Python application.

It may seem like such details wouldn't really matter because Python code is generally distributed as source code anyway. After all, compiled Python bytecode isn't compatible with all the various systems where the code might be used. But because the GPL also applies to any other applications that use the code, these details become important if, for example, a statically compiled application uses GPL Python code internally for some features. It has yet to be seen whether such use would trigger the GPL's requirements on the distribution of that new application's source code.

Because these restrictions must also be passed on to any other application that includes GPL code, the available licenses that can work with it are limited. Any other license you might consider must include at least the same restrictions as the GPL, though additional restrictions can be added if necessary. One example of this is the AGPL.

Affero General Public License (AGPL)

With the proliferation of the Internet, it's now quite common for users to interact with software without ever obtaining a copy of that software directly. Because the GPL relies on distribution of code to trigger the requirement to also distribute source code, online services such as Web sites and mail systems are exempt from that requirement. Some have argued that those exemptions violate the spirit of the GPL by exploiting a loophole in its provisions.

To close that loophole, the AGPL was created. This license contains all the restrictions of the GPL as well as the added feature that any user interacting with the software, even by way of a network, will trigger the distribution clause. That way, Web sites that incorporate AGPL code must divulge the source code for any modifications they've made and any additional software that shares common internal data structures with it.

■ **Note** Even though the terminology and philosophy of the AGPL are very similar to the GPL, its applicability to Python is a bit more clear. Because just interacting with the software triggers the terms of the license, it doesn't matter as much whether the code is compiled from a static language like C or built from a dynamic language like Python. This also has yet to be tested in court for Python cases, though.

Because the AGPL is more restrictive than the GPL itself, it's possible for a project that uses AGPL to incorporate code that was originally licensed with the standard GPL. All of the protections of the GPL remain intact, while some extra ones are added. There's also a variant of the GPL that incorporates fewer restrictions, called the LGPL.

GNU Lesser General Public License (LGPL)

Because the GPL states that statically linking one piece of code to another triggers its terms, many small utility libraries were used less often than they might otherwise have been. These libraries typically don't constitute an entire application on their own, but because their usefulness requires tight integration with the host application, many developers avoided them in order to avoid their own applications being also bound to the GPL.

The LGPL was created to handle these cases by removing the static linking clause. Thus a library released under the LGPL could be freely used in a host application without requiring the host be bound by the LGPL or any other specific license. Even proprietary, commercial applications with no intention of releasing any source code can incorporate code licensed with the LGPL.

All the other terms remain intact, though, so any modifications to the LGPL code must be distributed as source code if the code itself is distributed in any way. For this reason, many LGPL libraries have extremely flexible interfaces that allow their host applications as many options as possible without having to modify the code directly.

Essentially, the LGPL leans more toward using the notion of open source to foster a more open programming community than to protect the rights of the software's eventual audience. Further down that road is one of the most liberal open source licenses available: BSD.

Berkeley Software Distribution (BSD) License

The BSD license provides a way to release code with the intent of fostering as much adoption as possible. It does this by placing relatively few limitations on the use, modification and distribution of the code by other parties. In fact, the entire text of the license consists of just a few bullet points and a disclaimer. Referring to BSD as a single license is a misnomer, though, as there are actually a few variations. In its original form, the license consisted of four points.

- Distributing the source code to the program requires that the code retain the original copyright, the text of the license and its disclaimer.

- Distributing the code as a compiled binary program requires the copyright, license text and disclaimer be included somewhere in the documentation or other materials provided with the distributed code.

- Any advertising used to promote the final product must attribute the BSD-licensed code as being included in the product.

- Neither the name of the organization that developed the software nor the names of any of its contributors may be used to specifically endorse the product without explicit consent beyond the license itself.

Notice that this contains no requirement that the source code be distributed at all, even when distributing compiled code. Instead, it only requires that the appropriate attribution is retained at all times and that it remains clear that there are two separate parties involved. This allows BSD-licensed code to be included in proprietary, commercial products with no need to release the source code behind it, making it fairly attractive to large corporations.

The advertising clause caused some headaches with organizations trying to use BSD-licensed code, though. The primary problem is that as the code itself changed hands and was maintained by different organizations, each organization that had a hand in its development must be mentioned by name in any advertising materials. In some cases, that could be dozens of different organizations, accounting for a significant portion of advertising space, especially when software often contains quite a few other disclaimers for other reasons.

To address those concerns, another version of the BSD license was made, without the advertising clause. This license is called the New BSD license, and it includes all the other requirements of the original. The removal of the advertising clause meant that changes in management of the BSD-licensed code had very little impact on organizations using it, which broadened its appeal considerably.

One further reduction of the BSD license is called the Simplified BSD license. In this variation, even the non-endorsement clause is removed, leaving only the requirements that the text of the license and its disclaimer be included. In order to still avoid untrue endorsement, the disclaimer in this version includes an extra sentence that clearly states that the views of both groups are independent of each other.

Other Licenses

The options listed here are some of the more commonly chosen, but there are many more available. The Open Source Initiative maintains a list of open source licenses[2] that have been examined and approved as preserving the ideals of open source. In addition, the Free Software Foundation maintains its own list of licenses[3] that have been approved as preserving the ideals of free software.

■ **Note** The difference between free software and open source is primarily philosophical but does have some real-world implications. In a nutshell, free software preserves the freedom of users of that software, while open source focuses on the software development model. Not all licenses are approved for both uses, so you may need to decide which is more important to you.

Once you have a license in place, you can start the process of packaging and distributing your code to others who can make use of it.

Packaging

It's not very easy to distribute a bunch of files individually, so you'll first have to bundle them up. This process is called packaging, but it shouldn't be confused with the standard Python notion of a package. Traditionally, a package is simply a directory with an __init__.py file in it, which can then be used as a namespace for any modules contained in that directory.

---

[2] http://propython.com/osi-licenses/
[3] http://propython.com/fsf-licenses/

For the purposes of distribution, a package also includes documentation, tests, a license and installation instructions. These are arranged in such a way that the individual parts can be easily extracted and installed into appropriate locations. Typically, the structure looks something like this.

```
AppName/
    LICENSE.txt
    README.txt
    MANIFEST.in
    setup.py
    app_name/
        __init__.py
        ...
    docs/
        ...
    tests/
        __init__.py
        ...
```

As you can see, the actual Python code package is a subdirectory of the overall application package, and it sits as a peer alongside its documentation and tests. The documentation contained in the docs directory can contain any form of documentation you prefer, but is usually filled with plain text files formatted using reStructuredText, as described in Chapter 8. The tests directory contains tests such as those described in Chapter 9. The LICENSE.txt file contains a copy of your chosen license and README.txt provides an introduction to your application, its purpose and features.

The more interesting features of this overall package are setup.py and MANIFEST.in, which aren't otherwise part of the application's code.

setup.py

Inside your package, setup.py is the script that will actually install your code into an appropriate location on a user's system. In order to be as portable as possible, this script relies on the distutils package provided in the standard distribution. That package contains a setup() function that uses a declarative approach to make the process easier to work with and more generic.

Located within distutils.core, the setup() function accepts a wide array of keyword arguments, each of which describes a particular feature of the package. Some pertain to the package as a whole, while others list individual contents that are included in the package. Three of these arguments are required for any package to be distributed using standard tools.

- name—This string contains the public name of the package, as it will be displayed to those who are looking for it. Naming a package can be a complex and difficult task, but as it's highly subjective, it's well beyond the scope of this book.

- version—This is a string containing the dot-separated version number of the application. It's common for first releases to use a version of '0.1' and increase from there. The first number is typically a major version indicating a promise of compatibility. The second is a minor version number, representing a collection of bug fixes or significant new features that don't break compatibility. The third is typically reserved for security releases that introduce no new functionality or other bug fixes.

- url—This string references a Web site where users can learn more about the application, find more documentation, request support, file bug reports or other tasks. It typically serves as a central hub for information and activity surrounding the code.

In addition to these three required elements, there are several optional arguments that can provide further detail about the application.

- author—The name of the author of the application.

- author_email—An email address where the author can be reached directly.

- maintainer—If the original author is no longer maintaining the application, this field contains the name of the person now responsible for it.

- maintainer_email—An email address where the maintainer can be reached directly.

- description—This string provides a brief description of the purpose of the program. Think of it as a one-line description that could be shown in a list alongside others.

- long_description—As its name implies, this is a longer description of the application. Rather than being used in lists, this one is typically shown when a user requests more detail about the specific application. Because this is all specified in Python code, many distributions simply read the contents of README.txt into this argument.

Beyond this metadata, the setup() function is responsible for maintaining a list of all the files necessary to distribute the application, including all Python modules, documentation, tests and license. Like the other information, these details are supplied using additional keyword arguments. All paths listed here are relative to the main package directory where setup.py itself is located.

- license—This is the name of a file that contains the full text of the license under which the program is distributed. Typically that file is called LICENSE.txt, but by explicitly passing it in as an argument, it can be named whatever you prefer.

- packages—This argument accepts a list of package names where the actual code is located. Unlike license, these values are Python import paths, using periods to separate individual packages along the path.

- package_dir—If your Python packages aren't in the same directory as setup.py, this argument provides a way to tell setup() where to find them. Its value is a dictionary that maps a package name to its location in the filesystem. One special key you can use is an empty string, which will use the associated value as a root directory to look for any packages that don't have an explicit path specified.

- package_data—If your package relies on data files that aren't written in Python directly, those files will only get installed if referenced in this argument. It accepts a dictionary that maps package names to their contents, but unlike package_dir, the values in this dictionary are lists, with each value in the list being a path specification to the files that should be included. These paths may include asterisks to indicate broad patterns to match against, similar to what you can query on the command line.

There are other options for more complex configurations, but these should cover most of the bases. For more information, consult the distutils documentation.[4] Once you have the pieces in place, you'll have a setup.py that looks something like this.

```python
from distutils.core import setup

setup(name='MyApp',
      version='0.1',
      author='Marty Alchin',
      author_email='marty@propython.com',
      url='http://propython.com/',
      packages=['my_app', 'my_app.utils'],
)
```

MANIFEST.in

In addition to setup.py specifying what files should be installed on a user's system, a package distribution also includes a number of files that are useful to the user, without being installed directly. These files, such as documentation, should be available to users with the package but don't have any code value, so they shouldn't be installed in an executable location. The MANIFEST.in file controls how these files should be added to the package.

MANIFEST.in is a plain text file, populated with a series of commands that tell distutils what files to include in the package. The filename patterns used in these commands follows the same conventions as the command line, allowing asterisks to serve as a wildcard for a broad range of filenames. For example, a simple MANIFEST.in might include any text files in the package's docs directory.

```
include docs/*.txt
```

This simple instruction will tell disutils to find all the text files in the docs directory and include them in the final package. Additional patterns could be included by separating the patterns with a space. There are a few different commands available, each of which has an include and exclude version available.

- include—The most obvious option, this command will look for all files that match any of the given patterns and include them in the package. They'll be placed in the package at the same location as they were found in the original directory structure.

- exclude—The opposite of include, this will tell distutils to ignore any files that match any of the patterns given here. This provides a way to avoid including some files, without having to explicitly list every included file in an include command. A common example would exclude TODO.txt in a package that specifically includes all text files.

- recursive-include—This command requires a directory as its first argument, prior to any filename patterns. It then looks inside that directory and any of its subdirectories for any files that match the given patterns.

---

[4] http://propython.com/distutils-setup/

- recursive-exclude—Like recursive-include, this command takes a directory first, followed by filename patterns. Any files that are found by this command are not included in the package, even if they're found by one of the inclusion commands.

- global-include—This command finds all the paths in the project, regardless of where they may be within the path structure. By looking inside directories, it works much like recursive-include, but because it looks through all directories, it doesn't need to take any argument other than the filename patterns to look for.

- global-exclude—Like global-include, this finds matching files anywhere in the source project, but the files found are excluded from the final package.

- graft—Rather than looking for matching files, this command accepts a set of directories that are simply included in the package in their entirety.

- prune—Like graft, this command takes a set of directories, but it excludes them from the package completely, even if there were matching files inside.

With both setup.py and MANIFEST.in in place, distutils provides an easy way to bundle up the package and prepare it for distribution.

The sdist command

To finally create the distributable package, your new setup.py is actually executable directly from a command line. Because this script is also used to install the package later, you must specify what command you'd like it to carry out. Users who obtain the package later will use the install command, but to package up a source distribution, the command is sdist.

```
$ python setup.py sdist
running sdist
...
```

This command processes the declarations made in setup.py as well as the instructions from MANIFEST.in to create a single archive file that contains all of the files you've specified for distribution. The type of archive file you get by default depends on the system you're running, but sdist provides a few options that you can specify explicitly. Simply pass in a comma-separated list of formats to the --format option to generate specific types.

- zip—The default on Windows machines, this format creates a zip file.

- gztar—The default on Unix machines, including MacOS, this creates a gzipped tarball. To also create this archive on a Windows system, you'll need an implementation of tar installed, such as the one available through Cygwin.[5]

- bztar—This command uses the alternative bzip compression on the archive tarball. This also requires an implementation of tar installed.

- ztar—This uses the simpler compress algorithm to compress the tarball. As with the others, an implementation of tar is required to use this option.

---

[5] http://propython.com/cygwin/

- tar—Rather than using compression, this option simply bundles up a tarball if an implementation of the tar utility is available.

When you run the sdist command, archive files for each of the formats you specified will be created and placed inside a new dist directory within your project. The names of each archive will simply use the name and version you supplied in setup.py, separated by a hyphen. The example provided earlier would result in files such as MyApp-0.1.zip.

Distribution

Once you have these files in place, you'll need a way to distribute them to the public. One option is to simply host your own Web site and serve up the files from there. That's typically the best way to market your code to a wide audience because you have an opportunity to put the documentation online in a more readable way, show examples of it in use, offer testimonials from people who are already using it and anything else you can come up with.

The only problem with simply hosting it yourself is that it becomes fairly difficult to find using automated tools. Many packages will rely on the presences of other applications, so it's often useful to be able to install them directly from inside a script, without having to navigate to a Web site and find the right link to download. Ideally, they would be able to translate a unique package name into a way to download that package and install it without assistance.

This is where the Python Package Index (PyPI)[6] comes into play. It's an online collection of Python packages that all follow a standardized structure, so they can be discovered more easily. Each has a unique name that can be used to locate it, and the index keeps track of which version is the latest and references the URL to that package. All you need to do is add your package to the index and it will be much easier for your users to work with.

Uploading to PyPI for the first time requires registration on the site. A PyPI account will allow you to manage your application details later and upload new versions and updates. Once you have an account, you can run python setup.py register to set up a page for your application at PyPI. This is an interactive script that will offer you three options for registering your account.

- Use an existing PyPI account. If you've created an account on the PyPI Web site already, you can specify your username and password here.

- Register a new PyPI account. If you'd rather create an account at the command-line, you can enter your details here and have the account created during registration.

- Generate a new PyPI account. If you'd like to take a simpler approach, this option will take the username you're already using in your operating system, generate a password automatically and register an account for that combination.

Once you choose your option, the register script will offer to save your account information locally, so you won't have to go through that step every time. With an account in place, the script will register the application with PyPI, using the information in setup.py. In particular, the name and long_description fields will combine to form a simple Web page, with other details shown in a list.

With a page in place to hold the application, the last step is to upload the code itself using the upload command. This must be done as part of a distribution build, even if you had previously built a

---

[6] http://propython.com/pypi/

distribution. That way, you can specify exactly what type of distributions you'd like to send to PyPI. For example, you can upload packages for both Windows and non-Windows users in a single step.

```
$ python setup.py sdist --format=zip,gztar upload
```

The distribution files are named according to the name of the application and its version number at the time the distribution was created. The entry in PyPI also contains a reference to the version number, so you can't upload the same distribution type of the same version more than once. If you try, you'll get an error from `setup.py` indicating that you'll need to create a new version number in order to upload a changed distribution.

Taking It With You

As you can see, the process of packaging and distributing a Python application using PyPI is actually fairly straightforward. Beyond PyPI, it's usually a good idea to put together a dedicated project Web site, where you can better promote and support your code. Always remember that distribution isn't the last step. Your users will expect a certain amount of support and interaction as they use your code and hope to improve it, so it's best to find a medium that supports those goals for you and your users.

Applications of all different sizes, audiences and goals are fair game for distribution. It doesn't matter if you're writing a small utility to help automate common tasks or an entire framework to power a set of features for other users' code. The next chapter will show you how to build such a framework from start to finish, building on many of the techniques shown throughout this book.

CHAPTER 11

■■■

Sheets: A CSV Framework

Of course, the most important thing in programming is the program. Tools, techniques, philosophy and advice don't offer much at all if they're never applied to solve a real-world problem. Sometimes that problem is very specific, but other times it's merely a specific example of a more general problem. These general problems are typically the subject of libraries and frameworks, which can provide the base for a more specific application.

This puts frameworks in an interesting position because they're focused more on serving the needs of developers, rather than ordinary users. The goal is to provide a foundation and a set of tools to aid someone else in the development of a more specific application. Supporting a wider array of uses requires more advanced techniques than would ordinarily be used to solve the problem directly.

In order to be useful to other developers, though, the ideal goal is to provide a sort of translation service, so that the advanced techniques used by the framework allow other developers to use simpler techniques to perform those more advanced tasks. In this respect, framework design is very similar to other forms of design, but rather than focusing primarily on a visual user interface, the focus is on the application's programming interface, the API.

It's important to look at frameworks like this, because if you're writing a framework, your audience is looking for a tool to save them time and energy, so they can focus on their unique needs. The framework should provide a set of features in a way that encourages integration with other types of applications, so it's necessary to think in terms of how those other applications should work.

There are countless examples of frameworks in use already, serving a wide variety of needs. They all address a general class of problem, such as Django[1] for Web development, SQLAlchemy[2] for database interaction and Twisted[3] for working with network protocols. These each take different approaches with the style and form of the interfaces they expose to developers, highlighting the various ways a framework can operate.

This chapter will show a framework that uses a declarative syntax similar to the ones used in Django and Elixir.[4] The choice of this approach is based largely on style, and even though there are other approaches you could use, investigating one in detail will highlight many of the decisions that must be made when writing a framework. You'll see all the techniques shown in this book combine to form a single, cohesive whole, exposing a public API that provides a number of useful features.

The particular problem that this chapter will address is the need to work with files that store information as rows of comma-separated values, more commonly referred to as CSV files. It may seem like a simple format on the surface, but with multiple options available for tasks like separating values on a line, separating lines themselves and encoding individual values within each line, it becomes a very complex topic.

---

[1] http://propython.com/django/
[2] http://propython.com/sqlalchemy/
[3] http://propython.com/twisted/
[4] http://propython.com/elixir/

Python already does a lot to help with CSV files by providing a csv module.[5] Rather than attempting to duplicate its functionality, we can use csv to do most of the heavy lifting behind the scenes. What we're going to do instead is build a layer on top of csv to make it easier to work with and integrate with other applications. Essentially, we're just providing a new API on top of an existing one, in hopes that we can make it a bit friendlier.

Building a Declarative Framework

There are several steps involved in building a framework using a declarative syntax similar to that of Django or Elixir, but the process itself really isn't all that difficult. Making decisions along the way, however, is where things get tricky. In this chapter, I'll outline the various steps required to build such a framework, as well as many of the decisions you'll have to make, but I can't provide any such decisions because each will have to be made specifically for your own project.

You won't be all on your own, though. Each decision point along the way will outline the pros and cons of various options, so you can be confident about making an informed choice. Making the right decisions at the outset will help ensure that your framework will withstand future upgrades as well as criticisms from those who may not agree with you. Just make sure you have valid, real-world reasoning behind your decisions and you'll be fine.

Rather than leaving you with nothing but theory, this chapter will step through the creation of a framework that's simple enough to introduce the essential concepts, without having to dwell too long on matters specific to its purpose. It also needs to be a good example of when a declarative framework should be used, which first requires us to understand what it is we're really looking at.

Introducing Declarative Programming

At its core, a declarative framework is a helper to make declarative programming easier—or in some cases, possible. Of course, that definition is useless without defining what makes it declarative, but thankfully very little introduction is necessary. After all, you've already seen declarative programming in action, and have probably been using it for quite some time, perhaps without even realizing it.

Declarative programming is the practice of telling a program what you want (declaring), rather than telling it what to do (instructing). This distinction is really more about the programmer than the program, in that there are often no special syntax, parsing or processing rules and no single way to define what does and doesn't qualify. It's most often defined as the opposite of imperative programming, where the programmer is expected to outline every step the computer needs to perform.

With this in mind, it's easy to note that higher-level interpreted languages, like Python, are much better suited for declarative programming than their lower-level cousins, like C. In fact, many forms of it are built right in. Rather than having to declare a memory location, specify its type, then store a value in memory at that location, you can simply assign a variable and Python does the rest.

```
>>> foo = 'bar'
```

That's just one form of declarative programming, using one syntax. When we talk about declarative frameworks in Python, though, it usually refers to using a class declaration to configure the framework, rather than a long and complicated set of configuration directives. Whether or not that's the right approach for your needs requires a bit more discussion of the pros and cons.

---

[5] http://propython.com/csv-module/

To Build or Not to Build?

Declarative frameworks have been a rising trend in the Python world in the past few years, but it's important to understand that they're not always the best approach to a given problem. Like anything else, deciding whether to use a declarative framework requires understanding what it really is, what it does and what it means for your needs.

Declarative frameworks do a great job of wrapping a lot of complex behavior into a simple class declaration. This can be a great time-saver, but it can also seem a lot like magic, something the Python community is constantly battling against. Whether this is good or bad depends entirely on how closely your API matches what users will expect from a class declaration and how well you document the areas where those expectations may fail.

By having a class as the primary method of conveying your intentions to the framework, it's reasonable to expect that instances will have meaning. Most often, an instance refers to a specific set of data that conforms to a format defined by the class declaration. If your application acts on just a single set of well-defined data, there's little use in having individual instances.

Declarative classes are designed to create many different configurations using the same framework, each designed for a particular configuration of data. If you only have one data format to work with—even if you've got loads of data—it just doesn't make sense to write a framework built for configurability. Just write a solution for your type of data and use it.

In other cases, you may not be able to describe the structure of a data set in advance, but instead have to adjust the structure based on the data provided. In these cases, there's little value in offering a class declaration, since no single declaration would suffice for the needs of the data you're working with.

A primary value of objects is the ability to perform actions on their contents, by way of instance methods. Since a declarative framework results in customized classes that produce individual instances, it stands to reason that these instances should be able to perform useful tasks that would be more difficult without the framework's assistance. This not only increases their usefulness but it also helps ensure that the resulting instances match with users' expectations.

To review, a declarative framework is a valuable approach if you have:

- Many potential configurations

- Each configuration known in advance

- Many instances of any given configuration

- Actions that can be performed on a given instance

The CSV framework described in this chapter needs to deal with a vast array of possible configurations of columns and structure, with many example files of each type. Actions such as loading and saving data are common, while others are unique to specific configurations.

Once completed, this framework will allow applications to specify CSV configurations as classes like the following, and interact with them using methods automatically attached to the class.

```python
import sheets

class EmployeeSheet(sheets.Row):
    first_name = sheets.StringColumn()
    last_name = sheets.StringColumn()
    hire_date = sheets.DateColumn()
    salary = sheets.CurrencyColumn(decimal_places=2)
```

So let's get started.

Building the Framework

There are three primary components of any declarative framework, though one of them may come in different forms, or possibly not at all.

- A base class—Since declarative frameworks are all about declaring classes, having a common base class to inherit from gives the frame a place to hook in and process declarations as they're encountered by Python. A metaclass attached to this base class provides the necessary machinery to inspect the declaration at runtime and make the appropriate adjustments. The base class is also responsible for representing instances of whatever structure your framework encapsulates, often with various methods attached to simply common procedures.

- Various field types—Inside the class declaration are a number of attributes, typically called fields. For some applications, it may make more sense to call them something more specific, but for this discussion, fields will suffice. These fields are used to manage individual data attributes in the structures represented by your framework, and often come in different flavors, each tailored to a different general type of data, such as strings, numbers and dates. Another important aspect of fields is that they must be able to know the order in which they get instantiated, so the ordering specified in the declaration is the same ordering used later on.

- An options container—Not strictly a necessary component, most frameworks have use for some type of class-wide options, which shouldn't be specified on every individual field, as that wouldn't be very DRY. Since subclassing doesn't provide any options except the choice of base classes, some other structure must be used to manage these options. How these options are declared and processed can vary greatly from one framework to another; there's no syntactic or semantic standard whatsoever. As a matter of convenience, this container often also manages the fields attached to the class.

As a syntactic aid, most declarative frameworks also make sure that all three of these components can be imported from one single location. This allows end-user code to have a much simpler import block, while also containing all the necessary components on a single, identifiable namespace. The name of this namespace should be something meaningful, so it's easy to read in end-user code. The name of the framework itself is often an ideal choice, but it's important to be descriptive, so make sure it all makes sense when reading it over.

Although deciding what to call the framework can be deferred to later in the process, it helps to have a name in mind early on, if only to name the package that will contain the modules described below. Using a placeholder like csv would work fine for now, but since Python has its own csv module—which we'll be relying on as well—reusing this name would cause a great deal of problems. Since CSV files are commonly used to exchange data among spreadsheet applications, we'll call our little framework sheets.

It would seem that our journey should start with the base class, but really any of the three components can be a reasonable place to start. It often depends on which piece requires the most thought, does the most work or needs to be tested first. For this discussion, we'll start with the options container, as it can be created without relying on the implementation details of the other components. This avoids leaving too many vague references to functionality that hasn't been described yet.

Managing Options

The primary purpose of an options component is to store and manage options for a given class declaration. These options are not specific to any one field, but rather apply to the entire class or are used as default values that individual fields can optionally override. For now, we'll set aside the question of how these options will be declared and simply focus on the container itself and its associated needs.

On the surface, options are simply a map of names to values, so we could use a simple dictionary. After all, Python has a fantastic dictionary implementation and simple is most certainly better than complex. However, writing our own class affords us a few extra features that will be very handy.

For starters, we can validate the options that are defined for a given class. They can be validated based on their individual values, their combination with other options, their appropriateness for the given execution environment and whether or not they're known options at all. With a dictionary, we're stuck simply allowing any type of value for any option, even if it makes no sense.

Mistakes in options would then only be known when code that relies on them chokes because they're incorrect or missing, and those types of errors typically aren't very descriptive. Validating on a custom object means we can provide much more useful messages to users who try to use incorrect or invalid options.

Using a custom class also means we add our own custom methods to perform tasks that, while useful, are either repetitive or don't really belong anywhere else. A validation method can verify that all the included options are appropriate, displaying useful messages if not. Remember also that the options container often manages fields, so there are some methods that can be added for that purpose; these are described later in this section.

In fact, by combining those two features, the options class can even validate field declarations in the context of provided options. Try doing that with an ordinary dictionary.

Because it may end up encapsulating quite a bit of functionality, we'll set up a new module for our options container, unambiguously named `options.py`. Like most classes, the bulk of the work will be done in the __init__() method. For our purposes, this will accept all known options, store them away as attributes and set up some other attributes that will be used by other methods later on. Validation is generally only useful when actively defining options, so that belongs in its own method so as not to bog down this one.

And so we come to the next decision in your framework: what options should you accept? Different frameworks will obviously have different requirements, and it's important to lay them out as completely as you can at the outset. Don't worry, you can always add more later, but it's better to get them in place earlier than later.

One useful rule of thumb is that options should always have defaults. Asking your users to not only write a class and provide fields but also provide options every time will get frustrating, especially if the required option often has the same value. In general, if something is truly required and doesn't have some reasonable default, it should be supplied as an argument to the methods that require it, rather than defined as an option on the class.

We're building a framework to interface with CSV files, so there are a number of options available. Perhaps the most obvious is the character encoding of the file, but Python already converts file content to Unicode when the file is opened in text mode. The open() function accepts an encoding argument that allows all the same encodings available with a string's encode() method. It defaults to UTF-8, which should suffice for most common needs.

■ **Note** The encoding used when reading the file seems like a perfect candidate for an option, so you can override the default UTF-8 behavior. Unfortunately, the standard CSV interface requires that the file be already open when it's passed in, so if our framework follows the same interface, we have no control over the encoding. The only way to control it would be to change the interface to accept a filename rather than an open file object.

Compatibility: Prior to 3.0

The open() method became aware of character encodings in Python 3.0, so earlier versions required some extra effort to reliably get Unicode data. Because the main text of this chapter relies on Python 3.1, Unicode handling isn't mentioned at all. To achieve the same effect in older versions, you'll need to wrap your open() call in something else to handle the conversion to Unicode.

Python provides a codecs package that keeps track of all the character encodings available for Unicode conversion. The function we're most interested in for CSV is codecs.getreader(), which accepts an encoding as its argument. It returns a function that can then be used to wrap around an open file, so that when its read() method is called, it reads from the file and returns a decoded Unicode string.

To decode UTF-8 on the fly, which will work just like the default Python 3 behavior, first get a reader using codecs.getreader('utf8'). Then, simply open the file using reader(open(filename)) instead of just using open() on its own. From then on, the file you get from the reader will return Unicode strings suitable for use with the rest of this framework.

One common variation in CSV files is whether they contain a header row, containing titles for the various columns. Since we'll be defining columns as fields later on in the framework, we don't really need that header row, so we can skip it. But only if we know it's there. A simple Boolean, defaulting to False for the more common case, will do the trick nicely.

```
class Options:
    """
    A container for options that control how a CSV file should be handled when
    converting it to a set of objects.

    has_header_row
        A Boolean indicating whether the file has a row containing header
        values. If True, that row will be skipped when looking for data.
        Defaults to False.
    """

    def __init__(self, has_header_row=False):
        self.has_header_row = has_header_row
```

There we have a simple, but useful, options container. At this point the only benefit it has over a dictionary is that it automatically prohibits any options other than the ones we've specified. We'll come back and add a more rigorous validation method later.

If you're familiar with Python's csv module, you may already know that it contains a variety of options as part of its support for different dialects. Since sheets will actually defer to that module for much of its functionality, it makes sense to support all of the same options, in addition to our own. In fact, it even makes sense to rename our Options class Dialect instead, to better reflect the vocabulary already in use.

Rather than listing all of the options supported by csv separately, though, let's take a bit more forward-thinking approach. We're relying on code outside our control, and it's a bit of a maintenance hassle to try to keep up with any changes that code might introduce in the future. In particular, we can support any existing options as well as any future options, by simply passing any additional options straight to csv itself.

In order to accept options without naming them, we turn to Python's support for extra keyword arguments using the double-asterisk syntax. These extra options can be stored away as a dictionary, which will be passed into the csv functions later on. Accepting them as a group of keyword arguments, rather than a single dictionary, helps unify all of the options, which will be important once we actually parse options out of the class declaration.

```
class Dialect:
    """
    A container for dialect options that control how a CSV file should be
    handled when converting it to a set of objects.

    has_header_row
        A Boolean indicating whether the file has a row containing header
        values. If True, that row will be skipped when looking for data.
        Defaults to False.

    For a list of additional options that can be passed in, see documentation
    for the dialects and formatting parameters of Python's csv module at
    http://docs.python.org/library/csv.html#dialects-and-formatting-parameters
    """

    def __init__(self, has_header_row=False, **kwargs):
        self.has_header_row = has_header_row
        self.csv_dialect = kwargs
```

This class will grow some more features later on, but that's enough to get things started. We'll come back to it a few more times before we're done, but for now, let's move on to what may well be the meatiest part of our little framework: fields.

Defining Fields

Fields are generally just containers for specific pieces of data. Because it's such a generic term, different disciplines may use something more specific to refer to the same concept. In databases, they're called columns. In forms, they're often called inputs. When executing a function or a program, they're called arguments. To maintain some perspective beyond this one framework, this chapter will refer to all such data containers as fields, even though for sheets itself, the term "column" will make more sense when naming the individual classes.

The first thing to define is a base field class, which will describe what it means to be a field. Without any details of any particular data type, this base class manages how fields fit in with the rest of the system, what API they'll have and how subclasses are expected to behave. Since our framework is calling them columns, we'll start a new module called columns.py and get to work.

Fields are Python objects that are instantiated as part of the class declaration and assigned as attributes of the class. Therefore, the __init__() method is the first entry point into field functionality and the only point where the field can be configured as part of the declaration. Arguments to __init__() may vary depending on a field's type, but there are often at least a few arguments that are applicable to all fields, and can thus be processed by the base class.

First, each field can have a title. This allows for more readable and understandable code, but also provides a way for other tools to automatically document the fields with more useful information than just the field's attribute name. Planning for validation wouldn't hurt, so we'll also add a way to indicate whether the field is required.

```python
class Column:
    """
    An individual column within a CSV file. This serves as a base for attributes
    and methods that are common to all types of columns. Subclasses of Column
    will define behavior for more specific data types.
    """

    def __init__(self, title=None, required=True):
        self.title = title
        self.required = required
```

Notice that the title is optional. If no title is provided, a simple one can be gleaned from the attribute name the field is assigned to. Unfortunately, the field doesn't know what that name is yet, so we'll have to come back for that functionality later. We also assume that most fields will be required, so that's the default, to be overridden on a per-field basis.

■ **Tip** Required fields may not immediately seem to have much value for a CSV framework, since the data comes from files rather than directly from users, but they can be useful. For some things like sheets, it can eventually validate incoming files or the data that's about to be saved to an outgoing file. It's generally a good feature to include at the outset for any framework, to support features that can be added later.

You may already have other arguments in mind for your framework's fields. If so, feel free to add them in now, following the same basic pattern. Don't worry about planning for everything at the outset, though; there will be plenty of opportunity to add more later on. Next on the agenda is to get the fields properly connected to their associated classes.

Attaching a Field to a Class

Next, we need to set up the hook for getting additional data from the class the field is assigned to, including the field's name. This new attach_to_class() method is—as its name suggests—responsible for attaching the field to the class where it was assigned. Even though Python automatically adds the attributes to the class where they're assigned, that assignment doesn't convey anything to the attribute, so we'll have to do so in the metaclass.

First, we need to decide what information the attribute needs to know about how it was assigned. After preparing for a title in the previous section, it's clear that the attribute will need to know what name it was given when assigned. By obtaining that name directly in code, we can avoid the trouble of having to write the name out separately as an argument to the attribute instantiation.

The long-term flexibility of the framework will also depend on providing as much information as possible to attributes, so that they can easily provide advanced functionality by introspecting the classes they're attached to. Unfortunately, the name alone doesn't say anything about the class where the attribute now resides, so we'll have to provide that in the metaclass as well.

Lastly, the options that were defined earlier, such as encoding, will have some bearing on the attribute's behavior. Rather than expecting the attribute to have to retrieve those options based on the class that was passed in, it's easier to simply accept the options as another argument. This leaves us with an attach_to_class() that looks something like this.

```python
class Column:
    """
    An individual column within a CSV file. This serves as a base for attributes
    and methods that are common to all types of columns. Subclasses of Column
    will define behavior for more specific data types.
    """

    def __init__(self, title=None, required=True):
        self.title = title
        self.required = required

    def attach_to_class(self, cls, name, options):
        self.cls = cls
        self.name = name
        self.options = options
```

This alone will allow other methods of the attribute object to access a wealth of information, such as the name of the class, what other attributes and methods were declared on it, what module it was defined in and more. The first task we'll need to perform with that information is somewhat more mundane, though, as we still need to deal with the title. If no title was specified when the attribute was created, this method can use the name to define one.

```python
class Column:
    """
    An individual column within a CSV file. This serves as a base for attributes
    and methods that are common to all types of columns. Subclasses of Column
    will define behavior for more specific data types.
    """

    def __init__(self, title=None, required=True):
        self.title = title
        self.required = required

    def attach_to_class(self, cls, name, options):
        self.cls = cls
        self.name = name
        self.options = options
        if self.title is None:
            # Check for None so that an empty string will skip this behavior
            self.title = name.replace('_', ' ')
```

This addition takes an attribute name with underscores and converts it to a title using multiple words. We could impose other conventions, but this is simple enough to work with, accurate for most situations and fits in with common naming conventions. This simple approach will cover most use cases without being difficult to understand or maintain.

As the comment indicates, the if test for this new feature goes against standard idioms by explicitly checking for None rather than simply letting an unspecified title evaluate to False. Doing things "the right way" here would remove the ability to specify an empty string as a title, which can explicitly indicate that no title is necessary.

Checking for None allows empty strings to still retain that string as the title, rather than having it replaced by the attribute name. One example of the usefulness of an empty title would be as a way to indicate that the column doesn't need to be presented in a display of the file's data. It's also a good example of where comments can be crucial to understanding the intent of a piece of code.

■ **Tip** Even though this attach_to_class() method doesn't use the options that were provided, it's generally a good idea to include it in the protocol. The next section will show that the options will be available as an attribute of the class, but it's a bit more clear to pass it in as its own argument. If your framework needs to apply these class-level options to individual fields, it'll be easier to accept it as an argument than to extract it form the class.

Adding a Metaclass

With the attach_to_class() method in place, we must now move on to the other side of the equation. After all, attach_to_class() can only receive information; the metaclass is responsible for providing that information. Until now, we haven't even started looking at the metaclass for this framework, so we need to start with the basics.

All metaclasses start out the same, by subclassing type. In this case, we'll also add an __init__() method because all we need is to process the contents of the class definition after Python has finished with them. First up, the metaclass needs to identify any options that were defined in the class and create a new Dialect object to hold them. There are a few ways to go about this.

The most obvious option would be to simply define options as class-level attributes. That would make defining the individual classes easy later on, but it would impose some problems that may not be as obvious. For one, it would clutter up the main class namespace. If you tried to create a class to process CSV files containing information about coded documents, you might reasonably have a column named encoding. Because we also have a class option named encoding, we'd have to name our column something else in order to avoid one of them overwriting the other and causing problems.

On a more practical note, it's easier to pick out options if they're contained in their own namespace. By being able to easily identify which attributes are options, we can pass them all in as arguments to Dialect and immediately know if any were missing or if invalid names were specified. So the task now is to determine how to provide a new namespace for options, while still declaring them as part of the main class.

The simplest solution is to use an inner class. Alongside any other attributes and methods, we can add a new class, named Dialect, to contain the various option assignments. This way, we can let Python create and manage the extra namespace for us, so that all we have to do is look for the name Dialect in the attribute list and pull it out.

■ **Tip** Even though the inner `Dialect` class inhabits the main namespace alongside other attributes and methods, there's much less chance of a clash because it's only one name instead of several. Further, we use a name that starts with a capital letter, which is discouraged for attribute and method names, there's even less chance of collision. Because Python names are case-sensitive, you're free to define an attribute called `dialect` (note the small "d") on the class without fear of bumping into this `Dialect` class.

To extract this new `Dialect` class, we'll turn to the first implementation of a metaclass in this framework. Because this will help form the base class for future inheritance, we'll put the code into a new module, named `base.py`.

```python
from sheets import options

class RowMeta(type):
    def __init__(cls, name, bases, attrs):
        if 'Dialect' in attrs:
            # Filter out Python's own additions to the namespace
            items = attrs['Dialect'].__dict__.items()
            items = dict((k, v) for (k, v) in items if not k.startswith('__'))
        else:
            # No dialect options were explicitly defined
            items = {}
        dialect = options.Dialect(**items)
```

Now that the options have been pulled out of the class definition and have populated a `Dialect` object, we'll need to do something with that new object. We know from the definition of `attach_to_class()` in the previous section that it gets passed into that method for each field attribute that was defined, but what else?

In the spirit of retaining as much information as possible for later, we'll keep it assigned to the class itself. But since the capitalized name doesn't work as well as an attribute name, it's best to rename it to something more suitable. Since it also forms a private interface to the inner workings of the framework, we can prefix the new name with an underscore to further prevent any accidental name clashes.

```python
from sheets import options

class RowMeta(type):
    def __init__(cls, name, bases, attrs):
        if 'Dialect' in attrs:
            # Filter out Python's own additions to the namespace
            items = attrs.pop('Dialect').__dict__.items()
            items = {k: v for k, v in items if not k.startswith('__')}
        else:
            # No dialect options were explicitly defined
            items = {}
        cls._dialect = options.Dialect(**items)
```

This simple change removes it from the class namespace where it was given the original name and instead inserts it under a new name, _dialect. Both names avoid clashes with common attribute names, but this change makes it use a more standard private attribute name. Previously, it used the standard style for naming a class because that's how it's defined.

With that, we finally have all the pieces in places to continue working with the field attributes. The first task is to locate them in the class definition and call attach_to_class() on any that are found. This is easily accomplished with a simple loop through the attributes.

```python
from sheets import options

class RowMeta(type):
    def __init__(cls, name, bases, attrs):
        if 'Dialect' in attrs:
            # Filter out Python's own additions to the namespace
            items = attrs.pop('Dialect').__dict__.items()
            items = {k: v for k, v in items if not k.startswith('__')}
        else:
            # No dialect options were explicitly defined
            items = {}
        cls._dialect = options.Dialect(**items)

        for key, attr in attrs.items():
            if hasattr(attr, 'attach_to_class'):
                attr.attach_to_class(cls, key, cls._dialect)
```

This simple metaclass contains a loop that just checks each attribute to see if it has an attach_to_class() method. If it does, the method is called, passing in the class object and the name of the attribute. This way, all the columns can get the information they need very early on in the process.

Duck Typing

This metaclass uses hasattr() to check for the existence of an attach_to_class() method, rather than simply checking to see if the attribute is an instance of Column. All instances of Column should indeed have the necessary method, but by using hasattr() instead, we open it up for any type of object. You could add attach_to_class() to other types of attributes, descriptors and even methods and gain quick and easy access to more advanced functionality. The metaclass only checks for precisely what it needs, leaving the rest open for flexibility, which is a primary benefit of duck typing.

Now all that's necessary to fill out the rest of base.py is to include a true base class that individual CSV definitions can subclass. Since each subclass is a single row in a spreadsheet, we can name the base class Row to indicate its purpose. All it needs to do at the moment is include RowMeta as its metaclass, and it'll automatically get the necessary behavior.

```python
class Row(metaclass=RowMeta):
    pass
```

Bringing It Together

Technically, all the pieces are now in place to demonstrate at least the basics of a working system, but there's still one important piece to take care of. Currently, we have three different modules, each with some of the parts that need to be exposed in a public API. Ideally, all of the important bits should be available from one central import instead of three or potentially even more.

If you haven't already, create an __init__.py module in the same directory as the other scripts mentioned so far. That file can be empty and still have the ability to import all the packages individually, but with a little effort, it can be put to better use. Because this is the file imported when simply importing the package name directly, we can use that as a trigger to pull in the useful bits from all the other files. Open up __init__.py and put this code in it.

```
from sheets.base import *
from sheets.options import *
from sheets.columns import *
```

■ **Note** Ordinarily, using an asterisk to import everything is a bad idea because it can make it more difficult to identify what came from where. Since this module is only importing code and not doing anything with it, that problem doesn't really apply. As long as the package is imported on its own, such as `import sheets`, there won't be any confusion as to where the objects come from. And since we don't have to mention any of the objects by name, this will hold for anything we may add to those modules as well.

Now we have enough working parts to show that the framework can function, at least at a very basic level. If we create an `example.py` one directory up from the framework code itself, so that `sheets` is on the PYTHONPATH, we can now create a class that does some very simple work to show that it's starting to come together.

```
import sheets

class Example(sheets.Row):
    title = sheets.Column()
    description = sheets.Column()


if __name__ == '__main__':
    print(Example._dialect)
    print(Example.title)
```

All this really does so far is allow us to name the columns, though. In order to line them up with data in CSV files, we need to know the order in which the fields were defined in the class.

Ordering Fields

As it stands, the fields are all available as attributes of the class itself. This allows you to get some information about individual fields but only if you know the name of the field. Without a name, you'd have to inspect all the attributes on the class and check which of them are instances of Column or its subclasses. Even if you do that, though, you still don't know the order in which they were defined, so it's impossible to line them up with data from a CSV file.

In order to address both of those issues, we need to set up a list of columns, where each of the columns can be stored in the order in which it was defined. But first, we need to be able to identify that order at runtime, without the benefit of being able to ask the developer. There are at least three different ways to do this, each with its own benefits.

DeclarativeMeta.__prepare__()

Chapter 4 showed that metaclasses can control the behavior of the class namespace while Python is processing the block of code that makes up the class definition. By including a __prepare__() method on the declarative metaclass—in this case, RowMeta—we can provide an ordered dictionary, which can then keep the order of attribute assignments itself. It's as simple as importing an ordered dictionary implementation and returning it from a custom __prepare__() method.

```
from collections import OrderedDict

from sheets import options

class RowMeta(type):
    def __init__(cls, name, bases, attrs):
        if 'Dialect' in attrs:
            # Filter out Python's own additions to the namespace
            items = attrs.pop('Dialect').__dict__.items()
            items = {k: v for k, v in items if not k.startswith('__')}
        else:
            # No dialect options were explicitly defined
            items = {}
        cls._dialect = options.Dialect(**items)

        for key, attr in attrs.items():
            if hasattr(attr, 'attach_to_class'):
                attr.attach_to_class(cls, key, cls._dialect)

    @classmethod
    def __prepare__(self, name, bases):
        return OrderedDict()
```

That only gets us part of the way, though. Now the namespace dictionary contains all the class attributes, and it knows the order in which they were defined, but it doesn't address the issue of having a simple list of just the CSV columns. The namespace dictionary will also hold all the methods and other miscellaneous attributes that were defined, so we'll still need to grab the columns out of it and put them into another list.

One obvious way to do that would be to look at each attribute in the dictionary and check to see whether it's a column or not. That's the same process mentioned earlier in this section, but the difference with considering it now is that you can hide the complexity inside the metaclass.

Since __init__() gets run after the entire body has been processed, its attrs argument will be an ordered dictionary containing all the attributes. All that's left is to loop over them and pull out any columns that were found. Again, in the spirit of duck typing, we'll use the presence of attach_to_class() to determine which attributes are columns. In fact, we can use the existing loop and just inject the new code into the inner if block.

In order to use it in the real world, it'll need to be placed somewhere more useful, such as the Dialect object stored in the _dialect attribute of the class. Rather than simply assigning a list externally, it makes more sense to have Dialect manage that itself by giving it an add_column() method that we can call from the metaclass instead.

```
class Dialect:
    """
    A container for dialect options that control how a CSV file should be
    handled when converting it to a set of objects.

    has_header_row
        A Boolean indicating whether the file has a row containing header
        values. If True, that row will be skipped when looking for data.
        Defaults to False.

    For a list of additional options that can be passed in, see documentation
    for the dialects and formatting parameters of Python's csv module at
    http://docs.python.org/library/csv.html#dialects-and-formatting-parameters
    """

    def __init__(self, has_header_row=False, **kwargs):
        self.has_header_row = has_header_row
        self.csv_dialect = kwargs
        self.columns = []

    def add_column(self, column):
        self.columns.append(column)
```

Now that Dialect knows how to keep a record of fields, it's only a small matter to change RowMeta to add the columns to the dialect as they're found. Because the namespace is already sorted according to when the attributes were assigned, we can be sure that they'll be attached to the class in the right order. Thus, we can simply add a quick call to the dialect's add_column() in the column's attach_to_class() method.

```
class Column:
    """
    An individual column within a CSV file. This serves as a base for attributes
    and methods that are common to all types of columns. Subclasses of Column
    will define behavior for more specific data types.
    """

    def __init__(self, title=None, required=True):
        self.title = title
        self.required = required

    def attach_to_class(self, cls, name, dialect):
        self.cls = cls
        self.name = name
```

```
        self.dialect = dialect
        if self.title is None:
            # Check for None so that an empty string will skip this behavior
            self.title = name.replace('_', ' ')
        dialect.add_column(self)
```

■ **Note** This example also changes the name of the `options` attribute to `dialect` instead, to be consistent with the rest of the framework.

Now our code has an easy way to get at the columns that were provided to the class, in their original order. There's one fairly significant flaw with it, though: the __prepare__() technique is only available in Python starting with version 3.0. Because there was no equivalent functionality before then, any older versions will need to use a completely different approach to the problem.

We can make use of a basic principle of Python's class processing: the body of a class is executed as a block of code. That means that each of the column attributes are instantiated in the order they were written in the class definition. The Column class already has a block of code that runs when the attribute is instantiated, which can be extended a bit to keep track of each instantiation.

Column.__init__()

The most obvious choice is where we already have code: the __init__() method. It gets called for each Column object as it's instantiated, so it makes a convenient place to keep track of the order those objects are encountered. The actual process is fairly simple. All it takes is a counter that can be maintained in one place, regardless of which column is being processed and a small bit of code to increment that counter every time a new column is found.

```
class Column:
    """
    An individual column within a CSV file. This serves as a base for attributes
    and methods that are common to all types of columns. Subclasses of Column
    will define behavior for more specific data types.
    """

    # This will be updated for each column that's instantiated.
    counter = 0

    def __init__(self, title=None, required=True):
        self.title = title
        self.required = required
        self.counter = Column.counter
        Column.counter += 1

    def attach_to_class(self, cls, name, dialect):
        self.cls = cls
        self.name = name
        self.dialect = dialect
        if self.title is None:
```

```
        # Check for None so that an empty string will skip this behavior
        self.title = name.replace('_', ' ')
    dialect.add_column(self)
```

This code handles part of the problem. Now, each column has a counter attribute that indicates its position among the rest.

Simple is Better than Complex

Actually, that counter will be maintained across *all* columns, regardless of which class they're assigned to. Even though that's technically a bit of overkill, it doesn't actually hurt anything. Each group of columns will still be ordered appropriately among its peers, so they can be sorted properly without a problem. More importantly, resetting the counter for each class would significantly complicate the code.

First, we'd need a separate counter for each class that can have columns attached to it. Columns don't know about which class they're assigned to until attach_to_class() is called, so we'd have to put some code in there to determine when a new class is being processed. But since that takes place after the counter was already incremented in __init__(), it would need to reset the counter while assigning it to a new location for the new class.

It's definitely possible to keep a separate counter for each individual class, but doing so doesn't really add anything to the process. Because the simpler form is just as functional for most cases, the added complexity just isn't worth it. If you have a long-running process that creates Row subclasses dynamically on a regular basis, it's possible the counter will overflow and cause problems. In such a case, you'll need to take these additional steps to make sure everything continues to work properly.

The next step is to use that counter to force the ordering of the columns as they're stored on the Dialect object. In the __prepare__() approach, the namespace handled the ordering on its own, so there wasn't anything else to do. Here, we need to sort the list of fields explicitly, using the counter attribute to determine the order.

We can't do it right away in __init__() because that gets a dictionary of all the attributes, not just the columns. It doesn't know which attributes are columns until they're processed using their attach_to_class() methods. Sorting the list after processing all the columns with attach_to_class() instead would provide a complete list of just columns in the correct order. Here's what you'll need to add to the RowMeta class.

```
from sheets import options

class RowMeta(type):
    def __init__(cls, name, bases, attrs):
        if 'Dialect' in attrs:
            # Filter out Python's own additions to the namespace
            items = attrs.pop('Dialect').__dict__.items()
            items = {k: v for k, v in items if not k.startswith('__')}
        else:
            # No dialect options were explicitly defined
            items = {}
        cls._dialect = options.Dialect(**items)
```

```
for key, attr in attrs.items():
    if hasattr(attr, 'attach_to_class'):
        attr.attach_to_class(cls, key, cls._dialect)
```

 # Sort the columns according to their order of instantiation
cls._dialect.columns.sort(key=lambda column: column.counter)

This function call may look a little more complicated than it really is. It's just invoking a standard sort() operation but with a function that will be called to determine what value to use when sorting items. We could add a method to Column that just returns the counter and use that, but since it's only used here, a lambda function will do the same job inline.

Simple is Better than Complex

Another option is to actually sort the list while processing attach_to_class(). The default attach_to_class() implementation shown previously already calls add_column() on the provided Dialect object, so that's a good place to do the job. Unfortunately, doing so requires a few extra steps. It doesn't make sense to try to sort the whole list every time a new column is added, but we can use the bisect module in the standard library to keep the order more efficiently.

The bisect module provides an insort() method, which inserts a new item into an existing sequence while preserving a useful order to those items. Unlike a standard sort(), though, this function doesn't accept a key argument, but instead relies on comparing two items using the < operator. If one item compares as less than another, it gets placed further ahead in the sequence. That makes sense, but without the use of an explicit key, we'd need to implement an __lt__() method on the Column class to support insort().

Sorting after the fact only requires one additional line of code, while trying to sort throughout would introduce another import and another method on the Column class. The only thing we'd gain by going that route is the ability to see the order of all the columns that have been processed so far, but because new columns may be placed anywhere within that order, it's not really that useful until all the columns have been processed. Therefore, it's best to keep things simple and just sort the list once afterward.

Most of the code that was added in this approach is necessary whenever __prepare__() isn't available, regardless of any other preferences. The only area where we really have any room to use a different approach is where the counter value is updated. There are a few different ways to go about managing that value.

So far we've used the __init__() method of the Column class because that's always called during instantiation and it already had a basic implementation anyway. The trouble is that many __init__() methods are only used to save argument values as attributes on the object, so programmers have come to expect similar behavior. Aside from managing the counter, our own __init__() method matches that expectation perfectly.

So if a programmer wants to write a new column that doesn't use any of the same arguments as the base Column class, it's easy to write an __init__() method that simply doesn't call super(). Without using super() to fire the original __init__() method, that new column won't be ordered properly. Its counter attribute will always be the same as whatever was processed right before it, so sort() won't be able to reliably determine where it belongs.

You could argue that the problem here is with the programmers' assumption that __init__() doesn't do anything of value, but that's not a very productive approach to the problem. There are still a couple ways we can try to make things easier for users of the frameworks that can help avoid problems if someone neglects to use super().

Column.__new__()

Thinking about instantiation without __init__(), the next clear choice is __new__(), which is called earlier in the process. Using __new__() provides a chance to do the same work without competing with __init__(), so they can be independent of each other. The initialization of the object can still take place in __init__(), leaving __new__() to manage the counter value.

```python
class Column:
    """
    An individual column within a CSV file. This serves as a base for attributes
    and methods that are common to all types of columns. Subclasses of Column
    will define behavior for more specific data types.
    """

    # This will be updated for each column that's instantiated.
    counter = 0

    def __new__(cls, *args, **kwargs):
        # Keep track of the order each column is instantiated
        obj = super(Column, cls).__new__(cls, *args, **kwargs)
        obj.counter = Column.counter
        Column.counter += 1
        return obj

    def __init__(self, title=None, required=True):
        self.title = title
        self.required = required

    def attach_to_class(self, cls, name, dialect):
        self.cls = cls
        self.name = name
        self.dialect = dialect
        if self.title is None:
            # Check for None so that an empty string will skip this behavior
            self.title = name.replace('_', ' ')
        dialect.add_column(self)
```

The code in __new__() grows a bit from what was used in __init__() previously because __new__() is responsible for creating and returning the new object. Therefore, we need to create the object explicitly before assigning the counter to it. Then, the method needs to explicitly return the new object in order for it to be accessible by anything else.

Using __new__() instead of __init__() is merely a way to reduce the odds of colliding with a custom implementation. It may be less likely, but it's still possible for a subclass to provide __new__() on its own, and doing so without using super() would still cause problems. There's still one other option that separates the counting behavior even further.

CounterMeta.__call__()

There's still one other method that gets called when instantiating a class that you may not have considered. Technically, the class object itself is being called as a function, which means that there's a __call__() method somewhere that would be called. Since __call__() is only executed as an instance method, but instantiation takes place when calling a class, we need to look at the class as an instance of something else: a metaclass.

That means that we can create a metaclass to support the counter functionality entirely outside the Column class. A simple CounterMeta class with a __call__() method can keep track of the counter on its own, and Column can then use that as its metaclass. The body of this method looks essentially just like __new__() because it's called as pretty much the same part of the process. It needs to create the object by using super() and return it explicitly.

```python
class CounterMeta(type):
    """
    A simple metaclass that keeps track of the order that each instance
    of a given class was instantiated.
    """

    counter = 0

    def __call__(cls, *args, **kwargs):
        obj = super(CounterMeta, cls).__call__(*args, **kwargs)
        obj.counter = CounterMeta.counter
        CounterMeta.counter += 1
        return obj
```

Now that all of this functionality is isolated to a metaclass, the Column class gets a bit simpler. It can get rid of all the counter handling code, including the entire __new__() method. All it needs now to maintain the counting behavior is to use CounterMeta as its metaclass.

```python
class Column(metaclass=CounterMeta):
    """
    An individual column within a CSV file. This serves as a base for attributes
    and methods that are common to all types of columns. Subclasses of Column
    will define behavior for more specific data types.
    """

    def __init__(self, title=None, required=True):
        self.title = title
        self.required = required

    def attach_to_class(self, cls, name, dialect):
        self.cls = cls
        self.name = name
        self.dialect = dialect
        if self.title is None:
            # Check for None so that an empty string will skip this behavior
            self.title = name.replace('_', ' ')
        dialect.add_column(self)
```

In fact, this CounterMeta is now capable of providing this counting behavior for any class that needs it. By simply applying the metaclass, every instance of the given class will have a counter attribute attached to it. Then you can use that counter to sort the instances according to when they were instantiated, just like the columns in the sheets framework.

Choosing an Option

Of the options presented here, it's not always easy to determine which to choose. With each layer of added flexibility comes added complexity, and it's always best to keep things as simple as possible. If you're working in a Python 3 environment, __prepare__() is definitely the way to go. It doesn't require any additional classes to support it, it doesn't need to sort the list of columns after the fact and it works without touching the Column class at all.

The options for earlier versions of Python are more subjective. Which one you choose depends largely on how much you expect of your target audience and how much complexity you're willing to allow into your code. The simpler solutions require more vigilance on the part of your users, so you'll need to decide what's most important.

Since this chapter is designed for use with Python 3.1, the remaining examples of the code will use __prepare__(). Of course, the ability to order a set of fields is only useful once you have a collection of fields to work with.

Building a Field Library

In most declarative frameworks, sheets included, a primary function of fields is to convert data between native Python objects and some other data format. In our case, the other format is a string contained in the CSV file, so we need a way to convert between those strings and the objects the fields represent. Before we get into the details of specific field types, we need to set up a couple methods for managing data conversion.

The first method, to_python(), takes a string from the file and converts that string into a native Python value. This step is performed for each column, every time a row is read in from the file, to ensure that you can work with the correct type of value in Python. Because that behavior will be different for various types, delegating to a method like to_python() allows you to change this specific behavior on individual classes without having to do so all on one Column class.

The second method is to_string(), which works as an inverse to to_python() and will be called when saving a CSV file with values assigned in Python. Because the csv module works with strings by default, this method is used to provide any special formatting required by a particular CSV format. Delegating to this method means that each column can have its own options to suit the data that belongs in that field.

Even though each type of data behaves differently, the base Column class can support a simple use case by default. The csv module only works with files that are opened in text mode, so Python's own file access manages the conversion to Unicode while reading data. That means the value that comes from csv is already a string and can be used easily.

```
class Column:
    """
    An individual column within a CSV file. This serves as a base for attributes
    and methods that are common to all types of columns. Subclasses of Column
    will define behavior for more specific data types.
    """
```

```
    def __init__(self, title=None, required=True):
        self.title = title
        self.required = required

    def attach_to_class(self, cls, name, dialect):
        self.cls = cls
        self.name = name
        self.dialect = dialect
        if self.title is None:
            # Check for None so that an empty string will skip this behavior
            self.title = name.replace('_', ' ')
        dialect.add_column(self)

    def to_python(self, value):
        """
        Convert the given string to a native Python object.
        """
        return value

    def to_string(self, value):
        """
        Convert the given Python object to a string.
        """
        return value
```

Now we can start implementing them for individual data types.

StringField

The most obvious field to start with is a string because it can encompass any number of more specific forms of data. Titles, names, places, descriptions and comments are just some examples of the more specific values you might find in these fields, but from a technical standpoint they all work the same way. The sheets framework doesn't have to care what form of strings you'll be dealing with, only that they are in fact all strings.

The csv module provides strings on its own, so this class doesn't really have to do much. In fact, to_python() and to_string() don't need any custom implementation at all because they only need to return what they're given. The most important thing that's offered by a StringColumn is actually the name itself.

By having an attribute that's named according to the type of data it interacts with, the attribute becomes somewhat self-documenting. Rather than just using a generic Column to describe how strings are passed back and forth, you can use a StringColumn to be clear about how it works.

```
class StringColumn(Column):
    """
    A column that contains data formatted as generic strings.
    """

    pass
```

In fact, you could even call the base class StringColumn instead of just Column because it does the job on its own. Unfortunately, that would cause its own confusion when subclassing it, by requiring something like an IntegerColumn to subclass StringColumn. To keep things clearer, the base class will remain Column and each subclass will add only the necessary features on top of it, even though there's nothing useful to add beyond the name.

IntegerColumn

The next field type to add manages integers. Numbers are used quite a bit in spreadsheets, storing everything from ages to sales figures to inventory counts. Much of the time, those numbers will be plain integers that can be converted easily using the built-in `int()` function.

```
class IntegerColumn(Column):
    """
    A column that contains data in the form of numeric integers.
    """
    def to_python(self, value):
        return int(value)
```

IntegerColumn doesn't actually need to implement a `to_string()` method because the csv module automatically calls `str()` on whatever value is given to it. Since that's all we'd do in a `to_string()` method anyway, we can just leave it out and let the framework handle that task. As you'll see with other columns, `to_string()` is most useful when the column can specify a more explicit format to use. Simply writing out a number doesn't require that much flexibility.

FloatColumn

Many numbers in spreadsheets have finer granularity than integers, requiring additional information to convey the value beyond the decimal point. Floating point numbers are a decent way to handle those values, and supporting them as a column is just as easy as it was with IntegerColumn. We can simply replace all the instances of `int` with `float` and be done.

```
class FloatColumn(Column):
    """
    A column that contains data in the form of floating point numbers.
    """
    def to_python(self, value):
        return float(value)
```

Of course, floating point numbers have their share of problems when it comes to viewing them or adding them together in many cases. This is caused by a lack of defined precision in the decimal point: it floats around according to how well a given value can be represented in code. To be more explicit and avoid things like rounding errors, we turn to DecimalColumn.

DecimalColumn

Like FloatColumn, this can work with numbers beyond just the integers. Instead of working with floating point numbers, though, DecimalColumn will rely on the functionality of the decimal module providing with Python. Decimal values preserve as much detail in the original number as possible, which helps prevents rounding errors. This makes decimals much more suitable for use with monetary spreadsheets.

In Python, decimals are provided using the decimal module, which provides a Decimal class to manage individual numbers. Therefore, DecimalColumn needs to convert numbers from text in CSV files to Decimal objects in Python and back again. Like floats, Decimal already converts to strings well enough on its own, so the only conversion DecimalColumn really needs to do is from strings to Decimal when reading values. Since Decimal is designed to work with strings, it's just as easy as the other columns shown so far.

```
import decimal

class DecimalColumn(Column):
    """
    A column that contains data in the form of decimal values,
    represented in Python by decimal.Decimal.
    """

    def to_python(self, value):
        return decimal.Decimal(value)
```

There's one difference about this method from those in the other classes, though. Each of the others have the added side-effect of raising a ValueError if the value can't be properly converted, which we can use later to support validation. Decimal does validate during instantiation, but it raises an exception from the decimal module, InvalidOperation. In order to match the behavior of the others, we'll need to catch that and re-raise it as a ValueError.

```
import decimal

class DecimalColumn(Column):
    """
    A column that contains data in the form of decimal values,
    represented in Python by decimal.Decimal.
    """

    def to_python(self, value):
        try:
            return decimal.Decimal(value)
        except decimal.InvalidOperation as e:
            raise ValueError(str(e))
```

Even though DecimalColumn supports a more specialized data type, the code behind it is still fairly simple. Supporting dates, on the other hand, requires some added complexity.

DateColumn

Dates are also extremely common in spreadsheet documents, storing everything from employee paydays and holidays to meeting agendas and attendance. Like decimal values, dates require the use of a separate class to provide a native Python data type, but there's one significant difference: dates don't have a universally accepted string representation. There are some standards that are fairly well established, but there are still plenty of variations, from the placement of the date components to the punctuation used to separate them.

In order to support the necessary flexibility, a new DateColumn would need to accept a format string during instantiation, which can be used to parse values from the file as well as construct strings to store in the file. Python dates already use a flexible format string syntax,[6] so there's no need to invent a new

---

[6] http://propython.com/datetime-formatting/

one just for sheets. In order to specify the format during instantiation, though, we'll need to override __init__().

```
class DateColumn(Column):
    """
    A column that contains data in the form of dates,
    represented in Python by datetime.date.

    format
        A strptime()-style format string.
        See http://docs.python.org/library/datetime.html for details
    """

    def __init__(self, *args, format='%Y-%m-%d', **kwargs):
        super(DateColumn, self).__init__(*args, **kwargs)
        self.format = format
```

Notice that the format object has a default value, which makes it optional. It's usually best to provide defaults like this for field attributes, so users can get up and running quickly. The default value used here was chosen because it's fairly common and it places the values in order from the least specific to the most specific—from year to day, respectively. That helps reduce the ambiguity we might otherwise encounter across cultures that format dates differently. Since the goal is to work with existing data, though, it's always possible for a specific Row class to override this behavior with whatever format is used by a given file.

Compatibility: Prior to 3.0

Older versions of Python don't support the keyword-only argument syntax used here, so if you need to be compatible with versions prior to 3.0, you have a decision to make. One option would be to place the new format argument before *args, which provides a clear argument specification, but it also means that title will no longer be the first positional argument, which can be confusing among other fields. The other option is to simply accept *args and **kwargs; then pop 'format' out of kwargs before passing it into the super() call.

Either option will allow the necessary functionality, so the difference is mostly in style. You can either have a clean and clear argument list or you can have a keyword-only argument that stays out of the way of the positional arguments. This is one case where practicality may beat purity.

Having the format available on the DateColumn object, the next step is, as it was for the others, to make a to_python() method. Python's datetime object accepts each component of the date as a separate argument, but since to_python() only gets a string, we'll need another way to do it. The alternative comes in the form of a datetime class method called strptime().

The strptime() method accepts a string value as its first argument and a format string as its second. The value is then parsed according to the format string and a datetime object is returned. We don't actually need a full datetime, though, so we can also use that object's date() method to return just the date portion of the value as a date object.

```
import datetime

class DateColumn(Column):
    """
    A column that contains data in the form of dates,
    represented in Python by datetime.date.

    format
        A strptime()-style format string.
        See http://docs.python.org/library/datetime.html for details
    """

    def __init__(self, *args, format='%Y-%m-%d', **kwargs):
        super(DateColumn, self).__init__(*args, **kwargs)
        self.format = format

    def to_python(self, value):
        """
        Parse a string value according to self.format
        and return only the date portion.
        """
        return datetime.datetime.strptime(value, self.format).date()
```

■ **Note** datetime is the name of the module as well as the name of the class, so that's why it's written twice.

There's a subtle problem with to_python() as it's written here, though. All the other column types so far can accept both a string and a native object as values in to_python(), but strptime() will fail with a TypeError if you pass in a date object instead of a string. In order to construct a row in Python and save it in a file, we'll need to be able to accept a datetime object here, which will be converted to a string later, when saving.

Since to_python() is supposed to return a native object, this is a very simple task. All it takes is checking whether the value passed in is already a date object. If it is, to_python() can simply return that without doing any more work. Otherwise, it can continue on with the conversion.

```
class DateColumn(Column):
    """
    A column that contains data in the form of dates,
    represented in Python by datetime.date.

    format
        A strptime()-style format string.
        See http://docs.python.org/library/datetime.html for details
    """

    def __init__(self, *args, format='%Y-%m-%d', **kwargs):
        super(DateColumn, self).__init__(*args, **kwargs)
        self.format = format
```

```
    def to_python(self, value):
        """
        Parse a string value according to self.format
        and return only the date portion.
        """
        if isinstance(value, datetime.date):
            return value
        return datetime.datetime.strptime(value, self.format).date()
```

Writing the to_python() method was actually the most troublesome part of the DateColumn class. Converting an existing date value to a string is even simpler because there's an instance method, strftime(), available to do the job. It just accepts a format and returns a string containing the formatted value.

```
import datetime

class DateColumn(Column):
    """
    A column that contains data in the form of dates,
    represented in Python by datetime.date.

    format
        A strptime()-style format string.
        See http://docs.python.org/library/datetime.html for details
    """
    def __init__(self, *args, format='%Y-%m-%d', **kwargs):
        super(DateColumn, self).__init__(*args, **kwargs)
        self.format = format

    def to_python(self, value):
        """
        Parse a string value according to self.format
        and return only the date portion.
        """
        if isinstance(value, datetime.date):
            return value
        return datetime.datetime.strptime(value, self.format).date()

    def to_string(self, value):
        """
        Format a date according to self.format and return that as a string.
        """
        return value.strftime(self.format)
```

■ **Tip** A useful way to remember the difference between the two method names is that p stands for "parse" and f stands for "format."

We could go on adding more and more fields, but the ones shown here cover the basic forms of data found in most CSV files, as well as most of the techniques necessary to build your own field attributes in a declarative framework. Next, we'll need to set up the CSV functionality in order to bring these data types to life.

Getting Back to CSV

So far, this chapter has been fairly generic, showing tools and techniques that can be applied to any variety of declarative class frameworks. In order to put them to real-world use, we need to get back to the problem of parsing CSV files. Much of the work done in this section will also be applicable to other frameworks, but will be presented in a way specific to CSV.

The first thing to do is take a look at how Python's own csv module works. There's no sense completely reinventing the wheel. It's important to understand the existing interface so that we can match it as closely as possible. The csv module's functionality is provided in two basic object types: readers and writers.

Readers and writers are configured in similar ways. They both accept a file argument, an optional dialect and any number of keyword arguments that specify individual dialect parameters to override the main dialect. The main difference between readers and writers is that readers require a file to be opened for read access and writers require write access.

For readers, the file argument is typically a file object but may in fact be any iterable object that yields a single string for each iteration. Because the csv module also handles more complex newline usage, such as newlines encoded within a value, you should always open the file with the argument newline='' to make sure Python's own newline handling doesn't get in the way.

```
>>> import csv
>>> reader = csv.reader(open('example.csv', newline=''))
```

Compatibility: Prior to 3.0

As mentioned in the Managing Options section earlier in this chapter, earlier versions of Python didn't have very advanced text handling, including support for encodings or newlines. When working with those versions, you should make sure to open your files in binary mode ('rb') in addition to using the codecs module to get proper newline handling and Unicode support.

Once instantiated for use with a particular file and dialect, a CSV reader object has an extremely simple interface: it's an iterable object. Iterating over a reader will yield each row in the CSV file as a data structure that's usable outside the csv module. The standard csv.reader yields a list of values for each row, because the only thing it knows about is the position of each value in the row.

A more advanced options is csv.DictReader, which also accepts a sequence of column names during instantiation, so that each row can be produced as a dictionary. Our framework goes even further, yielding an object with each value from the file converted to a native Python data type and made available as an attribute.

Writer objects, on the other hand, are slightly more complex. Because simple iteration only allows reading values, rather than writing them, writers rely on a couple of methods to do the necessary work. The first, writerow(), writes out a single row to the file, as its name suggests. Its companion, writerows(), accepts a sequence of rows, which will be written to the file in the order they're found in the sequence.

Exactly what constitutes a row will differ based on what type of writer is used. As with readers, the csv module provides some different options. The standard `csv.writer` accepts a simple sequence of values for each row, placing each value on the row in the position it's found in the list. The more complex `DictWriter` accepts a dictionary, which uses the sequence of column names passed in during instantiation to determine where in the row each value should be written.

The interface for working with our framework should look as much as possibly like the interfaces to these standard readers and writers. A `sheets` reader should be an iterable object that yields instances of the custom class where all the column attributes were defined. Likewise, the writer should accept instances of that same class. In both cases, the order of the column attributes in the class definition will be used to determine where the values go.

One key factor of both the reader and the writer, though, is the notion of a row object. So far, we don't have any such object for the sheets framework, so we need to create one. As a class-based framework, `sheets` is already well-equipped to build an object that can represent a row. The columns and dialect are already defined on a class, so the ideal way to create an object would be to simply instantiate that class with a set of values. This will bring in aspects of the dialect and column classes described in earlier sections in order to produce a usable object.

The obvious place to implement this behavior is __init__(), but from there things get a little tricky. The first question is how to accept the values that will populate the attributes. Because we don't yet know anything about the layout of any particular `Row` subclass, we'll have to accept all arguments and deal with the requirements in the __init__() method itself.

Checking Arguments

As with any function, arguments to __init__() can be passed positionally or by keyword, but that decision has particular impact here because the object can be instantiated in one of two ways. When instantiating from a CSV file, as the next section will show, it's easiest to pass the values in positionally. When building an instance manually, though, it's highly convenient to be able to pass values in by keyword as well. Therefore, it's best to accept all positional and keyword arguments and manage them internally.

Two cases of invalid arguments are clear at the outset: too many positional arguments and keyword arguments that don't match any column names. Each of these cases requires a separate bit of code to support it, but they're both fairly easy to work with. For the positional case, we can simply check the number of arguments against the number of columns.

```
class Row(metaclass=RowMeta):
    def __init__(self, *args, **kwargs):
        # First, make sure the arguments make sense
        if len(args) > len(self._dialect.columns):
            msg = "__init__() takes at most %d arguments (%d given)"
            raise TypeError(msg % (len(self._dialect.columns), len(args)))
```

That takes care of the case where too many positional arguments are passed in, using the same error message Python would issue when the arguments are defined explicitly. The next step is to make sure that all of the provided keyword arguments match up with existing column names. This is easy to test by cycling through the keyword argument names and checking to see if each is also present in the list of column names.

Because the dialect only stores a list of columns, and not the list of column names, it's easiest to make a new list of column names here before testing them. Additional code to be added to __init__() later will also make use of this new list, so it's best to create it now.

```
class Row(metaclass=RowMeta):
    def __init__(self, *args, **kwargs):
        # First, make sure the arguments make sense
        column_names = [column.name for column in self._dialect.columns]

        if len(args) > len(column_names):
            msg = "__init__() takes at most %d arguments (%d given)"
            raise TypeError(msg % (len(column_names), len(args)))

        for name in kwargs:
            if name not in column_names:
                msg = "__init__() got an unexpected keyword argument '%s'"
                raise TypeError(msg % name)
```

That takes care of the obvious cases, but there's still one situation not yet covered: keyword arguments that target columns that also have positional arguments. To address this concern, we'll look at the behavior of Python itself. When confronted with an argument passed positionally and by keyword, Python raises a TypeError, rather than be forced to decide which of the two values to use.

```
>>> def example(x):
...     return x
...
>>> example(1)
1
>>> example(x=1)
1
>>> example(1, x=1)
Traceback (most recent call last):
  ...
TypeError: example() got multiple values for keyword argument 'x'
```

Providing that same behavior of our own __init__() is a bit more complex than the previous examples, but it's still fairly straightforward. We just need to look at each of the positional arguments and check whether there's a keyword argument matching the corresponding column name.

A useful shortcut for situations like this is to use a slice on the column name array to get only as many names as there are positional arguments. This way, we don't have to look through more names than necessary, and it eliminates the separate step of having to look up the column name by index inside the loop.

```
class Row(metaclass=RowMeta):
    def __init__(self, *args, **kwargs):
        # First, make sure the arguments make sense
        column_names = [column.name for column in self._dialect.columns]

        if len(args) > len(column_names):
            msg = "__init__() takes at most %d arguments (%d given)"
            raise TypeError(msg % (len(column_names), len(args)))

        for name in kwargs:
            if name not in column_names:
```

```
        msg = "__init__() got an unexpected keyword argument '%s'"
        raise TypeError(msg % name)

for name in column_names[:len(args)]:
    if name in kwargs:
        msg = "__init__() got multiple values for keyword argument '%s'"
        raise TypeError(msg % name)
```

With all the argument checking out of the way, __init__() can continue on with certainty that no invalid arguments were provided. From here, we can use those arguments to populate the values on the object itself.

Populating Values

There are actually two steps involved in populating the values on the object. The first is due to __init__() accepting both positional and keyword arguments. By offering both options, we now have arguments in two separate locations: args and kwargs. In order to set the values in one pass, we'll need to combine them into a single structure.

Ideally, that structure would be a dictionary because it combines the names and values, so we'll need to move positional arguments into the dictionary already provided by kwargs. For that, we'll need an index for each of the values passed in positionally and a reference to the corresponding column name, so the value can be assigned to the right name.

The last check from the previous section already provides that loop, so we can reuse that block to assign the value to kwargs. The only change we need to make to the loop is to use enumerate() to get the index of each column as well as its name. That index can then be used to get the value from args.

```
class Row(metaclass=RowMeta):
    def __init__(self, *args, **kwargs):
        # First, make sure the arguments make sense
        column_names = [column.name for column in self._dialect.columns]

        if len(args) > len(column_names):
            msg = "__init__() takes at most %d arguments (%d given)"
            raise TypeError(msg % (len(column_names), len(args)))

        for name in kwargs:
            if name not in column_names:
                msg = "__init__() got an unexpected keyword argument '%s'"
                raise TypeError(msg % name)

        for i, name in enumerate(column_names[:len(args)]):
            if name in kwargs:
                msg = "__init__() got multiple values for keyword argument '%s'"
                raise TypeError(msg % name)
            kwargs[name] = args[i]
```

Now kwargs has all the values passed into the constructor, each mapped to the appropriate column name. Next, we'll need to convert those values to the appropriate Python values before assigning them to the object. To do that, we'll need the actual column objects, rather than just the list of names we've been working with so far.

There's still one minor issue to consider. Looping through the columns gets us all the columns that were defined for the class, but kwargs only contains the values that were passed into the object. We'll need to decide what to do for columns that don't have a value available. When pulling in data from a CSV file, this won't usually be a problem because every row in the file should have an entry for each column. But when populating an object in Python, to be saved in a file later, it's often useful to assign the attributes after instantiating the object.

Therefore, the most flexible approach here is to simply assign None to any of the columns that don't have a value. Checking for required fields can be performed as a separate step later, when we get to validating fields for other things as well. For now, assigning None will work just fine.

```python
class Row(metaclass=RowMeta):
    def __init__(self, *args, **kwargs):
        # First, make sure the arguments make sense
        column_names = [column.name for column in self._dialect.columns]

        if len(args) > len(column_names):
            msg = "__init__() takes at most %d arguments (%d given)"
            raise TypeError(msg % (len(column_names), len(args)))

        for name in kwargs:
            if name not in column_names:
                msg = "__init__() got an unexpected keyword argument '%s'"
                raise TypeError(msg % name)

        for i, name in enumerate(column_names[:len(args)]):
            if name in kwargs:
                msg = "__init__() got multiple values for keyword argument '%s'"
                raise TypeError(msg % name)
            kwargs[name] = args[i]

        # Now populate the actual values on the object
        for column in self._dialect.columns:
            try:
                value = column.to_python(kwargs[column.name])
            except KeyError:
                # No value was provided
                value = None
            setattr(self, column.name, value)
```

With this functionality finally in place, you can see the Row class in action on its own. It's now capable of managing a set of columns, accepting values as inputs, converting them to Python objects while loading and assigning those values to the appropriate attributes.

```python
>>> import sheets
>>> class Author(sheets.Row):
...     name = sheets.StringColumn()
...     birthdate = sheets.DateColumn()
...     age = sheets.IntegerColumn()
...
>>> ex = Author('Marty Alchin', birthdate='1981-12-17', age='28')
>>> ex.name
'Marty Alchin'
>>> ex.birthdate
datetime.date(1981, 12, 17)
```

```
>>> ex.age
28
```

Now we can finally implement the code to actually interact with CSV files.

The Reader

Using the csv module directly, you obtain a reader by instantiating a class and passing in a file and the necessary configuration options. The sheets framework allows each custom Row class to specify all the columns and dialect parameters directly on the class, so that now contains everything we need. The direct analogy with csv would be to pass a file and a Row class into a function that then returns a reader object capable of reading the file.

The trouble with that approach is that it requires any code that wants to use the reader to import the sheets module in order to get the function that creates the reader object. Instead, we can get by with just the Row class itself by providing a class method that can do the necessary work. Then, the only argument that method needs to accept is the file to read. To match the existing csv naming conventions, we'll call this new method reader().

In order to work like the standard readers, our own reader() will need to return an iterable object that yields a row for each iteration. That's a simple requirement to fulfill, and it can be done without even involving any new objects. Remember that generator functions actually return an iterable object when they're first called. The body of a generator is then executed on each iteration of a loop, so that makes an ideal way to support a CSV reader.

In order to get the values from a CSV file, reader() can rely on the existing csv module's own reader functionality. The standard csv.reader returns a list for each row in the file, regardless of what the actual values mean or what their names should be. Since a row class can already process arguments that are stored in sequences such as lists, it's very simple to bind the two together.

```python
import csv

class Row(metaclass=RowMeta):
    def __init__(self, *args, **kwargs):
        # First, make sure the arguments make sense
        column_names = [column.name for column in self._dialect.columns]

        if len(args) > len(column_names):
            msg = "__init__() takes at most %d arguments (%d given)"
            raise TypeError(msg % (len(column_names), len(args)))

        for name in kwargs:
            if name not in column_names:
                msg = "__init__() got an unexpected keyword argument '%s'"
                raise TypeError(msg % name)

        for i, name in enumerate(column_names[:len(args)]):
            if name in kwargs:
                msg = "__init__() got multiple values for keyword argument '%s'"
                raise TypeError(msg % name)
            kwargs[name] = args[i]
```

```
        # Now populate the actual values on the object
        for column in self._dialect.columns:
            try:
                value = column.to_python(kwargs[column.name])
            except KeyError:
                # No value was provided
                value = None
            setattr(self, column.name, value)

    @classmethod
    def reader(cls, file):
        for values in csv.reader(file):
            yield cls(*values)
```

This neglects one important aspect of reading from CSV files, though. There are enough variations in how values are stored within a file that you may need to specify some options to control how the file is processed. Earlier, the Dialect class provided a way to specify those options on the Row class, so now we need to pass some of those options along in the call to csv.reader(). In particular, these are the options stored in the dialect's csv_dialect attribute.

```
    @classmethod
    def reader(cls, file):
        for values in csv.reader(file, **cls._dialect.csv_dialect):
            yield cls(*values)
```

That covers the options that the csv module already knows about, but remember that our own Dialect class allows for another option to indicate whether the file has a header row. In order to support that feature in the reader, we'll need to add some extra code that skips the first row if the dialect indicates that row would be a header.

```
    @classmethod
    def reader(cls, file):
        csv_reader = csv.reader(file, **cls._dialect.csv_dialect)

        # Skip the first row if it's a header
        if cls._dialect.has_header_row:
            csv_reader.__next__()

        for values in csv_reader:
            yield cls(*values)
```

Because all the reader needs to provide is an iterable that yields a row for each object, this method now does everything it needs to. It's not very forward-thinking, though. Since we're building a framework that may need to be improved later, it's always a good idea to at least consider future expansion.

Rather than relying solely on a generator function, a more flexible approach would be to create a new iterable class that will do the same job. As we'll see in the next section, the writer will need a separate class as well, so building this new iterable will create a pair of classes that will be easier to understand. First, the reader() method gets a whole lot simpler.

```
@classmethod
def reader(cls, file):
    return Reader(cls, file)
```

That delegates all the real work to a new Reader class, which must implement __iter__() and __next__() in order to function as an iterator. There are a few things that need to be stored away in __init__() first, though, including the row class that can create each instance and a csv.reader object to actually read the file.

```
class Reader:
    def __init__(self, row_cls, file):
        self.row_cls = row_cls
        self.csv_reader = csv.reader(file, **row_cls._dialect.csv_dialect)
```

The __iter__() method is easy to support because the Reader itself will be the iterator. Therefore, all that's necessary is to return self.

```
class Reader:
    def __init__(self, row_cls, file):
        self.row_cls = row_cls
        self.csv_reader = csv.reader(file, **row_cls._dialect.csv_dialect)

    def __iter__(self):
        return self
```

Because __next__() will get called for each iteration, its logic can be a bit simpler for the obvious task of returning individual row objects. All it needs to do is call __next__() on the csv.reader's iterator, passing the values into the row class that was stored in __init__().

```
class Reader:
    def __init__(self, row_cls, file):
        self.row_cls = row_cls
        self.csv_reader = csv.reader(file, **row_cls._dialect.csv_dialect)

    def __iter__(self):
        return self

    def __next__(self):
        return self.row_cls(*self.csv_reader.__next__())
```

You'll remember from Chapter 5 that when manually building an iterator, you have to be careful to raise a StopIteration exception in order to avoid an infinite loop. In this case, we don't have to do that directly because the csv.reader will do that on its own. Once it runs out of records, our own __next__() method just needs to let StopIteration go by without being caught.

The last feature to implement is the header row, which gets slightly more complex. In the generator function shown earlier, it's easy to just deal with the header row before getting into the real loop. As a manual iterator, we have to manage it separately because __next__() will get called from the beginning for each record.

To do so, we'll need to keep a Boolean attribute that indicates whether we still need to skip the header row. At the beginning, that attribute will be the same as the dialect's has_header_row attribute, but once the header row has been skipped, that attribute needs to be reset so that __next__() can yield a valid record every other time.

```
class Reader:
    def __init__(self, row_cls, file):
        self.row_cls = row_cls
        self.csv_reader = csv.reader(file, **row_cls._dialect.csv_dialect)
        self.skip_header_row = row_cls._dialect.has_header_row

    def __iter__(self):
        return self

    def __next__(self):
        # Skip the first row if it's a header
        if self.skip_header_row:
            self.csv_reader.__next__()
            self.skip_header_row = False

        return self.row_cls(*self.csv_reader.__next__())
```

You can test it by supplying a simple CSV file and reading it in. Consider a file containing a rough table of contents, with a column for the chapter number and another for the chapter title. Here's how you could write a Row to represent that file and parse the contents.

```
>>> import sheets
>>> class Content(sheets.Row):
...     chapter = sheets.IntegerColumn()
...     title = sheets.StringColumn()
...
>>> file = open('contents.csv', newline='')
>>> for entry in Content.reader(file):
...     print('%s: %s' % (entry.chapter, entry.title))
...
1: Principles and Philosophy
2: Advanced Basics
3: Functions
4: Classes
5: Protocols
6: Object Management
7: Strings
8: Documentation
9: Testing
10: Distribution
11: Sheets: A CSV Framework
```

This completes the transition from rows in a CSV file to individual Python objects. Because each of the rows in an instance of the Content class, you can also define whatever other methods you like and have those available when processing entries from the file. For the other side of the framework, we need a writer to move those objects back into a CSV file.

The Writer

Unlike the reader, the interface for a CSV writer requires some instance methods, so the implementation is a bit more complex. A generator method won't cut it this time around, so we'll need to add a new class to the mix in order to manage the file writing behavior. We can still rely on the csv module's own behavior to do most of the heavy lifting, so this new class only has to manage the additional features of the sheets framework.

The first part of the interface is simple. To mirror the availability of the reader, the writer should be accessible from a method on the Row subclass. This method will also take a file object, but this time it must return a new object rather than doing anything with that file right away. That makes the implementation of this writer() method simple on its own.

```
@classmethod
def writer(cls, file):
    return Writer(file, cls._dialect)
```

■ **Note** The SheetWriter can't get by with just the file because it's separate from Row and wouldn't otherwise have access to any of the dialect options.

This obviously doesn't do anything useful yet, though, so the main task is to create and fill out the SheetWriter class. There are two necessary methods to satisfy the writer interface, writerow() and writerows(). The former is responsible for taking a single object and writing out a row to the file, while the latter accepts a sequence of objects, writing them each out as a separate row in the file.

Before starting on either of those methods, Writer needs some basic initialization. The first obvious information it will need access to is the list of columns for the class. Beyond that, it'll also need the CSV options, but those are only necessary to create a writer using the csv module itself, just like the reader did. Lastly, it needs access to the one option that csv doesn't know about its own: has_header_row.

```
class Writer:
    def __init__(self, file, dialect):
        self.columns = dialect.columns
        self._writer = csv.writer(file, dialect.csv_dialect)
        self.needs_header_row = dialect.has_header_row
```

Before moving on to the all-important writerow() method, notice the header row option is actually named needs_header_row when assigned to the class. This allows writerow() to use that attribute as a flag to indicate whether the header row still needs to be written. If no row is needed in the first place, it starts as False, but if it comes in as True, it can be flipped to False once the header has actually be written to the file.

To write the header row itself, we can also defer to the csv.writer instead that will be used later to write the value rows. The csv module doesn't care what the overall structure of the file is, so we can pass in a row of header values and it'll be processed the same way as all the other rows. Those header values come from the title attribute of each column on the class, but we can use the string's title() method to make them a bit friendlier.

```
class Writer:
    def __init__(self, file, dialect):
        self.columns = dialect.columns
        self._writer = csv.writer(file, dialect.csv_dialect)
        self.needs_header_row = dialect.has_header_row

    def writerow(self, row):
        if self.needs_header_row:
            values = [column.title.title() for column in self.columns]
            self._writer.writerow(values)
            self.needs_header_row = False
```

With the header out of the way, writerow() can move on to write the actual row that was passed into the method. The code to support the header already lays out most of what needs to be done. The only difference is that, rather than getting the title of each column, the list comprehension needs to get the corresponding value from the row object that was passed in.

```
class Writer:
    def __init__(self, file, dialect):
        self.columns = dialect.columns
        self._writer = csv.writer(file, dialect.csv_dialect)
        self.needs_header_row = dialect.has_header_row

    def writerow(self, row):
        if self.needs_header_row:
            values = [column.title.title() for column in self.columns]
            self._writer.writerow(values)
            self.needs_header_row = False
        values = [getattr(row, column.name) for column in self.columns]
        self._writer.writerow(values)
```

Lastly, the writer also needs a writerows() method that can take a sequence of objects and write them out as individual rows. The hard work is already done, so all writerows() needs to do is call writerow() for each object that was passed into the sequence.

```
class Writer:
    def __init__(self, file, dialect):
        self.columns = dialect.columns
        self._writer = csv.writer(file, dialect.csv_dialect)
        self.needs_header_row = dialect.has_header_row

    def writerow(self, row):
        if self.needs_header_row:
            values = [column.title.title() for column in self.columns]
            self._writer.writerow(values)
            self.needs_header_row = False
        values = [getattr(row, column.name) for column in self.columns]
        self._writer.writerow(values)
```

```
def writerows(self, rows):
    for row in rows:
        self.writerow(row)
```

With a CSV reader and writer, the sheets framework is complete. You can add more column classes to support additional data types or add more dialect options based on more specific needs you may have, but the framework on the whole is intact. You can verify the full functionality by reading an existing file and writing it back out to a new file. As long as all the dialect parameters match the file's structure, the contents of the two files will be identical.

```
>>> import sheets
>>> class Content(sheets.Row):
...     chapter = sheets.IntegerColumn()
...     title = sheets.StringColumn()
...
>>> input = open('contents.csv', newline='')
>>> reader = Content.reader(input)
>>> output = open('compare.csv', 'w', newline='')
>>> writer = Content.writer(output)
>>> writer.writerows(reader)
>>> input.close()
>>> output.close()
>>> open('contents.csv').read() == open('compare.csv').read()
True
```

Taking It With You

In this chapter, you've seen how to plan, build and customize a framework using many of the tools Python makes available. What was a complicated task that would have had to be repeated multiple times has been reduced to a reusable and extendable tool. This is just one example of how the techniques in this book can combine for such a complex task, though. The rest is up to you.

PEP 8

■ ■ ■

Style Guide for Python

Authors: Guido van Rossum, Barry Warsaw

Introduction

This document gives coding conventions for the Python code comprising the standard library in the main Python distribution. Please see the companion informational PEP describing style guidelines for the C code in the C implementation of Python.[1]

This document was adapted from Guido's original Python Style Guide essay,[2] with some additions from Barry's style guide.[3] Where there's conflict, Guido's style rules for the purposes of this PEP. This PEP may still be incomplete (in fact, it may never be finished <wink>).

A Foolish Consistency is the Hobgoblin of Little Minds

One of Guido's key insights is that code is read much more often than it is written. The guidelines provided here are intended to improve the readability of code and make it consistent across the wide spectrum of Python code. As PEP 20[4] says, "Readability counts".

A style guide is about consistency. Consistency with this style guide is important. Consistency within a project is more important. Consistency within one module or function is most important.

But most importantly: know when to be inconsistent—sometimes the style guide just doesn't apply. When in doubt, use your best judgment. Look at other examples and decide what looks best. And don't hesitate to ask!

Two good reasons to break a particular rule:

1. When applying the rule would make the code less readable, even for someone who is used to reading code that follows the rules.

2. To be consistent with surrounding code that also breaks it (maybe for historic reasons)—although this is also an opportunity to clean up someone else's mess (in true XP style).

---

[1] http://propython.com/pep-7
[2] http://propython.com/python-style-guide/
[3] http://propython.com/warsaw-style-guide/
[4] http://propython.com/pep-20/

Code Layout

Indentation

Use 4 spaces per indentation level.

For really old code that you don't want to mess up, you can continue to use 8-space tabs.

Tabs or Spaces?

Never mix tabs and spaces.

The most popular way of indenting Python is with spaces only. The second-most popular way is with tabs only. Code indented with a mixture of tabs and spaces should be converted to using spaces exclusively. When invoking the Python command line interpreter with the -t option, it issues warnings about code that illegally mixes tabs and spaces. When using -tt these warnings become errors. These options are highly recommended!

For new projects, spaces-only are strongly recommended over tabs. Most editors have features that make this easy to do.

Maximum Line Length

Limit all lines to a maximum of 79 characters.

There are still many devices around that are limited to 80 character lines; plus, limiting windows to 80 characters makes it possible to have several windows side-by-side. The default wrapping on such devices disrupts the visual structure of the code, making it more difficult to understand. Therefore, please limit all lines to a maximum of 79 characters. For flowing long blocks of text (docstrings or comments), limiting the length to 72 characters is recommended.

The preferred way of wrapping long lines is by using Python's implied line continuation inside parentheses, brackets and braces. If necessary, you can add an extra pair of parentheses around an expression, but sometimes using a backslash looks better. Make sure to indent the continued line appropriately. The preferred place to break around a binary operator is *after* the operator, not before it. Some examples:

```python
class Rectangle(Blob):

    def __init__(self, width, height,
                 color='black', emphasis=None, highlight=0):
        if width == 0 and height == 0 and \
           color == 'red' and emphasis == 'strong' or \
           highlight > 100:
            raise ValueError("sorry, you lose")
        if width == 0 and height == 0 and (color == 'red' or
                                           emphasis is None):
            raise ValueError("I don't think so -- values are %s, %s" %
                             (width, height))
        Blob.__init__(self, width, height,
                      color, emphasis, highlight)
```

Blank Lines

Separate top-level function and class definitions with two blank lines.

Method definitions inside a class are separated by a single blank line.

Extra blank lines may be used (sparingly) to separate groups of related functions. Blank lines may be omitted between a bunch of related one-liners (e.g. a set of dummy implementations).

Use blank lines in functions, sparingly, to indicate logical sections.

Python accepts the control-L (i.e. ^L) form feed character as whitespace; Many tools treat these characters as page separators, so you may use them to separate pages of related sections of your file.

Encodings (PEP 263)

Code in the core Python distribution should always use the ASCII or Latin-1 encoding (a.k.a. ISO-8859-1). For Python 3.0 and beyond, UTF-8 is preferred over Latin-1, see PEP 3120.

Files using ASCII (or UTF-8, for Python 3.0) should not have a coding cookie. Latin-1 (or UTF-8) should only be used when a comment or docstring needs to mention an author name that requires Latin-1; otherwise, using \x, \u or \U escapes is the preferred way to include non-ASCII data in string literals.

For Python 3.0 and beyond, the following policy is prescribed for the standard library (see PEP 3131[5]): All identifiers in the Python standard library MUST use ASCII-only identifiers, and SHOULD use English words wherever feasible (in many cases, abbreviations and technical terms are used which aren't English). In addition, string literals and comments must also be in ASCII. The only exceptions are (a) test cases testing the non-ASCII features, and (b) names of authors. Authors whose names are not based on the latin alphabet MUST provide a latin transliteration of their names.

Open source projects with a global audience are encouraged to adopt a similar policy.

Imports

Imports should usually be on separate lines, e.g.:
Yes:

```
import os
import sys
```

No:

```
import sys, os
```

It's okay to say this though:

```
from subprocess import Popen, PIPE
```

Imports are always put at the top of the file, just after any module comments and docstrings, and before module globals and constants. Imports should be grouped in the following order:

1.   standard library imports

2.   related third party imports

3.   local application/library specific imports

You should put a blank line between each group of imports. Put any relevant __all__ specification after the imports.

---

[5] http://propython.com/pep-3131/

Relative imports for intra-package imports are highly discouraged. Always use the absolute package path for all imports. Even now that PEP 328[6] is fully implemented in Python 2.5, its style of explicit relative imports is actively discouraged; absolute imports are more portable and usually more readable.

When importing a class from a class-containing module, it's usually okay to spell this

```
from myclass import MyClass
from foo.bar.yourclass import YourClass
```

If this spelling causes local name clashes, then spell them

```
import myclass
import foo.bar.yourclass
```

and use `myclass.MyClass` and `foo.bar.yourclass.YourClass`.

Whitespace in Expressions and Statements

Pet Peeves

Avoid extraneous whitespace in the following situations:

- Immediately inside parentheses, brackets or braces.

Yes:

```
spam(ham[1], {eggs: 2})
```

No:

```
spam( ham[ 1 ], { eggs: 2 } )
```

- Immediately before a comma, semicolon, or colon:

Yes:

```
if x == 4: print x, y; x, y = y, x
```

No:

```
if x == 4 : print x , y ; x , y = y , x
```

Immediately before the open parenthesis that starts the argument list of a function call:
Yes:

```
spam(1)
```

No:

```
spam (1)
```

Immediately before the open parenthesis that starts an indexing or slicing:
Yes:

---

[6] http://propython.com/pep-0328/

```
dict['key'] = list[index]
```

No:

```
dict ['key'] = list [index]
```

More than one space around an assignment (or other) operator to align it with another.
Yes:

```
x = 1
y = 2
long_variable = 3
```

No:

```
x             = 1
y             = 2
long_variable = 3
```

Other Recommendations

- Always surround these binary operators with a single space on either side: assignment (=), augmented assignment (+=, -= etc.), comparisons (==, <, >, !=, <>, <=, >=, in, not in, is, is not), Booleans (and, or, not).

- Use spaces around arithmetic operators:

Yes:

```
i = i + 1
submitted += 1
x = x * 2 - 1
hypot2 = x * x + y * y
c = (a + b) * (a - b)
```

No:

```
i=i+1
submitted +=1
x = x*2 - 1
hypot2 = x*x + y*y
c = (a+b) * (a-b)
```

- Don't use spaces around the = sign when used to indicate a keyword argument or a default parameter value.

Yes:

```
def complex(real, imag=0.0):
    return magic(r=real, i=imag)
```

No:

```
def complex(real, imag = 0.0):
    return magic(r = real, i = imag)
```

- Compound statements (multiple statements on the same line) are generally discouraged.

Yes:

```
if foo == 'blah':
    do_blah_thing()
do_one()
do_two()
do_three()
```

Rather not:

```
if foo == 'blah': do_blah_thing()
do_one(); do_two(); do_three()
```

- While sometimes it's okay to put an **if**/**for**/**while** with a small body on the same line, never do this for multi-clause statements. Also avoid folding such long lines!

Rather not:

```
if foo == 'blah': do_blah_thing()
for x in lst: total += x
while t < 10: t = delay()
```

Definitely not:

```
if foo == 'blah': do_blah_thing()
else: do_non_blah_thing()

try: something()
finally: cleanup()

do_one(); do_two(); do_three(long, argument,
                             list, like, this)

if foo == 'blah': one(); two(); three()
```

Comments

Comments that contradict the code are worse than no comments. Always make a priority of keeping the comments up-to-date when the code changes!

Comments should be complete sentences. If a comment is a phrase or sentence, its first word should be capitalized, unless it is an identifier that begins with a lower case letter (never alter the case of identifiers!).

If a comment is short, the period at the end can be omitted. Block comments generally consist of one or more paragraphs built out of complete sentences, and each sentence should end in a period.

You should use two spaces after a sentence-ending period.

When writing English, Strunk and White apply.

Python coders from non-English speaking countries: please write your comments in English, unless you are 120% sure that the code will never be read by people who don't speak your language.

Block Comments

Block comments generally apply to some (or all) code that follows them, and are indented to the same level as that code. Each line of a block comment starts with a # and a single space (unless it is indented text inside the comment).

Paragraphs inside a block comment are separated by a line containing a single #.

Inline Comments

Use inline comments sparingly.

An inline comment is a comment on the same line as a statement. Inline comments should be separated by at least two spaces from the statement. They should start with a # and a single space.

Inline comments are unnecessary and in fact distracting if they state the obvious. Don't do this:

```
x = x + 1                 # Increment x
```

But sometimes, this is useful:

```
x = x + 1                 # Compensate for border
```

Documentation Strings

Conventions for writing good documentation strings (a.k.a. "docstrings") are immortalized in PEP 257.[7]

- Write docstrings for all public modules, functions, classes, and methods. Docstrings are not necessary for non-public methods, but you should have a comment that describes what the method does. This comment should appear after the def line.

- PEP 257 describes good docstring conventions. Note that most importantly, the """ that ends a multiline docstring should be on a line by itself, and preferably preceded by a blank line, e.g.:

```
"""Return a foobang

Optional plotz says to frobnicate the bizbaz first.

"""
```

- For one liner docstrings, it's okay to keep the closing """ on the same line.

---

[7]http://propython.com/pep-0257/

Version Bookkeeping

If you have to have Subversion, CVS, or RCS crud in your source file, do it as follows.

```
__version__ = "$Revision: 68852 $"
# $Source$
```

These lines should be included after the module's docstring, before any other code, separated by a blank line above and below.

Naming Conventions

The naming conventions of Python's library are a bit of a mess, so we'll never get this completely consistent—nevertheless, here are the currently recommended naming standards. New modules and packages (including third party frameworks) should be written to these standards, but where an existing library has a different style, internal consistency is preferred.

Descriptive: Naming Styles

There are a lot of different naming styles. It helps to be able to recognize what naming style is being used, independently from what they are used for.

The following naming styles are commonly distinguished:

- `b` (single lowercase letter)

- `B` (single uppercase letter)

- `lowercase`

- `lower_case_with_underscores`

- `UPPERCASE`

- `UPPER_CASE_WITH_UNDERSCORES`

- `CapitalizedWords` (or CapWords, or CamelCase—so named because of the bumpy look of its letters[8]). This is also sometimes known as StudlyCaps.

■ **Note** When using abbreviations in CapWords, capitalize all the letters of the abbreviation. Thus `HTTPServerError` is better than `HttpServerError`.

- `mixedCase` (differs from CapitalizedWords by initial lowercase character!)

- `Capitalized_Words_With_Underscores` (ugly!)

---

[8] http://propython.com/camelcase

There's also the style of using a short unique prefix to group related names together. This is not used much in Python, but it is mentioned for completeness. For example, the `os.stat()` function returns a tuple whose items traditionally have names like `st_mode`, `st_size`, `st_mtime` and so on.

(This is done to emphasize the correspondence with the fields of the POSIX system call struct, which helps programmers familiar with that.)

The X11 library uses a leading X for all its public functions. In Python, this style is generally deemed unnecessary because attribute and method names are prefixed with an object, and function names are prefixed with a module name.

In addition, the following special forms using leading or trailing underscores are recognized (these can generally be combined with any case convention):

- `_single_leading_underscore`: weak "internal use" indicator. E.g. `from M import *` does not import objects whose name starts with an underscore.

- `single_trailing_underscore_`: used by convention to avoid conflicts with Python keyword, e.g.

`Tkinter.Toplevel(master, class_='ClassName')`

- `__double_leading_underscore`: when naming a class attribute, invokes name

- mangling (inside class `FooBar`, `__boo` becomes `_FooBar__boo`; see below).

- `__double_leading_and_trailing_underscore__`: "magic" objects or

- attributes that live in user-controlled namespaces. E.g. `__init__`,

- `__import__` or `__file__`. Never invent such names; only use them as documented.

Prescriptive: Naming Conventions

Names to Avoid

Never use the characters `l` (lowercase letter el), `O` (uppercase letter oh), or `I` (uppercase letter eye) as single character variable names.

In some fonts, these characters are indistinguishable from the numerals one and zero. When tempted to use `l`, use `L` instead.

Package and Module Names

Modules should have short, all-lowercase names. Underscores can be used in the module name if it improves readability. Python packages should also have short, all-lowercase names, although the use of underscores is discouraged.

Since module names are mapped to file names, and some file systems are case insensitive and truncate long names, it is important that module names be chosen to be fairly short—this won't be a problem on Unix, but it may be a problem when the code is transported to older Mac or Windows versions, or DOS.

When an extension module written in C or C++ has an accompanying Python module that provides a higher level (e.g. more object oriented) interface, the C/C++ module has a leading underscore (e.g. `_socket`).

Class Names

Almost without exception, class names use the CapWords convention. Classes for internal use have a leading underscore in addition.

Exception Names

Because exceptions should be classes, the class naming convention applies here. However, you should use the suffix `Error` on your exception names (if the exception actually is an error).

Global Variable Names

(Let's hope that these variables are meant for use inside one module only.) The conventions are about the same as those for functions.

Modules that are designed for use via `from M import *` should use the `__all__` mechanism to prevent exporting globals, or use the older convention of prefixing such globals with an underscore (which you might want to do to indicate these globals are "module non-public").

Function Names

Function names should be lowercase, with words separated by underscores as necessary to improve readability.

mixedCase is allowed only in contexts where that's already the prevailing style (e.g. `threading.py`), to retain backwards compatibility.

Function and Method Arguments

Always use `self` for the first argument to instance methods.

Always use `cls` for the first argument to class methods.

If a function argument's name clashes with a reserved keyword, it is generally better to append a single trailing underscore rather than use an abbreviation or spelling corruption. Thus `print_` is better than `prnt`. (Perhaps better is to avoid such clashes by using a synonym.)

Method Names and Instance Variables

Use the function naming rules: lowercase with words separated by underscores as necessary to improve readability.

Use one leading underscore only for non-public methods and instance variables.

To avoid name clashes with subclasses, use two leading underscores to invoke Python's name mangling rules.

Python mangles these names with the class name: if class `Foo` has an attribute named `__a`, it cannot be accessed by `Foo.__a`. (An insistent user could still gain access by calling `Foo._Foo__a`.) Generally, double leading underscores should be used only to avoid name conflicts with attributes in classes designed to be subclassed.

■ **Note** there is some controversy about the use of __names (see below).

Constants

Constants are usually declared on a module level and written in all capital letters with underscores separating words. Examples include `MAX_OVERFLOW` and `TOTAL`.

Designing for Inheritance

Always decide whether a class's methods and instance variables (collectively: "attributes") should be public or non-public. If in doubt, choose non-public; it's easier to make it public later than to make a public attribute non-public.

Public attributes are those that you expect unrelated clients of your class to use, with your commitment to avoid backward incompatible changes. Non-public attributes are those that are not intended to be used by third parties; you make no guarantees that non-public attributes won't change or even be removed.

We don't use the term "private" here, since no attribute is really private in Python (without a generally unnecessary amount of work).

Another category of attributes are those that are part of the "subclass API" (often called "protected" in other languages). Some classes are designed to be inherited from, either to extend or modify aspects of the class's behavior. When designing such a class, take care to make explicit decisions about which attributes are public, which are part of the subclass API, and which are truly only to be used by your base class.

With this in mind, here are the Pythonic guidelines:

- Public attributes should have no leading underscores.

- If your public attribute name collides with a reserved keyword, append a single trailing underscore to your attribute name. This is preferable to an abbreviation or corrupted spelling. (However, notwithstanding this rule, `cls` is the preferred spelling for any variable or argument which is known to be a class, especially the first argument to a class method.)

■ **Note** See the argument name recommendation above for class methods.

- For simple public data attributes, it is best to expose just the attribute name, without complicated accessor/mutator methods. Keep in mind that Python provides an easy path to future enhancement, should you find that a simple data attribute needs to grow functional behavior. In that case, use properties to hide functional implementation behind simple data attribute access syntax.

■ **Note 1** Properties only work on new-style classes.

■ **Note 2** Try to keep the functional behavior side-effect free, although side-effects such as caching are generally fine.

■ **Note 3** Avoid using properties for computationally expensive operations; the attribute notation makes the caller believe that access is (relatively) cheap.

- If your class is intended to be subclassed, and you have attributes that you do not want subclasses to use, consider naming them with double leading underscores and no trailing underscores. This invokes Python's name mangling algorithm, where the name of the class is mangled into the attribute name. This helps avoid attribute name collisions should subclasses inadvertently contain attributes with the same name.

■ **Note 1** Note that only the simple class name is used in the mangled name, so if a subclass chooses both the same class name and attribute name, you can still get name collisions.

■ **Note 2** Name mangling can make certain uses, such as debugging and __getattr__(), less convenient. However the name mangling algorithm is well documented and easy to perform manually.

■ **Note 3** Not everyone likes name mangling. Try to balance the need to avoid accidental name clashes with potential use by advanced callers.

Programming Recommendations

- Code should be written in a way that does not disadvantage other implementations of Python (PyPy, Jython, IronPython, Pyrex, Psyco, and such).

For example, do not rely on CPython's efficient implementation of in-place string concatenation for statements in the form a+=b or a=a+b. Those statements run more slowly in Jython. In performance sensitive parts of the library, the ''.join() form should be used instead. This will ensure that concatenation occurs in linear time across various implementations.

- Comparisons to singletons like None should always be done with is or is not, never the equality operators.

Also, beware of writing `if x` when you really mean `if x is not None`—e.g. when testing whether a variable or argument that defaults to `None` was set to some other value. The other value might have a type (such as a container) that could be false in a boolean context!

- Use class-based exceptions.

String exceptions in new code are forbidden, because this language feature is being removed in Python 2.6.

Modules or packages should define their own domain-specific base exception class, which should be subclassed from the built-in `Exception` class. Always include a class docstring. E.g.:

```python
class MessageError(Exception):
    """Base class for errors in the email package."""
```

Class naming conventions apply here, although you should add the suffix `Error` to your exception classes, if the exception is an error. Non-error exceptions need no special suffix.

When raising an exception, use `raise ValueError('message')` instead of the older form `raise ValueError, 'message'`.

The paren-using form is preferred because when the exception arguments are long or include string formatting, you don't need to use line continuation characters thanks to the containing parentheses. The older form will be removed in Python 3000.

- When catching exceptions, mention specific exceptions whenever possible instead of using a bare `except:` clause.

For example, use:

```python
try:
    import platform_specific_module
except ImportError:
    platform_specific_module = None
```

A bare `except:` clause will catch `SystemExit` and `KeyboardInterrupt` exceptions, making it harder to interrupt a program with Control-C, and can disguise other problems. If you want to catch all exceptions that signal program errors, use `except Exception:`.

A good rule of thumb is to limit use of bare `except` clauses to two cases:

1. If the exception handler will be printing out or logging the traceback; at least the user will be aware that an error has occurred.

2. If the code needs to do some cleanup work, but then lets the exception propagate upwards with `raise`. `try...finally` is a better way to handle this case.

- Additionally, for all try/except clauses, limit the try clause to the absolute minimum amount of code necessary. Again, this avoids masking bugs.

Yes:

```python
try:
    value = collection[key]
except KeyError:
    return key_not_found(key)
else:
    return handle_value(value)
```

No:

```
try:
    # Too broad!
    return handle_value(collection[key])
except KeyError:
    # Will also catch KeyError raised by handle_value()
    return key_not_found(key)
```

Use string methods instead of the string module.

String methods are always much faster and share the same API with unicode strings. Override this rule if backward compatibility with Pythons older than 2.0 is required.

- Use `''.startswith()` and `''.endswith()` instead of string slicing to check for prefixes or suffixes.

startswith() and endswith() are cleaner and less error prone. For example:

Yes:

```
if foo.startswith('bar'):
```

No:

```
if foo[:3] == 'bar':
```

The exception is if your code must work with Python 1.5.2 (but let's hope not!).

- Object type comparisons should always use `isinstance()` instead of comparing types directly.

Yes:

```
if isinstance(obj, int):
```

No:

```
if type(obj) is type(1):
```

When checking if an object is a string, keep in mind that it might be a unicode string too! In Python 2.3, str and unicode have a common base class, basestring, so you can do:

```
if isinstance(obj, basestring):
```

In Python 2.2, the types module has the StringTypes type defined for that purpose, e.g.:

```
from types import StringTypes
if isinstance(obj, StringTypes):
```

In Python 2.0 and 2.1, you should do:

```
from types import StringType, UnicodeType
if isinstance(obj, StringType) or \
   isinstance(obj, UnicodeType) :
```

- For sequences, (strings, lists, tuples), use the fact that empty sequences are false.

Yes:

```
if not seq:
if seq:
```

No:

```
if len(seq)
if not len(seq)
```

- Don't write string literals that rely on significant trailing whitespace. Such trailing whitespace is visually indistinguishable and some editors (or more recently, `reindent.py`) will trim them.

- Don't compare boolean values to `True` or `False` using ==

Yes:

```
if greeting:
```

No:

```
if greeting == True:
```

Worse:

```
if greeting is True:
```

Copyright

This document has been placed in the public domain.

PEP 10

■ ■ ■

Voting Guidelines

Author: Barry Warsaw

Abstract

This PEP outlines the python-dev voting guidelines. These guidelines serve to provide feedback or gauge the "wind direction" on a particular proposal, idea, or feature. They don't have a binding force.

Rationale

When a new idea, feature, patch, etc. is floated in the Python community, either through a PEP or on the mailing lists (most likely on python-dev[1]), it is sometimes helpful to gauge the community's general sentiment. Sometimes people just want to register their opinion of an idea. Sometimes the BDFL wants to take a straw poll. Whatever the reason, these guidelines have been adopted so as to provide a common language for developers.

While opinions are (sometimes) useful, but they are never binding. Opinions that are accompanied by rationales are always valued higher than bare scores (this is especially true with -1 votes).

Voting Scores

The scoring guidelines are loosely derived from the Apache voting procedure,[2] with of course our own spin on things. There are 4 possible vote scores:

- +1 I like it
- +0 I don't care, but go ahead
- -0 I don't care, so why bother?
- -1 I hate it

You may occasionally see wild flashes of enthusiasm (either for or against) with vote scores like +2, +1000, or -1000. These aren't really valued much beyond the above scores, but it's nice to see people get excited about such geeky stuff.

---

[1] http://propython.com/python-dev/
[2] http://propython.com/apache-dev/

Copyright

This document has been placed in the public domain.

PEP 20

The Zen of Python

Author: Tim Peters

Abstract

Long time Pythoneer Tim Peters succinctly channels the BDFL's guiding principles for Python's design into 20 aphorisms, only 19 of which have been written down.

The Zen of Python

Beautiful is better than ugly.
Explicit is better than implicit.
Simple is better than complex.
Complex is better than complicated.
Flat is better than nested.
Sparse is better than dense.
Readability counts.
Special cases aren't special enough to break the rules.
Although practicality beats purity.
Errors should never pass silently.
Unless explicitly silenced.
In the face of ambiguity, refuse the temptation to guess.
There should be one—and preferably only one—obvious way to do it.
Although that way may not be obvious at first unless you're Dutch.
Now is better than never.
Although never is often better than *right* now.
If the implementation is hard to explain, it's a bad idea.
If the implementation is easy to explain, it may be a good idea.
Namespaces are one honking great idea—let's do more of those!

Easter Egg

```
>>> import this
```

Copyright

This document has been placed in the public domain.

P E P 257

■ ■ ■

Docstring Conventions

Authors: David Goodger, Guido van Rossum

Abstract

This PEP documents the semantics and conventions associated with Python docstrings.

Rationale

The aim of this PEP is to standardize the high-level structure of docstrings: what they should contain, and how to say it (without touching on any markup syntax within docstrings). The PEP contains conventions, not laws or syntax.

> "A universal convention supplies all of maintainability, clarity, consistency, and a foundation for good programming habits too. What it doesn't do is insist that you follow it against your will. That's Python!"
>
> —Tim Peters on comp.lang.python, 2001-06-16

If you violate these conventions, the worst you'll get is some dirty looks. But some software (such as the Docutils[1] docstring processing system[2][3]) will be aware of the conventions, so following them will get you the best results.

Specification

What is a Docstring?

A docstring is a string literal that occurs as the first statement in a module, function, class, or method definition. Such a docstring becomes the __doc__ special attribute of that object.

All modules should normally have docstrings, and all functions and classes exported by a module should also have docstrings. Public methods (including the __init__ constructor) should also have

---

[1] http://propython.com/docutils/
[2] http://propython.com/pep-256/
[3] http://propython.com/pep-258/

docstrings. A package may be documented in the module docstring of the `__init__.py` file in the package directory.

String literals occurring elsewhere in Python code may also act as documentation. They are not recognized by the Python bytecode compiler and are not accessible as runtime object attributes (i.e. not assigned to `__doc__`), but two types of extra docstrings may be extracted by software tools:

1. String literals occurring immediately after a simple assignment at the top level of a module, class, or `__init__` method are called "attribute docstrings".

2. String literals occurring immediately after another docstring are called "additional docstrings".

Please see PEP 258, "Docutils Design Specification", for a detailed description of attribute and additional docstrings.

For consistency, always use `"""triple double quotes"""` around docstrings. Use `r"""raw triple double quotes"""` if you use any backslashes in your docstrings. For Unicode docstrings, use `u"""Unicode triple-quoted strings"""`.

There are two forms of docstrings: one-liners and multi-line docstrings.

One-Line Docstrings

One-liners are for really obvious cases. They should really fit on one line. For example:

```
def kos_root():
    """Return the pathname of the KOS root directory."""
    global _kos_root
    if _kos_root: return _kos_root
    ...
```

Notes:

- Triple quotes are used even though the string fits on one line. This makes it easy to later expand it.

- The closing quotes are on the same line as the opening quotes. This looks better for one-liners.

- There's no blank line either before or after the docstring.

- The docstring is a phrase ending in a period. It prescribes the function or method's effect as a command ("Do this", "Return that"), not as a description; e.g. don't write "Returns the pathname ...".

- The one-line docstring should NOT be a "signature" reiterating the function/method parameters (which can be obtained by introspection). Don't do:

```
def function(a, b):
    """function(a, b) -> list"""
```

This type of docstring is only appropriate for C functions (such as built-ins), where introspection is not possible. However, the nature of the return value cannot be determined by introspection, so it should be mentioned. The preferred form for such a docstring would be something like:

```
def function(a, b):
    """Do X and return a list."""
```

(Of course "Do X" should be replaced by a useful description!)

Multi-Line Docstrings

Multi-line docstrings consist of a summary line just like a one-line docstring, followed by a blank line, followed by a more elaborate description. The summary line may be used by automatic indexing tools; it is important that it fits on one line and is separated from the rest of the docstring by a blank line. The summary line may be on the same line as the opening quotes or on the next line. The entire docstring is indented the same as the quotes at its first line (see example below).

Insert a blank line before and after all docstrings (one-line or multi-line) that document a class—generally speaking, the class's methods are separated from each other by a single blank line, and the docstring needs to be offset from the first method by a blank line; for symmetry, put a blank line between the class header and the docstring. Docstrings documenting functions or methods generally don't have this requirement, unless the function or method's body is written as a number of blank-line separated sections -- in this case, treat the docstring as another section, and precede it with a blank line.

The docstring of a script (a stand-alone program) should be usable as its "usage" message, printed when the script is invoked with incorrect or missing arguments (or perhaps with a -h option, for "help"). Such a docstring should document the script's function and command line syntax, environment variables, and files. Usage messages can be fairly elaborate (several screens full) and should be sufficient for a new user to use the command properly, as well as a complete quick reference to all options and arguments for the sophisticated user.

The docstring for a module should generally list the classes, exceptions and functions (and any other objects) that are exported by the module, with a one-line summary of each. (These summaries generally give less detail than the summary line in the object's docstring.) The docstring for a package (i.e., the docstring of the package's __init__.py module) should also list the modules and subpackages exported by the package.

The docstring for a function or method should summarize its behavior and document its arguments, return value(s), side effects, exceptions raised, and restrictions on when it can be called (all if applicable). Optional arguments should be indicated. It should be documented whether keyword arguments are part of the interface.

The docstring for a class should summarize its behavior and list the public methods and instance variables. If the class is intended to be subclassed, and has an additional interface for subclasses, this interface should be listed separately (in the docstring). The class constructor should be documented in the docstring for its __init__ method. Individual methods should be documented by their own docstring.

If a class subclasses another class and its behavior is mostly inherited from that class, its docstring should mention this and summarize the differences. Use the verb "override" to indicate that a subclass method replaces a superclass method and does not call the superclass method; use the verb "extend" to indicate that a subclass method calls the superclass method (in addition to its own behavior).

Do not use the Emacs convention of mentioning the arguments of functions or methods in upper case in running text. Python is case sensitive and the argument names can be used for keyword arguments, so the docstring should document the correct argument names. It is best to list each argument on a separate line. For example:

```
def complex(real=0.0, imag=0.0):
    """Form a complex number.
```

```
        Keyword arguments:
        real -- the real part (default 0.0)
        imag -- the imaginary part (default 0.0)

        """
        if imag == 0.0 and real == 0.0: return complex_zero
        ...
```

The BDFL[4] recommends inserting a blank line between the last paragraph in a multi-line docstring and its closing quotes, placing the closing quotes on a line by themselves. This way, Emacs' fill-paragraph command can be used on it.

Handling Docstring Indentation

Docstring processing tools will strip a uniform amount of indentation from the second and further lines of the docstring, equal to the minimum indentation of all non-blank lines after the first line. Any indentation in the first line of the docstring (i.e., up to the first newline) is insignificant and removed. Relative indentation of later lines in the docstring is retained. Blank lines should be removed from the beginning and end of the docstring.

Since code is much more precise than words, here is an implementation of the algorithm:

```
def trim(docstring):
    if not docstring:
        return ''
    # Convert tabs to spaces (following the normal Python rules)
    # and split into a list of lines:
    lines = docstring.expandtabs().splitlines()
    # Determine minimum indentation (first line doesn't count):
    indent = sys.maxint
    for line in lines[1:]:
        stripped = line.lstrip()
        if stripped:
            indent = min(indent, len(line) - len(stripped))
    # Remove indentation (first line is special):
    trimmed = [lines[0].strip()]
    if indent < sys.maxint:
        for line in lines[1:]:
            trimmed.append(line[indent:].rstrip())
    # Strip off trailing and leading blank lines:
    while trimmed and not trimmed[-1]:
        trimmed.pop()
    while trimmed and not trimmed[0]:
        trimmed.pop(0)
    # Return a single string:
    return '\n'.join(trimmed)
```

The docstring in this example contains two newline characters and is therefore 3 lines long. The first and last lines are blank:

---

[4] Guido van Rossum, Python's creator and Benevolent Dictator For Life.

```
def foo():
    """
    This is the second line of the docstring.
    """
```

To illustrate:

```
>>> print repr(foo.__doc__)
'\n    This is the second line of the docstring.\n    '
>>> foo.__doc__.splitlines()
['', '    This is the second line of the docstring.', '    ']
>>> trim(foo.__doc__)
'This is the second line of the docstring.'
```

Once trimmed, these docstrings are equivalent:

```
def foo():
    """A multi-line
    docstring.
    """


def bar():
    """

    A multi-line
    docstring.
    """
```

Copyright

This document has been placed in the public domain.

Acknowledgments

The "Specification" text comes mostly verbatim from the Python Style Guide[5] essay by Guido van Rossum.

This document borrows ideas from the archives of the Python Doc-SIG.[6] Thanks to all members past and present.

---

[5] http://propython.com/python-style-guide/
[6] http://propython.com/doc-sig/

■ ■ ■

Backwards Compatibility Policy

Author: Benjamin Peterson

Abstract

This PEP outlines Python's backwards compatibility policy.

Rationale

As one of the most used programming languages today,[1] the Python core language and its standard library play a critical role in thousands of applications and libraries. This is fantastic; it is probably one of a language designer's most wishful dreams. However, it means the development team must be very careful not to break this existing 3rd party code with new releases.

Backwards Compatibility Rules

This policy applies to all public APIs. These include:

- Syntax and behavior of these constructs as defined by the reference manual

- The C-API

- Function, class, module, attribute, and method names and types.

- Given a set of arguments, the return value, side effects, and raised exceptions of a function. This does not preclude changes from reasonable bug fixes.

- The position and expected types of arguments and returned values.

- Behavior of classes with regards to subclasses: the conditions under which overridden methods are called.

Others are explicitly not part of the public API. They can change or be removed at any time in any way. These include:

---

[1] http://propython.com/programming-community-index/

- Function, class, module, attribute, method, and C-API names and types that are prefixed by _ (except special names). The contents of these can also are not subject to the policy.

- Inheritance patterns of internal classes.

- Test suites. (Anything in the Lib/test directory or test subdirectories of packages.)

This is the basic policy for backwards compatibility:

- Unless it is going through the deprecation process below, the behavior of an API must not change between any two consecutive releases.

- Similarly a feature cannot be removed without notice between any two consecutive releases.

- Addition of a feature which breaks 3rd party libraries or applications should have a large benefit to breakage ratio, and/or the incompatibility should be trivial to fix in broken code. For example, adding an stdlib module with the same name as a third party package is not acceptable. Adding a method or attribute that conflicts with 3rd party code through inheritance, however, is likely reasonable.

Making Incompatible Changes

It's a fact: design mistakes happen. Thus it is important to be able to change APIs or remove misguided features. This is accomplished through a gradual process over several releases:

1. Discuss the change. Depending on the size of the incompatibility, this could be on the bug tracker, python-dev, python-list, or the appropriate SIG. A PEP or similar document may be written. Hopefully users of the affected API will pipe up to comment.

2. Add a warning.[2] If behavior is changing, a the API may gain a new function or method to perform the new behavior; old usage should raise the warning. If an API is being removed, simply warn whenever it is entered. `DeprecationWarning` is the usual warning category to use, but `PendingDeprecationWarning` may be used in special cases were the old and new versions of the API will coexist for many releases.

3. Wait for a release of whichever tree (trunk or py3k) contains the warning.

4. See if there's any feedback. Users not involved in the original discussions may comment now after seeing the warning. Perhaps reconsider.

5. The behavior change or feature removal may now be made default or permanent in the next release. Remove the old version and warning.

---

[2] http://propython.com/warnings-module/

Copyright

This document has been placed in the public domain.

P E P 3000

■ ■ ■

Python 3000

Author: Guido van Rossum

Abstract

This PEP sets guidelines for Python 3000 development. Ideally, we first agree on the process, and start discussing features only after the process has been decided and specified. In practice, we'll be discussing features and process simultaneously; often the debate about a particular feature will prompt a process discussion.

Naming

Python 3000, Python 3.0 and Py3K are all names for the same thing. The project is called Python 3000, or abbreviated to Py3k. The actual Python release will be referred to as Python 3.0, and that's what `python3.0 -V` will print; the actual file names will use the same naming convention we use for Python 2.x. I don't want to pick a new name for the executable or change the suffix for Python source files.

PEP Numbering

Python 3000 PEPs are numbered starting at PEP 3000. PEPs 3000-3099 are meta-PEPs—these can be either process or informational PEPs. PEPs 3100-3999 are feature PEPs. PEP 3000 itself (this PEP) is special; it is the meta-PEP for Python 3000 meta-PEPs (in other words, it describe the process to define processes). PEP 3100 is also special; it's a laundry list of features that were selected for (hopeful) inclusion in Python 3000 before we started the Python 3000 process for real. PEP 3099, finally, is a list of features that will not change.

Timeline

See PEP 361,[1] which contains the release schedule for Python 2.6 and 3.0. These versions will be released in lockstep.

---

[1] http://propython.com/pep-361/

■ **Note** Standard library development is expected to ramp up after 3.0a1 is released.

I expect that there will be parallel Python 2.x and 3.x releases for some time; the Python 2.x releases will continue for a longer time than the traditional 2.x.y bugfix releases. Typically, we stop releasing bugfix versions for 2.x once version 2.(x+1) has been released. But I expect there to be at least one or two new 2.x releases even after 3.0 (final) has been released, probably well into 3.1 or 3.2. This will to some extent depend on community demand for continued 2.x support, acceptance and stability of 3.0, and volunteer stamina.

I expect that Python 3.1 and 3.2 will be released much sooner after 3.0 than has been customary for the 2.x series. The 3.x release pattern will stabilize once the community is happy with 3.x.

Compatibility and Transition

Python 3.0 will break backwards compatibility with Python 2.x.

There is no requirement that Python 2.6 code will run unmodified on Python 3.0. Not even a subset. (Of course there will be a tiny subset, but it will be missing major functionality.)

Python 2.6 will support forward compatibility in the following two ways:

- It will support a "Py3k warnings mode" which will warn dynamically (i.e. at runtime) about features that will stop working in Python 3.0, e.g. assuming that `range()` returns a list.

- It will contain backported versions of many Py3k features, either enabled through `__future__` statements or simply by allowing old and new syntax to be used side-by-side (if the new syntax would be a syntax error in 2.x).

Instead, and complementary to the forward compatibility features in 2.6, there will be a separate source code conversion tool.[2] This tool can do a context-free source-to-source translation. For example, it can translate `apply(f, args)` into `f(*args)`. However, the tool cannot do data flow analysis or type inferencing, so it simply assumes that apply in this example refers to the old built-in function.

The recommended development model for a project that needs to support Python 2.6 and 3.0 simultaneously is as follows:

1. You should have excellent unit tests with close to full coverage.

2. Port your project to Python 2.6.

3. Turn on the Py3k warnings mode.

4. Test and edit until no warnings remain.

5. Use the 2to3 tool to convert this source code to 3.0 syntax. Do not manually edit the output!

6. Test the converted source code under 3.0.

---

[2] http://propython.com/2to3/

7. If problems are found, make corrections to the 2.6 version of the source code and go back to step 3.

8. When it's time to release, release separate 2.6 and 3.0 tarballs (or whatever archive form you use for releases).

It is recommended not to edit the 3.0 source code until you are ready to reduce 2.6 support to pure maintenance (i.e. the moment when you would normally move the 2.6 code to a maintenance branch anyway).

PS. We need a meta-PEP to describe the transitional issues in detail.

Implementation Language

Python 3000 will be implemented in C, and the implementation will be derived as an evolution of the Python 2 code base. This reflects my views (which I share with Joel Spolsky[3]) on the dangers of complete rewrites. Since Python 3000 as a language is a relatively mild improvement on Python 2, we can gain a lot by not attempting to reimplement the language from scratch. I am not against parallel from-scratch implementation efforts, but my own efforts will be directed at the language and implementation that I know best.

Meta-Contributions

Suggestions for additional text for this PEP are gracefully accepted by the author. Draft meta-PEPs for the topics above and additional topics are even more welcome!

Copyright

This document has been placed in the public domain.

---

[3] http://propython.com/spolsky-on-rewrites/

PEP 3003

■ ■ ■

Python Language Moratorium

Authors: Brett Cannon, Jesse Noller, Guido van Rossum

Abstract

This PEP proposes a temporary moratorium (suspension) of all changes to the Python language syntax, semantics, and built-ins for a period of at least two years from the release of Python 3.1. In particular, the moratorium would include Python 3.2 (to be released 18-24 months after 3.1) but allow Python 3.3 (assuming it is not released prematurely) to once again include language changes.

This suspension of features is designed to allow non-CPython implementations to "catch up" to the core implementation of the language, help ease adoption of Python 3.x, and provide a more stable base for the community.

Rationale

This idea was proposed by Guido van Rossum on the python-ideas[1] mailing list. The premise of his email was to slow the alteration of the Python core syntax, builtins and semantics to allow non-CPython implementations to catch up to the current state of Python, both 2.x and 3.x.

Python, as a language is more than the core implementation—CPython—with a rich, mature and vibrant community of implementations, such as Jython,[2] IronPython[3] and PyPy[4] that are a benefit not only to the community, but to the language itself.

Still others, such as Unladen Swallow[5] (a branch of CPython) seek not to create an alternative implementation, but rather they seek to enhance the performance and implementation of CPython itself.

Python 3.x was a large part of the last several years of Python's development. Its release, as well as a bevy of changes to the language introduced by it and the previous 2.6.x releases, puts alternative implementations at a severe disadvantage in "keeping pace" with core python development.

Additionally, many of the changes put into the recent releases of the language as implemented by CPython have not yet seen widespread usage by the general user population. For example, most users are limited to the version of the interpreter (typically CPython) which comes pre-installed with their

---

[1] http://propython.com/moratorium-proposal/
[2] http://propython.com/jython/
[3] http://propython.com/ironpython/
[4] http://propython.com/pypy/
[5] http://propython.com/unladen-swallow/

operating system. Most OS vendors are just barely beginning to ship Python 2.6—even fewer are shipping Python 3.x.

As it is expected that Python 2.7 be the effective "end of life" of the Python 2.x code line, with Python 3.x being the future, it is in the best interest of Python core development to temporarily suspend the alteration of the language itself to allow all of these external entities to catch up and to assist in the adoption of, and migration to, Python 3.x

Finally, the moratorium is intended to free up cycles within core development to focus on other issues, such as the CPython interpreter and improvements therein, the standard library, etc.

This moratorium does not allow for exceptions—once accepted, any pending changes to the syntax or semantics of the language will be postponed until the moratorium is lifted.

This moratorium does not attempt to apply to any other Python implementation meaning that if desired other implementations may add features which deviate from the standard implementation.

Details

Cannot Change

- New built-ins

- Language syntax—The grammar file essentially becomes immutable apart from ambiguity fixes.

- General language semantics—The language operates as-is with only specific exemptions (see below).

- New __future__ imports—These are explicitly forbidden, as they effectively change the language syntax and/or semantics (albeit using a compiler directive).

Case-by-Case Exemptions

- New methods on built-ins—The case for adding a method to a built-in object can be made.

- Incorrect language semantics—If the language semantics turn out to be ambiguous or improperly implemented based on the intention of the original design then the semantics may change.

- Language semantics that are difficult to implement—Because other VMs have not begun implementing Python 3.x semantics there is a possibility that certain semantics are too difficult to replicate. In those cases they can be changed to ease adoption of Python 3.x by the other VMs.

Allowed to Change

C API—It is entirely acceptable to change the underlying C code of CPython as long as other restrictions of this moratorium are not broken. E.g. removing the GIL would be fine assuming certain operations that are currently atomic remain atomic.

- The standard library—As the standard library is not directly tied to the language definition it is not covered by this moratorium.

- Backports of 3.x features to 2.x—The moratorium only affects features that would be new in 3.x.

- Import semantics—For example, PEP 382. After all, import semantics vary between Python implementations anyway.

Retroactive

It is important to note that the moratorium covers all changes since the release of Python 3.1. This rule is intended to avoid features being rushed or smuggled into the CPython source tree while the moratorium is being discussed. A review of the NEWS file for the py3k development branch showed no commits would need to be rolled back in order to meet this goal.

Extensions

The time period of the moratorium can only be extended through a new PEP.

Copyright

This document has been placed in the public domain.

Index

■ Symbols and Numerics

!= operator, 154
!r format, strings, 202
!s format, strings, 202
symbol, comments, 208
% operator, string substitution, 199
%r/%s formats, 199
* (asterisk)
   using all option to customize imports, 47
_ *see* underscore (_) character
+ operator, concatenation, 198
== operator, 154
@ syntax, decorators, 68–69
` (backtick) character
   linking multiple documents, ReST, 213
~ operator
   bitwise inversion, 149
< operator, 154
<< bitwise operator, 149
<<< (doctests), 218
> operator, 154
>> bitwise operator, 149
2to3 tool, 16
   version compatibility, 192, 196

■ A

abs method, 154
add method, 145
   sets, 40
add_column method, 257, 260
addition operation, 151
addTypeEqualityFunc method, 225, 226, 230
AGPL (Affero General Public License), 234–235
algorithms
   C3 algorithm, 109–115

all option, modules
   customizing imports, 47–48
AND bitwise comparison operation, 149, 152
and operator
   conditional expressions, 32
annotation_processor function
   factoring out boilerplate code, 86
annotations
   see also function annotations
   annotating with decorators, 90
annotations value, 61
anonymous links, ReST, 213
append method
   lists, 40
   sequences, 162
applications
   distribution, 241–242
   licensing, 233–236
   packaging, 236–241
   supporting multiple languages, 197
archive files
   sdist command, 241
args value, 61
   decorators with optional arguments, 74
   populating values, csv, 273
argument annotations
   type safety, 79
   type safety as decorator, 90
arguments, functions, 53–67
   checking init arguments, 271–273
   decorators with, 72–74
      optional arguments, 74–75
   default values, 53, 62, 63, 64, 65, 66, 74, 84
   docstrings explaining, 209
   function annotations, 78
   get_arguments function, 62–66, 67
   getargspec function, 62
   getfullargspec function, 61, 62
   identifying argument values, 62–66

arguments, functions (*cont.*)
    introspection, 61
    keyword arguments, 53, 54
        adding default values for, 65
    memoization, 76
    optional arguments, 63, 66
        decorators with, 74–75
    overriding, 54
    partial function, 61
    passing in different order to function
        definition, 53, 54
    planning for flexibility, 54
    preloading, 61
    required arguments, 63, 66, 67
    type safety as decorator, 90
    validate_arguments function, 66–67
    validating, 66–67
    variable positional arguments, 54
    zip function, 63
arithmetic operations, 145
arithmetic operators, 145
    whitespace, 287
as clause, with statement, 30
as keyword
    accessing exceptions, 23, 24
ASCII, 195
    text encoding, 197, 285
assert keyword, 222
assertAlmostEqual method, 224
assertDictContainsSubset method, 227
assertDictEqual method, 225
assertEqual method, 224, 225
assertFalse method, 222
assertGreater method, 226
assertGreaterEqual method, 226
assertIn method, 227
assertion methods
    overriding to change test behavior, 230
AssertionError exception, 224, 230
assertIs method, 229
assertIsNone method, 229
assertIsNot method, 229
assertIsNotNone method, 229
assertLess method, 226
assertLessEqual method, 226
assertListEqual method, 225
assertMultiLineEqual method, 227
assertNotAlmostEqual method, 224
assertNotEqual method, 224
assertNotIn method, 227
assertRaises method, 227, 228, 229

assertRaisesRegexp method, 228
assertRegexpMatches method, 227
assertSameElements method, 227
assertSequenceEqual method, 225
assertSetEqual method, 225
assertTrue method, 222
assertTupleEqual method, 225
asterisk (*)
    using all option to customize imports, 47
attach_to_class method, 250, 251, 252
    checking existence of, 254
    ordering fields, declarative frameworks,
        257, 259, 260
attributes
    see also fields, declarative frameworks
    attaching field to class, declarative
        frameworks, 250
    doc attribute, 209, 303
    failureException class attribute, 230
    hasattr method, 226
    naming conventions, 292, 293
attributes, functions
    func attribute, 133
    im_func attribute, 132, 133
attributes, objects, 126–131
    accessing, 126
    bases attribute, 118
    customized access using methods, 173
    dealing with, magic methods, 138–140
    delattr method, 127, 139
    getattr method, 126, 138–139, 173
    instances sharing single namespace, 170
    metaclass attribute, 122
    mro attribute, 118, 119
    properties, 127–129
    self-caching properties, 173–176
    setattr method, 126, 139, 173
attrs argument, init method
    ordering fields, declarative frameworks,
        257
author argument
    setup function, distutils, 238

■ **B**

b prefix, byte strings, 191, 192, 196
backtick (`) character
    linking multiple documents, ReST, 213
backwards compatibility, 15
    Python 3.0, 314

backwards compatibility policy, 309–311

base class, declarative frameworks, 246, 249

base.py module, 253, 254

bases attribute
inheritance, classes, 118

beauty, Zen of Python, 2

behaviors, objects
instances sharing single namespace, 170

Berkeley Software Distribution (BSD)
license, 235–236

big-endian values, bytes, 194

binary operations, 151, 152

binary operators, whitespace around, 287

bisect module
ordering fields, declarative frameworks, 260

bitwise inversion, 149
in-line/right-side methods, 152

bitwise operations, 148–149, 151, 152

blank lines, code layout, 284

block comments, 289

blocks see code blocks

boilerplate code, factoring out, 86–88

bool method, 143

Borg pattern, 170–173

bound methods, 132–133

break statement
iterators, 156
using with while loop, 29

BSD license, 235–236

Bushido, 13

byte string literals
b prefixing quoted literal, 191

byte strings, 191–195

bytes
chr function, 192
complex conversion of, 193–195
eight-byte values, 195
endianness, 194
four-byte values, 195
ord function, 192
ordering multiple-byte numbers, 195
primary use of, 192
strings, 191–195
struct module, 193–195
values spanning multiple bytes, 194

bytes type, 192

bztar type, 240

■ C

C3 algorithm
Method Resolution Order (MRO), 109–115

cachedproperty function, 175, 176

caching, 20
self-caching properties, 173–176

call method
CallCounter class, 165
CounterMeta class, 262–263

callables, 165–166

CamelCase style, 290

candidate classes, identifying, 109

CapitalizedWords style, 290

ceil method, 153

chain function, 38, 80

chaining iterables together, 38

chains
C3 algorithm, 111
exception chains, 24–26
explicit/implicit chains, 25

chr function, 192

class attribute, 130
failureException class attribute, 230

class declaration
creating classes, 119
metaclasses, 125
options container, 247
responsibility controlling namespace dictionary, 126

class methods, 133–134

classes
assigning functions to, 135
attaching call method to class definition, 165
attributes, 126–131
automatic subclasses, magic methods, 137–138
built-in types and, 103
creating, 119–126
at runtime, 120–121
controlling namespace, 125–126
defaultdict class, 45
descriptors, 129–131
docstrings, 305
identifying candidate classes, 109
inheritance, 103–119
C3 algorithm, 109–115
multiple inheritance, 105–106

classes (*cont.*)
    instances sharing single namespace, 170
    introspection, 117–119
    issubclass function, 118
    magic methods, 135–142
    metaclasses, 121–122
    Method Resolution Order (MRO), 106–109
    methods, 131–135
    naming conventions, 292
    object type, 169
    objects and, 103
    OrderedDict class, 44
    passing control to other classes, 115–117
    plugin framework, 122–125
    plugins, 124
    ref class, weakref module, 180
    subclasses method, 118
    super function, 115–117
classes, declarative frameworks
    attaching field to class, 250–252
    base class, 246
    Column class, 250, 251
    declarative classes, 245
    Dialect class, 249
    metaclass, 246
    Options class, 248
    RowMeta metaclass, 253, 254
classmethod decorator, 133, 134
clear method, sets, 41
closures, 69–70
    wrappers, 70–72
cls namespace
    instances sharing single namespace, 173
cmp method, 155
code blocks
    creating classes, 119
    except keyword, 22
    Zen of Python, 4
code layout, 284–285
code, importing, 45–51
codecs package, 248
coding
    avoiding repetition, 12
    style guide for Python, 283
    Zen of Python, 6
coerce_arguments decorator, 88, 89
coercion, type, 88–89
collect function, gc module, 179

collections, 39–45
    dictionaries with default values, 44
    named tuples, 43
    ordered dictionaries, 44
    sets, 39–43
collections module, 45
Column class, 250, 251
    checking existence of attach_to_class method, 254
    init method, 258–261
    new method, 261
    ordering fields, 260, 262
    to_python method, 263
    to_string method, 263
column classes
    DateColumn class, 266–270
    DecimalColumn class, 265–266
    FloatColumn class, 265
    IntegerColumn class, 265
    StringColumn class, 264–265
columns.py module, 249
comments, 208, 288–289
    block/inline comments, 289
comparison operations, 154–155
    bitwise comparison operations, 149
comparison tests, 224–226
compatibility
    backwards compatibility, 15, 309–311
complex method, 153
complexity, Zen of Python, 3, 11
comprehensions
    dictionary comprehensions, 37
    list comprehensions, 35
    set comprehensions, 37
concatenation, string substitution, 198
conditional expressions, 31–32
    and/or operators, 32
consistency, Python style guide, 283
constants
    naming conventions, 293
Contact class
    inheritance, 104–105
contains method, sequences, 163
context managers, 166–167
    enter/exit methods, 166
    with statement, 30, 166
control flow, 21–32
    catching exceptions, 21–24
    conditional expressions, 31–32
    exception chains, 24–26

if/else blocks, 31
    proceeding after exceptions, 27–28
    try/except blocks, 26–27
    while loops, 29
    with statement, 29–31
copy function, copy module, 187
copy method, 188
    dictionaries, 187
copy module, 187
    copy function, 187
    deepcopy method, 188, 189
copying objects, 186–189
    deep copies, 188–189
    shallow copies, 187–188
counter attribute, columns, 259
CounterMeta class
    call method, 262–263
coupling, loose, 13
CSV framework, 245, 270–281
    see also declarative frameworks; sheets
        framework
    checking init arguments, 271–273
    CSV files containing header row, 248
    CSV reader, 275–278
    CSV writer, 279–281
    populating values, 273–275
    required fields, 250
csv module, 244, 264, 270–271
    DictReader, 270
    DictWriter, 271
    reader method, 275
    readers, 270, 275–278
    writerow method, 270, 279, 280
        needs_header_row option, 279
    writerows method, 270, 279, 280
    writers, 270, 279–281
csv_dialect attribute, 276
cyclical references
    garbage collection, 178–180

■ D

data conversion methods, 263
data storage, 182
    retrieving data, 183
data structures
    exporting to strings, 182
DateColumn class, 266–270
    to_python method, 267, 268, 269

datetime class
    strptime method, 267
decimal module, 265
DecimalColumn class, 265–266
declarative classes, 245
declarative frameworks
    see also CSV framework; sheets
        framework
    adding metaclass, 252–254
    attaching field to class, 250–252
    base class, 246
    building, 244–245
    building field library, 263–270
    columns.py module, 249
    components of, 246
    CSV framework, 245
    DateColumn class, 266–270
    DecimalColumn class, 265–266
    declarative programming, 244
    default values for framework options,
        247
    defining fields, 249–250
    field types, 246
    FloatColumn class, 265
    import block, 246
    IntegerColumn class, 265
    managing options, 247–249
    metaclass attached to base class, 246
    namespace, 246
    naming, 246
    options container, 246, 247–249
    ordering fields, 256–263
    StringColumn class, 264–265
    to build or not to build, 245
    valuable prerequisites for, 245
declarative programming, 244
DeclarativeMeta class
    prepare method, 256–258, 263
decode method, strings, 198
decorator function
    property decorator function, 127
    type safety as decorator, 93
decorators, 61, 67–78
    @ syntax, 68–69
    annotating with, 90
    decorator creating decorators, 77–78
    memoization, 75–76
    type coercion, 88
    type safety as decorator, 90–94

decorators (*cont.*)
    with arguments, 72–74
    with optional arguments, 74–75
    wrappers, 70–72
decorators, list of
    classmethod, 133
    coerce_arguments, 88, 89
    memoize, 76
    property, 174
    repeatable, 159
    staticmethod, 134
    suppress_errors, 68
    typesafe, 87, 90–94
    wraps, 71
deep copies
    copying objects, 188–189
deepcopy method, copy module, 188, 189
defaultdict class, 45
defaults value, 61
    identifying argument values, 64
del method, 177
    cyclical references, 178–180
del statement, 177
delattr method, 127, 139
delete method, descriptors, 131
deleter methods, 128, 129
delitem method, sequences, 163
description argument
    setup function, distutils, 238
descriptors, 129–131
    class attribute, 130
    delete method, 131
    get method, 129, 131
    set method, 130
design, framework, 243
deterministic functions, 75
development
    Python 3000 development, 313–315
    Python language moratorium, 317–319
    Test-Driven Development (TDD), 217
    voting guidelines, 299–300
    Zen of Python, 6, 10, 11
dialect attribute, 257, 258
Dialect class
    adding metaclass, 252, 253
    base.py module, 253
    class declaration, 249
    csv_dialect attribute, 276
    header rows, 276
    ordering fields, 257, 259
    renaming Options class, 249

dict attribute, objects, 170
dict function, 38
dictionaries, 38
    assertDictContainsSubset method, 227
    assertDictEqual method, 225
    copy method, 187
    default values, 44
    DictReader class, csv, 270
    namespace dictionary, 170–176
    ordered dictionaries, 44
    update method, 40
dictionary comprehensions, 37
DictReader class, csv module, 270
DictWriter class, csv module, 271
difference method, sets, 42
discard method, sets, 41
distribution, 241–242
    Python Package Index (PyPI), 241
    sdist command, 240–241
distutils package
    setup function, 237–239
division
    divmod method, 147, 151
    floordiv method, 146, 151
    floor/true division, 146, 151
    in-line method, 152
    modulo operation, 146, 151
    remainder, 146
    truediv method, 146, 151
divmod method, 147
Django, 243
doc attribute, 209, 303
docstrings (documentation strings), 208–210, 303–307
    describing functions, 209
    explaining arguments, 209
    getdoc function, 100
    including exceptions, 210
    including return value, 209
    indentation, 306–307
    introspection, 99–101
    multi-line docstrings, 305–306
    PEP-257 (docstrings), 289
    one-line docstrings, 304–305
    using triple double quotes, 304
doctest module, 220
doctests, 218–221
    formatting code, 218
    integrating with documentation, 219
    representing output, 218–219
    running tests, 220–221

documentation, 207
  comments, 208
  docstrings, 208–210
  docutils package, 211
  external documentation, from code,
      210–211
  installation and configuration, 210
  integrating doctests with, 219
  linking multiple documents, ReST, 213–
      214
  packaging, 237
  proper naming, 207–208
  reference documents, 210
  tutorials, 210
  utilities assisting with, 211–215
  Zen of Python, 11
documentation strings *see* docstrings
docutils package, 211
  reStructuredText (ReST), 211, 214
DRY (don't repeat yoursefl) principle
  creating classes at runtime, 120
duck typing, 254
dump/dumps functions, pickle module, 182

■ **E**

elif keyword, 4
else keyword, 4
  if/else blocks, 31
  try/except blocks, 27
encode method, strings, 197, 198
encoding
  ASCII, 197
  open function, 247
  PEP-263, 285
  text, 196–198
  Unicode-focused encodings, 197
  Zen of Python, 9
endianness, bytes, 194
enter method, context managers, 166
EnvironmentError exception, 22, 23, 24
eq method, 154
equality tests, 224–225
error handling
  working with overridden attributes,
      140
  Zen of Python, 7
except clause/keyword, 9, 22
  see also try/except blocks
exception chains, 24–26

exceptions
  accessing, 23
  catching, 21–24
  docstrings including, 210
  naming conventions, 292
  proceeding after, 27–28
  programming recommendations, 294
  raising, 22
  StopIteration exception, 156
  testing, 227–229
  try/except blocks, 26–27
  working with overridden attributes, 140
  Zen of Python, 7, 8
exclude command
  MANIFEST.in file, 239
exit method, context managers, 166
explicit arguments, 54
  type safety, function annotations, 82, 83
explicit chains, 25
explicit code
  importing with asterisk notation, 48
  Zen of Python, 2, 9
exponentiation, 147, 151
expressions
  conditional expressions, 31–32
  generator expressions, 36–37
  list comprehensions, 35
  readability of, 31
  whitespace in, 286–288
  Zen of Python, 3

■ **F**

fail method, TestCase, unittest, 222
failureException class attribute, 230
fallback imports, 45–46
fields, declarative frameworks
  attaching field to class, 250–252
  base field class, 249
  building field library, 263–270
    DateColumn class, 266–270
    DecimalColumn class, 265–266
    FloatColumn class, 265
    IntegerColumn class, 265
    StringColumn class, 264–265
  call method, CounterMeta class, 262–
      263
  data conversion methods, 263
  defining, 249–250
  field types, 246

fields, declarative frameworks (*cont.*)
    init method, Column class, 258–261
    new method, Column class, 261
    ordering fields, 256–263
    prepare method, 256–258, 263
    required fields, 250
    to_python method, 263
    to_string method, 263
file handling, context managers, 166
finally keyword, try/except blocks, 27, 29
flat structures, Zen of Python, 4, 5
float method, 153
FloatColumn class, 265
floor division, 146, 147, 151
floor function/method, 153
floordiv method, 146
format method, strings, 201–202, 203,
   205
format option, sdist command, 240
formatting
    reStructuredText (ReST), 212
formatting code, doctests, 218
formatting strings, 201–206
    alignment of output string, 203
    custom format specification, 205–206
    distinguishing types of strings, 202
    looking up values within objects, 202
    nesting argument references, 204
    padding output with spaces, 203
    plain text table of contents, 204–205
    standard format specification, 203–204
framework design, 243
frameworks, 243
    building declarative framework, 244–245
    CSV framework, 270–281
Free Software Foundation licenses, 236
    GNU General Public License (GPL), 233
fromlist argument, import function, 49
func attribute, 133
function annotations, 78–94
    annotating with decorators, 90
    argument annotations, 79
    factoring out boilerplate code, 86–88
    return value annotation, 92
    type coercion, 88–89
    type safety, 79
    type safety as decorator, 90–94
function type, 53
functions
    see also arguments, functions
    @ syntax, decorators, 68–69
    assigning functions to classes and
        instances, 135
    closures, 69–70
    creating weak reference inside, 181
    decorator creating decorators, 77–78
    decorators, 61, 67–78
    deterministic functions, 75
    docstrings, 305
        introspection, 101
    docstrings describing, 209
    functions relying on iteration, 33
    generators, 94–96
    lambdas, 96
    memoization, 75–76
    methods and, 131
    naming conventions, 292
    Python, 53
    robustness principle, 15
    wrappers, 70–72
    x prefixed functions, 33
functions, list of
    annotation_processor, 86
    cachedproperty, 175, 176
    chain, 38, 80
    chr, 192
    collect, 179
    copy, 187
    decorator, 93
    dict, 38
    dump/dumps, 182
    floor, 153
    get_arguments, 62–66
    getargspec, 62
    getdoc, 100
    getfullargspec, 61, 62
    globals, 49
    hours_and_minutes, 147
    import, 49–51
    import_module, 51
    import_path, 50, 51
    isinstance, 80, 117
    issubclass, 118
    iter, 155
    load/loads, 183
    locals, 49
    min, 35
    namedtuple, 43
    open, 30, 31
    ord, 192
    pack, 193–194
    partial, 61

property, 127, 129
range, 33, 96, 156
returns, 94
reversed, 160
round, 153
set, 37, 40
split, 34
str, 199
super, 115–117
typesafe, 79, 80, 82
unpack, 193, 194
validate_arguments, 66–67
xrange, 33, 96
zip, 38, 63
functools module
    partial function, 61
    wraps decorator, 71
future module
    importing code, 46–47

■ G

garbage attribute, 179
garbage collection, 176–182
    cyclical references, 178–180
    reference counting, 177
    weak references, 180–182
gc module, 179
generator expressions, 36–37, 94
generators, 94–96
    repeatable generators, 158–159
    yield statement, 94
get method
    descriptors, 129, 131
    Zen of Python, 10
get_arguments function, 62–66
getargspec function, 62
getattr method, 138–139
    accessing attributes, 126, 173
    mixins, 105
getdoc function, 100
getfullargspec function, 61, 62
    identifying argument values, 63, 64
getitem method, 157, 160
getmro method, 119
getreader function, codecs, 248
getstate method, 183, 184
getter methods, 127
    naming setter as, 128
global variables, naming, 292

global-exclude command, MANIFEST.in
    file, 240
global-include command, MANIFEST.in
    file, 240
globals argument, import function, 49
globals function, 49
GNU Lesser General Public License (LGPL),
    235
GPL (GNU General Public License), 233–234
    Affero General Public License (AGPL),
        234–235
graft command, MANIFEST.in file, 240
gt method, 154
gztar type
    format option, sdist command, 240

■ H

has_header_row attribute, 277, 279
hasattr method, 226, 254
header rows
    CSV framework, 248
    Dialect class, 276
    has_header_row attribute, 277, 279
    needs_header_row option, 279
hours_and_minutes function, 147

■ I

i method prefix, 151
id function, objects, 169
identity, objects, 169
    instances sharing single namespace, 170
    testing, 229
if/else blocks, 31
    Zen of Python, 4
im_func attribute, 132, 133
implicit chains, 25
implicit code
    importing with asterisk notation, 48
    Zen of Python, 2, 9
import block
    declarative frameworks, 246, 255
import function, 49–51
import_module function, 51
import_path function, 50, 51
ImportError exception, 45, 46
importing code, 45–51
    fallback imports, 45–46
    future module, 46–47

importing code (*cont.*)
    import function, 49–51
    importlib module, 51
    relative imports, 48
    using all option to customize imports,
        47–48
importlib module, 51
imports
    style guide for Python, 285–286
in keyword, sets, 40
include command, MANIFEST.in file, 239
indentation
    docstrings, 306–307
    style guide for, 284
index method, 152
IndexError exception, 161
inequality operator, 154
inheritance, 103–119
    bases attribute, 118
    C3 algorithm, 109–115
    Contact class, 104–105
    Method Resolution Order (MRO), 106–
        109
    mro attribute, 118, 119
    multiple inheritance, 105–106
    naming conventions, 293
    object type, 103
init method
    checking arguments, csv, 271–273
    Column class, 258–261
    fields, 250
    instances sharing single namespace, 170
    metaclasses, 121, 122
    objects, 136–137, 170
    plugins, 125
    readers and writers, csv, 271–273
init method, test case class
    adding addTypeEqualityFunc method
        to, 225
    overriding assertion methods, 230
init module
    creating __init__.py module, 255
inline comments, 289
inner functions, closures, 69–70
in-place operators, 151
InputValidator class, 123, 125
insert method, sequences, 162
insort method, bisect module, 260
inspect module
    getargspec function, 62
    getdoc function, 100

getfullargspec function, 61, 62
getmro method, 119
instance variables, naming, 292
instances *see* objects
instantiation, 136
int method, 153
IntegerColumn class, 265
integers
    chr function, 192
    ord function, 192
interfaces, Zen of Python, 3
intersection method, sets, 42
introspection, 97–101
    classes, 117–119
    docstrings, 99–101
    function arguments, 61
    identifying object types, 98
    isinstance function, 117
    modules, 98
InvalidOperation exception, 266
inversion, bitwise, 149, 152
invert method, 149
IOError exception, 22, 23
is not operator, 154
is operator, 154
    object comparison, 169
isinstance function
    introspection, 117
    programming recommendations, 296
    type safety, function annotations, 80
issubclass function, 118
issubset method, 42
issuperset method, 42
items method
    dictionaries, 80
    mappings, 165
iter function, 155, 157
iter method, 155
    Reader class, 277
    repeatable generators, 158
iteration, 33–39
    chaining iterables together, 38
    dictionary comprehensions, 37
    functions relying on, 33
    generator expressions, 36–37
    generators, 94–96
    list comprehensions, 35
    programming concepts, 19
    sequence unpacking, 34
    sequences, 33
    set comprehensions, 37

StopIteration exception, 277
x prefixed functions, 33
zipping iterables together, 38
iterators, 155–159
break statement, 156
next method, 155, 156
range function, 156
repeatable generators, 158
StopIteration exception, 156
iteritems/iterkeys methods, 165
itertools module
chain function, 80
itervalues method, 165

■ K

KeyError exception
dictionaries with default values, 44
removing items from sets, 40
keys
mappings, 164
ordered dictionaries, 44
keys method, mappings, 164
keyword arguments, 53, 54
accept options without naming, 249
adding default values for, 65
checking init arguments, 271, 272
format method, strings, 201
identifying argument values, 62, 63, 64
protocol, 183
setup function, distutils, 238
type safety, function annotations, 80, 82,
83
Zen of Python, 2
keywords
as, 23, 24
assert, 222
else, 27
except, 22
finally, 27
protocol, 183
raise, 22
test, 222
try, 22
with, 30
Knuth, Donald, 14
kwargs value, 74, 81, 82, 83, 273
kwonlyargs value, 61
kwonlydefaults value, 61, 64

■ L

lambdas, 96
languages
applications supporting multiple, 197
Python language moratorium, 317–319
left binary shift operation, 151
left-hand methods, 150
len method, 144, 160
level argument, import function, 49
LGPL (GNU Lesser General Public License),
235
license argument
setup function, distutils, 238
LICENSE.txt file, 237
licensing, 233–236
Affero General Public License, 234–235
Berkeley Software Distribution, 235–236
Free Software Foundation, 236
GNU General Public License, 233–234
GNU Lesser General Public License, 235
Open Source Initiative licenses, 236
line length, maximum, 284
linking multiple documents, ReST, 213–214
list comprehensions, 35
lists
append method, 40
assertListEqual method, 225
little-endian values, bytes, 194
load/loads function, pickle module, 183
locals argument, import function, 49
locals function, 49
log files, exception chains, 25
loops
while loop, 29
loose coupling, 13
lshift method, 149
lt method, 154, 260

■ M

magic methods, 135–142
automatic subclasses, 137–138
creating instances, 136–137
dealing with attributes, 138–140
delattr method, 139
getattr method, 138–139
init method, 136–137
new method, 137
setattr method, 139

magic methods (*cont.*)
  str method, 140–142
  string representations, 140–142
  subclasses method, 137
main function, unittest module, 223
maintainer argument
  setup function, distutils, 238
MANIFEST.in file, 239–240
  sdist command, 240
mappings, 164–165
  items method, 165
  iterxyz methods, 165
  keys method, 164
  values method, 165
mathematical operations, 144–148
memoization, 75–76
memoize decorator, 76
memory management
  garbage collection, 176–182
metaclass attribute, 122
metaclasses, 121–122
  call method, CounterMeta, 262–263
  class declaration, 125
  declarative frameworks, 252–254
  init method, 258–261
  new method, 261
  plugins, 124
  prepare metaclass, 125
  prepare method, 125, 256–258, 263
  RowMeta metaclass, 253, 254
metadata
  setup function, distutils, 237, 238
Method Resolution Order *see* MRO
methods, 131–135
  applying @property decorator to, 174
  assigning functions to classes and
    instances, 135
  bound methods, 132–133
  class methods, 133–134
  data conversion, 263
  docstrings, 303, 305
  functions and, 131
  i prefix after underscores, 151
  in-line methods, 151
  left-hand methods, 150, 151
  magic methods, 135–142
    automatic subclasses, 137–138
    creating instances, 136–137
    dealing with attributes, 138–140
    string representations, 140–142

  naming conventions, 292
  r prefix after underscores, 150, 151
  right-hand methods, 150, 151
  static methods, 134–135
  unbound methods, 131–132
methods, list of
  abs, 154
  add, 40, 145
  append, 40
  attach_to_class, 250
  bool, 143
  call, 165
  ceil, 153
  clear, 41
  cmp, 155
  complex, 153
  contains, 163
  copy, 187, 188
  decode, 198
  deepcopy, 188, 189
  del, 177, 178–180
  delattr, 139
  delitem, 163
  difference, 42
  discard, 41
  divmod, 147
  encode, 197, 198
  enter, 166
  eq, 154
  exit, 166
  float, 153
  floor, 153
  floordiv, 146
  format, 201–202
  get, 10
  getattr, 138–139, 173
  getitem, 157, 160
  getmro, 119
  getstate, 183, 184
  gt, 154
  hasattr, 226
  index, 152
  init, 136–137, 170, 271–273
  int, 153
  intersection, 42
  invert, 149
  issubset, 42
  issuperset, 42
  items, 165
  iter, 155, 158

iteritems, 165
iterkeys, 165
itervalues, 165
keys, 164
len, 144, 160
lshift, 149
lt, 154
mod, 146
mul, 145
ne, 154
neg, 154
new, 137, 171–173
next, 155
nonzero, 144
pop, 41
pos, 154
pow, 147
remove, 40, 163
repr, 142
reversed, 160
round, 153
rshift, 149
setattr, 139, 173
setitem, 162
setstate, 185, 186
sorted, 188
str, 140–142
strptime, 267
sub, 145
subclasses, 118, 137
symmetric_difference, 42
to_python, 263
to_string, 263
truediv, 146
unicode, 141
union, 42
update, 40
values, 165
min function
    generator expressions, 36
    list comprehensions, 35
mixedCase style, 290
mixins
    inheritance, 171, 172
    multiple inheritance, 105
mod method, 146
    string substitution, 199
module attribute
    creating classes at runtime, 121
    namespaces, 126

modules
    docstrings, 303, 305
    import function, 49–51
    import_module function, 51
    introspection, 98
    naming conventions, 291
    programming recommendations, 295
    using all option to customize imports,
        47–48
modules, list of
    base.py, 253, 254
    bisect, 260
    collections, 45
    columns.py, 249
    copy, 187
    csv, 244, 264, 270–271
    decimal, 265
    doctest, 220
    functools, 61, 71
    future, 46–47
    gc, 179
    importlib, 51
    init, 255
    inspect, 61, 62
    itertools, 80
    options.py, 247
    pickle, 182
    struct, 193–195
    tests.py, 223
    this, 1
    unittest, 221–230
    weakref, 180
modulo operation, 146, 151
    divmod method, 147
    in-line method, 152
mount point, plugin framework, 123
MRO (Method Resolution Order)
    C3 algorithm, 109–115
    classes, 106–109
    getmro method, 119
    identifying candidate classes, 109
    introspection, 117–119
    super function, 115–117
mro attribute, 118, 119
MRO lists, removing items from, 112
mul method, 145
multiple inheritance, classes, 105–106
multiplication operation, 151

■ N

name argument
    import function, 49
    setup function, distutils, 237
named tuples, 43
namedtuple function, 43
namespace dictionary, 170–176
    accessing, 126
    Borg pattern, 170–173
    creating classes at runtime, 120
    descriptors, 131
    instances sharing single namespace,
        170, 172
    ordering fields, declarative frameworks,
        256
    responsibility controlling, 126
    self-caching properties, 173–176
namespaces
    creating classes, 125–126
    declarative frameworks, 246
    prepare method, metaclasses, 125
    Zen of Python, 12
naming conventions, 290–294
    attributes, 292, 293
    classes, 292
    constants, 293
    descriptive, 290–291
    exceptions, 292
    functions, 292
    global variables, 292
    inheritance, 293
    instance variables, 292
    methods, 292
    modules, 291
    packages, 291
    prescriptive, 291–294
    proper naming, documentation, 207–
        208
naming styles, 290–291
    underscore (_) character, 291
ne method, 154
needs_header_row option, 279
neg method, 154
nesting, Zen of Python, 4
new method
    Column class, 261
    instances sharing single namespace,
        170, 171–173

    objects, 137
next method
    iterators, 155, 156
    metaclasses, 121
    Reader class, 277, 278
nonzero method, 144
numbers, 152–155
    comparison operations, 154–155
    ordering multiple-byte numbers, 195
    sign operations, 154

■ O

object management, 169
    copying objects, 186–189
    cyclical references, 178–180
    garbage collection, 176–182
    namespace dictionary, 170–176
        Borg pattern, 170–173
        self-caching properties, 173–176
    pickling, 182–186
    reference counting, 177
    weak references, 180–182
object type
    inheritance, 103
    introspection, 98
    programming recommendations, 296
Object-Relational Mapper (ORM)
    self-caching properties, 174
objects, 169
    assigning functions to classes and
        instances, 135
    attributes, 126–131
    classes and, 103
    copying, 186–189
    creating instances, magic methods, 136–
        137
    dict attribute, 170
    getattr method, 173
    getstate method, 183, 184
    id function, 169
    identity, 169
    inheriting from object, 103
    init method, 170
    injecting into strings, 199
    instances sharing single namespace, 170
    instantiation, 136
    looking up values within, 202
    new method, 171–173
    pickling, 182–186

removing references to, 177
setattr method, 173
setstate method, 185, 186
type, 169, 170
value, 169
open function
    encoding argument, 247
    using in with statement, 30, 31
Open Source Initiative licenses, 236
    GNU General Public License (GPL), 233
operations, 143–152
    arithmetic operations, 145
    bitwise comparison operations, 149
    bitwise operations, 148–149
    changing argument ordering, 150
    comparison operations, 154–155
    left-hand methods, 150
    mathematical operations, 144–148
    modulo operation, 146
    right-hand methods, 150
    shifting operations, 149
    sign operations, 154
operators
    == operator, 154
    and operator, 32
    arithmetic operators, 145
    inequality operator, 154
    in-place operators, 151
    is not operator, 154
    is operator, 154
    or operator, 32
    whitespace, 287
options attribute
    ordering fields, declarative frameworks,
        258
Options class, declarative frameworks, 248
options container
    accepting options without naming, 249
    declarative frameworks, 246, 247–249
    default values for options, 247
options.py module, 247
OR bitwise comparison operation, 149, 152
or operator, conditional expressions, 32
ord function, 192
ordered dictionaries, 44
OrderedDict class, 44
ordering fields, declarative frameworks,
    256–263
    call method, CounterMeta, 262–263
    choosing option, 263
    init method, Column, 258–261

new method, Column, 261
    prepare method, metaclasses, 256–258,
        263
OSError exception, 22, 23
output
    representing, doctests, 218–219
overriding, function arguments, 54

■ P

pack function, struct module, 193–194,
    195
    endianness, 194
package_data argument
    setup function, distutils, 238
package_dir argument
    setup function, distutils, 238
packages see modules
packages argument
    setup function, distutils, 238
packaging, 236–241
    adding files to package, 239
    MANIFEST.in file, 239–240
    sdist command, 240–241
    setup.py script, 237–239
Pareto Principle, 14
partial function, 61
paths
    import_path function, 50, 51
    relative imports, 48
patterns
    Borg pattern, 170–173
PEP-10 (voting guidelines), 299–300
PEP-20 see Zen of Python
PEP-257 see docstrings
PEP-258 (Docutils Design Specification),
    304
PEP-263 (encodings), 285
PEP-3000, 313
PEP-3003 (Python language moratorium),
    317–319
PEP-3099, 313
PEP-3100, 313
PEP-361, 313
PEP-387 see backwards compatibility policy
PEP-8 see style guide for Python
performance
    memory or CPU usage, 95
Peters, Tim, 1

pickle module, 182
　　dump function, 182
　　dumps function, 182
　　load function, 183
　　loads function, 183
pickling, 182–186
　　getstate method, 183, 184
　　setstate method, 185, 186
placeholders, 199
　　%r format, 199
　　%s format, 199
　　format method, strings, 201
　　injecting objects into strings, 199
　　rearranging in substitution string, 200
plugin framework, 122–125
　　InputValidator class, 123
　　mount point, 123
plugins, 122–125
　　classes, 124
pop method, sets, 41
pos method, 154
positional arguments
　　checking init arguments, 271, 272
　　format method, strings, 201
　　identifying argument values, 62, 63
　　type safety, function annotations, 80
　　variable positional arguments, 54
pow method, 147
practicality, Zen of Python, 6
preloading arguments, 61
prepare method
　　metaclasses, 125, 256–258, 263
print function
　　representing output, doctests, 219
programming
　　backward compatibility, 15
　　declarative programming, 244
　　recommendations, 294–297
programming concepts
　　caching, 20
　　collections, 39–45
　　control flow, 21–32
　　importing code, 45–51
　　iteration, 19, 33–39
　　transparency, 21
programming philosophies *see* Zen of
　　Python
properties
　　attributes, 127–129
　　descriptors, 129–131
　　self-caching properties, 173–176

property decorator
　　applying to methods, 174
property decorator function, 127
property function, 129
protocol keyword
　　retrieving data from storage, 183
prune command, MANIFEST.in file, 240
punctuation, Zen of Python, 2
Py3k (Python 3000), 313
PyPI (Python Package Index), 241
Python
　　2to3 tool, 16
　　base.py module, 253, 254
　　columns.py module, 249
　　creating __init__.py module, 255
　　functions, 53
　　GNU General Public License (GPL), 234
　　introspection, 61
　　keyword arguments, 53, 54
　　MANIFEST.in file, 239–240
　　options.py module, 247
　　programming philosophies, 1–17
　　setup.py script, 237–239
　　style guide for, 283
　　tests.py module, 223
　　Zen of Python, 1–12, 301–302
Python 3.0
　　background to, 16
　　backwards compatibility, 314
　　catching exceptions prior to, 24
　　language moratorium, 317–319
Python 3000 development, 313–315
Python Enhancement Proposal (PEP), 1
Python Package Index (PyPI), 241
PYTHONPATH
　　relative imports, 48

■ R

r method prefix, 150, 151
raise keyword, 22
　　exception chains, 24
range function, 33, 96, 156
　　generator expressions, 36
　　sequences, 160
read method, codecs, 248
readability
　　expressions, 31
　　style guide for Python, 283
　　Zen of Python, 5

Reader class, 277, 278
reader method, 275
reader, CSV framework, 275–278
readers
    csv module, 270, 275–278
    DictReader, 270
    sheets reader, 271
README.txt file, 237
recursive-exclude command, MANIFEST.in
    file, 240
recursive-include command, MANIFEST.in
    file, 239
ref class, weakref module, 180
reference counting
    cyclical references, 178–180
    garbage collection, 177
    removing references to objects, 177
    weak references, 180–182
reference documents, 210
regular expressions
    assertRaisesRegexp method, 228
    assertRegexpMatches method, 227
relative imports, 48
remainder, division, 146
remove method
    sequences, 163
    sets, 40
repeatable decorator, 159
repeatable generators, 158–159
repetition, avoiding, 12
repr function
    representing output, doctests, 219
repr method, 142
    %r format, 199
    byte string literals, 191
ReST (reStructuredText)
    distinguishing between paragraph and
        block of code, 212
    docutils package, 211
    formatting, 212
    linking multiple documents, 213–214
    Sphinx, 214
return value annotation
    type safety as decorator, 92
return values
    docstrings including, 209
    function annotations, 78
returns function
    type safety as decorator, 94
reversed function, 160
reversed method, sequences, 160

right binary shift operation, 152
right-hand methods, 150
robustness principle, 14, 88, 110
round function, 153
round method, 153
Row class, sheets, 275
RowMeta metaclass, 253
    declarative frameworks, 253, 254
    prepare method, 256–258, 263
rshift method, 149
rules, Zen of Python, 6
runtime
    creating classes at, 120–121

■ S

scripts, docstrings, 305
sdist command, 240–241
self-caching properties
    object management, 173–176
sequence unpacking, 34
sequences, 33, 159–164
    append method, 162
    assertIn method, 227
    assertNotIn method, 227
    assertSameElements method, 227
    assertSequenceEqual method, 225
    contains method, 163
    delitem method, 163
    DictReader, csv, 270
    getitem method, 160
    insert method, 162
    iteration, 33
    len method, 160
    programming recommendations, 296
    remove method, 163
    retrieving items, 160
    reversed method, 160
    setitem method, 162
    slicing syntax, 161
set comprehensions, 37
set function, 37, 40
set method, descriptors, 130
setattr method, 139
    accessing attributes, 126, 173
setitem method, sequences, 162
sets, 37, 39–43
    add method, 40
    assertSetEqual method, 225
    clear method, 41

sets (*cont.*)
　　combining sets, 41
　　difference method, 42
　　discard method, 41
　　in keyword, 40
　　intersection method, 42
　　issubset method, 42
　　issuperset method, 42
　　pop method, 41
　　remove method, 40
　　removing all items from set, 41
　　removing any item from set, 41
　　removing specific item from set, 40
　　representing empty set, 41
　　symmetric_difference method, 42
　　union method, 42
　　update method, 40
setstate method, 185, 186
setter methods, 127, 129
　　naming as getter, 128
setup function, distutils, 237–239
　　metadata, 237, 238
setUp method, unittest, 221–222, 230
setup.py script, 237–239
shallow copies, objects, 187–188
sheets framework
　　see also CSV framework; declarative
　　　　frameworks
　　naming declarative frameworks, 246
　　readers, csv, 275
　　required fields, 250
　　using csv module functionality, 249
sheets reader, 271
SheetWriter class, 279
shifting operations, 149
sign operations, 154
simplicity, Zen of Python, 3, 12
slicing syntax, sequences, 161
sort operation, columns
　　declarative frameworks, 260
sorted method, 188
source code, Zen of Python, 5
spaces, style guide for, 284
Sphinx
　　reStructuredText (ReST), 214
split function, 34, 45, 50
SQLAlchemy, 243
state
　　getstate method, 183, 184
　　setstate method, 185, 186

statements
　　in-place string concatenation, 294
　　whitespace in, 286–288
static methods, 134–135
staticmethod decorator, 134
StopIteration exception, 156, 277
storing data, 182
　　retrieving data from storage, 183
str function, 199
　　representing output, doctests, 219
str method, 140–142
　　%s format, 199
str type, 192
string literals, docstrings, 304
string methods
　　programming recommendations,
　　　　296
string substitution, 199
StringColumn class, 264–265
strings
　　alignment of output string, 203
　　assertMultiLineEqual method, 227
　　byte strings, 191–195
　　custom format specification, 205–206
　　decode method, 198
　　distinguishing types of, 202
　　encode method, 197, 198
　　exporting data structures to, 182
　　format method, 201–202
　　formatting, 201–206
　　injecting objects into, 199
　　in-place string concatenation, 294
　　nesting argument references, 204
　　padding output with, 203
　　placing multiple values into, 199
　　programming recommendations, 297
　　standard format specification, 203–204
　　string representations, magic methods,
　　　　140–142
　　Unicode strings, 196
　　version compatibility, 192, 200, 202
strptime method, datetime, 267
struct module, 193–195
　　pack function, 193–194, 195
　　unpack function, 193, 194, 195
style guide for Python, 283–297
　　code layout, 284–285
　　comments, 288–289
　　docstrings, 289
　　imports, 285–286

naming conventions, 290–294

naming styles, 290–291

programming recommendations, 294–297

setUp method, 222

version bookkeeping, 290

sub method, 145

subclasses method, 118, 137

subclasses, automatic subclasses

magic methods, 137–138

substitution, 198–200

rearranging placeholders in substitution string, 200

string substitution, 199

subtraction operation, 151

super function

common mistake using, 117

metaclasses, 121

passing control to other classes, 115–117

super method, 170, 171

suppress_errors decorator, 68

decorator creating decorators, 78

decorators with arguments, 73

decorators with optional arguments, 74, 75

wrappers, 70, 71

symmetric_difference method, sets, 42

■ **T**

t/tt options, command line, 284

tabs, style guide for, 284

tar type

format option, sdist command, 241

TDD (Test-Driven Development), 217

tearDown method, unittest, 229

test keyword, TestCase class, 222

TestCase class, unittest, 221

adding test to test framework, 225

addTypeEqualityFunc method, 225

assert keyword, 222

assertAlmostEqual method, 224

assertDictContainsSubset method, 227

assertDictEqual method, 225

assertEqual method, 224, 225

assertFalse method, 222

assertGreater method, 226

assertGreaterEqual method, 226

assertIn method, 227

assertIs method, 229

assertIsNone method, 229

assertIsNot method, 229

assertIsNotNone method, 229

assertLess method, 226

assertLessEqual method, 226

assertListEqual method, 225

assertMultiLineEqual method, 227

assertNotAlmostEqual method, 224

assertNotEqual method, 224

assertNotIn method, 227

assertRaises method, 227, 228, 229

assertRaisesRegexp method, 228

assertRegexpMatches method, 227

assertSameElements method, 227

assertSequenceEqual method, 225

assertSetEqual method, 225

assertTrue method, 222

assertTupleEqual method, 225

creating subclass of, 221

ensuring consistent environment, 222

fail method, 222

methods describing how code works, 222

providing custom test class, 230

setUp method, 221–222, 230

executing test methods, 222

tearDown method, 229

test keyword, 222

testNumber method, 223

writing tests, 222–226

Test-Driven Development (TDD), 217

testing

doctests, 218–221

overriding assertion methods, 230

providing custom test class, 230

unittest module, 221–230

version compatibility, 226, 227, 229

writing tests, 222–226

testmod function, doctest module

testNumber method, unittest, 223

tests

adding test to test framework, 225

equality/comparison tests, 224–226

packaging, 237

representing failures and errors, 223

storing, 223

testing exceptions, 227–229

testing identity of objects, 229

testing sequences, 227

testing strings, 226

tests.py module, 223
text, 195–198
    encoding, 196–198
    plain text table of contents, 204–205
    Unicode strings, 196
this module, 1
title method, strings, 279
to_python method, 263, 264
    DateColumn class, 267, 268, 269
to_string method, 263, 264, 265
Transmission Control Protocol, 14
transparency, 21
true division, 151
truediv method, 146
try/except blocks, 26–27
    catching exceptions, 22
    else keyword, 27
    finally keyword, 27, 29
    programming recommendations, 295
tuples
    assertTupleEqual method, 225
    getfullargspec function, 61
    named tuples, 43
    namedtuple function, 43
    sequence unpacking, 34
tutorials, documentation, 210
Twisted, 243
type coercion, 88–89
type function
    creating classes at runtime, 120, 121
    metaclasses, 121
type safety
    as decorator, 90–94
    function annotations, 79
type, objects, 169, 170
TypeError exception
    catching exceptions, 23, 24
    DateColumn class, 268
    sequence unpacking, 34
types
    built-in types and classes, 103
    bytes type, 192
    duck typing, 254
    function type, 53
    programming recommendations, 296
    str type, 192
typesafe decorator, 87, 90–94
typesafe function, 79, 80, 82
    type coercion, 89

■ U

u prefix, Unicode strings, 196
unbound methods, 131–132
underscore (_) character
    linking multiple documents, ReST, 213
    naming styles, 291
Unicode
    UTF-8 encoding, 197
unicode method, 141
Unicode strings, 196
union method, sets, 42
unittest module, 221–230
    adding test to test framework, 225
    assertTrue/assertFalse methods, 222
    assertXyz methods, 224–229
    equality/comparison tests, 224–226
    fail method, 222
    main function, 223
    providing custom test class, 230
    representing failures and errors, 223
    setUp method, 230
    setup tasks, 221–222
    tearDown method, 229
    TestCase class, 221
    writing tests, 222–226
unpack function, struct module, 193, 194, 195
    endianness, 194
update method
    dictionaries, 40, 65
    sets, 40
url argument
    setup function, distutils, 238
UTF-8
    decoding UTF-8 on the fly, 248
    encoding argument, open function, 247
    encodings (PEP-263), 285
    Unicode-focused encodings, 197

■ V

validate_arguments function, 66–67
validating arguments, 66–67
    type safety, function annotations, 80
value, objects, 169
ValueError exception
    catching exceptions, 24
    DecimalColumn class, 266

exception chains, 25
sequence unpacking, 34
values method, mappings, 165
varargs value, 61
variable arguments
    type safety, function annotations, 81, 82
    variable positional arguments, 54
variables, naming, 292
varkw value, 61
version argument
    setup function, distutils, 237
version bookkeeping, 290
version compatibility
    backwards compatibility, 309–311
    keyword-only argument syntax, 267
    open method, 248
    testing, 226, 227, 229
    text handling, 270
voting guidelines, 299–300

■ **W**

weak references
    garbage collection, 180–182
weakref module, 180
while loop, 29
whitespace
    blank lines, 285
    in expressions and statements, 286–288
    Zen of Python, 5
with keyword, 30
with statement, 29–31
    as clause, 30
    context managers, 166
wrappers, 70–72
wraps decorator, 71
    decorators with arguments, 72
    decorators with optional arguments, 74
Writer class, 279
writer, CSV framework, 279–281
writerow method, csv, 270, 279, 280
    needs_header_row option, 279

writerows method, csv, 270, 279, 280
writers, csv module, 270, 279–281
    DictWriter class, 271
    SheetWriter class, 279

■ **X**

x prefixed functions, 33
X11 library, 291
XOR bitwise comparison operation, 149, 152
xrange function, 33, 96

■ **Y**

yield statement, generators, 94

■ **Z**

Zen of Python, 1–12, 301–302
    avoid ambiguity, 9
    beauty, 2
    complexity, 3, 11
    error handling, 7
    exceptions, 7, 8, 14
    explicit code, 2
    flat structures, 4
    loose coupling, 13
    namespaces, 12
    Pareto principle, 14
    practicality, 6
    readability, 5
    repetition, 12
    robustness, 14
    rules, 6
    simplicity, 3, 12
    whitespace, 5
zip function
    identifying argument values, 63
    type safety, function annotations, 80
    zipping iterables together, 38
zip type
    format option, sdist command, 240
ztar type
    format option, sdist command, 240